Second Chances

BOOKS BY JUDITH S. WALLERSTEIN, PH.D.

*Surviving the Breakup: How Children and
Parents Cope with Divorce,*
with Joan Berlin Kelly, Ph.D.

*Second Chances: Men, Women, and Children
a Decade After Divorce,*
with Sandra Blakeslee

Second Chances

MEN, WOMEN, AND CHILDREN
A DECADE AFTER DIVORCE

JUDITH S. WALLERSTEIN, Ph.D.,
AND
SANDRA BLAKESLEE

TICKNOR & FIELDS • NEW YORK

For information about permission to reproduce selections
from this book, write to Permissions, Ticknor & Fields,
215 Park Avenue South, New York, New York 10003.

Library of Congress Cataloging-in-Publication Data

Wallerstein, Judith S.
Second chances : men, women, and children a decade after
divorce / Judith S. Wallerstein and Sandra Blakeslee.
p.   cm.
Bibliography: p.
Includes index.
ISBN 0-89919-648-9
ISBN 0-89919-949-6 (pbk.)
1. Divorced people — United States — Longitudinal studies.
2. Children of divorced parents — United States — Longitudinal
studies.   I. Blakeslee, Sandra.   II. Title.
HQ834.W358   1989   88-23320
306.8'9 — dc19   CIP

Printed in the United States of America

Book design by Robert Overholtzer

VB 11 10 9 8 7 6 5 4 3 2

*To the men, women, and children
who gallantly led the way by
sharing their experiences with us
so that others could learn*

Contents

PART IV
New Ties and Old Ties

PART V
Danger and Opportunity

Introduction

THEY HAD BEEN childhood sweethearts. Like so many of their generation, Christina and Nicholas Moore got married right after college graduation and raised a family. Their three children were stunned when, in 1971, after twenty years of marriage, Nicholas filed for divorce.

In the years that followed, the children struggled with intense feelings of anger and sorrow. Ruth, the oldest, felt deprived of her adolescence as she dutifully took up the role of mother's helper and confidante. Denise, the second-born, seemed unfazed by the divorce until she went away to college, tried to commit herself to a young man, and came face to face with her long-buried feelings. Sammy, the youngest, struggled through elementary school, as teacher after teacher complained about his aggressive behavior and poor schoolwork. When I last saw the family in 1988, Sammy and Ruth were finally doing well, psychologically and socially. Denise, however, remained troubled.

Christina had been a slender, lively woman in her early forties at the time of the breakup. But for many years after the divorce, she felt dead inside. The last time I ran into Nicholas and his second wife, he made his way across a large banquet hall to find me. "Judy," he said, grinning. "I want you to understand that I am happier now than I have ever been in my life, happier than I ever dreamed would be possible for me."

*

There are winners and losers in the years after divorce. In some families, particularly where there has been longstanding conflict or physical violence, everyone may be better off. But in most families divorce tends to benefit one of the adults much more than the other. For that one person — most often the one who sought the divorce — the quality of life can be greatly enhanced, even beyond his or her expectations. But for the other person, divorce can have tragic consequences — five, ten, and even fifteen years after the event. And for the children of divorce, growing up is unquestionably harder every step of the way, although many emerge as compassionate adults, concerned about their parents and eager for an enduring relationship.

I first met the Moores more than fifteen years ago when they participated in a study I was conducting on sixty families, with 131 children, who were going through divorce.[1] At that time, my colleagues and I interviewed each family member at length, face to face, on two to four separate occasions over several weeks. We asked the adults about the breakdown of their marriages, and we asked the children what they understood about what had happened to their families. We wanted to record faithfully their views of the experience and their feelings about the impact of divorce on their lives. They told us how divorce felt to them and they discussed their hopes, frustrations, fears, and disappointments. After these first interviews, I followed the sixty families over the course of time, interviewing them again, face to face and at length, one, five, ten, and fifteen years after divorce.[2] The result is the longest study tracking divorced families ever conducted, with no counterpart in the world. The conversations and the insights we drew from them provide a dynamic picture of divorce unlike any we have had before. As we stayed in touch with our families over the years, we saw — for the first time and at first hand — exactly how divorce affects men, women, and children over the long haul. The result is this book — the first ever written on the long-term consequences of divorce on the American family.

When I started the study in 1971, very little was known about how people cope with divorce psychologically. According to the prevailing view at the time, divorce was a brief crisis that would soon resolve itself. By the end of the decade, however, several researchers including myself had begun to recognize that divorce is a much more serious trauma.[3] Children in particular were showing severe reactions at the time their parents' marriages broke up and during the immediate aftermath. Record numbers of children and adolescents from divorced families were being referred into psychological counseling services. Schools were reporting that boys from divorced families were in serious trouble. While we had learned quickly about the acute effects of divorce — knowledge that was useful in helping people better prepare for the difficulties they inevitably faced — I realized that the most critical question about divorce had not yet been asked or answered: Granted that divorce is stressful, does it engender long-term effects, and if so, what are they and for whom? Over the long haul, what factors influence "good outcomes" — that is, what leads adults and children to turn out reasonably happy and psychologically well adjusted? On the down side, what influences "bad outcomes" — what leads adults to have continuing problems in their relationships and children to suffer continuing low self-esteem and hurt feelings?

These were the questions people were asking me themselves: How long will I hurt? Will she always be this angry at me? Will he ever forgive me? I'm forty-two years old and starting all over again; what's going to happen to me? Will I make the same mistake if I ever get married again? Or, about the children: What will happen to my children? How will they turn out? Are they going to be damaged for life? Are they going to get divorced when they grow up because of my divorce? Will I be able to take care of my children?

Divorce has two purposes. The first is to escape the marriage, which has grown intolerable for at least one person. The second is to build a new life. Everyone who initiates a divorce fervently hopes that something better will replace the failed marriage — and this second-life-building aspect of divorce turns out to be far more important than the crisis. It is the long haul of divorce that matters. How people succeed in translating the hope for a better life into a reality is the critical, unexamined issue in the postdivorce years.

The idea that divorce can have long-lasting effects comes as a surprise to many people, including many mental health experts. Most Americans find comfort in the belief that time heals all wounds. The effects of divorce, it is said, last two or three years and no more. This notion stems in part from observations of the symptoms that children and adults develop at the time of marital separation. Little children often have difficulty falling asleep at bedtime or sleeping through the night. Older children may have trouble concentrating at school. Adolescents often act out and get into trouble. Men and women may become depressed or frenetic. Some throw themselves into sexual affairs or immerse themselves in work. But after a time, most men, women, and children outwardly seem to get their lives back on track. We have found that it takes women an average of three to three and one-half years and men two to two and one-half years to reestablish a sense of external order after the separation.

Getting one's external life back on track, however, does not begin to resolve the profound internal changes that people experience in the wake of divorce. Children's fundamental attitudes about society and about themselves can be forever changed by divorce and by events experienced in the years afterward. These changes can be incorporated permanently into their developing characters and personalities. The postdivorce family and the remarried family are radically different from the original intact family. Relationships are different. Problems, satisfactions, vulnerabilities, and strengths are different. People may get their lives back on track, but for most the track runs a wholly different course than the one they were on before divorce.

Divorce is deceptive. Legally it is a single event, but psychologically it is a chain — sometimes a never-ending chain — of events, relocations, and radically shifting relationships strung through time, a process that forever changes the lives of the people involved.

I first became interested in divorce after I moved to California from the Midwest more than twenty years ago with my husband and children. The high California divorce rate struck me immediately, but it was a conversation on a Sunday morning that galvanized me into action.

My daughter's new friend Karen, age nine, had slept over and we were having breakfast. Karen put her spoon into her mouth and stared off into space. "I wonder," she said, laying aside the spoon, "if my mother is going to marry Mr. O'Brien."

I said with genuine surprise, "Karen. Do you really call him Mr. O'Brien?"

She said, "Of course I do." She then revealed that this would be her mother's fourth marriage.

Karen was a bright, charming, and animated little girl. It intrigued me that she could be so happy amid the instability and number of changing relations in her family, and I was surprised that she would use a formal name for someone about to become her stepfather. I began to think about divorce not with the notion that children are necessarily damaged by it, but with the idea that today's children might negotiate their way through and come out as charming and open as Karen. It was an intriguing idea.

More profoundly, though, I was influenced by my own childhood. My father died of cancer when I was eight years old, leaving my mother at the age of twenty-nine with two children, several years of college education, little money, and few marketable skills. No doubt my lifelong professional interest in helping children, especially those suffering loss and separation, has its roots in my own continued mourning for my father and in my compassion for my mother's gallant struggles to protect my younger brother and me from the economic and personal hardships that she faced daily.

After my conversation with Karen, I began to search the literature and found that very little had been written about divorced families and children who were not in psychological treatment. Almost no one had looked in depth at the consequences for normal people, and there had been no studies conducted at close range over time.

About this time, I was invited to become a consultant to develop community mental health programs in a suburban county of the San Francisco Bay Area. Amid a steep rise in divorces, we were getting a lot of phone calls from worried parents and bewildered teachers asking for advice. What should we tell the children about divorce? How do we deal with their fears? What should we do about the angry little boys who are out of control on the playground? Or about the little girls with nightmares? There was no place to refer these callers. There was no body of knowledge, no experts.

So I went to the Zellerbach Family Fund in San Francisco and asked for money. Many on the board were concerned grandparents themselves and were willing to help. I teamed up with a colleague, Joan Berlin Kelly, and we designed a study that would examine how normally healthy people cope with divorce. We hired a small staff of professional psychologists and clinical social workers highly skilled in working with children and families, and we began to look for clients. We had lunch with the judge on the family court bench and spoke with members of the bar. In record time, we had more people willing to talk to us than we knew what to do with. When we had sixty families, with 131 children from the ages of two to eighteen, we closed the study to newcomers. It was spring 1971.

None of the children and adults in our study were referred to us for psychological counseling. The children were at the appropriate grade level in school and had never been referred for mental health services. Those who suffered chronic emotional disturbance or severe learning disabilities were screened out of our study and referred elsewhere. If anything, the children we selected had many strengths. All of these boys and girls were functioning within their parents' failing marriages; despite the anxiety and unhappiness associated with their parents' divorces, they were an able group of children.

Many of the adults had seen marriage counselors, especially near the end of the marriage. But with a few exceptions, they were not seeking help for other reasons; as a group, they were not a population in treatment. These couples and their children seemed to be doing well or reasonably well and thus were representative of the way normal people from a white, middle-class background cope with divorce. About a quarter of the men in the study are doctors, lawyers, or top management executives; 10 percent are blue-collar workers; and the remainder are in sales or white-collar positions or are owners of small businesses. A third of the women have college degrees, including some graduate degrees; in all, 75 percent of the women have had at least some college education. Half the participating families belong to churches or synagogues. Almost all were raised in traditional, intact families with middle-class values stressing hearth and home. For almost all, this was the first divorce on either side of the family. While a few went on welfare immediately after divorce, not one of the adults is on welfare today.

From the outset it was our intention to select families from within a fairly homogeneous population, specifically one that would enable us to see the effects of divorce itself in bold relief. Families from a white, middle-class community are less likely to suffer the stresses of poverty, racism, immigration issues, and wide cultural variation — factors that could obscure our focus on divorce. We looked for functioning nuclear families where the mother and father had lived together continuously with children under one roof and where there was no severe social pathology, illiteracy, or criminality. Beyond this, however, we took into the study a wide range of families, including well-functioning individuals and others suffering the effects of alcoholism, depression, chronic unemployment, family violence, and other problems that often contribute to divorce.

We settled upon the number of families very carefully — a group large enough to enable us to do valid statistical analysis but small enough to allow us to get to know everyone well. We decided against going after a larger group via telephone interviews or questionnaires because we wanted to develop close, face-to-face relationships that would let us capture their experiences through their eyes, in the context of their true feelings. We wanted to understand their hearts as well as their minds.

This, then, is divorce under the best of circumstances. Indeed, for middle-class children like those you are about to meet, divorce is likely to be the greatest stress they face while growing up. They do not have to deal with war, racism, hunger, violence, or the grinding poverty of the inner city. Yet when the little children came to the playroom at our center, they acted out stories of starving animals whose food was being snatched by monsters. Because these children were well fed and cared for, we took this to mean that they were afraid of not being cared for and of not being fed. Knowing all about them, we could separate their fantasies and their fears from the real conditions in their lives. Because these children grew up in relatively stable, protected homes in which most had been well cared for, the effects of the marital failure and of divorce stood out clearly. When they told us they were suddenly afraid they would wake up in the morning and find no adults at home, we linked their new fear to the recent divorce.

The study was supposed to last one year, for we believed that normal, healthy people would be able to work out their problems following divorce in about one year's time. They would solve the issues and get on with their lives, and we would be able to chart their recoveries and look at the ways that children mastered troubling family events. Indeed, we did not question the commonly held assumption that divorce was a short-lived crisis.

But when we conducted follow-up interviews one year to eighteen months later, we found most families still in crisis. Their wounds were wide open. Turmoil and distress had not noticeably subsided. Many adults still felt angry, humiliated, and rejected, and most had not gotten their lives back together. An unexpectedly large number of children were on a downward course. Their symptoms were worse than before. Their behavior at school was worse. Their peer relationships were worse. Our findings were absolutely contradictory to our expectations.

This was unwelcome news to a lot of people, and we got angry

letters from therapists, parents, and lawyers saying we were undoubtedly wrong. They said children are really much better off being
released from an unhappy marriage. Divorce, they said, is a liberat-
ing experience.

But that is not what we were hearing from our families. There was
a whole group of youngsters who did not believe the divorce was
really happening until a year or so later. In many instances, these
were children who had come home one day to find one parent crying
and the other angry. The parents then announced without warning
that the marriage had come apart. A third of the younger children
did not believe what they were told.

When we first saw seven-year-old Ned, he brought his family album to the office. He showed us picture after picture of himself with
his father, his mother, and his little sister. Smiling brightly, he said,
"It's going to be all right. It's really going to be all right." A year later
Ned was a very sad child. His beloved father was hardly visiting and
his previously attentive mother was angry and depressed. Ned was
doing poorly in school, was fighting on the playground, and would
not talk much to his mother. He told us a story about his two rabbits.
One day, both rabbits got lost after the cage that he had carefully
constructed was torn apart by wild dogs. In despair, Ned went looking for them, worried that they would be eaten by dogs. But he could
not find them. Sometime during the year that followed, however,
Ned went for a walk and found one rabbit. It was no longer tame. It
had become wild and was taking care of itself. At this point in his
tale, Ned broke down and cried.

We took the story to be about Ned and his sister, about his sense
that he was not being appropriately cared for. The rabbit hutch was
broken open by marauding dogs — powerful figures, not unlike his
parents. Like the rabbits, Ned and his sister felt unprotected in the
wild. He would have to take care of himself. As Ned finally confronted the divorce, he seemed very troubled, gallantly holding on to
the notion that his father would return, his mother would be happy,
and the family he had always known and loved would be fully restored. But he no longer believed it.

Dismayed by such findings, I went back to the Zellerbach Family
Fund to report that what we were finding looked entirely different
than anything we expected. The children are not recovering, I said.
The adults have not settled their problems. We need to watch these

families for a few more years to see how and when these difficulties subside. The Fund agreed to support a five-year follow-up, and in 1975 and 1976 we managed to contact and interview fifty-six out of the sixty families in our original study. Based on these interviews we wrote a book, *Surviving the Breakup.*[4] To provide continuity in the life stories, a few of the anecdotes related in the earlier book have been incorporated into *Second Chances.*

We found that the psychological condition of children and adolescents was related to the overall quality of life in the postdivorce family. Five years after divorce, one-third of the children were clearly doing well and were maintaining good relationships with both parents, who no longer fought with such high intensity. They had come to accept the divorce as something better than the failing marriage, and on balance these youngsters seemed to be back on track. Some were better off than they had been during the failing marriage.

At the same time, though, we were deeply concerned about a large number of youngsters — well over a third of the whole group — who were significantly worse off than before. Clinically depressed, they were not doing well in school or with friends. They had deteriorated to the point that some early disturbances, such as sleep problems, poor learning, or acting out, had become chronic.

We also found, in this five-year follow-up, that the majority of children still hoped that their parents would reconcile. They would misinterpret snippets of conversation between themselves and parents to mean that reconciliation was possible. Even if there had been a remarriage, they held on to reconciliation fantasies based on the logic that "if they can get divorced once, they can do it again." After the first five years they were also intensely angry at their parents for giving priority to adult needs rather than to their needs. Few children were truly sympathetic or really understood why their parents divorced, even when the parents thought it was obvious.

At the five-year mark, the majority of adults felt they were better off, but a surprisingly large number did not. Half the men and two-thirds of the women were more content with the quality of their lives. The rest, however, were either stalled or felt more troubled and unhappy than they had during the marriage. Many had experienced a great deal of loneliness. One woman complained that her health was failing and speculated that it might be related to her built-up anger.

She said, "I have no one to take care of me, no one to check on me. I am totally alone. My children have no compassion and my ex-husband is an icicle."

Economically, half the men were solidly upper or middle class while, with few exceptions, women were poorer. Yet to a surprisingly high degree compared with the rest of the nation, two-thirds of the men in our study regularly paid court-ordered child support at this juncture. Unfortunately, the child support in many instances did not cover even the cost of child care for the working mother.

Nearly one-third of the children were party to intense bitterness between the parents. True, some couples were no longer standing in the same kitchen screaming at one another; they were screaming on the telephone instead. Or they fought face to face while dropping off or picking up children. The illusion we had held — that divorce brings an end to marital conflict — was shattered.

In 1980, I spent a year at a think tank, the Center for Advanced Study in the Behavioral Sciences in Stanford, California. My thinking about divorce was shifting. Early on I had been interested in the initial experience of divorce and its immediate aftereffects, in how children and adults were coping or failing to cope. But now I began to wonder about such long-term effects as changes in attitude and self-image. These changes would not manifest themselves as symptoms, such as bed hopping in adults or bedwetting in children, but would more likely be deeply embedded into each person's world view vis-à-vis their relationships and expectations. While more elusive than behavioral changes, such changes in attitude are, in the long run, more important for the individual and for society.

Evidence was accumulating in other areas of experience that a brief trauma in childhood could affect an individual's long-term attitudes toward life and death. For example, the collapse of a West Virginia dam left adults and children feeling that they could have virtually no influence over future life events.[5] And a very brief kidnapping of a busload of children, in which no one was hurt, left the children feeling that another catastrophe was lurking in wait. In fact, as researchers learned from a later follow-up, these children shared the shocking notion that they would not live past age thirty-five.[6]

I wondered therefore what attitudes children of divorce might carry with them into adulthood and into their own adult relationships and marriages. Would adolescence be different for these young people? Finally, I wanted to return to and recast the earlier questions I'd asked in observing my daughter's friend Karen — questions about how children and adults *master* different experiences. How does mastery of divorce differ from that of bereavement? How does mastering an experience affect a person's subsequent world view, attitude toward relationships, and future expectations? And most of all, could we use what we learn about how people master divorce to develop programs to help them avoid its detrimental effects?

I returned to the Zellerbach Family Fund with a request for support in conducting a ten-year follow-up, pursuing these questions, with the same sixty families in our original study. At the five-year interviews, many of the teenagers had asked, "Will you call on me again in five years?" I was intrigued with the notion of seeing them again and wondered how they had negotiated entry into young adulthood. This is a critical psychological passage for all young people, and it had never been studied within the framework of divorce.

The ten-year follow-up was directed as much at those children who succeeded and benefited from divorce as at those who did not do well. We also sought to study those adults who were able to restructure their lives through various mechanisms and those who failed to do so. Working with most of the same staff, we interviewed our original families throughout 1981 and 1982.[7] (Because it took two years to conduct the ten-year follow-up interviews, many of the people were seen eleven and almost twelve years after the divorce.)

These are the first and only ten-year reports on the psychological effects of divorce on men, women, and children. Throughout the study and in the course of writing this book, I have been profoundly struck by the major changes taking place all around us, not only for the individuals described here but for society as well. Even though the divorce rate began to rise in the early 1970s and has remained high for a full generation, there is an extraordinary reluctance to acknowledge its seriousness and its enormous impact on all our lives. We have been afraid to look at what is happening in our midst.

In 1980 I founded the Center for the Family in Transition, to provide services for people who are separating, divorcing, and remarrying. My staff and I counsel more divorcing families than any other agency in America, and my concern about divorce has been amplified by this experience. Having worked with more than two thousand troubled families since 1980, I have to say that things are not getting better and divorce is not getting easier. If anything, it's getting worse. The experiences of these families are relevant to everyone in our society.

In 1987 and 1988, we went back to many of the children and adults once again to ask permission to use their experiences — with appropriate disguises — in a book designed to help other people cope with divorce. We could not resist, however, the opportunity to sit down with them all once more, for interviews lasting several hours each, to begin a fifteen-year follow-up of the same group. Observations from these fifteen-year interviews are included here where they shed light, both good and bad, on the continuing legacy of divorce among these families. The bulk of the book, however, is based on fully analyzed data from the ten-year follow-up. At this point, much of our data from the fifteen-year follow-up is impressionistic and awaits systematic analysis. Although we have seen some fascinating changes and turnabouts, our most recent findings do not run counter to our observations at ten years.

The collective experiences of the people in *Second Chances* make up a body of wisdom that we have not had before. Although each person's story is unique, reflecting the way just one person copes with divorce, all the stories taken together constitute an invaluable guide to others. The guide can be used prospectively, for people anticipating divorce (If I do this, how can I protect myself and my children?), and retrospectively, for people who have already experienced a divorce (Why do I feel the way I do? How did I get where I am? Am I different from others in my position?).

The families in our study have followed many different paths over the years, and their experiences make up a broad network of possibilities. Now, at the ten- and fifteen-year marks, we can look back and determine patterns; we can see where people are likely to succeed or to fail. The choices they have made and the paths they have taken have been shaped over time, as the children pass through important developmental stages of life and their parents move into middle or old age. We now know at what ages the children are likely to encounter difficulties, what the difficulties are, and how they differ for boys and girls. We know the obstacles encountered by men and women as they try to pull away from their failed marriages and rebuild their lives. Most important, we know that roads can widen and fork at particular places, opening new vistas, new opportunities, and ways to head off trouble ahead.

I hope that the stories that follow will help others avoid many of the unhappy psychological and economic consequences of divorce that are reported here. There are, as we shall see, far too many casualties; too many people, young and old, have gotten lost along the way. My goal is to prevent, or at least substantially reduce, the casualty list by providing an accurate map of the roads' windings, the mistakes that can be avoided and the obstacles that need to be overcome. This map is entirely drawn from the experiences of the men, women, and children who have shared their lives with us over the last fifteen years, and this book is dedicated to them — not as a token bow, but truly to acknowledge that they are our teachers.

Divorce has ripple effects that touch not just the family involved, but our entire society. As the writer Pat Conroy observed when his own marriage broke up, "Each divorce is the death of a small civilization." When one family divorces, that divorce affects relatives, friends, neighbors, employers, teachers, clergy, and scores of strangers. Although more people stay married than get divorced, divorce is not a *them* versus *us* problem; everyone, in one way or another, has been touched by it. Today, all relationships between men and women are profoundly influenced by the high incidence of divorce. Children from intact families are jittery about divorce. Teachers from all over the country tell me that their students come to school wide-eyed with fear, saying that their parents quarreled the night before and asking in terror, "Does that mean they are going to divorce?" Radical changes in family life affect all families, homes, parents, children, courtships, and marriages, silently altering the social fabric of the entire society. This book, therefore, is intended for us all.

PART 1

Second Chances

1

The Nature of Divorce

DIVORCE IS A MAJOR turning point for men and women. The questions it forces them to ask and the changes that it brings affect every aspect of life. Some are external: Where will I live? How much money will I have? Should I go back to school? Should I sell the house? What kind of job can I get? Who will be living in the house with us? Whom can I count on for support?

Other changes are internal. People again must ask themselves, Who am I? What do I want? Whom do I want? How can I undo what happened and how can I avoid repeating my mistakes? What are my priorities? Because a man's or woman's identity is often tied to a spouse, especially if the marriage has lasted many years, divorce may shake adult identity to the core.

People consider divorce for many reasons. They may be eager to escape a relationship that has become stressful, demeaning, or intolerable. At least one of the partners in the marriage may think that almost any option would be preferable to feeling trapped — by law, economic need, love, guilt, compassion, hate, concern about the effects of divorce on children, or a host of similar reasons that keep people entangled in relationships. They conclude that the only solution to their unhappiness is divorce.

But whatever the reasons behind the decision, most people ending a marriage hope to improve the quality of life for themselves and for their children. They hope to find a new love, a more enriching relationship, a more responsive sexual partner, a more supportive companion, a better provider. Failing that, they hope to establish a single life that will provide greater opportunity for self-respect, contentment, and serenity or, at the least, less turbulence, intrusiveness, and hurt.

Divorce is much more than the coup de grâce of a stressful marriage. It is a new beginning that offers people second chances. It is no more and no less than an opportunity to rebuild lives. And there's the rub.

People want to believe that divorce will relieve all their stresses — back we go to square one and begin our lives anew. But divorce does not wipe the slate clean. Some second chances come with three small children, a low-paying job, and the ghosts of the failed marriage. Some come with a sense of having been torn away from one's children and not knowing how to reestablish a home. Some second chances begin with loneliness and a feeling of being unloved and unlovable. Some bring on acute problems that turn into chronic problems. A second chance at age forty-five is not equivalent to a second chance at age thirty-two.

Other second chances bring new hope that better solutions are possible. Some come with a sense of courage that stems from having ended a demeaning relationship. Some allow people to pursue a more meaningful relationship with another person. Our second chances are not created equal.

Few adults anticipate accurately what lies ahead when they decide to divorce. Life is almost always more arduous and more complicated than they expect. It is often more depleting and more lonely for at least one member of the marriage. At the time of divorce, people are intent on getting rid of their unhappiness, and they find it difficult to conjure up understanding for something they have never experienced. It is hard for them to imagine the multiple changes that divorce will bring in its wake. Eventually they do learn, however, that the changes we make from divorce are hard-won.

What happens at this first turning point of divorce and at the turning points that follow determines the life trajectories of men, women, and children in the years to come. Divorce can be a profound catalyst for psychological, social, and economic change. It can also be a stumbling block against such change or the beginning of psychological, social, and economic deterioration. Divorce opens up or closes off a multitude of opportunities. As ever, the journey begins with the first step — and the direction of that first step governs each step that follows.

Some people use divorce to reexamine assumptions about why the marriage failed; about roles and relationships; about who they are, how they feel, and what they are capable of doing. As Margaret told me at our ten-year meeting, "I cried for two years after Scott left. He said I couldn't do anything right. So then I finally decided out of anger that I would show him. And I began to do just that. Gradually, as I began to be successful, I looked back at my life and I began to remember a whole lot of things about me that I had forgotten, including how competent I had been as a teenager and how many people had admired my ability at that time. And this I had really forgotten — how, when I got engaged, my old parish priest took me aside and warned me that maybe it would be a mistake to marry Scott." Reaching into her past, Margaret recaptured a long-forgotten self-image to bolster her new self-image. In calling upon old roots for new self-esteem, she made good, constructive use of her second chances.

"It's only in my second marriage that I'm realizing how important fathers are," said Martin. "My stepdaughter and my second wife have taught me so much about what fathers can do. I've gotten to know my own daughter for the first time." Martin also used his second chances to expand and grow.

Unfortunately, many others don't even recognize their second chances. "Look," said Jessica, "I'm forty-five and the truth is I'm no good in bed."

"Is that what your ex-husband said?" I asked her.

She nodded.

I am constantly amazed at how many divorced men and women carry inside them the nagging voices of their former spouses. Jessica had internalized and completely accepted her husband's negative view of her. Long after the divorce, she retained images that had been forged in the marriage — of the world as a treacherous place and of herself as flawed and undesirable. She continued living by the rules of the failed marriage, as if the marriage were still in place.

Bob was tearful as he explained why he was seeing less of his children. "They don't need me," he said. "After all, they've got their mother and Charlie, who's there in my place. They're probably better off if I don't come by."

Following the collapse of his marriage, Bob forfeited a chance to build a close relationship with his children that would have been of great value to him as an adult and that would have been central to the children's happiness and self-esteem.

Sometimes we think of one crisis as resembling all the others and all stressful events as having a great deal in common. But the truth is that in a family with children, there is no experience like divorce. In some respects, the closest thing to it is death and bereavement, for they each spur internal and external life changes: Each involves loss and mourning; each brings in its wake lasting changes in the fabric of daily life and intimate relationships. But divorce is different. Unlike death, divorce involves choice, and the long-lasting changes it effects carry the promise of positive outcomes. Unlike bereavement, divorce is intended to relieve stress and reduce unhappiness in family members. These intended effects may or may not be realized, but in either case, divorce at the outset comprises a special category of life crisis in that it simultaneously engenders new solutions and new problems. Divorce is also unique in that it gives rise to the central passions of human life.

Feelings of loss and grief commingle with those of love and hate. Sexual jealousy is triggered and reinforced by a sense of betrayal. Relief is tinged with guilt. Narcissistic rage is precipitated by humiliation. Acute depression rides on the heels of rejection. When long-lasting marriages break up, a person's very identity may be threatened. These feelings, and the internal conflicts they arouse, are not amenable to a quick fix or short recuperation. People do not forget that divorce is rarely a mutual decision or that it is a voluntary act, an entirely man-made and woman-made act.

When we fall in love, we idealize the object of our love; at the point of leaving, however, we de-idealize and sometimes dehumanize the loved one. Divorce is really the opposite of falling in love and it inevitably marshals anger and sometimes intense rage — rage that people feel is justified. *It is a rage that feels good.* Rooted in a sense of having been exploited and humiliated to the core, this anger flows from wounded self-esteem and helps us defend ourselves against feelings of depression, unlovableness, and abandonment. It is the kind of anger that helps people deny responsibility for the marriage's failure. The "bad guy" is he or she who wants the divorce; the "good guy" is he or she who wants to continue the family. What other life crisis engenders the wish to kill? In what other life crisis are children used as bullets? Divorce is unique in that it unleashes our most primitive and most profound human passions — love, hate, and jealousy.

No-fault divorce is a legal concept that has gained acceptance in this country, but I have yet to meet one man, woman, or child who emotionally accepts "no-fault" divorce. In their hearts, people believe in fault and in the loss associated with the decision to end a marriage. Adults almost inevitably blame each other, but, as we shall see, they rarely blame themselves. Children, on the other hand, feel that their parents are to blame for having failed at one of life's major tasks, which is to maintain marriage and family for richer or for poorer, for better or for worse.

Divorce is different from other life crises in that anger more often erupts into physical and verbal violence, violence that can cause serious psychological harm for many years. It spills onto the children and into the legal system. In fact, judges, lawyers, and police are in more danger of being shot or killed by angry family members than by criminals.

In most crisis situations, such as an earthquake, flood, or fire, parents instinctively reach out and grab hold of their children, bringing them to safety first. In the crisis of divorce, however, mothers and fathers put children on hold, attending to adult problems first. Divorce is associated with a diminished capacity to parent in almost all dimensions — discipline, playtime, physical care, and emotional support. Divorcing parents spend less time with their children and are less sensitive to their children's needs. At this time they may very well confuse their own needs with those of their children.

Divorce is also the only major family crisis in which social supports fall away. When there is a death in the family, people come running to help. After a natural disaster, neighbors rally to assist those who have been hurt. After most such crises, clergymen may call on the family to console adults or speak with children who are badly shaken. But not so with divorce. Friends are afraid that they will have to take sides; neighbors think it is none of their business. Although half the families in our study belong to churches or synagogues, not one clergyman came to call on the adults or children during divorce. Grandparents may be helpful but are apprehensive about getting caught in the crossfire. They often live far away and feel their role is limited. When a man and a woman divorce, many people tend to act as if they believe it might be contagious. The divorced person is seen as a loose cannon. We have names for them: rogue elephant, black widow. Despite the widespread acceptance of divorce in modern society, there remains something frightening at its core. It is as if married people are afraid that another's divorce will illuminate the cracks in their own relationships. On a visceral level, every divorce threatens to erode our own marriages.

Stages of Divorce

The emotional process of divorce takes several years to negotiate, occurring in three broad, overlapping stages. Unfortunately, there is no inevitable progression from one stage to the next; a family or an individual may remain stuck in one stage for many years.

The acute, or first, stage begins with escalating unhappiness within the failing marriage and crests with the decision to divorce and the departure of one parent from the household. This is the period where the stage is set for the spilling of anger and sexual impulses, depression and disorganization in the family. This behavior, which has been called "crazy making," sheds light on the nature of marriage itself. Psychologically, the very structure of the marriage helps maintain adulthood. When the marriage collapses, many impulses are no longer contained.

During this acute stage of divorce, well over half of the children in our study witnessed physical violence between their parents. Before this time, 75 percent of the children had never seen physical violence at home. A bank president shoves his wife into the hall closet and locks the door as she screams and the children plead. An elementary school teacher hurls a lamp at her husband as he turns to leave the room. In both instances, the children watch. Violent behavior, in fact, most often occurs in the presence of children. I have found no evidence that boys or girls are protected from such scenes. To the contrary, it seems that adults may need an audience to witness the expression of these feelings or perhaps to restrain them from causing greater harm to one another.

As people are catapulted back into the sexual marketplace, they may seem to return to adolescence. The men, as one of my colleagues so aptly puts it, often become "hip, hirsute, and horny." Many adults are also obsessed with sexual fantasies during this acute stage. Alice, a genteel suburban matron in her mid-forties, describes her feelings graphically: "I am walking down the street and an image suddenly flashes into my head, of me wearing only underpants sitting on a half-made bed in a sleazy hotel. And I am all alone." She asks urgently, "Judy, what's wrong with me. These ideas are haunting me. Why can't I get them out of my head?"

As we talk, I gradually learn that, although she initiated the divorce, the undoing of her marriage was very frightening; it made her fear a loss of control over her sexuality. She was afraid that without a sexual partner she would be alone but would continue to have sexual impulses. At the same time, she worried that others would make sexual passes toward her. This so frightened her that she felt humiliated and demeaned. Her obsessive sexual fantasies mirrored these fears and perhaps her wishes as well.

At this stage, men and women often act out their sexual feelings: A fifty-year-old professional woman takes on a series of young lovers; a forty-two-year-old man seduces the teenage babysitter. These short, somewhat frantic sexual liaisons are usually a short-lived phenomenon. People act in very uncharacteristic ways, feeling as if their lives are proceeding under strobe lights. Once again, though, children become frightened — they do not know that the behavior is temporary, nor do they make connections between the parents' behavior and the family breakup. To them, it appears that Mom or Dad has gone mad.

This stage usually lasts for several months to a year or two following the separation. If the separation has taken place in a climate of mutual trust and concern for each other, the acute stage is much less chaotic. On the other hand, it may last for many years. Sooner or later, however, most divorcing families proceed to the second, or transitional, stage of the divorcing process.

At this point, adults and children become involved in unfamiliar roles and relationships within the new family structure. They make efforts to solve problems and experiment with new lifestyles in new settings. Adults may go back to school, attempt a new relationship, move to a new home, or pick up old ties. It is a time of alternating progress and regression, a time of trial and error and fluctuating moods. Children often move to new communities, schools, and friends. They are uprooted.

Life may be unstable and home may be unsettled for several years. The family has permeable boundaries. It must absorb new people, new schools, new lovers, good and bad choices. It is not clear through all this who is in the family and who is out of the family. Many families move several times during this period.

The third stage is marked by a renewed sense of stability. The divorced family is reestablished as a new, secure, functioning unit. In the normal course of events, relationships settle down. Long-term visiting and child support patterns become established. We saw comparatively little change in visiting and child support at the ten-year mark compared with the five-year mark. With time, living and schooling arrangements grow stable.

At the same time, we find that single-parent families are particularly vulnerable, seeming to experience more emergencies than intact families. Arrangements over the children tend to break down as children enter new developmental stages and as adults enter new relationships. Adolescence is much more difficult for the single parent and for the children, both boys and girls. Second marriages with children from a first marriage are more prone to divorce. Half the children in our study experienced at least two divorces by their mother or father in the ten-year period. Men and women tell us very clearly at the ten-year mark that the stress of being a single parent never lightens and that the fear of being alone never ceases. Because many single parents are financially strapped, they have less leeway when emergencies strike, no backup for illness, crisis, or loss. They have fewer resources to help solve a problem. And when a second marriage occurs, the family is again thrown onto a teeter-totter. New issues come along with new relationships and life is rearranged once again as the families confront their second chances.

The Children of Divorce

The experience of divorce is entirely different for parents and for children. Many people have wanted to believe that what is good for adults will be good for their children. It is seductively simple to think that a child's psychological problems are mainly a reflection of family problems — as if children were not people with reactions of their own, separate from those of adults. As a parent puts his or her life together in the postdivorce years, they say, the children will inevitably improve. Because an unhappy woman often has a hard time being a good mother, they argue, it follows that a happy woman will be a good mother.

But this argument just does not jibe with my experience. It is often true that an unhappy adult finds it hard to be a nurturing parent, for unhappiness can deplete the adult's capacity to provide the care and understanding that children need. But it does not follow that a happy or happier adult will necessarily become a better parent. The "trickle down" theory is not relevant to parent-child relationships. An exciting love affair or a gratifying career advance may make for a much happier adult, but there is no reason to expect that the adult's greater happiness will lead to a greater sensitivity or greater concern for his or her children. To the contrary, circumstances that enrich an adult's life can easily make that adult less available to children. Unfortunately, the genuine love and tenderness between adults in a second marriage is not always shared with the children who come from a previous marriage.

Although the decision to divorce is rarely mutual, adults generally do agree about the state of the marriage. It is uncommon — although it surely happens — for one spouse to be genuinely surprised when the other presses for divorce. Most of the time both adults acknowledge, openly or secretly, that there are flaws and tensions in a marriage on the brink. They may disagree about how to remedy those troubles, but they rarely disagree that the troubles exist. Children, however, can be quite content even when their parents' marriage is profoundly unhappy for one or both partners. Only one in ten children in our study experienced relief when their parents divorced. These were mostly older children in families where there had been open violence and where the children had lived with the fear that the violence would hurt a parent or themselves. Even so, few children truly expect their parents to divorce. When there is fighting in the household, children hope against hope that the fighting will vanish, and they look forward to a more peaceful time. They do not prepare themselves for divorce, and when they are told that a divorce is imminent, many refuse to believe it.

Divorce is a different experience for children and adults because the children lose something that is fundamental to their development — the family structure. The family comprises the scaffolding upon which children mount successive developmental stages, from infancy into adolescence. It supports their psychological, physical, and emotional ascent into maturity. When that structure collapses, the children's world is temporarily without supports. And children, with a vastly compressed sense of time, do not know that the chaos is temporary. What they do know is that they are dependent on the family. Whatever its shortcomings, children perceive the family as the entity that provides the support and protection that they need. With divorce, that structure breaks down, leaving children who feel alone and very frightened about the present and the future.

The human newborn is one of the most helpless creatures on earth. Human children need their parents far longer than any other animal species, and children are tragically aware of this fact — they know how absolutely dependent they are on adults. Accordingly, they have a very primitive, very real fear of being left on their own. A child's immediate reaction to divorce, therefore, is fear. When their family breaks up, children feel vulnerable, for they fear that their lifeline is in danger of being cut. Their sense of sadness and loss is profound. A five-year-old enters my office and talks about divorce with the comment "I've come to talk about death." Children grieve over the loss of the family, the loss of the parent who has left home, and the imagined loss of both parents. Their grief may even seem unrelated to the relationship that they had with the parent who left — children cry over parents that they were close to and parents who were distant.

Children are profoundly concerned not only for themselves but for the welfare of their parents. It is upsetting to see a parent in tears. A ten-year-old girl says, "Mom thinks no one worries about her. But I do!" Children long intensely for the parent who has left home and worry that he or she might never come back. One seven-year-old was told that his father had moved to Oakland. "Where is Oakland?" wailed the boy. "Is Oakland in Mexico? Where is Mexico?"

Children of all ages feel intensely rejected when their parents divorce. When one parent leaves the other, the children interpret the act as including them. "He left Mom. He doesn't care about me." Or "She left Dad. I must not be what she wanted."

Children get angry at their parents for violating the unwritten rules of parenthood — parents are supposed to make sacrifices for children, not the other way around. Some keep their anger hidden for years out of fear of upsetting parents or for fear of retribution and punishment; others show it. Little children may have temper tantrums; older children may explode, like the fifteen-year-old girl in our study who put her fist through a wall. Related to the anger is a sense of powerlessness. Children feel that they have no say, no way to influence this major event in their lives. Despite ongoing fantasies that things will magically get better, they cannot prevent divorce, fix it, rescue mom or dad, or rescue the marriage. No one gives priority to their wishes, concerns, and fears.

Children feel intense loneliness. It amazes me how little support they get at this time, even from grandparents. Divorce is an acute, painful, long-remembered experience that children must often negotiate with the sense that they are alone in the world. All supports, even their parents, seem to fall away. There may be no one to talk to, nowhere to turn. A child will remember for many years the neighbor down the block who was kind during the divorce. In our study, fewer than 10 percent of the children had any adult speak to them sympathetically as the divorce unfolded.

Loyalty conflicts, sometimes flipping from one parent to the other and back again, are a common experience for children of divorce. Many children conceptualize divorce as a fight between two teams, with the more powerful side winning the home turf, and will root for different teams at different times. Even when children are encouraged not to take sides, they often feel that they must. However, when they do take sides to feel more protected, they also feel despair because they are betraying one parent over the other. If they do not take sides, they feel isolated and disloyal to both parents. There is no solution to their dilemma.

Many children feel guilty, and some feel that it is their duty to mend the marriage. One seven-year-old believed for five years that she caused her parents' divorce because she failed to deliver a message from one parent to the other. A little boy thought it was his fault because his dog was noisy.

The devastation children feel at divorce is similar to the way they feel when a parent dies suddenly, for each experience disrupts close family relationships. Each weakens the protection of the family; each begins with an acute crisis followed by disequilibrium that may last several years or longer; and each introduces a chain of long-lasting changes that are not predictable at the outset. But divorce may well be a more difficult tragedy for the child to master psychologically.

Loss due to death is final; the dead person cannot be retrieved. Only a very young child or someone with a psychotic illness can deny, for any length of time, the finality of death. Moreover, death always has an identifiable calendar date and usually a clear cause, no matter how long and drawn out or unanticipated it might be. The

impact of divorce is different. Finality is not present in the same way
as in death, and children logically assume that the divorce can be
undone at any time. Divorce is often preceded by several separations,
each of which may seem decisive but turn out not to be final. These
can confuse children and lead them to expect reconciliation, if not
immediately, then eventually. Moreover, divorce is usually a partial
loss, and most children tend to see the departed parent for many
years afterward. As a result, children who experience divorce are
more likely to feel a persistent, gnawing sense that the loss of the
intact family is not final; maybe it can be repaired. People who divorce can remarry. People who separate can rejoin. Thus children's
capacity to cope with divorce is very much decreased by the uncertainty of the event itself, by its elusive causes, and by what children
regard and keep alive as its potential reversibility. Perhaps the most
important factor in keeping alive children's hope for reconciliation is
their intense need to think of their parents as mutually affectionate
and together.

This feeling can endure for decades. A middle-aged woman whose
parents had divorced thirty years earlier sought counseling from a
female psychologist on my staff for her periodic depressions. After a
while, she confessed that she was also seeing a male psychologist at
another location. Her fervent wish was to bring both psychologists
together in one room, to have them hold hands, with her present, so
that they might symbolically restore the intact family that she had lost
when she was five years old. We had a difficult time persuading this
intelligent but depressed woman that staging her fantasy would not
cure her depression.

Second chances hold different meanings for parents and for children. For adults, there is a chance to fall in love, to make a better
choice, and to succeed in another relationship or a second marriage.
There is the chance to achieve new dignity, to undo a mistake, to
redefine one's adulthood, one's goals, and to make use of what was
learned during the first marriage. There is an opportunity for psychological growth and a chance to be a better parent, with or without
a new partner.

Children do not perceive divorce as a second chance, and this is
part of their suffering. They feel that their childhood has been lost
forever. Divorce is a price *they* pay, as forfeiture to their parents' failures, jeopardizing their future lives. But children of divorce do have
second chances, in the very futures they are worried about. In the

years after divorce, especially in adolescence and later as they enter young adulthood, children have opportunities to negotiate different and better solutions in their own lives and to reinterpret their earlier experiences in light of newfound maturity. They may re-create the kinds of traumatic relationships that they witnessed in their parents' marriage or, as they consciously or unconsciously dredge up past hurts, they may master longstanding fears of repeating their parents' mistakes. They have a chance to choose better and to resolve the un-resolved issues of a childhood that included the trauma of divorce. Many children are able to do just this. Sadly, many others fail.

I was surprised to discover that the severity of a child's reactions at the time of the parents' divorce does not predict how that child will fare five, ten, and even fifteen years later. All of our programs for children of divorce make the opposite assumption — if we help chil-dren acknowledge or recognize their feelings at the time, they'll do better in the years to come. But from what we saw ten and fifteen years later, this is not the case. Some of the most troubled, depressed, and fretful children in our study turned out fine ten years later, while some of the least troubled, seemingly content, and calmest children were in poor shape ten and fifteen years later. *One cannot predict long-term effects of divorce on children from how they react at the outset.* This new finding has important implications for the mental health and le-gal professions. Much of our energy and effort is focused on the crisis of divorce rather than the long term. But as we talked to our families through the years, we began to think of the postdivorce period as a tapestry made of many threads, with no one thread accounting for all that we saw. As the years went by, we discovered that themes and patterns shifted with each developmental stage. A color that showed little at the outset might later come to dominate the design.

The Divorce-Marriage Mirror

It is time to take a long, hard look at divorce in America. And in the looking, we find surprises, because divorce is the mirror image of marriage. By looking at divorce, we gaze at no less than our most fundamental values — the values by which we measure the meaning and worth of human relationships, of love, of the family itself. And profound changes in the family can only mean profound changes in society as a whole.

As our attitudes about divorce have changed in the second half of this century, so have our attitudes about marriage and family. With divorce comes an erosion of commitments to our partners and to the institution of marriage itself. With divorce comes a weakening of our unspoken moral commitments to our children. Today we expect more from marriage than previous generations did and we respect it less. The divorce-marriage mirror reflects an image that is shockingly different from any we have seen before, and we cannot hope to break the mirror or to make it reflect the time that was.

To recognize that divorce is an arduous, long-lasting family trauma is not to argue against it. Divorce is a useful and necessary social remedy. Given the egalitarian nature of American life and the rights of individuals, divorce is here to stay. And the fact is that most divorces with children are not impulsive. People may be wretched and lonely for years before summoning up the courage to separate, and most worry about the effects of divorce on their children. There is considerable evidence that a conflict-ridden marriage is not in the best interests of the children. There is evidence, too, that children benefit from dissolution of such marriages.[1] Nor do most people consider that their divorce was a mistake a decade after the fact.

It is important to realize, however, that the experience of growing up in America is radically different today than it was just a generation ago. Parent-child relationships have changed, relationships between men and women are different, family structure is different, grandparenting has new challenges — and institutions are failing to keep up with the changes.

Superficially — in our mind's eye and in political speeches — we maintain the illusion that our society is as it was before. We try to convince ourselves that the family is intact and that commitment is forever. Weddings are whiter and veils are longer than ever. We deplore the fact that children today do not know literature and history, have never heard of the Magna Charta — as if we adults know or make much use of such information ourselves. The truth is that we refuse to acknowledge the widening gap between our belief systems and our everyday lives. But the family *has* changed. The illusion is not the reality. And every parent and child in America knows this. Divorce is both cause and effect of the changes.

Let's look for a moment at the world we actually inhabit today.

• It is a world in which our trust in the reliability of relationships has been shaken, especially those that are most fundamental and intimate. "I'm afraid to use the word *love*," says a young adult who remembers her parents' divorce as if it happened yesterday. "You can hope for love, but you can't expect it."

• Relationships between men and women are infused with anxiety, especially during courtship. People who grow up in divorced families are more eager for lasting relationships and more worried about ever achieving them. This anxiety spreads to their contemporaries who never directly experienced divorce.

• It is a world wherein divorced adults, as they explore their second chances, wonder whether anybody will want them. The woman or man who is rejected by a spouse often accepts the judgment of herself or himself as being unattractive, damaged, and unlovable.

• There is rising anger and greater freedom to express that anger between the sexes. The amount of anger that men feel toward women who have hurt them is matched only by the anger that women feel toward men who have hurt them. Adults carry around angers that last and last. This war being fought in legislative halls and in courts is fueled by polemic. Economic issues are disguised as ideology. People claim they are talking about benefits for the children, while they are really talking about money, sexual jealousy, revenge, or longing for the lost marriage.

• It is a world in which relations between children and their parents have changed. Many children assume responsibilities well beyond their years as they undertake to psychologically advise and physically nurture a troubled parent.

• Single parents, mothers and fathers alike, are stressed to the breaking point as they find their incomes falling and responsibilities rising. To raise children without a partner is emotionally and physically exhausting. Although there have been changes in patterns of custody, close to 90 percent of children remain in their mothers' primary custody after divorce.

• The visiting parent is a new kind of parent, and there are no proven guidelines for how to maintain this relationship successfully. Few visiting parents and children do not have some question, as they part, about the forthcoming visit. Will you choose the school dance over seeing me next Saturday? If I misbehave, will you be there next Sunday?

• Behavioral scientists find themselves confronted by uncharted territory. Because our understanding of child development and family life is almost entirely based on the intact family, the divorced family has been looked at as a variation on or departure from the intact family. But now we are finding that the divorced family is an entirely new family form, one that needs to be looked at entirely on its own. The reality we observe in today's divorced families does not fit the psychological ideas that we were brought up with professionally. Instead of guessing as we go, we need to develop new theory and understanding to match the new reality.

• It is a world in which we see a threatened erosion of the economic and social status of white, middle-class children. Many children who grow up in divorced families are not climbing the ladder as high as their parents. As we shall see, 40 percent of the young men in our study are drifting. While two-thirds of the college-age children are entering college or other post-secondary education, many drop out because they cannot afford to pay their own tuition. Only half manage to stay in school, even though they grew up in affluent communities in which 85 percent of their graduating classes go on to college, with many students receiving full financial support from their parents. Universities are avoiding the financial hardships posed by divorce. Financial aid forms asking for the mother's and father's income rarely acknowledge divorce or the fact that many divorced fathers who are well able to do so do not support their children after age eighteen, especially when there are children in a second marriage.[2]

• On a positive note, this new world is one in which we have opportunities to rectify our mistakes, to seek second chances. We can reject demeaning, lonely, conflicted, or unloving relationships. Battered wives can turn away from their neurotic husbands. Children may be able to live apart from an exploitive parent. We live in a society that widely assumes that men and women have the right to expect a happy marriage and that if a marriage does not work, no one has to stay trapped. This certainly was not true of our grandparents' generation, when marriage was often an economic necessity and dominant religious and community values made divorce taboo.

With this new world have come dilemmas that our society has failed to face squarely or bravely.

Dilemma: The psychological needs of children do not change just because there are changes in the family structure.

Dilemma: Our fragile family structures have gotten out of sync with our emotional needs. The family is supposed to be an oasis, a restorative place where children and adults find respite from the stresses of the workplace and school. Home is where a preschooler hides his head in Mommy's lap. Home is where an adolescent regroups after taking risks that lead to both failures and successes. Home is an adult metaphor for a safe place.

Dilemma: The needs and certainly the wishes of adults and children are often in conflict with regard to the decision to divorce. The terrible dilemma for parents is what to do about this conflict.

Dilemma: What may be good for one member of the marriage is not necessarily good for the other. In most families with children, divorce is a unilateral decision.

Dilemma: As widely reported elsewhere, the economic burden of divorce is falling on women and children. Professor Lenore Weitzman of Harvard University found that on average, women with minor children experienced a 73 percent decline in standard of living during the first year after divorce whereas their husbands experienced a 42 percent increase in their standard of living. The researcher predicts a two-tier society with women and children as an underclass.[3]

Dilemma: Although children need parents and parents want to continue good relationships with their children, parent-child relationships are forever altered by divorce.

Dilemma: Divorce reflects our democratic ethos that the rights of the individual are as important as the rights of the group. It stresses the needs of the individual over the needs of the family. How do we set priorities? Which is more important in given situations, the individual or the family? Either way we choose, ethical dilemmas are raised for society.

These dilemmas and the profound shifts in family and marital relationships are reflected in our popular culture. In *E.T.*, one of the highest-grossing movies in history, the father has just run off to Mexico with his girlfriend, and the mother breaks down and cries whenever the children mention him. The youngest boy in the family meets a little alien creature stranded on earth who becomes his alter ego. Like the extraterrestrial, the little boy is lonely and baffled. Both are rootless, unconnected, and lost. *E.T.* was one of the first instances in which our popular culture acknowledged the problem of the family unraveling — and it was acknowledged only in passing! We are almost persuaded to feel that it is neither unnatural nor unexpected for a father to run off with his girlfriend and to leave his wife in tears and his child lonely and baffled.

The film captures an important part of the American experience today: Adults are alienated from children, while children are baffled by adults. Adults are portrayed as incompetent and unavailable; they are too busy, too unhappy and self-absorbed to be useful. So the child, both alien and human, is left to his own resources, escape, and fantasies.

It is furthermore no accident that the most popular television series in many years is about loving fatherhood in an intact family. Nor is it an accident that Bill Cosby, a.k.a. Cliff Huxtable, presents us with an idealized view of the family in which, to our great relief, love, virtue, and gentleness inevitably triumph over and resolve the minor daily crises of life. This is what we think we have lost. It is what we yearn for in our fantasies, even though as we watch the screen, we know better — we know it doesn't exist, if in fact it ever did. And yet how eager we are to be seduced by this pseudoreality that proffers comfort, not truth.

When I set out to interview the families in our study at the ten-year mark, I expected that most adults would say that divorce was a closed book. For children, it would be ancient history. After all, most had spent the major part of their lives in divorced or remarried families. I expected to find a range of ways in which people had put their lives back together — with some doing well and others chronically unhappy — and I was braced for a few tears, nostalgia, reluctance to look back, lingering attachments, and maybe occasional regret that a divorce had ever happened. But I did not expect the experience to endure so fully for so many, with high drama, passions, vivid memories, fantasy relationships, jagged breaks in development, intense anger, and profound discrepancies in quality of life. Nor did I anticipate the problems that so many young people would encounter upon entering young adulthood. Although I thought I was being realistic, nothing prepared me for what I found.

2

Getting in Touch

TEN YEARS LATER

TEN YEARS after their parents had separated and filed for divorce, we are able to track down 116 out of the 131 children in our original study. The youngest is eleven, the oldest twenty-nine. Finding them is not always easy, but once contact is made they come willingly, even eagerly, to be interviewed.

The children remember us with startling clarity, providing tiny details about our first meetings a decade ago. Because we were with them at the major crisis in their lives, when they felt most alone and beleaguered, we seem to be special to them still, to hold an established place in their world as people who are genuinely interested in them and can be trusted. As we sit down to renew our friendships and refresh our memories, it feels as if we belong to an extended family.

We meet in restaurants, at our office, in their homes, at airports, or wherever it is most convenient for them. My staff and I spend two to four hours talking face to face with each person, asking for details of their current lives, including broad questions that open up windows into their relationships, feelings, conflicts, attitudes, hopes, and dreams. How do you view yourself now and in the future? How self-confident do you feel? What do you worry about? Do you expect to marry? Do you have a boyfriend or girlfriend and what is he or she like? Do you want children of your own? Although we have the full record of what transpired during and after their parents' divorces, we ask them many questions about the past, to tap into their changing perspectives. How do you feel that the divorce has affected your relationships and plans? What do you think, on balance, was the effect of divorce on you and your parents? How are your relationships with each parent, with stepparents and siblings, and how have these changed in recent years? What do you remember about the divorce? How important is it in your life today? What advice do you have for parents in divorcing families and for other young people, both at the time of the divorce and afterward?

The experience seems cathartic. I am struck by the ready availability of strong feelings, especially feelings of sadness. Several young men begin the interview with a cool pose but, in recalling events from the past, drop their defenses, letting the tears flow.

Many are curious about how they behaved at different times over the years, and thus love hearing about themselves and their siblings as small children, as if we are providing lost pages of the family album. They ask how other young people in the study are doing, even though they have never met. And they seem very eager to have their pain and efforts acknowledged, showing gratitude when they feel that they are understood.

After some initial shyness, children reveal how often and how soberly they have thought about their parents' divorces over these ten years. It turns out that everyone has made some connection between the experiences of growing up in a divorced family and the experiences that they are having today. In describing their insights, these young people express themselves carefully and thoughtfully, making sure that their exact feelings are conveyed and correcting us when they feel that we are not grasping a nuance of meaning.

After our meetings are over, many of them are reluctant to let go. One woman in her twenties stands tearfully on the sidewalk, slowly waving as I drive off. Others reach out and hug me as interviews end. The responsiveness of these children of divorce, as well as their pleasure in our interest, is profoundly moving. Perhaps we are tapping into the widespread existential loneliness of young people in our society — or perhaps loneliness among the children of divorce is special.

Despite the varied pathways they have taken, the children of divorce share many attitudes, feelings, and expectations. In various ways, they tell me that they think of themselves as belonging to a special group. They are children of divorce, even though they have shed their childhoods. It has become a fixed identity and a self-definition that strongly affects their current and future relationships.

This is surprising. We have come to associate fixed identities with certain kinds of traumas that affect well-defined groups. Vietnamese boat people, for example, may all undergo similar, terrifying experiences and thereafter have shared feelings that become part of their identities, both as individuals and as a group. On the other hand, we do not associate feelings of fixed identity with bereavement. A child who loses a parent through death does not go through life feeling a common bond and mutual identification with all other children who have lost parents the same way. But the children of divorce do feel that kind of bond. They carry the experience throughout their lives and feel a kinship with all other children of divorce, claiming an identity that sets them apart from their peers.

Not only do they seem to feel that they are survivors of tragedy, the children of divorce project this identity onto their own *as yet unborn* children. In discussing the future, they each say that they will delay having children until they are sure that their marriage is working. Their idea is to protect their children from having the same experience they had. "No one should have to go through what I went through," says a twenty-three-year-old man. "You can undo a marriage, but you can't undo a child," says a twenty-year-old woman.

In myriad ways, they tell us that growing up is harder for children of divorce, every step of the way. As if by collusion, they say that their lives have been overshadowed by their parents' divorces and that they feel deprived of a range of economic and psychological supports. They feel that they did not get the kind of support that they imagine children from happy, intact families take for granted.

Even though they no longer have any illusions that their parents could ever remarry, their sense of loss and wistful yearning persists, and their emotions run deep and strong. They feel less protected, less cared for, less comforted. In addition to their sense of shared identity, these children share vivid, gut-wrenching memories of their parents' separations.

"I'm nineteen years old, but I still wake up when I hear loud talking or yelling," says Betty. "And I cry."

"I saw my dad beat up my mom," says twenty-two-year-old Tom. "That is a scar I think of every day." *Every day.* Like many children of divorce, Tom's vivid and painful memories are part of his daily life. We have to keep reminding ourselves that these young people are talking about events from a decade ago. We like to think that, over time, doors close, memories fade — but for these young people, the door is still ajar.

Fighting and screaming are especially remembered. Jason, who is now twenty-three, recalls one event from his parents' divorce fifteen years ago: "Mom and Dad were fighting in the bathroom and Mom ran out into the bedroom and Dad went after her. I tried to stop Dad and he belted me across the room. And I could hear him punching her. And I could hear her gasping in the bedroom." He says now, "I don't know how anyone can *do* that." Jason is haunted by this memory, which for him lives on in the present.

Most remember in great detail the day that the family separated for good. "I remember the day Mom left without telling Dad. We drove all day and all I could think of was how much it would hurt him when he came home that night to find the house empty with us gone," says a nineteen-year-old girl.

Children of divorce also share a morality, one that is more conservative than their parents. As a group, they want what their parents did not achieve — a good marriage, commitment, romantic love that lasts, and faithfulness. The word *faithful* comes up again and again in our interviews. However, their hopes, as we shall see, are shadowed by the sorrowful sense that they are unlikely to achieve their goals of an enduring love and marriage. Their anxiety about not achieving these goals, of being betrayed and rejected in their relationships with the opposite sex, is intense and pervasive.

To avoid their parents' mistakes, they tell us that they will live with the person they love before getting married. They all agree — again as if by collusion — that marriages should not happen early and impulsive marriages should be avoided. After having thought endlessly about how to select the right partner to avoid divorce, they say:

"I learned from my parents' mistakes. I want a long-term relationship because sex without love is animal passion. I want to be in love. There is more to be gained from a long-term relationship."

"Marriage is good. Fidelity is good. Don't cheat. Talk about everything. Don't split up."

"Ideally I would like to find someone to settle down with forever. It's a lot of work, but I think I can, and I have to. I have to be willing to put temptation in anyone else aside. I believe that marriage should be a permanent thing."

The children of divorce have an old-fashioned view of the rules of marriage. They are disdainful of concepts like serial monogamy and open marriage, and compared with their parents, they are a morally conservative group. Their return to more traditional values, however, is not rooted in theology but stems from their own gut-wrenching unhappiness over the experience of divorce. Only one in eight saw both parents recover from divorce in happy remarriages.

Many of these children enter adolescence and young adulthood with deep reservoirs of unresolved feelings, particularly anger about how their parents behaved during their marriage. These emotions have extraordinary staying power. Although most children accept the divorce after ten years, a significant number were furious at the time and are still angry at how their parents acted during marriage and at the separation. This kind of anger does not necessarily reflect the parents' continued hostilities. Rather, it stems from the young people's patient and careful observations of adult behavior over many years. "My parents each gave too little and asked too much," says fifteen-year-old Laura. Young people come to conclusions like this independently. Although parents like to think that their children are brainwashed by others, it's often not the case; the children truly feel that one or both parents acted badly.

"My parents lied and cheated on each other."

"Dad was irresponsible. That's why I hate irresponsibility so much. I haven't forgiven him. I still feel distaste and bitterness."

"I am bitter about all the turmoil in my life. I wish it hadn't happened. I was hurt."

They remain intensely critical of parents who they feel betrayed the marriage. As Eloise, age twenty-one, lies dying from an incurable melanoma, she turns to her mother and says, "I want Dad to know that I'm still angry at him for what he did to you." The mother is stunned. Her husband left ten years ago, but in ensuing years Eloise and her father had grown close. There was never any indication that the girl still felt strongly about her father's infidelity. The mother discourages Eloise from saying anything to her father, knowing that it would break her ex-husband's heart. The girl dies without telling her father her secret feelings.

While children are angry at their parents' failure and may judge them harshly, they are also aware of their parents' suffering. Despite their own neediness and anger, the children of divorce express an extraordinary sympathy when talking about their parents' failings, and as young adults they seem more aware of their parents' limitations as human beings. If at one time they took one side or another in the ongoing quarrels, they now feel embarrassed about it. Some feel that ongoing fights were a nuisance, something to be stepped over, while others say that the ongoing fights were the biggest traumas in their lives, worse than the divorce itself.

I have been astonished by how many of the children of divorce possess a frankness, candor, gentleness, and sweetness that does not reflect the way they feel they have been treated. While many feel rejected and deprived, their own relationships are surprisingly empathic, even generous. While they fear rejection in relationships with the opposite sex, most are not shallow or cynical about these relationships; they care about issues of right and wrong. They are responsive to our interest and willing to talk so that other young people might be helped by their experiences.

As a group, the children of divorce do not feel a sense of entitlement. Knowing that their needs may have to take lower family priority, they accept conditions set down by a harried single parent and understand that they have to share, that resources are limited, and that they must act fairly with others.

Oddly enough, I find more mixed feelings among the adults than among their children about meeting once again, ten years after their divorces. Some are absolutely delighted by my overture. One woman, after driving three hours, sweeps into my office and throws her arms around me; a man kisses me impulsively on both cheeks and says, "What you're doing is wonderful." But I soon begin to realize that we are tapping into two melodies: one is "Yes, I'd love to see you," and the other is "I don't want to reopen that chapter in my life." About half of the parents in our study fall into the latter group and seem reluctant to talk with us. Despite assurances of anonymity, the adults place a high value on privacy, finding it hard to understand how their experiences might be useful to others. Men, in particular, want to know ahead of time what it is I want to ask them.

Why adults should find it so difficult to discuss a decade-old divorce is not clear. Parents and children experience tremendous stress when a marriage breaks down; divorce is equally painful for both. Yet when we reach out at ten years, the adults seem far more defensive than the children. Not one child in our study expresses this kind of suspiciousness when we call them to make an appointment for the ten-year follow-up. There has been much public discussion about children's feelings of responsibility for divorce, yet I suspect that some of the reticence we see among adults may reflect a persistent, underlying guilt related to their children or their former spouse.

In fact, what ultimately brings most of the men and women through our door is enduring concern for their children. Because we are meeting concurrently with every family member, we offer to give parents general feedback about their children's lives if, of course, the children consent and if we think it can help the family. Every young person ultimately grants our request to give feedback to his or her parents. One teenage boy tells us, "Tell my mom that she is wrong. She thinks she shouldn't give me man of the house responsibilities. But I should have more responsibilities — anything to restore normal times. She should know that."

As a group, the adults show a palpable need to put their best foot forward, to cover their failures, and to disguise their unhappiness. After all, they are supposed to be living proof that divorce is the solution to one's problems.

"Everything is easier for all of us," says Laura, dressed in an expensive print dress and pearls, her hair in a chignon. "Life is improving steadily, and all it takes is time, if we had only realized that at the start." As the interview proceeds, however, I learn that Laura's daughter has just had a second abortion and that her own second marriage is on the brink of falling apart.

As many interviews proceed, efforts to convince me that life is "simply wonderful" begin to crumble, giving way to a starker picture of the past five and ten years. Indeed, life has been far more difficult than most imagined it would be. No single question gets at this truer picture; instead, it emerges slowly over the course of each interview.

"I've had only a couple of short-term relationships in the past years," says a man now in his early fifties. "The only woman I was excited about ended up marrying someone else, and I didn't even know he existed."

"I miss being a housewife," says a forty-eight-year-old woman. "I'm tired of wearing all the hats like the full-time job hat, the full-time side activities hat, and the full-time single parent hat." Taking a deep breath, she says, "I've always had a boyfriend. We'll probably stay together for some time." As the breath is fully exhaled, she adds, "But it's not positive."

Before we began talking to people, we expected that ten years would be plenty of time to resolve most issues associated with divorce. Five years after divorce, many adults are admittedly still struggling with questions of what to do with their lives, but most have begun the third stage of divorce, entering new jobs and second marriages and taking up various other second chances. Surely, we thought, the vast majority of men and women in our study will, *after ten years*, have put the divorce well behind them. The dust will have settled and we will now have a chance to see how people really resolve the difficult issues of postdivorce life.

Although divorce begins with stress in the marriage, peaks at separation with filing of divorce papers, and is followed by years of transition, its effects do not vanish at the two-year or five-year mark or, as we are discovering, even at the ten- and fifteen-year marks. For many people, the feelings and memories of marital rupture are vivid and fresh ten and fifteen years following the breakup. The quality of the initial period after the separation does not predict the long-lasting consequences of divorce. These may endure a lifetime.

To get at how these men and women have tackled their problems, we knew we'd have to examine the zigs and zags of people's lives, the pathways they've followed, and the choices they have made. The true measure of divorce is found long after the shouting stops and the lawyers go home; it is calibrated according to how people feel about themselves years later, how their lives have changed, for better or worse.

We had interviewed all of these people at length when their marriages were breaking up, again one year to eighteen months later, and again five years later. Now, after ten years, we have taken the reams of information we gathered and have begun to look for patterns in their feelings, memories, attitudes, and relationships. In our conversations, we try to ascertain whether they are hopeful or discouraged, generally content with their lives, or disappointed in the way things have turned out. We examine their family lives, work lives, sex lives, and social networks. Finally, we subject all our observations to statistical analysis to tease out connections between parts of the present and parts of the past.

In measuring an individual's quality of life, we use yardsticks that accurately reflect how they assess their own lives. Because we want to combine their comments with our own observations of how they are doing, our measures combine subjective and objective reports.

We are interested in how people feel now about decisions made after the divorce. Have they used the failure of the first marriage to make better decisions? Or have they written the same novel over the ten years? Do they live the same fantasy as before? Did they marry an alcoholic the second time around? Or have they developed a more realistic self-image, one that no longer accepts as valid the criticisms of the ex-spouse? Are they making more realistic choices in life?

Because we are opening painful areas, we avoid direct questions that might discourage the free flow of innermost thoughts, memories, and feelings. Instead, we follow each person's lead, supporting the conversation with neutral comments, letting it flow so that we can capture their thoughts and observations about divorce. In this way, we encourage them to make their own connections and self-revelations. Above all, we are interested in their views of what happened and the connections they make between the past and present.

Incredibly, one-half of the women and one-third of the men are still intensely angry at their former spouses, despite the passage of ten years. Because their feelings have not changed, anger has become an ongoing, and sometimes dominant, presence in their children's lives as well.

About half of the men and women in the study are happy with their present lives. For them, the divorce is a closed book over which they have no regrets. To our astonishment, however, divorce continues to occupy a central, emotional position in the lives of many adults ten and fifteen years later. They are not back on track but are still grappling with the aching consequences of a decade-old divorce. Many continue to have very strong feelings about the failed marriage and have not given up the hopes and disappointments attached to it. Some have experienced second divorces, chronic loneliness, poor relationships with their children, or enduring feelings of betrayal and abandonment. A third of the women and a quarter of the men, mostly the older ones, feel that life is unfair, disappointing, and lonely. It is sobering to see how unhappy they are at this stage.

I knew that divorce is not an event that can be gotten over if one simply waits long enough, but even I was surprised at the staying power of feelings after divorce. The great American scenario was that men and women would reconstruct their lives, pull up their socks, and get on with their lives. They'd meet a better man or a better woman and get a better job. They'd have enough money for their

children, and fathers would pay college tuition if only children visited
regularly and were nice to them. They would avoid the mistakes of
the first marriage in a second one.

With typical American optimism, we wanted to believe that time
would mute feelings of hurt and anger, that time itself heals all
wounds, and that people by nature are resilient. But there is no evidence that time automatically diminishes feelings or memories; that
hurt and depression are overcome; or that jealousy, anger, and outrage will vanish. Some experiences are just as painful ten years later;
some memories haunt us for a lifetime. People go on living, but just
because they have lived ten more years does not mean they have
recovered from the hurt.

Divorce for most people is predicated on the assumption that they
have the capacity to make use of their second chances and to rebuild
their lives at any time during adulthood. As it turns out, this is not
always true. Some can, especially with a little help or luck, and some
cannot or, more important, some do not. The dominant pattern of
remarriage in our former couples is for one to find a lasting second
marriage while the other has a second or perhaps third divorce or
never remarries at all.

An adult is more likely to succeed after divorce if he or she has
some history of competence, some earlier reference point to serve as
a reminder of earlier independence and previous successes. For all,
recovery from crisis is an active process. It can be facilitated by the
luck of the draw or by a chance meeting, but it involves active effort,
planning, and the ability to make constructive use of new options and
to move ahead. It helps to have talent, marketable skills in a good
marketplace, and social skills that catalyze support networks. The
lucky ones have families and children willing and able to help and
money saved up or available. Such things make it easier. But there
are no guarantees of success. As we shall see, many things — age,
sex, money, good looks, courage, luck, and countless decisions made
along the way — frame our second chances.

Throughout the book, I have focused on three families whose lives
illustrate the complex problems and opportunities posed by divorce.
The Moores are a traditional, upper-middle-class family in which
both parents are well educated; the father is a physician. The marriage, which lasted twenty years, occupied a major portion of Nicholas's and Christina's adult lives. Nicholas sought the divorce and

remarried soon after it was final. Christina, who opposed it, has stayed single for the past fifteen years. Both continue to maintain stable homes, with the mother in the traditional role of homemaker and the father as economic provider. Their three children, Ruth, Denise, and Sammy, experienced very little conflict during the marriage and divorce but are showing long-term effects to this day.

The Burrelles divorced in their thirties for reasons that I have never been able to understand fully. Betty moved from California to New Mexico with her three children, Steve, Tanya, and Kyle, while Dale, an up and coming hospital administrator, was promoted and moved to New York. Convinced that he was doing the best he could for them, he sent sporadic child support but never sought greater contact with his children than an occasional letter or telephone call. Betty struggled as a single parent — economically, socially, and psychologically responsible for her three children. Divorce shattered their comfortable middle-class living standard and thrust them into poverty.

The Catalanos, who married when Rosemary was eighteen and Bob was twenty-one, are from a lower-middle-class background. Each had a high school education and Bob went on to become a television repairman. After six years of marriage, Rosemary sought the divorce, citing irreconcilable differences. Acknowledging those differences, Bob opposed the divorce but went along with his wife's wishes. Rosemary went back to school, worked full-time, raised her two children, and emerged a new person. Her remarriage has been especially successful, as has a new business venture that she owns and operates. Although Bob had trouble putting his life back together after his first divorce, he too married again, but that marriage failed after seven years. The children, Billy and Kelly, have seen their father erratically over the years. They grew up in a household headed by their stepfather, who was close to Kelly but not to Billy.

Clearly, three families cannot capture the whole experience of divorce, and you will hear many other voices throughout *Second Chances*. These families do, however, reflect some of the major findings of our study and bring familiarity and coherence to the multifaceted subject of divorce.

The stories that follow are true. I have carefully disguised each person to protect his or her privacy, but the words they speak are not changed. Except for disguises, every quote is real.

PART 2

Winners and Losers

3

Nicholas and Christina Moore

NICHOLAS MOORE AND CHRISTINA WOODWARD were childhood sweethearts. They married soon after college graduation in 1951 but delayed having children until he finished medical school. Eventually the young Dr. Moore joined a lucrative radiology practice in San Francisco.

Today neither of them can really say what made them decide to get married. Christina was and is very pretty. Her father was president of an Ivy League school, her upbringing genteel and protected. On her wedding night, she was a virgin. Nicholas, the product of a poor but respectable family in the same town, used a small inheritance from his maternal grandmother to help pay for medical school at the University of Nebraska. Although he courted Christina all through college, Nicholas always found other women very attractive. On their wedding night, he was no virgin.

In all outward appearances, the marriage was successful from the start. Nicholas became quite wealthy, and Christina created the kind of home he had always wanted, establishing an ambiance of harmony, security, and conservative elegance. She did not work outside her home.

Although their twenty years of marriage were not particularly loving, it was only Nicholas who wanted the divorce. Christina opposed it in a befuddled way. At no time could either of them remember being passionate with one another, and sex was a disappointment for both of them from the start. When I met Nicholas for the first time, just after they separated in 1971, he said, "She doesn't want sex. First it was too cold. Then it was too hot. Then it wasn't here. Then it wasn't there. We finally stopped having sex altogether."

According to Christina, her husband left much to be desired. "Nicholas is a very dominating and opinionated man who has a short temper and expects instant perfection," she said. "I can do nothing right in his eyes." When I asked her about their sex life, she surprised me by saying, "He's just not interested in sex. We have not made love for the last three years." Her tone implied that she would have liked more sex, which is not what Nicholas had led me to believe. "I used to be a very passive person," she added. "Now that I assert myself more, he likes it less."

The Moores did not share a social life beyond the obligatory entertainment imposed by his professional work. Christina skillfully organized formal dinner parties for ten or twelve guests, but informal social gatherings with close friends were never part of their married life together. Casual get-togethers made Christina fluttery and anxious. She did not ever want people to drop by the house unannounced.

The marriage lasted for two decades primarily because Nicholas and Christina recognized their social bond, loved their three children, and enjoyed being parents. Each child was a joy. Daughters Ruth and Denise — age fourteen and ten at the divorce — were the kind of youngsters who are praised and cherished by teachers, ministers, and relatives. They provided an enormous sense of gratification to both parents. Their son Sammy, who was seven at the divorce, was overshadowed by his high-achieving sisters, but was certainly the son that his father had always hoped for.

When Nicholas decided to divorce, he announced his intention to Christina. Then, in a typical interaction for this family, they summoned the children to the living room, where Nicholas turned to Christina and said, "You tell them." After she did so awkwardly, he criticized her for her approach. Ruth and Sammy began to cry.

Nicholas stayed at home one week following the announcement and then moved to a nearby apartment house. If he had any misgivings about leaving, they centered on his role with his children. If he was not *pater in situ*, how would he remain *pater familiaris*? Without daily authority over the children, what authority would he have?

At our first meeting, Nicholas struck me as an attractive, urbane, and personable man. Tall and muscular, with curly blond hair, he was soft-spoken and exceedingly responsive to any suggestions I made regarding his children, whipping out a pencil to write down everything I said. He had close, strong relationships with them and shared separate hobbies with each — he took Ruth to the theater, Denise sailing, Sammy on fossil hunts. He pumped me with questions about the impact that divorce might have on the children, but he was particularly worried about Sammy, who was getting into fight after fight at school. He was also worried about Ruth. How would he be able to set rules for her or be a parent during her adolescence? Nicholas found it difficult to relinquish control.

At the same time, Nicholas showed very little interest in his wife's reaction to the divorce, detaching from her with amazing rapidity. He did, however, maintain a strong sense of obligation. After all, she was the mother of his children. One of the very few men who did not take his attorney's advice as to how he could legally minimize his financial obligations, he insisted on supporting Christina after the divorce. Her life would not be up to her previous standards of elegance, but she would not suffer.

At our five-year interview, Nicholas looked wonderful, tanned and weathered from all the sailing, tennis, and fossil hunting. With even, white teeth, sun-bleached hair, and a winning smile, he could easily have passed for much younger than forty-seven. Three years earlier, he had married a forty-three-year-old nurse, Connie, who worked in his hospital, and had bought her a grand new house not far from his children. Nicholas had followed all my suggestions, spending individual time with each child, with extra attention for Sammy.

He was a much happier man. His work was going well and he did not fight with Christina. "It's the best decision I could have made," he said. "I should have done it years ago. My marriage is happy, my new wife is a lovely woman, the children are doing well, and I am not in the least sorry for my decision." There was only one problem: "Hardly any of the children have contact with Connie. The relationship is very strained."

Nicholas found himself caught in a conflict between his second wife and his children, especially his daughters. From his perspective, he was the man in the middle. His new wife wanted him to spend time with her. His daughters, while always well behaved and civil, did not like his wife and wanted him for themselves. Their frequent visits were tense and uncomfortable. On one level, however, Nicholas was not displeased. His discussions about the situation suggested that this type of jealous feuding for his favor, while trying at times, was not lacking in its rewards.

At the ten-year follow-up Nicholas still looks dapper and healthy. He is a successful, affluent physician who exudes confidence and prosperity. As he enters my office, he mentions several recent achievements in my professional career; he is the kind of man who makes it a point to find out such things.

His second marriage remains a success. "Connie is a good wife," he says with pride. "She's been active with the local March of Dimes and has done volunteer work at Children's Hospital, and she's very good at running the house. All in all, I am much happier. I've never regretted getting divorced."

The children are fine, he reports. "I've been keeping up with everyone. Denise is away at college, but I must admit I am a little worried about her. She's changed so much since she went away, but I think it's the school she's in and some boy she met there. Ruth's changed, too. I hoped that she'd go directly to graduate school, but she seems to be marking time. I drop by Christina's every Friday to give Sammy his allowance. You wouldn't believe the change in him, Judy. The last few years, he's become downright civilized and we're seeing a lot more of each other. All the kids call me and I think they have come to accept my house as their second home."

"Really? Are they on better terms with Connie?"

"Well, not really. That has been a disappointment for me," he says in his formal manner. He does not betray the depth of feeling I know is there.

Pursuing this, I ask, "Do you think the situation will improve?"

"Mostly I'm a very happy man," he says, skirting my question. Not a man whose boundaries are easy to cross, he is reluctant to discuss this topic any further. Nicholas does, however, express some concern for Christina.

"I hope she'll be able to go out and get work, remarry, or do something more useful with her life. It's none of my business, but she seems to be in pretty much the same place she was ten years ago. I don't know what she'll do with herself when Sammy leaves for college next year."

As always, Nicholas is pleasant. He thanks me for my continuing efforts on his behalf and on behalf of his family. I tell him how impressed I am by his ability to maintain a reliable presence in their lives and for supporting each child through college. He is proud of them and loves them.

Nicholas Moore is a winner in the postdivorce decade. At the height of his career and holding high rank in two professional associations, he has maintained an extraordinarily stable life over the last ten years. His new wife is more responsive to his needs, particularly his sexual wishes. They travel, entertain, and look forward to a comfortable retirement. Nicholas misses his children but sees them regularly. Aware of their continued but courteous, unspoken criticism of him and his decision to leave Christina, he recognizes that he can probably no longer influence them in this regard. Nevertheless, the failure of his first marriage is behind him, a mistake that he has undone. With high self-esteem and not a shadow of loneliness in his life, Nicholas on balance has gained far more from divorce than he has lost.

In families with children, divorce is rarely a mutual decision. One person wants out, while the other goes along reluctantly or opposes it moderately or vigorously. In our study, 65 percent of the women and 35 percent of the men actively sought to end the marriage in the face of opposition.[1] Only one couple decided to divorce by truly mutual agreement.

As our ten-year follow-up interviews proceed, I begin to notice marked differences — physically, emotionally, and socially — between the members of formerly married couples: their lifestyles, careers, socioeconomic status, and relationships with children, lovers, new wives, and new husbands are different. Slowly, a pattern emerges.

In two-thirds of the former couples, one person is much happier a decade after divorce. These individuals enjoy a better-quality life than that which existed in their failing marriages. They have successfully constructed a gratifying relationship or a network of relationships; they are relatively free from anxiety and depression and other symptoms of emotional distress; and they have been able to achieve a degree of economic stability that protects them against daily worry. Many accomplish this within a successful remarriage, while others find it in a strong, postdivorce family outside of marriage.

The other partners in these couples have not succeeded in improving the overall quality of life ten years after their divorce. They feel unhappy much of the time, often suffer from loneliness, anxiety, or depression, and may be preoccupied with financial concerns as a regular part of daily life. In only 10 percent of couples do *both* husband and wife reconstruct happier, fuller lives by the decade mark. For the remaining quarter, neither the man nor the woman is better off, on balance (or they are actually worse off), than they had been during the marriage. This reflects their own subjective judgment and is in accord with our observations. Looking closely, we find that by and large the person who wanted the divorce is the one doing well, while the one who opposed it is doing less well. His or her forebodings have been realized.

I did not expect to discover that there are winners and losers in the years after divorce; and I certainly did not expect to find gross discrepancies within each couple. To cross-check the discovery, I looked at hundreds more divorce cases being followed since 1980 at our Center for the Family in Transition. The pattern of winners and losers is beginning to be evident there, too. In some instances, people gain a great deal in pride and competence by holding the family together, juggling career and family, and maintaining commitments to their children. At the same time, though, they experience an impoverished quality of life, with fewer friends and limited relationships. Despite the pride in their achievements, they are more lonely, unhappy, and worried.

When I first saw this pattern of winners and losers, I was dismayed, for it runs counter to common expectations about divorce. Divorce is presumed to do two things — undo mistakes from the first marriage and improve the quality of life for both partners. Clearly it lives up to its first expectation. At the ten-year mark, 80 percent of the women and 50 percent of the men affirm the divorce decision. They do not claim to be satisfied with their current lives, but they *are* happy to be out of the former marriage. If the purpose of divorce is to escape a particular stressful relationship, then most people succeed.

But for many people divorce does not live up to its second expectation. Ten years down the road, almost half of the women and two-thirds of the men have no better or a worse quality of life than before the divorce. If the purpose of divorce is to enhance, create, or achieve a quality of life that is richer and happier than what was had in the failing marriage, then the odds of succeeding are far less than is commonly believed.

Many hope for a better life within a happy second marriage. Here, too, the odds are less favorable than generally expected. Most of the time, only one of the former partners found a stable second marriage while the other tried and failed or never remarried. In one-fifth of the couples, neither person remarried during the ten years. In only one in seven of the former couples did the former wife and husband experience stable second marriages.

In assessing the thoughts and feelings as well as the intimate and social relationships, work, family life, and economic stability of men and women ten years after divorce, we find explanations for why some win and some lose.

Age makes a difference. Well-established men who divorce in their thirties and forties tend to be winners in the postdivorce decade. Not surprisingly, most are approaching or have reached the peak of their earning power and are financially secure at the decade mark. They tend to have a higher self-esteem and are happier than men in their twenties. Most of these older men pay child support regularly, although at levels set by the court ten years earlier. As their children grow into adolescence, very few offer to increase child support payments even though they are earning far more than before. One man who was earning close to $200,000 a year voluntarily increased his payments from $150 a month to $200 when his only son became a teenager. The son calls it "a tip."

As a group, older men seem more willing than women to accept responsibility for failure in the first marriage, admitting to mixed feelings and strong regrets about the divorce. Indeed, when such regrets are heard, they come mostly from older men.

On the other hand, I was fascinated by the apparent ease with which Nicholas and other older men left their wives of ten, fifteen, or twenty years. Perhaps they had been gradually detaching themselves over the years, but I must admit — and here I show my prejudices — that the final pulling away was shockingly complete in many cases. Nicholas Moore is a good man, a man of strong commitments who at one time loved his former wife. While he behaves responsibly toward her now, he is more inclined to indifference, with no remaining sense of affection and only general concern. Other older men were much less responsible than Nicholas, and many treated women cruelly after long years of marriage. Many of these

husbands who pull away after fifteen or twenty years of marriage talk
about their wife's age as an important factor in the decision to divorce. They admit that they are repelled by the changes in her face
and body, by the inevitable sags and wrinkles. I have the sense, as
they speak, that they are frightened by an indirect vision of their own
mortality. In seeking a younger woman, as many do, they seem to be
trying to delay their own aging and eventual death.

The most important influence on an older man's sense of well-
being and happiness ten years after divorce is a successful second
marriage. Compared with single or divorced men, the remarried men
had more ties to the community, were twice as likely to have friends,
tended to get more support at work, and lived altogether more stable
lives.

At the ten-year mark, less than one-third of the men now over fifty
and one-half of those now in their forties continue to be happily remarried. Many found new wives in the first year after divorce and
most who remarried did so within three years. Men like Nicholas
seem to have learned from their experience. In taking up their second
chances, they chose women whom they perceive to be sexier, less
critical, more responsive, more giving. They know what they want.

The men who divorced while in their thirties are the happiest
group in our study. They are less lonely, have more friends, and have
established, through mostly excellent second marriages, high self-
esteem. More have children living with them, and most are economically secure. As a group they have maintained or improved their
standard of living over the past five years.

For a host of reasons, men undergo less psychological change than
women in the wake of divorce. Like Nicholas Moore, their lives are
remarkably continuous. Many women are completely different people ten years after divorce. Not so the men. For one thing, male social
roles tend to be defined by employment, whereas women tend to
separate work and family roles. After divorce, a man's job, status,
and contacts at work are relatively unchanged, so a major part of his
life remains stable.

The most common pattern after divorce is for the man to move into
an apartment, leaving his wife and children in the home until the
divorce arrangements are worked out. Men, therefore, are less likely
to assume the task of singlehandedly caring for children and running
a household after divorce. The task of raising children and taking
them successfully through the different stages of growing up pro-

motes psychological growth in adults. The visiting role does not provide the same opportunities, denying many men an important stimulus for change.

For cultural and economic reasons, the divorced man tends to have a larger pool of potential mates than the divorced woman, with a better chance of finding a new partner who will match his wishes, needs, faults, and foibles. When a divorced woman establishes a relationship with a man, she may be tempted to meet him more than halfway because her choice of available men is narrower. Given his wider choices, the man may not have to think about meeting a new woman more than halfway. Overall, he faces less pressure to change, to accommodate another person's needs.

Although some men had adventurous flings with younger women soon after divorce, few men in our study became dedicated, carefree bachelors; most find it very difficult to create a gratifying home — a home that they love — for themselves without the help of a woman. This does not mean, of course, that men are incapable of creating a homey atmosphere, but many are convinced that they cannot make a home without a woman at their side. Men after divorce can be extremely lonely — and instead of drawing on their own inner resources or relying on a network of friends to provide needed comfort in their lives, they tend to seek female companionship.

Half of the older men in our study, those over forty at separation, did not remarry in the decade after divorce, and in our follow-up interviews they paint a picture of intense isolation and deprivation.

As I walk into David Norris's Optical Shoppe in San Jose, I am cheered by how well he looks. Trim and fit at sixty-one, David is quite distinguished in his white lab coat. We go into his office at the back of the store where David offers me a comfortable chair.

It is soon apparent, however, that he is not comfortable with this interview. His answers are brief and his manner skittish, until near the end of the hour, when he begins to ask me questions that have long been on his mind.

As we talk, I learn that David Norris is a lonely man. When his wife, Alice, divorced him ten years ago she took away his child, most of their friends, and his entire social network. David puts in long hours at his optical business because he has no real reason to go home after work. His ex-wife puts everything she has to say to David in writing.

When I ask about the divorce, he says it had to happen. His wife is so rigid. When I ask if he dates, he makes me feel that I've over-stepped propriety, but says he did date one lady.

"What happened?"

"She became interested in someone else."

"That must have hurt you."

"Well, you never know about another person," he says. "I've put it away."

"Do you think about the future?"

"I've thought about that. But you can't plan. You have no control. I'm going to retire in four or five years. I may travel a little."

David wishes that he had kept the house. His wife took it because she claimed his daughter needed it, but he is not comfortable in an apartment and regrets not buying another house for himself. He hears that his ex-wife is now thinking of selling the house. "It's sad that no one from the family will live there anymore," he says. "I'd buy it if I could."

David asks me to tell him about Alice. He sometimes worries about her and hopes that she remarries. His daughter tells him that she smokes too much.

Five years later, at our fifteen-year follow-up, David seems un-changed. Now sixty-six, he is selling his business but has no idea of what to do with the rest of his life.

I am especially concerned and saddened as he talks about his only child. "She has a job that doesn't allow her to enjoy life very much. But what can you do? I told her that I wanted her to finish school, and it kind of bothered me that she didn't." He seems helpless.

"She and I aren't close," he says. "She doesn't come over much, and I don't like to call because her hours aren't regular. I don't like to wake her so I leave it to her to call me, which is seldom. I'd like her to be in touch, but . . . life goes by and it's gone and never comes back."

About his social life he now says, "I'm sort of a loner. I don't think that I'll ever remarry. There's perhaps twenty-five percent of my life left and I guess I want to live it that way. What I miss most is watch-ing my daughter grow up. She'd come over but it's not like living with her." Then, bitterly, he adds, "It's gone. It will never come back. That's what I regret the most. It's like a death, only worse. In a death, a person is gone and fades away. But not in a divorce."

David impresses me with feelings of emptiness and sadness. Our limited conversations may have been the most meaningful interactions that he has had in the last five years. An unhappy, constricted, lonely man who seems much older and more rigid than he was ten and fifteen years earlier, he is resigned to finishing out the rest of his life in the same isolated fashion, as if in mourning for what he has given up and for what he will never rebuild.

David Norris represents a group of older men whose relationships depend on family ties. Although David's marriage was impoverished and his wife says she never loved him, it provided David with the social network that he needed. When his wife left, he never was able to rebuild those networks on his own, for himself. Ten years later, his twenty-year-old daughter, with tears running down her face, says, "He never asked about what I wanted to do and because he didn't ask, I thought he didn't care."

Older women rebuild nests and networks but continue to feel lonely, yet the plight of many older men is worse. Uninterested in clubs, churches, political organizations, and community associations, they have no life outside work and even have trouble reaching out to their children. A decade after divorce, a quarter of the older men in our study remain isolated.

In the final analysis, men seem to undergo much less change after divorce than women, but there may be important changes in men that are going undetected, changes that are not picked up by the questions we ask or the attitudes we bring to the study of divorce.

I am frankly surprised by the chorus of people who say that, compared with women, the men in our society don't have access to their feelings and are incapable of intimacy, love, affection, self-searching, or empathy. On the contrary, many of the men we know from this study — and we know them well — suffered, bled, and cried in the wake of divorce. They sorely missed their children, wives, and home lives, feeling as if they had nowhere to turn. If anything, they felt trapped because their only source for love, praise, sharing, establishing a home, and self-esteem was either through a woman or through their children. After divorce, both sources were blocked or were more difficult to reach. It is no coincidence that every man who sought a divorce in this study had another woman waiting in the wings.

*

When Nicholas demanded the divorce, Christina was stunned. Their marriage had its problems, but Christina never imagined that the tensions between them could lead to this. She had been brought up in an ordered world where people keep commitments, where they do what they are supposed to do. If Christina had any faults, it was that she was too nice, too civilized and dignified. When I saw her soon after Nicholas left, Christina was frantic. Behind the fashionable blond coiffure and Chanel suit sat a terrified woman. She carried two how-to books and three pamphlets on divorce, had just taken a Parent Effectiveness Training course, and was thinking of taking it again.

Christina could not make any decisions. She said repeatedly, "How can I get Denise to her oboe lessons? What shall I do with the children over the summer?" The summer was several months away. What she did or did not "do with the children over the summer" was hardly the critical issue, but Christina could think of nothing else. It was as if she could not take responsibility for planning even the smallest aspect of her life. Yet she was being called on to take unprecedented responsibility for both herself and her children.

There was a pathetic and ironic quality to Christina as she talked. She had tried all her life to do what was right. She read Spock, Gesell, and other child psychologists. She spoke to her pediatrician regularly. In a hundred different ways she repeated that she was only trying to be a good mother, a good wife. Yet her heroic efforts had failed. Now she faced the breakup of her marriage — the smashing of her plans to provide the ideal home in which serenity and gracious living would prevail.

Christina tried to put on a bright face, and indeed she looked very beautiful by all external measures. But the escalating events of recent weeks seemed to crush her self-confidence and cripple her ability to make decisions and plans. Floating on a sea of platitudes, Christina described her marriage and divorce vaguely, abstractly. Underneath her facade, I felt there was a very hurt, bitter woman who was hardly in touch with the enormity of her anger, humiliation, and lack of reward for so much effort over the years. She spoke breathlessly, with a fluttering quality. "I never cry," she said, "except in the movies where it is dark. I try to avoid things that make me feel out of control."

Although Christina was aware of problems in the marriage, she opposed the divorce with all her heart. Having always lived with her family or her husband, with no experience living as an independent adult, she was realistically frightened about raising three children alone. During our first meeting, she raised question after question about children — what to do about their misbehavior at the dinner table, about bedtime now that her husband was gone, about Ruth's breaking curfew, about Sammy's refusal to go to school, about how to set up new household routines.

Christina had sought psychological counseling and I urged her to continue with it for a while longer. After she left my office, I worried if she would be able to meet her new responsibilities, given her need for external structure to feel calm inside.

When I called Christina five years later, she greeted me as if we had talked the day before. She came to my office, again well coiffed and in a chic suit, smiling and laughing with girlish charm. I had forgotten how tall and stunning she was. Christina assured me that everything was fine. "I'm living about ten minutes from where I used to live," she said. "The girls and I went looking for the house together. Ruth crawled under the porch and decided that it had a really good foundation. She really surprised the agent."

Christina bit her bottom lip and sighed. "Sammy is still my biggest problem. He didn't learn anything in elementary school, and now that he's starting junior high I don't know if he'll be able to ever catch up. He still punches other children and is hard to discipline. Sometimes I think it would have been better if he lived with Nicholas after the divorce. But then I know that all of Nicholas's rules and regulations would drive Sammy up the wall."

Not much else had changed with Christina. "I'm really going to have to look for a job," she said, "but I'm so busy with the children, getting the house fixed up, doing the garden and all. I give occasional piano lessons. But it's hard to plan much more."

I asked her about the house.

"It's nothing like my other home," she said. "But I've tried to help the children adjust to it."

Did she have a social circle of friends? Was she dating?

"I'm not so interested. I went to a Parents Without Partners meeting, but that's not an ambiance for me. What will happen will happen when I'm ready for it to happen."

There were no serious money pressures. "My lawyer did very well for me, and Nicholas was fair," Christina said. "The children's needs are covered, and whenever I need financial advice I call Nicholas and he is happy to advise me."

When Christina left after this visit, I still felt worried about her. Although she looked much better, even more attractive, I realized that her life was at a very low ebb. As she herself said, there was virtually no change following the divorce, except that she was a single parent and lived in a different house. This is not how she hoped her life would turn out.

At the ten-year interview, I am again disturbed by how little Christina has changed. "I'm a full-time mother," she says. "I haven't had time for dating and I guess you could say my social life is pretty limited. I play some bridge. And Sammy takes up a lot of my time. He's really begun to grow up this past year. We went through so much but I think he's going to be okay."

Sammy is seventeen. He has just added a pet iguana, two parakeets, and a kitten to his already impressive "private zoo collection." Christina drives thirty miles round trip each week to buy live crickets for the iguana from a specialty pet shop across the bay.

"What is your relationship with Nicholas these days?" I say, shifting the subject away from children.

"We talk on the phone now and then, but the only time I've seen him in person was four years ago. Denise was up at Clear Lake, hiking with some friends. We heard on the radio that a major forest fire had broken out in the area. Nicholas and I drove up together to find her. Thank God, she was okay."

What does she now think about divorce?

"We couldn't have continued to live together," she says. "He was in love with another woman. Anyhow, he and I didn't agree on a lot of things. We have different views on discipline and how to raise children. He's really a man who doesn't like women, and I couldn't meet his demands. He treated me the way he treats so many people. Now he's got his house just the way he wants it. But I don't know. Maybe he's a better father this way."

I think to myself how little bitterness she is showing, how generous she is in spirit — and how out of touch she is in her inability to recognize the constriction of her life. She seems unable to plan for Sammy's departure.

"I've considered taking some classes in a master's program," she says. "I might go for an M.A. in music theory or for an advanced degree in music history. I went over and talked to the dean at the University of San Francisco. They have a good music department."

"That sounds like a good idea," I say. "What would it involve?"

As she answers, I realize that it is very unlikely she will be able to carry through this plan. She sees herself as a homemaker and mother. Her attitudes and role in life have not changed over the decade. She is still putting unlimited time into the care of the one child still at home.

Unlike her former husband, Christina Moore has lost more than she has gained in the decade after divorce. True, she is no longer married to a man who was hypercritical of her and she is more independent. But when her son leaves for college, she faces increasing loneliness, continued singlehood, sexual deprivation, and fewer opportunities to meet people or begin a new career. In the years ahead, her primary social contacts will be with children who have left home. If she is ever to have a better life, she will have to make heroic efforts to help herself. She remains economically dependent on her ex-husband, and her self-esteem is resting on fragile supports.

Age is a crucial factor for women who divorce. In our study, every woman who was forty or older at marital separation remained unmarried ten years later. Now in their fifties, some had had recent love affairs or sexual encounters, but not one had a stable love relationship at the ten-year mark. By contrast, half of their former husbands were remarried at the ten-year mark. Two of the ex-husbands were in homosexual relationships.

I was really taken aback when I found how much our figures vary from national estimates, which hold that 75 percent of divorced women and 80 percent of divorced men remarry. Could our study be so far off the mark? I asked Dr. Arthur Norton, assistant chief demographer of the United States.[2] He thought not. Few people, he said, realize how such population figures are derived. For example, the census figures are averages that include many eighteen-, nineteen- and twenty-year-old women who tend to remarry readily after divorce. Older women who have been married ten or twenty years encounter very different odds.

A 1985 Census Bureau survey shows that 65 percent of all women who have divorced once remarried. There was a major discrepancy in age: 48 percent remarried in their twenties, 33 percent in their thirties, and 11 percent in their forties. Only 3 percent of divorced women remarried in their fifties. Clearly, older women have a very different postdivorce life than younger women.

Women who are forty and older at separation and divorce fall into two groups. In our study, about half sought the divorce. They felt demeaned and belittled or had been intensely lonely in the marriage. One was physically abused. A few felt that it was their last chance to get out of the marriage. They were not necessarily expecting to marry again but felt drained and debilitated by this relationship. It was worth taking a chance on a better life, and some succeeded. When her daughter finished high school, Alice Norris moved to Vancouver to work with the Greenpeace movement. Although living on a shoestring, she loves her work and is dedicated to the cause. At our ten-year interview, she is, at fifty-four, very happy and relaxed and says that she talks to her daughter mostly by telephone. Her advice to others: "If the relationship is harmful, get out. I'm very much at peace with my divorce. Beforehand I felt responsible for my husband, not for me. I was always doing what other people wanted me to do, not what I wanted." Unlike Christina, she detaches from her former responsibilities, including her child, about whom she says, "I really don't know what my daughter is thinking and that's one reason why I wanted to talk to you. Perhaps you can tell me."

The other half of the older women felt their lives were disrupted, after reasonably happy long-term marriages, when their husbands filed for divorce. Many of these women really loved their husbands, were happy with their lives, and loved their homes, which they considered to be extensions of themselves. For many, the home was a metaphor for happiness and fulfillment of childhood fantasies, expanding their personal boundaries. They liked raising their children and enjoyed their economic stability. Life had a great many built-in serenities and continuities that allowed them to live in accord with their expectations. Some were not happy in the sexual or personal relationships in their marriages but nevertheless were living in full harmony with the values of their earlier hopes and dreams. For them, divorce was a most unwelcome and unexpected shock.

Ten years after divorce, the older women stand out from other groups in our study. With one or two major exceptions, they undergo much less psychological change, explore fewer second chances, and have less sense of pride or accomplishment than their younger counterparts. They do not shift gears psychologically or socially. Eighty percent are insecure financially and almost half experienced a decline in their standard of living in the five previous years. Younger women, by contrast, mostly improved their financial status in those years, often through successful remarriages or new careers.

Tragically, many courts, not recognizing the greater difficulty that divorce poses for older women, treat them as no different from thirty-year-olds, with the admonition "You are able-bodied, so go out and sell your house, get a job, and carry your own weight in society." This attitude overlooks the psychological, economic, and social barriers that older divorced women face. Ironically, many dating services are more realistic; men *willing* to date women over fifty are invited to join at half price.

The economic discrepancy between former wives and husbands in this group is shocking and deplorable. Although most of the women are working, they have experienced a mixture of full- and part-time work interspersed with periods of unemployment. Only one woman works at the professional level for which she was academically prepared. Although many trained as teachers, they are working as sales clerks, dressmakers, drafters, or cashiers at levels not appropriate to their intellectual capabilities. While they like working with people, the work itself is unrewarding in terms of interest or financial gain. They improvise to meet basic expenses. Many former husbands, on the other hand, are at the peak of their professional and business careers, and the majority are well off financially. Only a handful of the older women are financially secure ten years after divorce. As an added burden, many face the physical deterioration, terminal care, and death of elderly parents. In this, too, they feel beleaguered and alone, getting very little support from children or ex-husbands. Caring for an elderly parent can be just as stressful as caring for a toddler, with greater anxieties and fewer rewards.

These women find support in friends, clubs, and churches; some are involved in interest groups, hobby groups, and community activities that bring them in contact with other women. Even though they are not isolated socially, they are intensely lonely. In comparing their lives today with their married years, they express a terrible feeling of loss. These women loved and cherished the roles of wife, mother, homemaker, and nurturer. They laid out the holiday decorations, cooked the traditional feasts, and passed the carving knife to the man of the house. Since the divorce, they still put out the decorations and cook the feasts for the children. But it is not the same. While they may not miss the warmth of their ex-husband's body in bed, they miss the warmth of traditional family life. The flawed marriage was still congruent with the roles they wanted to play in their lives, and they approved of themselves despite the stresses in the relationship.

Ten and fifteen years of heading a household does not erase the sense of loss these older women feel or their anxiety about living alone. Older single women in our society are indeed more vulnerable and have reason to be fearful of their future alone. When the youngest child leaves home, their role as homemaker will diminish. Some women are honest about their fears, worrying that they might induce their children to stay at home to protect their own needs. "I need Jimmy," says Corrine. "I think I keep my children around for me, and that's not good for them and that worries me." Other women are incapable of acknowledging the conflict between their own wishes and the needs of their children; they may lean heavily on children, who in turn fear leaving their mothers alone. Such conflicts make the already difficult task of leaving home much more difficult for the children and, indeed, some do not escape.

Like Christina Moore, many older women are wrapped up in identifications stemming from their long years of marriage. A sense of "we-ness" emerges out of a stable marriage, as each person identifies with some of the other person's values and attitudes. Self-esteem is based on one's inner standards and the partner's standards plus standards created within the identity of the marriage — each person wants the other to be proud of his or her achievements, and each is eager to win approval and praise along with love. As the years go by, these identifications strengthen and a new marital identity is formed. As it becomes difficult for one or both partners to think of themselves outside the context of the marriage, a superordinate identity is created. In a good marriage, each person contributes to the new entity, which operates in a conjoined orbit. Out of this partnership one gains a comfortable sense of identity that is different from the identity one had as a single person.

In more traditional marriages, like the Moores', mutual identity stems from the powerful personality or career path of just one of the partners. Some wives, for example, define themselves as the "doctor's wife" (like Christina) or the "business executive's wife." When such marriages last for many years and then come apart in middle age, there can be serious loss and confusion, especially for the wife, who may have an extraordinarily difficult time reestablishing an identity separate from the marriage.

Half of the women in our study who did not remarry report a deteriorating sense of physical well-being as they cope with the many problems that arise in the decade after divorce. They have more bodily complaints, including colds, headaches, backaches, constipation, migraines, colitis, high blood pressure, and jaw pain. Indeed, these complaints are not confined to older women but are widely reported by single, divorced women. (Remarried women do not report a wide range of somatic symptoms.) Others have psychological problems but cannot afford therapy. Many, it seems, lay their hands on a refillable Valium prescription in lieu of the treatment they need.

Some men and women seem to be held together by marriage; it brings order and security to their lives, and the structure itself provides their raison d'être and their highest level of adult adjustment. For both men and women, marriage in middle or later life has an additional and very important function: It provides an internal buffer against the anxieties of aging, of being old and alone, and of facing the inevitability of death. It also provides external supports to cope with the increasing disabilities and infirmities of old age. When the structure is removed, they are left feeling extremely vulnerable, and the external symptoms of physical deterioration are symbolic of internal conflict and emotional distress. Not everyone can be expected to reconstruct a happy life following divorce. Not everyone is possessed of the inner resources, or the youth and beauty, to attract external supports. The capacity to change is not a given and cannot be taken for granted.

4

Denise Moore

PLAYING THE QUEEN OF HEARTS

IN MANY YEARS of studying divorce, I have been haunted by a scene from a French surrealist film called *The Blood of a Poet*. A man and a woman are sitting opposite each other playing cards. Next to the man is a cloaked figure. Under the table is a dead child. The woman, who is beautiful, reaches across the table, smiles invitingly, and says, "What you need is the queen of hearts." As the man looks at his hand, beads of sweat appear on his forehead. He does not have the queen of hearts and is seized with anxiety. Then, surreptitiously, he reaches under the table and finds the queen of hearts in the breast pocket of the dead child. He slams down the card. The masked figure next to him then hands him a gun. The man shoots himself.

As a psychologist, I am fascinated by this scene because it symbolizes a key dilemma of many young people today. As I see it, the queen of hearts represents the capacity to love. The adult man is missing this card in his deck but understands that he possessed it in childhood. Time is running out. If he is to win the beautiful woman, he must find the queen of hearts. But as he reaches into his past to play the card, he is overcome with fear, guilt, and memories attached to his childhood. Unable to deal with them, he chooses self-destruction.

This does not mean of course that young adults are literally shooting themselves over childhood conflicts. But many who experienced divorce as children are entering adult heterosexual relationships with the feeling that the deck is stacked against them. As they reach into the past, children of divorce find the queen of hearts wrapped in a cocoon of memories — memories of broken hearts, angry conflicts, ugliness, and sometimes violence; memories of wretchedness, abandonment, and betrayal; memories that are sometimes real, sometimes imagined.

The entry into young adulthood occurs roughly between the ages of eighteen and twenty-three, and it is a difficult time for all young people, divorce or no divorce. To become an adult, one must have established in adolescence the sense of a separate identity. One must have the courage to try new ventures, to take chances. One must be able to seek out and establish an intimate and committed relationship. It helps enormously to have imprinted on one's emotional circuitry the patterning of a successful, enduring relationship between a man and a woman. Since the family provides such relationships sui generis, it is parents who carve the deepest impressions on children.

All young people are profoundly afraid of making irrevocable mistakes while crossing the Rubicon into adulthood. New ventures can be perilous, and decisions are inherently riskier than they were at younger ages. When one choice is made, other choices are closed off, perhaps forever. The changing roles of men and women, greater sexual freedom, and the high rate of divorce make courtship riskier. Adolescents feel the effects of these changes in society, and they are afraid of rejection, failure, and disappointment.

The children of divorce are likewise afraid, but more so. It is never easy to play the queen of hearts, but the children of divorce have a dead child under the table; their entry into young adulthood is encumbered by an inescapable need to reexamine the past. What they see are the long shadows cast by their parents, who failed to maintain a loving relationship. Now that it is time to venture forth, to trust, and to make a commitment, the children of divorce find that their search for love and intimacy is ghost-ridden. In adolescence they think about these issues, but in young adulthood anxiety about them hits full force. They fear betrayal. They fear abandonment. They fear loss. They draw an inescapable conclusion: Relationships have a high likelihood of being untrustworthy; betrayal and infidelity are probable. Of course, young people can find a great deal of evidence in our society to support this conclusion. The suspicion that betrayal can come at any time without warning spills into our modern culture. I think most of us attending a wedding these days mutter somewhere in the back of our minds, "I wonder how long this will last."

It is clear from talking to the young people in our study that the transition into young adulthood is especially difficult in ways that they did not anticipate. Even those who do very well in high school and who have many friends and stable relationships say that they experience rising anxiety in their late teens and early twenties. Feelings and memories about their parents' divorce arise with new intensity at this time. Like all young people their age, they ask, What kind of adult will I be? Whom will I marry? What can I expect out of life? But the children of divorce also ask, What kind of relationships will I have? Am I doomed to repeat my parents' mistakes? Or, as one young man puts it, "Must I take a leaking ship into the storm of life?"

The behavior of children of divorce is often at odds with their philosophy of high hopes and high morality. They seem propelled by despair and anxiety as they search for what they fear they will never find. They abhor cheating yet find themselves in multiple relationships that lead to cheating. They want marriage but are terrified of it. They detest divorce but end up divorced. They believe in love but expect to be betrayed. Such grave inconsistencies make life difficult. Unable to resolve these internal conflicts, they are driven to self-destructive behaviors.

At entry into young adulthood, every child in our study is afraid of repeating his or her parents' failure to maintain a loving relationship. The extent to which this fear dominates their lives, as a conscious concern or as an undercurrent, varies greatly. The extent to which they are led unconsciously to seek out relationships that will confirm their fears of loss and rejection also vary. But all hold two traits in common: fear of rejection and betrayal and a lifelong vulnerability to the experience of loss.

The Sleeper Effect

I am looking forward to my meeting with Denise Moore. She is the first youngster in our study to be interviewed at the ten-year mark, and I must confess she is one of my favorites. Her mother, Christina, tells me that Denise is getting good grades in college and that she has a boyfriend. I wonder what major she has decided on and what her boyfriend is like. I remember her blond hair, apple cheeks, and innocence at age sixteen, when last we met.

As Denise enters my office, she greets me warmly. With a flourish-ing sweep of one arm, she says, "You called me at just the right time. I just turned twenty-one!" Then, as I settle in to hear all the news, she startles me. Denise's expression turns serious. She says, "I'm into pain."

This is the last thing in the world I expected her to say.

I first met Denise when she was eleven. She was chubbier then, a well-built, sturdy, charming youngster who had the aura of a child who has been well cared for and protected. I knew from her parents and teachers that she was very highly regarded as an honors student and a gifted musician and that she was involved in a busy round of activities including oboe lessons, school sports, and sailing. Taught by a nationally acclaimed oboist from San Francisco, Denise was a star in the school orchestra and hoped for a career in music.

Denise came willingly to my office that first time ten years ago. She answered questions easily and directly, emphasizing how little had changed since her father left home. Mom was "happier" and played the piano more. Dad was happier, although Denise was afraid that he might remarry or move away. But if Dad has a girlfriend, she said, "I'll have to decide if I like her."

I asked Denise at that first interview, "Is there anything recently that's troubled you?"

"You mean from the divorce?"

"Whatever."

"The divorce didn't upset me," said Denise. "I was not surprised because I knew my parents weren't getting along. I used to get up every morning to see if the beds were pushed together or apart," she said with a mischievous smile. "Anyway, I like it better because now I don't have to pretend that I don't hear fights in the bedroom."

Denise then volunteered a touching story of a lost puppy she had found on her way home from school. No one seemed to be taking care of it so she brought it home. Her parents were sorry it was lost and had no one to care for it, but they would not let her keep the puppy. As Denise told the story, she was visibly upset and on the verge of tears. Then she seemed to slam a door. She straightened up and said, matter-of-factly, "I realized there wasn't anything I could do about it."

I assumed that Denise had displaced some of her feelings about the divorce onto the puppy and her parents' rejection of the stray animal.

While the puppy episode must have hurt, as Denise told the story her obviously strong grief was short-lived. A pragmatic, well-controlled youngster, I thought to myself — perhaps too well controlled.

I gave Denise some crayons and paper. "Would you like to draw your family?"

"I'd rather not, " she said primly and drew a contrived still life with flowers and fruit. Again I thought to myself, This child is holding feelings in conscious check.

Denise was willing to talk about school and friends but not about her parents or her future. Preoccupied with today, she wanted to stay in the same house, go to the same school, have the same friends.

Now, ten years later, Denise sits across a table, her flaxen hair cut short, and recounts recent events in her life. When she says that she is "into pain," I am frankly puzzled. Denise is the one child in our study who we all thought was "most likely to succeed" in the aftermath of divorce. Despite my concern that she denied her feelings to an extreme degree, she was a prime candidate for full recovery because she had so much going for her, including high intelligence, many friends, supportive parents who did not engage in internecine warfare, plenty of money, and good college support. As we began our ten-year interviews, we knew very little about what the characteristics of successful coping and recovery from divorce would be, but if anyone had made it through the gauntlet, I expected it to be Denise.

As Denise sits telling her story, I find myself drawn into unexpected intricacies of her life and, by extension, into the lives of many other children of divorce. After graduating from high school with honors, Denise was admitted to the UCLA music department and did very well in her freshman year. Then, for the first time in her life, she fell apart. As she tells it, "I met my first true love." The young man, her age, so captivated Denise that she decided it was time to have a fully committed love affair. But on her way to meet him in Montana to spend summer vacation with him, "my courage failed," says Denise. "I went to New York instead. I hitchhiked across the country. All the time I didn't know what I was looking for. I thought I was just passing time. I didn't stop and ponder. I just kept going, recklessly, all the time waiting for some word from my parents. I guess I was testing them. You see, I wanted them to acknowledge my pain. But no one — not my dad, not my mom — ever asked me what I was doing there on the road alone."

"How do you explain that?"

"I don't think they brought me up with honesty," says Denise. "There's another chapter in this that I might as well tell you. I stopped eating and my weight dropped to ninety-seven pounds. Then, one day in the dorm, a friend made me look in the mirror and I got real scared. I realized how depressed I was and what I was doing to myself. I began to get angry. I'm still very angry. I'm angry at my parents for not facing up to the emotions, to the feelings in their lives, and for not helping me face up to the feelings in mine. They never asked about or acknowledged my pain." Denise looks ready to cry. "I try, Judy. I really try. But I have a hard time forgiving them."

"I'm sorry to hear how much you've been suffering. When did you discover you were angry?"

"You'll laugh," she says. "It was in my karate class. I loved it. I loved hitting. I found I couldn't stop hitting. Then I realized I was angry and had been for a very long time."

"Denise, when I first met you, you admitted to so little feeling. You've shown little feeling over the years. Should I have pushed you then or later? Would that have helped?"

She smiles patiently and says, "I don't think so. That was exactly the point. All those years I denied feelings. I wasn't consciously lying, but I always had the sense I was passing time, passing through, never thinking about what was happening. I lived with the absolute thought that I could live without love, without sorrow, without anger, without pain. That's how I coped with the unhappiness in my parents' marriage. And that's why I didn't get upset at the divorce. That's why I looked so good to you when I was little. Only that year, when I met Frank, did I become aware of how much feeling I was sitting on all those years. I was afraid to love him because I was afraid I'd lose him, afraid he wouldn't stay mine. Before I met Frank I always said to myself that I would never let anyone or anything hurt me. But it didn't work when I fell in love. You see, Judy, it takes practice to let pain happen."

Denise is holding nothing back. "I'm able to cry now, for the first time. Life isn't easy. It isn't easy to dredge up these feelings from the past. I've felt deceived. That's why I said I'm into pain. At least maybe I can face it now, do you think?"

Three and a half hours have gone by. I am sobered by her outpouring. Will other young women bring similar surprises?

Little in Denise's childhood predicted her present dilemma. She was capable, handling the divorce with aplomb. Indeed, she was every parent's dream of the perfect daughter — competent, pretty, award-winning, and smart. Nothing predicted the storm that lay ahead. My only inkling was an early concern that she did not have access to her feelings as an eleven-year-old. She felt she had no permission from herself or from her parents to grieve, to feel sorrow or anger. She also felt an enormous need to conform, partly to protect her parents and to hold the family together.

In love and looking for intimacy, Denise was frightened of not getting what she wanted, of never finding a steadfast relationship that would last. It was time for Denise to commit herself to another, to love someone, to reveal herself, to risk, to enter the kind of relationship in which her parents failed — and she was terrified. Afraid of not finding commitment, she couldn't commit herself. Denise's acute depression and her anorexia occurred not coincidentally just at the point where she was on her way to continue and to consummate her first love affair. Denise could not go forward to meet her young man, nor could she go back home again. For the first time she confronted the fears, anxieties, guilt, and concerns that she had suppressed over the years. Called upon to play the queen of hearts, she was stymied because all of her buried feelings came into play.

She embarked instead on a pilgrimage to nowhere, in what looked like aimless wandering. It was, in reality, the equivalent of an inner search for feelings buried a decade ago. Denise was obsessed with the notion that her parents should have shown concern for her, should have fed her, nurtured her, and given her permission to feel. But what she really needed was permission from herself to experience love — even though to experience love is to risk its loss. Until she can accept that, she cannot play the queen of hearts.

The Moores' divorce produced in Denise deep-seated anxieties about relationships, fears that she banished to the farthest recesses of her mind. But the feelings endured, only to resurface ten years later. In a true sense, this can be considered a sleeper effect, a delayed reaction to an event that happened many years earlier. We saw many young women with acute, delayed depression that is certainly a sleeper effect of divorce and that can be very dangerous. Denise experienced the sudden onset of a depression that was expressed in a close brush with a potentially serious eating disorder and aimless hitchhiking by a girl who was not street-smart and whose only defense was her naiveté.

The sleeper effect is particularly dangerous because it occurs at the crucial time when many young women make decisions that have long-term implications for their lives. Entering young adulthood, they are faced with issues of commitment, love, and sex in an adult context — and they are aware that the game is serious. If they tie in with the wrong man, have children too soon, or choose harmful lifestyles, the effects can be long-lasting and tragic. Suddenly overcome by fears and anxieties, they begin to make connections between these feelings and their parents' divorce:

"I'm so afraid I'll marry someone like my dad."

"How can you believe in commitment when anyone can change his mind anytime?"

"I am in awe of people who stay together."

There are many other manifestations of the sleeper effect.

I first met Ellen when she was fourteen. Like Denise, she had led a protected life in a traditional middle-class family. The divorce was "civilized," the most civilized in our study, which led me to hope that divorce might have had less impact on Ellen. Ten years later I heard through the grapevine that she was an assistant editor at *Ms.* magazine and was going places fast. She flew in from New York on business, so I grabbed the opportunity to see her. Ellen is very much in accord with my expectations. At twenty-four, she is well dressed, warm, expressive, and funny. As she recounts a spate of social and political jokes making the rounds in New York, I wonder if we'll be able to move on to more intimate conversation. Ultimately, a particularly bitter joke about the relationships between men and women gets us onto serious ground. Ellen talks for ten minutes about her current boyfriend, with whom she has shared an apartment for two years. After she extols his many virtues, I decide to venture what I imagine to be a simple question. "You know, Ellen, I'm interested that you haven't used the word *love*."

She freezes. After a long silence, she says, "I'm afraid to use that word."

Realizing I have hit a raw nerve, I approach her with another question. "Are you afraid to use it with me? Or are you afraid with you?"

"With both of us," she says, responding with a gush of words and feelings. "I'm afraid to use the word *love* because relationships are too uncertain. You can hope that a relationship is going to be permanent, but you can't expect it. My problem is that I'm jealous. I'm always afraid that if my boyfriend is thirty minutes late he is with another woman. He works with a female employee. I wonder all the time whether sex would be better with her and whether he will fall in love with her and whether they will fall in love with each other. I never feel sure of him. I guess it's a rare couple that goes through life without one of them being sexually involved with someone else. It's a bummer."

Ellen puts her head in her hands. "How can you ask anyone for a commitment when anyone can change his mind anytime?" She looks up with wet eyes. "I'm respected. I have friends. I keep busy, but it doesn't work. I get very depressed."

A significant number of young women are living with an intolerable level of anxiety about betrayal. So preoccupied are they with expectations of betrayal that they really suffer minute to minute, even though their partners may be completely faithful. I was shocked when Ellen said she worries when her boyfriend is even thirty minutes late. This fear of betrayal is different from Denise's fear of getting involved. Ellen has both — the fear that commitment is impossible plus intense jealousy verging on obsession. Both of these concerns rise to prominence as young women move into later adolescence and young adulthood, when the developmental task is to establish an intimate, loving relationship. Held back at this crucial point, they suffer very much. Such anxieties occur and persist in many young women who are, by most standards, extremely successful. Ellen has a good academic record, high ambitions, and a fast-track job. And yet young women like Ellen and Denise are preoccupied by their fears of betrayal. Accordingly, their relationships bring them far less pleasure than they might. Career achievements are nice but, by their own account, not enough. Promotions are important but have a hollow ring.

Even though they bravely say, "What happened to my mother won't happen to me," and even though they try, as every generation does, to separate from their parents, we see that they are deeply worried about their relationships. Their situation is especially painful because they want to believe in commitment and love, they want to marry and have children, and they want to choose right the first time around. There is a poignant quality to their desire, for they want so desperately what they most fear.

The sleeper effect primarily affects young women, in part because girls seem to fare much better psychologically immediately after divorce than boys. Because girls appear so much better adjusted socially, academically, and emotionally every step of the way after divorce, much of the research about the effects of divorce on children emphasizes the good recovery of girls compared with the more troubled experience of boys.

As young men enter adulthood, their behavior is more congruent with their pasts, reflecting difficulties encountered throughout their high school years. Many girls may seem relatively well adjusted even through high school and then — wham! Just as they undertake the passage to adulthood and their own first serious relationships, they encounter the sleeper effect. I have not seen a counterpart of the sleeper effect among boys, nor do boys have as much anxiety over relationships with girls. Although they worry about the same issues, their fears seem less pervasive.

Ours is the first report of the sleeper effect in children of divorce — it was simply not known to exist until we had the opportunity to follow these children for at least ten years after their parents separated. Because they were well adjusted during adolescence and performed so well throughout high school, the troubles they are experiencing now at entry into young adulthood came as a complete surprise. It was Denise's saying "I'm into pain" that first alerted us to look for this long-delayed reaction in others.

Recognition of the sleeper effect may change our assumption that boys generally suffer more from divorce; perhaps the risk is equalized over the long term. The fact that girls look good in the wake of divorce may have more to do with our research questions than with reality. If we were to enter the schools and ask girls different questions — delving into their inner feelings and subtle issues in their relationships — we would be likely to find major differences between girls who experience divorce and girls from intact, reasonably happy families. Such questions, however, are harder to ask. It is easier to examine academic grades and observe rambunctious playground behavior.

The fear of betrayal that Denise and Ellen describe overwhelms the lives of all too many young women. Girls who have never been betrayed by either parent fear betrayal. Girls who have never been betrayed or abandoned by a lover fear betrayal and abandonment. This fear so colors their relationships that many young women find maladaptive ways to cope. Some take many lovers at one time. Others seek out older men who are less likely to betray a younger woman. Some become trapped in unsatisfactory relationships and are unable to break off because of their fear. Many are derailed from satisfying their ambitions and achieving career plans. All of these behaviors arise out of the young woman's conscious or unconscious wish to protect herself against abandonment, betrayal, and rejection. As Denise says, "I thought that I didn't need love."

What could be safer? What could be sadder?

The Hungry Child

While waiting for Dolores in a Chicago restaurant, I have time to go over notes of earlier meetings. She was a youngster who, at the time of her parents' divorce, told us how often her father was away from home during the marriage and how much she had missed him. The children lived with their mother in a neat duplex in a tidy working-class neighborhood on the north side of Chicago. Because their mother worked sixty hours a week as the manager of a dry cleaning shop, the children never saw enough of her. I remember Dolores as a needy, affection-starved teenager. What would she be like today?

Minutes later, a slender twenty-three-year-old woman with short black hair, chiseled features, and dark eyes comes to my table.

"Hello, Dr. Wallerstein. I hope I haven't kept you waiting very long. I just got off work."

"Why, Dolores, you look wonderful. Come sit down. Would you like something to eat? It's so good to see you again."

Soon we are talking about our shared memories, people we know in common, and how the divorce study is progressing. The memories seem to make Dolores ravenous. As she demolishes a twelve-ounce steak, I watch her and think that much of what she is telling me fits with the theme of hunger, with the fact that divorce creates children hungry for affection and nurturing.

Dolores says that she moved out of her mother's house soon after high school graduation and within a few months began living with a man. "He put me on a pedestal. He wanted all my attention, so he basically drove me crazy. I had to leave after three months." She has had many boyfriends since then. "Some relationships last a few months and then I move on," she says airily. "Actually, I like older men. Some of it is a father complex. I've had many surrogate fathers.

Also, older men don't fall in love with you right away. Young men are ga-ga and sticky sweet. Most guys I go out with are older. Mostly they last six months."

Dolores's current relationship, which has lasted more than a year, is with a forty-five-year-old man, who is older than her father. As she describes him, he is not great looking or particularly rich, but he has a certain charm.

"What do you like most about him?"

"He treats me like a queen," Dolores replies. "He takes care of me and cares about me. He's like my dad. Dad used to teach me things. And my boyfriend does, too. He's sometimes sticky and abrupt, but he always puts me first, although he has had many others."

Dolores has found another way to resolve fears of betrayal and commitment. A whole group of young women in our study were attracted primarily to older men. These are not one-night stands. The women describe close relationships with these men and stress that they are well treated and cared for while the relationships last. The women all work, albeit mostly at low-paying jobs, and are not financially dependent on their older lovers. In fact, they go out of their way to make it clear that they are not "kept women." While they may accept gifts, especially if the older lover is wealthy, they make a real effort to maintain psychological independence by holding on to financial independence.

By hooking up with older men, these young women avoid the emotional complications that can accompany courtship with younger men: falling in love, jealousy, infidelity, and so on. An older man does not tie as many knots into the heartstrings of a younger woman, and he may be more reliable, more willing to stay at home, and less likely to disappear. For the young woman, then, the relationship is less risky than one with a young man nearer her age. An older man is more likely to be there when she comes home, and it is less likely that a forty-five-year-old man will betray a twenty-five-year-old woman. She feels safer.

Another motivation is the young woman's search for a parent. I suspect that many of the older men in these relationships are loving in a paternal or even maternal way. They no doubt have strong, protective, compassionate feelings for their young lovers, and although these are sexual relationships, they may not be primarily sexual from the young woman's point of view. The psychological value of an older lover to the child of divorce is complex and satisfying. The child, grown into a young woman, still yearns for someone to take care of her. By taking an older lover, she combines a sexual relationship with a parent-child relationship. Her lover is caretaker in loco parentis, a good father and a good mother rolled into one. When women talk about their older lovers, the emphasis is not on sex but on nurturing. As Dolores says, "He takes care of me and cares about me."

These women are young and attractive, and they are not after money or sugar daddy security. But, afraid that they would lose a diamond, they settle for rhinestones. They may even describe their lovers in negative terms: "He's ugly, but he's nice to me." Their choices in men reflect their own depreciated self-esteem; they believe that this is all they deserve.

Not all relationships between younger women and older men fit this analysis, for such relationships can be based on mutual respect and love. But for most of the young women in our study, the relationships with older men represent primarily the search for the parent they never had. They have no conscious memories of being continuously well parented as little girls, and so they miss the sense of having been loved, taken care of, and esteemed. Trading sex for closeness now, they want to be held and cuddled by their older lovers, as if they are trying to recapture — or to experience for the first time — the physical nearness that very young children seek by crawling into daddy's lap.

It is important to note that the young women in our study who experienced intense anxiety in their relationships with men had not actually been abandoned: They had ongoing relationships with their fathers. In fact, almost half of those between the ages of nineteen and twenty-three continued to see their fathers approximately once a month or more, often over dinner — visits that appeared to be a combination of attraction and continuing disappointment. One twenty-five-year-old calls her father daily; if by chance she forgets, he calls her.

When these young women describe their father-daughter relationships, it sounds as though they are describing dating relationships with young men. And it may well be that the tradition of meeting alone in restaurants over the years without the presence of the mother has unconsciously reinforced the erotic aspects of these relationships.

Despite the frequent contacts with their fathers, the young women do not feel that their fathers love or value them, and they speak about their fathers with a curious mix of affection and disdain. They go on at length about how little they trust them as parents and are openly critical with me of their fathers' attitudes about and relationships with women. Doubtless the basic father-daughter relationship serves as a template for the relationships these women anticipate with other men. As one young woman whom we will meet later says so clearly, "I never had a stable father figure in my life."

The Constricted Boy

Ten years after divorce, close to one-half of the boys, who are now between the ages of nineteen and twenty-nine, are unhappy and lonely and have had few, if any, lasting relationships with young women.

Robert begins our ten-year interview by handing me his résumé. The gesture is typical of him. I glance at it, seeing that he has won scholarships all the way through school and that his grades are superb. He became interested in science during high school, winning a Westinghouse award for a project on bioluminescence, and he is still fascinated by fireflies, tropical fish, and anything that glows in the dark. Fully supported by grants and scholarships, he is now working on his doctorate in biology at Stanford University.

Robert's father is not an educated man. Although they have visited over the years and once went on a canoeing trip together, Robert is noncommittal about his feelings. In fact, there is a blankness and cautiousness to all of his conversation. His rigid posture seems an outward manifestation of his absorption with bioluminescence — a phenomenon of light without warmth. I try to break the shell, to get Robert in touch with his feelings, but he does not respond.

We talk first about his interest in biology and how it developed. Robert describes with respect and admiration a high school teacher who encouraged him. "I guess one thing just led to another," he says in summing up his choice of career. "I think the field really chose me. One is recommended and ends up following a set course."

I ask about other interests.

He mentions running.

What about friends?

He says, "I'm probably more solitary than average. On a typical day I run first thing in the morning, start work at seven-thirty, and am in the lab most nights until eleven or midnight. My experiments need checking every few hours and I guess I don't trust anyone else to do it for me, but I don't mind."

I wait for him to go on. He waits for my next question.

"How is your dad?"

"He's okay. We see each other. Things are not bad. Considering how much I've been away from home, it's pretty close."

"How's your mom?"

"She's pretty busy. She sees my brother."

There is a staccato quality to this conversation. My attempts to put him at ease are of no use — he has no small talk. I decide to try asking about the past. What are his memories about his parents' divorce? Robert was fifteen when the break came and so it boggles me when he says, "I really don't remember the year of the divorce at all. Since this is the ten-year follow-up, it was probably ten years ago." Robert stiffens in his chair and I sense that all his feelings — whatever they are — about divorce have been sealed behind this cool exterior. I ask about his social life, more specifically about girls. Does Robert go out on dates?

"Not very much. I'm too busy most of the time. I've done a little dating. But I don't have a girlfriend. Actually, if it happens, it happens. If I met someone, then I suppose I would just start to see more of her. Then I'd have to see. Especially with the way things are these days. Marriage is more of a legal commitment than an emotional one."

"Robert, what if you do get married?"

"Well, I'd be married, that would be it. I'd expect to know her for several years. As you know," he says solemnly, "college professors have a higher than average divorce rate. Two-thirds of the people in my profession get divorced. That's a pretty poor record."

I don't know where Robert found those statistics. They are sheer nonsense. I continue to press him.

He says, "If I knew someone well enough to get married, I wouldn't have divorce on my mind. I hope that it wouldn't come up." From his tone, it is clear that Robert believes he is speaking of something unreachable.

By now it is obvious to me that Robert has placed an unbridgeable distance between his feelings and his conscious thought. "How did the divorce affect your life, Robert?"

"I'm sure I've become far more hesitant," he says. "If my family had stayed together I'd probably be less cautious. One never knows."

Robert represents a group of young men who partly succeed in meeting the demands of adulthood. They establish careers, but they don't come close to locating, much less playing, the queen of hearts.

Robert's career choice is excellent. In high school he used a mentor to help formulate his plans, worked successfully, and achieved recognition in a field appropriate to his talents. Aiming higher than his parents in professional and educational goals, he continues to feel encouraged and supported by them. As part and parcel of this, he is unhaunted by memories; in fact, his memories are extraordinarily dim. He has repressed and denied the impact of the divorce experience while rescuing just enough psychological energy for his upward climb.

My concern about Robert and young men like him is that they have little conscious recognition of their emotional constriction. Robert is inhibited, socially withdrawn, and celibate. At twenty-five, he leaves a major part of his life entirely unaddressed. This intelligent young man is able to remember complex scientific material, yet he cannot remember important episodes of his own life. Undoubtedly there are many boys like Robert who do not come from divorced families. Once again, however, Robert's experiences fit a pattern among the young men in our study.

Robert's shyness at age fifteen has since been reinforced by the way he handles major events, including the major event of his adolescence, his parents' divorce. It is too early to say if this will be a lifelong pattern, but obviously this internal constriction of emotion and external social isolation may not change in future years. He could marry, but he will remain an inhibited man, with limited access to his own feelings. —

Young men and women respond differently to feelings that flow from the divorce experience over the years. Although there is no evidence that one sex feels more or less pain than the other, women tend to express their feelings more easily. Yet, as we saw earlier, girls who buried or denied their feelings at the time can fall prey to the sleeper effect. Those repressed feelings come back to haunt them in unexpected ways. Many young men, however, seem to be able to shut their emotions away. As they mature, they too pay a price for this denial.

Uncomfortable in social situations, these young men are awkward with women and hold back on dating, even casual dating. When they do ask for a date and reach out for a relationship, they are incredibly vulnerable to rejection and are easily hurt by minor or imagined slights. As a result, they tend to live inhibited, lonely lives in which they may not acknowledge the loneliness. It is difficult to know how consciously unhappy Robert feels with his isolation.

Moreover, young men like Robert are cut off from their feelings and memories, as if a major part of their psychological life is not available to them. To avoid the pain of some feelings, they shut out all feelings. To avoid the pain of some memories, they banish whole segments of their lives from ready recall. As a result they are tragically constricted, suffering an inhibition that makes intimacy difficult to establish. Unable to share deeply hidden feelings, they build lifestyles of solitary interests and habits to protect these inhibitions from being tested.

Of course, inhibition is not unique to children of divorce; but I am distressed by how much psychic energy is invested in keeping painful memories at bay. When children must spend so much energy protecting themselves from the past, they may not have enough left over to deal successfully with the present. Whatever its roots, this kind of holding back seems to be a male pattern of coping with the fear of rejection. As one young man says poignantly, "I'm afraid to have a girlfriend. When she gets to know me, she won't love me."

When it comes to playing the queen of hearts, boys and girls have different timetables and different solutions to similar problems. Relationships seem to play a more central role in the lives of women, affecting all aspects of their lives. The young men in our study seem psychologically more reserved. Some hold back from relationships, concentrating on careers instead. Unlike the women, who are worried about betrayal, the men seem worried that they won't find true love, and they deal with this issue in several ways. Some simply do not play the game. They say "what will happen will happen." Others commit to a first relationship, giving high priority to fidelity and trust. Some play the field; others, including many of our delinquents, physically and verbally demean or abuse their girlfriends.

Before they can play the queen of hearts, the children of divorce must peel through layers of feelings associated with their parents' breakup. There are ruminations of guilt: If I had not been there or if I had tried harder, maybe they would not have gotten divorced. There are constellations of fear: What if she really gets to know me and does not love me? What if he marries me and later says he no longer loves me? There are expectations of failure: If I play the queen of hearts, I will be betrayed and abandoned. My capacity to love will be trumped.

5

Sammy Moore
BOYS LEAVING HOME

WHEN SAMMY MOORE, age seven, learned that his father was leaving for good and that he would be left at home with his mother and two older sisters, he took a marking pen and wrote "Fuck mom" on the refrigerator.

His reaction didn't surprise me in the least. Unlike his sisters, Sammy had no clue that his family was about to collapse; when the separation occurred, he was stunned and then intensely angry. I have seen many boys this age express anger at their parents in oblique, unpredictable ways. Moreover, they are likely to blame the mother when things go wrong. Some boys refuse to go to bed, do homework, complete chores, or perform a variety of other previously routine tasks, while others displace their anger onto a younger brother or sister. For Sammy, a well-behaved boy from a polite household, the outrageous act of writing on the refrigerator was the opening salvo in a barrage of aggressive behavior.

The first time I met Sammy, he was dressed in jeans and a t-shirt with wild mustangs on the back. With blue-gray eyes and sandy-colored hair, he looked remarkably like his father, Nicholas — a fact that seemed to please them both.

Sammy did not want to talk directly about the divorce. As we sat in the playroom at the center, he seemed uninterested in the toys and somewhat antsy about being there. Even so, this first visit yielded several clues about his feelings.

Asked if he was having any difficulties, he said gravely, "I have trouble going to sleep at night. Sometimes it takes me four hours. But last night my sister Ruth gave me a coloring book and I fell asleep coloring."

Asked if he had wishes, he said, "I think about antigravity paint and a spray gun that makes me invisible." Later he said, "I want my hair cut real short, because I want to look like a man."

A little later Sammy drew a picture of his family, with himself splashing alone in a big swimming pool while his mother and sisters stood nearby, holding hands. He drew Nicholas as a tiny figure, almost off the page.

After Sammy left, I called his teacher to hear her impressions of the boy. In a worried tone, she said that Sammy was clinging to her in the classroom but that out on the playground he was punching other children and had lost most of his friends. Lowering her voice, as if to keep us from being overheard, she said, "Yesterday he told me, 'Sometimes I think things are breaking up inside me and I want them to break all the way out.' Can you imagine, Dr. Wallerstein, how he must be feeling? Just a couple of weeks ago he said that he was sad for fifteen minutes every day, but for the rest of the day he's mad. Yes, I am concerned about Sammy."

At our second interview a few weeks later, Sammy volunteered as he entered the office, "I don't miss my dad. I see him every day. It's just like always." (At this time Sam was seeing his father once a week.) He then refused to talk any further about his father or about the divorce.

This time, Sammy allowed himself to explore all the toys in the playroom but again did not seem able to play with any of them. At the end of the hour, when it was time to go, Sammy was defiant. "Why? Why do I have to go? I'm not ready. I don't want to go."

As I later learned from Christina, even though Sammy had hardly talked to me, our interview opened a floodgate of anxious questions on the way home — questions he had never dared ask before but which had clearly been on his mind for some time: "Are you ever going to get back together? Is Daddy going to get married again? Will he have other children?"

At our third interview, Sammy was friendlier and more relaxed. We played a board game, which he handily won by bending all the rules. And afterward, he built a cannon out of Tinker Toys and began to talk about his father's sailboat. "The mast blew over, you see," he said, aiming the cannon at an imaginary boat. "Like this." Making explosive noises, Sammy enacted the disaster for both of us to see.

One year later, I learned that Sammy was still not doing well in many aspects of his life. To his mortification, he was occasionally wetting his pants at school. Following each such episode, Sammy refused to return to school, complaining of a variety of physical symptoms. The teacher reported that he was still extremely aggressive and would run headlong into groups of other children, arms flailing, striking out indiscriminately. In the classroom, his attention span was short and he was not learning. The school year had begun with a bang. When Sammy found out who his teacher was, he stormed into the principal's office and demanded that he be assigned to another class. Sammy wanted a man teacher.

Sammy was able to talk with me very directly at our one-year visit, and the sadness underlying his anger was more visible. "My parents don't get along," he said. "They used to argue about me all the time when they were married. I guess I caused them a lot of trouble by not wanting to go to school and all. I didn't mean to make them argue . . ." Sammy's voice trailed off. With that, his eyes filled with tears and he asked to go home. Concerned about the boy's suffering, I decided to talk with him directly about his feeling of responsibility for the divorce. I said, "It sounds like you think that maybe you caused a lot of the trouble between your parents." We talked about this for quite a while. I tried to assure him that the divorce was not caused by anything he did, but it was apparent that he was not able to hear me and was holding firm to his guilt. This little boy was hurting very much.

"If you had three wishes, Sammy," I said sometime later during our visit, "what would they be?"

He said, "I wish they'd get back together. That's wish one, two, and three." Bursting into tears, he said, "That's all I want."

Despite Sammy's good fortune in having loving, concerned parents and despite their very civilized divorce, it was clear to me that his initial distress, sadness, and anger had continued and were in danger of becoming chronic.

I was not surprised that I could not help Sammy with his enduring feelings of responsibility for his parents' divorce. When these feelings last, a simple explanation is not likely to change a child's inner conviction. A child often prefers feeling responsible for the divorce to feeling powerless, for at the root of this imagined guilt is a sense of utter helplessness that is even more disturbing. In other words, it is less threatening to feel evil and responsible than it is to feel powerless. At other times, feelings of guilt are linked to "bad" thoughts or fantasies, and the child sees the divorce as punishment for being naughty. A child can make a connection between a minor infraction like not cleaning his room and causing the divorce. Sometimes a child's sense of responsibility for the divorce is caused by the child's real wish that he be close to one parent and that the other parent disappear; when this occurs and the rival disappears, the child is terrified at what he regards as the omnipotence of his secret wishes.

While their family physician recommended psychotherapy at this time for Sammy, Nicholas and Christina decided to wait, in the hope that his symptoms would abate.

Five years after his parents' divorce, Sammy was somewhat improved. Now twelve and still boyish, he was beginning to show the early blush of adolescence in his body movements, and there was no doubt he would be sturdy like Nicholas, with the same athletic build and sun-bleached hair.

Certain problems, however, had persisted, the most prominent of which was that Sammy was frequently anxious about going to school. Many mornings he complained that his throat hurt, his head ached, his stomach churned, or that he was afraid to walk to school because bullies would grab him en route. Christina dealt with the complaints patiently but firmly, so on most days Sammy made it to school despite his fears. "He's always had problems getting off to school," Christina said. "When he first started nursery school, he wouldn't let me leave. We had a terrible time."

After the five-year follow-up, Sammy's parents decided to pursue the recommendation for psychotherapy and he began weekly individual treatment, which lasted over a two-year period. Following therapy, his schoolwork very much improved and his ability to concentrate was restored. One of his teachers said, "He's a neat kid, with a good sense of humor. He can sometimes figure out something faster than anyone else in the class." His relationship with his peers was restored as well.

Most heartening was Sammy's deepening interest in zoology, which developed during his adolescence. He loved animals and hoped — after seeing a television documentary that captured his imagination — to establish himself as an expert in captive breeding programs of wild animals. When I saw him at the termination of his treatment (at Christina's request), we spent most of our time talking about his animals. Sammy had at home a chameleon, seven zebra finches, a tarantula, a sheep dog, two cats, an "incredibly smart" white rat named Zorro, a lop-eared rabbit, a box turtle, an ant farm, and, as soon as his mother said yes, he was going to get a ferret. "It's not legal to buy or sell ferrets in California," he told me knowingly, "but you can get them anyway. I met a guy at the Renaissance Faire last fall who had a ferret and he let me take care of it for half the day. They're real slinky."

"You must need your mom's help with all those animals."

"She's great," Sammy said. "We turned the back sun porch into a vivarium so I can keep a lot of my cages and supplies in one place. I wish we lived out in the country so I could get some exotic animals. You know, a llama or something like that. But we live in the 'burbs, so I'll have to wait."

This time when I asked about the divorce, Sammy said, "I liked it better when they were married. For a long time I sat in class and thought about it and I used to figure out how they'd be punished and then how I'd be punished. Most of all, I used to think that except for me they would still be together. But now I don't think about it. I used to think I was the only one like me in my family. Like, my mom and sisters are all girls. But I don't think about that so much anymore."

Sammy spoke at length about his best friend, David, who also collected animals. "We're like brothers," he said, "except his parents aren't divorced."

And his dad?

"I like seeing my dad when we're alone, but I don't like going over to his house a whole lot," Sammy said. "I don't feel comfortable with Connie. In fact, I never appreciated Mom as much until Dad got married again. At my house I can leave my turtle in the sink, but over at the other house Connie freaks out. I like it at home because my room is my room. I mean, for a mom, my mom is pretty good."

Ten years. As we talk over his glass of Coke and my glass of wine, Sam describes a high school career that includes membership on the track team and vice presidency of the ski club. He has blossomed into a competent, self-assured young man. Like most seventeen-year-olds in our divorced families, and despite his father's wealth, he has a part-time job, working ten hours a week as a busboy at a salad bar. Unlike many other teenage boys in our study, however, Sam talks enthusiastically about his college plans.

"I like San Diego," he says, "and tuition in the University of California system is really reasonable. I'm positive I can line up a job at the Wild Animal Park, and they've got the best captive breeding program in the world. One reason I feel so confident that I'm going to do well my freshman year is that Mom has pretty much raised me to make my own decisions. I think that'll make college easier." His voice drops as he picks up the subject of his mother and her vulnerability. "It's leaving that's a bitch. My mom and I get along pretty good these days. Sometimes we argue but she's a great mom, and she gives me a lot of time, even though she has lots to think about. If there were other men around it would be a lot easier for her." It is not clear to me if by "other men" Sam is referring to his father or to himself. "She wouldn't be so uptight," he says with genuine concern. "I'm really worried about her, Dr. Wallerstein. Once we had this fire in the kitchen and it was lucky I was there because I called the fire department. She just stood there sort of paralyzed and didn't seem to know what to do."

Sam looks restless and begins to bite his thumbnail. "My leaving is going to be hard on her. I try to do a lot of stuff around the house but I just don't know who's going to help her when I'm gone. Denise is gone. Ruth visits, and it's good for Mom that she came back after college. But I think it's going to be much harder on her than on me." Suddenly, Sammy blurts, "She's going to be alone."

"You're concerned about her."

"I wish she'd get married," says Sam. "But I don't think it's going to happen. She hasn't dated much. You know, I think she would have been more into dating if I hadn't been there. I think she's been trying to take care of me."

When we change the subject to Nicholas, Sam lights up. "Dad and I have gotten really close this past year," he says. "I used to think that he didn't care about me when he came to visit. And for a long time I was absolutely convinced that he left Mom because of me." Sam looks down, as if to give me a moment to absorb this insight. "It took me years to realize that it wasn't true," he says, looking back up, as if for confirmation from me.

"Of course not," I say, pleased that he has come to grips with this longstanding issue.

Sam smiles and continues, "He taught me how to drive last year after I got my learner's permit and from then on, we just started hanging out a lot more together. We both like the outdoors, even though Dad is not much of an animal lover."

After a shaky start, Sammy is well on his way.

Boys who are six, seven, and eight years old when their parents divorce have a particularly difficult time adjusting to the changes in their lives. In our work and in studies conducted in different areas of the country, many little boys cannot concentrate at school and either withdraw from their peers or clobber everyone in sight. Either way, academically and socially they quickly begin to lose ground compared with boys in intact families.

How much of this behavior is related to the boy's anxiety at being left in custody of his mother, just when he is developing strong identifications with his father and consolidating his own masculinity, is difficult to determine. But Sammy certainly showed signs of this connection.

When Nicholas left, Sammy was clearly terrified of being overpowered by his mother and older sisters. When he drew his family, the female figures dominated while Sammy was drowning and his father was nearly out of the picture. His aggressive behavior may have reflected his fear of being weak and dominated by the three women. Certainly, Sammy's march into the principal's office to demand a male teacher and his wish for a short haircut reflected a concern that his masculinity was threatened.

Sammy was anxious because in an immature way, he saw Christina as a powerful figure who drove Nicholas off the home turf. Unlike his sisters, Sammy could not identify with his mother, could not feel protected and reassured by being like her, because that would have compromised his masculinity. The protective relationship that mothers and daughters develop — being close and being alike — does not extend to little boys. Terrified by his feelings and angry at his parents for putting him in such a vulnerable position, Sammy lashed out at the world.

Sammy also confessed a year later that he felt guilty for having caused the divorce. After all, if his parents hadn't argued about him so much — if he had been better behaved — perhaps they would not have divorced. Sammy thought he drove the final wedge between his parents.

The real source of Sammy's guilt probably lay deeper in his psyche. As everyone in this family told us, Sammy and Christina were exceptionally close. She lavished attention on her last baby, the only boy, and turned to him for the love and affection that she was not getting from Nicholas. As a preschooler, Sammy was quite understandably in love with his mother and felt, as is normal at this developmental stage, rivalry with his father. Sammy was just outgrowing these feelings when suddenly the divorce shattered his world. Deep down, in a place he could only feel but not understand, Sammy believed that the divorce fulfilled his earlier wish of having Christina all to himself. He felt twice guilty — for making his parents fight and for driving his father away.

Eventually, however, Sammy benefited from the love and continued protection of both his parents and from individual psychotherapy. Although I was not privy to the content of his psychotherapy, it is likely that he and the therapist were able to explore together his guilt, his anger, and his fear of punishment, all of which probably underlay his symptoms in the years immediately following the divorce. Most of all, the therapy was able to allay the child's suffering. While his grade school memories are undoubtedly the most miserable of his life, Sammy was back on track by midadolescence. Nicholas and Christina both deserve a lot of the credit for this turn of affairs.

As Sammy entered adolescence, he was supported by his mother's close but not too close interest, by her respect for his burgeoning masculinity, and by her catering to his interests and welcoming his relationship with his father. Without her support, he could not have done so well. Just as important was her giving the boy room to develop his own interests and friendships, not intruding on his life despite her own neediness. Christina was able to separate her anger at Nicholas and keep it from spilling onto her son. In fact, she relied on Sammy's strength and respected his ability to protect her in emergencies.

Nicholas played an equally important role in his son's recovery. At age sixteen, Sammy reached out and found a confident father who fully supported his move into young manhood and who would help him reach his goals. Father and son forged a much closer relationship at this juncture, which helped Sammy plan his move away from home. While Nicholas lived nearby through the years, Sammy felt blocked by his stepmother and did not draw close to his father until he was old enough so that he and his father could establish an independent friendship.

Sam is sad and worried about leaving home and feels sorry for his mother, but his departure — although difficult for him — is not a severe emotional or moral crisis, for several reasons.

Because his mother is financially secure, he does not have to worry that she will become destitute.

Although he is concerned about her psychological condition — especially her vulnerability in emergencies — the availability of his older sister Ruth alleviates his sense of responsibility.

Finally, with his mother's support, Sam enjoys a close relationship with his father. Confident of emotional and financial backing, he does not feel he is being thrown out into the world without help.

Other boys find leaving home much more difficult, as the next story illustrates.

Like Sammy Moore, Carl Patton was also seven years old when his father, an airline pilot, left home. I remember him as the little boy who wouldn't take off his heavy air force jacket, even though it was a sizzling hot day, because his father had given it to him for Christmas that year.

Before the divorce, Carl was a happy, well-cared-for child. After it, he and his older brother and sister visited their father regularly and frequently. After several years, however, the children realized that their father's attention was elsewhere when they visited. Almost always, there would be other adults around or adult activities planned. Carl watched hundreds of hours of television at his father's house, feeling more and more alone and removed from his earlier visions of family life.

I vividly remember my visit with Carl at the five-year mark. It was late on a winter afternoon that he invited me into his living room and asked me if I liked cats. When I said yes, he handed me a large tabby cat and then he picked up a smaller gray one. We sat in the twilight, each stroking a cat, talking about Carl's life.

He began in an adult, serious tone, "I know you saw my brother Kedric. He said you gave him an article about teenagers and divorce."

Attempting to match his serious style, I offered to provide him with an article about children his age and divorce. I said, "I take it you're getting along better with your brother."

"Yes, Kedric and I get along better. He's not cruel or kind. He's just in his own world doing his own thing." A grandfather clock chimed just then from its sentry post in the front hallway. "If I weren't so busy," Carl said, "I would notice the quietness of the house. Everybody here is going their own way. It seems like our family is breaking up but it's better because the fights aren't here." Carl implied that the quiet and sadness were related. He talked about school, his friends, and after a while I asked about his father.

"It's gotten a little better. Maybe he's a little more interested in me. I like to see him and sometimes I think he's reaching out to me."

"Does that still upset your mother?"

"No," he said, with a philosophical shake of the head. "That's changed. She encourages me to do what I want now that she has her own jewelry design business and has all that gold to fool around with. I remember how I used to feel that I was in the middle and how I worried about being disloyal to both Mom and Dad. Mom seemed to me the most hurt and angry. I couldn't stand to see her unhappy. So I stuck by her side to make her happy."

"Carl," I said. "If a boy whose parents just got divorced walked into this room right now, what would you tell him?"

"I'd tell him not to feel hopeless. The situation is hard and it gets worse. But with time and help from his parents, everything will be all right." I could not make out his features in the dim light but Carl's voice was sad. "I remember how I thought I was losing everything important," he said. Carl went on to describe how over the years his mother interrogated the children after each visit to their father's house. The other children made a pact not to answer her, but Carl could not go along. He felt sorry for his mother and broke ranks. "I couldn't stand it," he said. "She was so sad. I hope she gets married because then I'd feel better about leaving home. Mom would not be lonely and would have a life of her own."

Other family members had just told me that Carl's mother leaned heavily on her youngest child. These were difficult years, in which she experienced several business deals that did not work out, and she had sustained a serious back injury that put her in traction for two months. Always, Carl could be counted on to come to his mother's assistance, and she looked to him as the major support figure in her family.

About his father, Carl said, "I'm angry that his girlfriends are always there when I'm there. I'd like some privacy. My dad is hard to talk to, you know, and he's still a perfectionist. If you don't abide by his ways you're out."

Five years later, at the ten-year follow-up, I am impressed by Carl's gentleness and the careful way he chooses his words. But I am shocked at the way Carl, now seventeen, has rewritten history. He is spending more time with his father and has a whole new view of his mother. As he speaks, it is clear to me that he has shifted 180 degrees. His earlier concern and compassion for his mother are gone, and he has entirely revamped his assessment of her, including his feelings and her feelings.

To my utter amazement, he says, "I never could understand how Dad could marry Mom after she forced him to leave the East Coast and move out here." This is an entirely new version of family history that neither parent has ever mentioned. "I still haven't figured out the divorce," says Carl. "Maybe Mom doesn't like men." (I can hardly believe my ears.) "I wonder whether Mom is gay, because she did not like my dad or me."

Considering that Carl's mother opposed the divorce because she deeply loved her husband and that she loves her children very much, I am dumbfounded by Carl's comments. Jane Patton is affectionate with Carl and closely attached to Kedric and their sister. I am very troubled by this grave distortion of reality.

He says, "My dad and I have become very good friends. He is like me and tells me both sides of the story." Carl explains, "I feel very disappointed in Mom. She works sixty hours a week designing her jewelry and I guess she's doing okay. But I don't want a mom who's a cash register. I want somebody who's interested in me." He also explains, with some disappointment but no evident resentment, "I'm really worried about money for college next year. I'll be a freshman." It turns out that Carl's father, who is a wealthy man, is not helping with college tuition. "I don't understand why Dad won't help me," he says vaguely. "But his wife is having another baby next spring and I guess the new family is taking up most of his life."

The problems boys face in leaving home are qualitatively different from and more complex than those experienced by girls. First, boys and their mothers usually do not exhibit the same kind of close, mutual, emotional dependence found in mothers and daughters. Mothers and sons are caught in a powerful psychological dance in which they are mutually drawn close to each other and then pushed apart, back and forth in a classic pas de deux. One of our expectations was that divorced women would turn to their sons to take the ex-husband's place, treating them as heads of household. While I have seen some of this, I have seen more of the other extreme, where boys feel pushed away. Sometimes boys feel depreciated for their maleness or rejected because they remind their mothers of their fathers.

A mother sends several messages to her son and asks for certain things in return. First and foremost, she wants his help, sympathy, and support in running the household. At the same time, she wants him to be an ally, to reinforce her beliefs about how badly her husband behaved. She feels a need for the boy to hold her hand and say, "You were right, Mom."

But many women realize that it is detrimental for them to become emotionally dependent on their sons. One hand beckons while the other pushes him away. Some mothers, out of genuine concern for their sons, push them consciously. Says one mother, "I do not want to lean on him too much."

Many boys, however, misunderstand this attempt by their mothers to protect the distance between them and interpret it as rejection. As Carl says, "My mother is a cash register. She doesn't care about me." In the cash register image, he captures the complaint of many boys who feel they do not get enough attention and affection from their working mothers. This neediness is often reinforced by the disappointments inherent in the visiting father-child relationship. A boy may actively pull away in response to his mother's distancing. He may also need to pull away even while feeling love and respect.

This interaction between mother and son often reaches a crescendo just at the time of adolescent separation, when the boy is ready to leave home. Anchored by a profound moral obligation to his mother, he has a terrible time jumping ship, so much so that leaving home is actually experienced as a serious moral and emotional crisis.

In psychological terms, however, both mother and son are behaving in expectable ways in this pas de deux. Boys perceive that it is psychologically dangerous for them to become too close to their mothers. Ultimately, they are frightened of being drawn into the mother's orbit, of being a mama's boy, of not doing the manly thing. Since they are not protected by a father living in the same household, they are afraid of being emasculated. They resent and fear being disciplined by a woman.

The experience of leaving home is different for boys in intact families. Over the years, the young man detaches gradually from his parents, moving back and forth from being a little boy to being an adult and back again, sometimes in any one day. His primary emotional investment fluctuates from home to school, from friends to parents, from past to future. With time he establishes an independent stance, a more detached relationship with parents. This is part of normal adolescent development; it is in part what makes adolescence so maddening and incomprehensible to parents, unless they can think back on their own adolescence for help in understanding.

In a divorced family, adolescence is more complex and can be more painful. There is less opportunity to detach gradually from a relationship with a single parent, which is likely to be both more central and more encompassing than in intact families. Nor is it easy to be the son of a woman who is alone. The rising sexuality of the adolescent boy is very frightening to him, and he wants to get away from his mother; without his father present, he feels unprotected from his own impulses and fantasies.

Some young people solve the issue by detaching rapidly, often before they are ready. Others remain close to their mothers, delaying psychological departure. Boys who are so close to their mothers, however, are generally less prepared emotionally for the momentous separation. It is much harder to make the break without the help and support of an older man, preferably the father or stepfather.

During their adolescence, over one-third of the boys and girls went to live with their fathers. Of these, half stayed about one year, growing disenchanted with what they found and realizing after a short time that they had been following a fantasy. My observation is that this is a fairly widespread phenomenon, with adolescents moving between the two homes several times in high school, essentially customizing their custody with or without their parents' approval. Of those who went to live with their fathers during adolescence, the half that stayed made the father's home the steppingstone to independence. In some dramatic instances, the youngster chose correctly, moving away from a stormy relationship with the mother into a more supportive household with the father. This move was never easy for parent or child, and all acknowledge that it took time and effort.

Sometimes the teenager took credit for having helped the father evolve as a parent.

At the ten-year follow-up, Edward, age sixteen, describes how he took the initiative and moved to his father's home. Describing his life with his mother, he says, "There was yelling and screaming every day. I had to leave because there was no harmony in the house. Since I left I have had some sad realizations having to do with the whole concept of what a mother is and should be. I started to realize that I was not an extension of my mom, that I was my own person. My mom is dominant and has a hard time accepting that a person has other things in his life besides his mom." Ed continues to talk in detail about his move to his father's home, the early difficulties that they had, and the resolutions they achieved. "My dad is loving and caring, but he has been disconnected in the past. He had not grown up, and he had some growing up to do since the divorce, but he came to see that he wants to be with me, not just every weekend, not just as a sugar daddy. My dad is very valuable to me. He is a good and generous man. He is a loving and caring friend. He is proud of me and I love him very much."

I was astonished to find that boys from divorced families experience an intense, rising need for their fathers during adolescence — even if the divorce occurred ten years earlier. Divorced fathers play a heretofore unappreciated role in the lives of their sons at this juncture. To take those first slippery steps toward independence, to pull away from the mother-son pas de deux, a boy needs a supportive father. Edward and his father and Nicholas and Sammy provide excellent examples of how this relationship can work well. But what if fathers are emotionally or physically unavailable? What if they fail to provide this support and no one else — a stepfather, grandparent, or mentor — is there to assume this role?

As Carl moves into midadolescence, a metamorphosis occurs. Preparing to leave home and make his move into young manhood, he turns to his father to help him define his own sense of masculinity and separateness. His most powerful need at this time is for a strong relationship with his dad, which would give him confidence to loosen his close ties to his mother. Instead he finds a father who — caught up in a new marriage with young children — is uninterested in him. And so Carl transforms the real, disappointing father he has into the image he needs, creating a phantom father. He turns against his mother even as he completely loses sight of his father's many failings.

Carl, for example, does not allow himself to consciously resent his father's refusal to help with college or even to question it. Perhaps he is afraid to feel anger because he needs his father so much. Perhaps he feels powerless in the face of his eighteenth birthday, at which time his father's legal obligations cease. Caught in this bind, Carl rewrites the history of his relationship with his mother. She becomes the negative foil for his father's idealization, and he uses anger at her to help him leave home. Unfortunately the fantasy is not enough to hold the boy into manhood. Sixteen years after his parents' divorce, this bright and gentle young man is floundering badly at age twenty-three and has no stable base and no clear direction in his life.

Carl's older brother, Kedric, although raised in the same family, faced different issues at the time of his parents' divorce and followed a different route.

The Pilot's Oldest Son

As I step off the airplane in Seattle to meet Kedric Patton for our ten-year interview, he gives me a huge, wonderful grin. His first sentence is "I didn't get into the Air Force Academy, Judy. I got married instead. I'm into the lumber business. I guess that's it." He laughs with an afterthought. "Oh, I've got a new Irish wolfhound."

Although Kedric is very much a man now, he still has the look, at twenty-six, of a lanky boy tripping over himself wherever he goes. He exudes self-confidence, speaks with a brusque candor, and has a way of reducing things to their essentials. I react to him strongly, and throughout our several hours of talking I feel that I am highly privileged to know him. This is a young man who talks rarely, yet in our conversation he gives freely of himself. I find this very moving. Despite Kedric's maturity, I want to reach out to him, to assure him and to tell him what an impressive young man he is. In this sense, he conveys a sadness that he does not express. He has made a very good adjustment in life, but he has consciously done so — at a price.

"How happy are you, Kedric?"

"I like what I do," he says, "but not entirely. Donna and I got married four years ago. I worry about being a good husband. She says she never knows what I'm thinking and that frightens her. I don't know if I'll ever have children, Judy, at least not now. There are some feelings I don't seem able to reach, some gentle, loving feelings that have to do with being a good husband and a good father. I prefer not to think about it. But I think she's right. And I know what you're going to ask me. Yes, it does have to do with my parents' marriage and divorce and with my relationship with my mom."

I first met Kedric when he was sixteen, the oldest of three children, his father's favorite. His mother was distraught over the divorce and tried to lean on him, but Kedric turned away. At one point he went into another room, put out the lights, and sat in the dark for a long time. "There are feelings," he says of this memory. "I couldn't be what she needed. I felt a great pity for her, but I couldn't help."

Fully expecting to follow in his father's footsteps as an air force jet pilot and later as a captain of 747s for a major U.S. airline, Kedric majored in aeronautical engineering at the University of Colorado, earning a near four-point average. He flew a Cessna 172 on weekends and completed check-out rides in a Lear jet. His ROTC instructors gave him the highest recommendations possible, and at basic flight school in Lubbock, Texas, Kedric was one of the most promising candidates to step into a flight suit — that is, until his interview with the squadron commander. A few days after his arrival, Kedric sat in a room and answered questions from a panel of senior officers. In classic Chuck Yeagerese, the commander asked Kedric why he wanted to fly for the air force. "Sir," said Kedric, "because there is no better way to get away from people and probably no cleaner way to die." The startled officer asked Kedric several more questions, and Kedric went out of his way to give outrageous answers. The panel had no choice but to ask him to leave flight training school.

Full of conflicts about pursuing his father's career, Kedric did not express them until the eleventh hour. Then, still angry about his father's betrayals and infidelities, Kedric sabotaged himself. He went back to California for a while, giving flying lessons at a friend's private flight school. He had no clear direction in life until he turned to someone he loved very much.

The winter of his twenty-second birthday, Kedric called Donna, an independent young woman he had been dating for several years in Colorado.

"Marry me," he said.

"You're kidding."

"No, I'm not. Hey, this is Valentine's Day. Marry me."

"Put it in writing."

"So I did," says Kedric. "I love her. She's stubborn. She stands up for herself. She doesn't go around saying yes, yes, yes to anything I ask."

"Like your mom did with your dad?"

"You got it. If she wants something, I want her to have it. If I want something, she wants me to have it. I like that she stands up for herself and I want her to be happy. She's intelligent, she's pretty, and we get along very well."

I'll never forget Kedric's expression of intense anger when I brought up the subject of his father. "Someday I will say to my dad, 'Are you proud of what you have done with your life?' But," Kedric said, "what can he answer me?"

Unlike his younger brother, Carl, Kedric entertains no illusions about his father; indeed, in getting himself thrown out of flight school he made a conscious break with much that his father represented. His marriage, by design, bears no resemblance to that of his parents. What are the factors that account for Kedric's capacity to move ahead?

First, he was older than many youngsters in our study at the time of his parents' divorce. At sixteen, he was well into adolescence, had already considered career choices, and had begun the process of separation. He came to divorce, therefore, from a position of strength, having already negotiated many of the major developmental hurdles. From the start he was considered bright and talented, a good-looking boy who had mastered skills admired by his peers. One of the first things he told me at sixteen was "I'm a better tennis player than my dad."

Furthermore, Kedric had been raised in a stable family, with clear values about right and wrong. Without this background, he could have been more disoriented by reports of his father's repeated infidelities; as it was, Kedric never questioned his judgment that his father's behavior was wrong. Despite his intense unhappiness, Kedric was able to maintain enough discipline to keep up his schoolwork and keep an eye on his career goals. Besides his being older, Kedric was largely helped by his capacity to distance himself from his family and the turbulence of divorce. He had an advantage over his younger siblings in this regard, although he did not feel more fortunate at the time. I remember how lonely and frightened he really was beneath his cool manner at our first meeting and how much he wanted to keep talking as we sat in the park and later in my car.

Kedric also benefited from being secure in the knowledge that he was his father's favorite child and that he was loved and esteemed by both parents. Unlike many children of divorce, Kedric resisted the crossfire between his parents. Each of them loved him and allowed him to stay on the sidelines of their battle. A child who feels loved holds on to a sense of self-esteem, an inner vision of self, and to the hope that things will get better. Even though the marriage was unhappy for both his parents, Kedric felt good about himself, about his family, and about family traditions, excluding his father's behavior. Unlike many other children, his self-esteem did not suffer with the divorce; it had not been eroded by years of family conflict.

Another protective factor is Kedric's mother. Before the divorce, Jane Patton spent her time baking bread and raising children. After the divorce, she suddenly found herself thrust into the unfamiliar role of winning bread for three children, which she eventually did by establishing her own jewelry design business. She was agitated and depressed for the first few years, turning to Kedric for help with household logistics and moral support. Indeed, she looked to her eldest child to become her friend, confidant, and strong supporter — someone to help her through the greatest crisis of her life, to play the role of "other."

But Kedric refused to play this role for his mother. He maintained his distance, not out of meanness or lack of compassion, but because he intuitively sensed that he could not become the other person she so desperately needed without impairing his own integrity and his own developmental need to move out of the family stronghold. What protected him, aside from his own instincts to pull back, was that his mother responded by permitting him the distance he needed. Despite her disappointment that he would not come closer, she let him go and did not reject him or invade the boundaries that he set. (Instead she turned directly to her youngest son, Carl, for the support that she needed.) To his great credit, Kedric pushed his mother away without crippling his own moral integrity. It hurt to turn away from her; he felt that he was being uncompassionate and unloving, but he fought appropriately to maintain his distance. The price he has paid — as he identifies it — is that gentle, loving feelings are not available in his relationship with his wife ten years later. He has become used to keeping all his feelings under tight control.

Yet another factor in Kedric's ability to pull his life together involves issues of identification. Kedric is able to draw on his relationship with his father to define himself as a young man on his way in the world and to distance himself from his mother. He has no confusion whatsoever about his manhood. At the same time, Kedric struggles against identifying with the father whose immoral behavior he finds unforgivable, and so he rejects the goals and professional ambitions set by his father's example. It is no accident that Kedric got himself tossed out of pilot training — he was tormented by the thought of following in his father's footsteps and by the thought of not following in those footsteps. Because he was a talented student, he easily completed required college courses, but at the final step his anger and rejection of his father's conduct caused him to destroy his pilot training goal. He decided to change his life course and married early, fully aware that he was choosing a woman who is not like his mother.

Such decision making requires a conscious rejection of parental identification. Summoning courage, Kedric chose not to identify with the father whose behavior was abhorrent. Although he now stays in touch with his parents, he has developed the more important relationships of his young adulthood with his wife's mother, father, and siblings. He also brings his considerable talents to his father-in-law's lumber business. At age twenty-six, Kedric confidently holds an executive position supervising a large staff.

Young men like Kedric are living fully in accord with their own standards and expectations of life. They are working very hard and feel they have taken responsibility for themselves. They seek women who will help them work through their divorce experience, discussing every detail in depth. Such marriages can be especially close.

A number of other young people in our study dramatically turned away from their parents' examples, going home only for brief, obligatory visits on holidays. Most of all, they turned their backs on their parents' values, having weighed those values and found them wanting. They continue to be angry, disdainful, or moderately amused by the infidelities of one or both parents, and they may be very critical of the parenting that they or their siblings received.

As Kedric now says, "I'm not angry at Dad anymore. Just amused. He gets this itch and can't help himself."

When young people turn away deliberately from identifying with their parents, they actually redefine their own life values, goals, expectations, and relationships. Arriving at a measured decision that rejects a parent's path is a painful process, for one does not turn one's back on a parent without feeling anger and guilt, without mourning the relationship that could have or should have been. Such a step requires courage because it involves taking a chance on new relationships and on new role models. In a strange way, this is an achievement that both depends on and enormously increases independence and self-esteem. Establishing independence different from the parental model is often a goal of psychotherapy, especially when a young person has identified with an abusive or demeaning parent. The process is both conscious and unconscious and requires time to evolve. Early identifications are powerful and can be broken only from a position of strength. Turning away from identification with a tyrannical parent is particularly difficult to do alone because the relationship itself destroys self-esteem, and high self-esteem is requisite to breaking from the past. People sometimes find strength in other relationships, but it is always painful to disavow a parent — for it means, of course, disowning a part of oneself.

Finally, Kedric is protected because he is able to create a loving relationship with a young woman whom he respects. Instead of imitating his father's demeaning treatment of his mother, he treats his wife with love and dignity, thereby consolidating his own growth into manhood. He has learned from his parents' mistakes. His capacity to love and to be loved are powerful protective factors in helping him to complete his internal maturation process and to hold fast to his independence from his father's example. He also embraces the values of his wife's family, who welcome him warmly. In them he finds a synchrony of views, a stability, and a sense of family that was lacking in his own life during and after the breakup of his parents' marriage.

Boys within the same family can and usually do have different relationships with each parent. Many of the siblings in our families not only had different relationships with each parent but turned out very differently in the decade after divorce. In fact, we saw increasing disparity in siblings in terms of who did well and who did poorly in psychological adjustment and relationships. Even though siblings usually visited their father together during their growing-up years and spent roughly the same amount of time with him, they felt differently about him and perceived his attentions differently. Even though they were raised by the same mother, their experiences and relationships with her were all different. The sibling who had the closer relationship with the mother fared much better than the sibling with the less close relationship. The sibling with the better relationship considered the divorce a closed chapter of his or her life, while the other kept it alive in his or her present thinking.[1]

Carl and Kedric Patton are nine years apart, and their growing-up experiences varied enormously in the years after divorce. At sixteen, Kedric was his father's favorite son, all that Carl wanted to be. Kedric rejected his mother's attempts to lean on him with firmness but with great inner conflict and a continued sense of guilt at having failed her. Kedric in anger also turned away from identifying with his father. Carl, being much younger, spent most of his growing-up years closely attached to his mother, tenderly concerned for her happiness, but feeling increasingly peripheral to her career. At the same time, he felt unloved by his father, taking second place to his father's emotional investment in his new family.

Although both are sensitive and gifted, the boys showed marked psychological differences and made different conscious and unconscious choices all through their growing-up years. Not surprisingly, they look, think, and feel differently about themselves, their family, and about the divorce when they enter young adulthood.

When I call Kedric at the fifteen-year mark to ask permission to use his earlier interviews, his wife, Donna, answers the phone. She sounds charming, just as Kedric described her, and tells me their news right away: They have a little girl, Angela, who is now almost three. "Kedric is a wonderful father," says Donna. "It's a good thing I'm around, though, because without me to balance things out Angela would be spoiled rotten by her daddy. He reads to her every night, puts her to bed, and is really very indulgent."

I take the opportunity to ask Donna how she thinks Kedric's life has been going the past five years. "You'll be pleased to hear this, Dr. Wallerstein," she says. "Kedric was doing great in the lumber yard, as you know, but all he ever talked about was flying. He'd take me and Angela down to the airport to watch the planes come in, and if there was a flying show within a day's drive, we'd always go to it. Finally I said, 'If this is what you want to do, Kedric, then do it!' I guess he finally listened to me because he went and renewed his pilot's license and opened a flying school. Things are changing and he's happier than I've ever seen him." I think to myself that at last Kedric really *has* let go of his anger at his father. He's able to take what he wants and admires about his father and to leave the rest.

Minutes later I am talking to Kedric on the telephone. He affirms that he has made a major career change and that his marriage is strong and happy. "One thing stands out in my mind," he says after a while. "You remember, Judy, that I wasn't sure that I wanted to have children? And how I felt that there were a whole lot of feelings that I couldn't reach inside me? Well, since Angela was born I've got them. And it's wonderful."

Feeling goose bumps, I realize that none of these triumphs or insights have been handed to Kedric on a silver platter. This young man worked hard for his second chances, and he has truly made the best of them.

Sammy Moore and Carl and Kedric Patton reacted differently to divorce and found different ways to incorporate the experience into their lives over the ten years that followed. Sammy was just beginning to move out of his mother's orbit and into the world of school and peers when his parents separated. At a time when he was still struggling with feelings of rivalry with his father, the divorce seemed to answer his forbidden secret wishes. As a result, he felt guilty for having caused the divorce. His reaction, although severe, was appropriate given what he was worried about. Over the years, as he is assured by Nicholas's continuing presence, Christina's loving parenting, and several years of therapy, his fears diminish and he recovers.

Divorce interrupted Carl Patton's developmental course at the same time as it did Sammy's, but Carl took on a much closer, more supportive role for his hard-working mother. Unlike Sammy, he was not buffered by his older siblings. In the dynamics of his family, he became his mother's helper — out of love and gentleness. But he felt rebuffed, rejected, and replaced in his father's life. In effect, his own inner fears did seem to materialize. Carl continued to reach out to his father but felt that he drew no response. Now, when it is time for him to leave home, he feels depleted and disadvantaged psychologically. Unlike Sammy, he cannot detach gradually. Instead, he retreats into fantasy to help make the break and invents a rejecting mother and a phantom father who is loving and encouraging. In distorting reality, he is poorly prepared for his move into adulthood.

Kedric is probably the most fortunate. At sixteen, he was already fairly mature when his parents divorced and was more or less detached emotionally from them. By virtue of his own achievements, his self-esteem was high and he was very aware that his parents loved and valued him. Nevertheless, the divorce threatened to derail him. His relationship with his father was profoundly shaken by moral issues surrounding the divorce, and his first steps toward independence were threatened by his mother's intense need for help. And yet Kedric was able to move forward by rejecting his father as an identification figure and by turning instead toward his wife and her family. When he becomes a parent himself, he is finally able to express the gentle, loving feelings he feared were lost to him.

6

Ruth Moore

DAUGHTERS AND MOTHERS

RUTH MOORE was nearly fourteen years old when her parents divorced. The oldest of the three children in the family, Ruth was the last to come to see me as the Moores' marriage was falling apart. She was the final piece in our first complete picture of this family.

"Thank God it's over," said Ruth, dressed in jeans and a batik jacket she had just bought at an art fair. "Now we don't have to walk on eggs anymore." I looked at her closely. With long blond hair pulled into a neat ponytail, she seemed like a much younger version of her genteel mother. Ruth was a polite, well-bred teenager who was just beginning to make her first moves away from the very traditional family in which she had been raised. Christina was upset because Ruth had broken curfew and hitchhiked into San Francisco during a recent transit strike. But her behavior, while disturbing to her mother, seemed no cause for alarm. Ruth was doing the normal things that fourteen-year-olds do, and she hung out with a good crowd of kids.

As Ruth and I talked, it became clear to me that she had begun to distance herself from her parents. She told me that she had won battles to extend her curfew and to take public transportation and not to have to report on her telephone calls and other activities.

"I'm different," said Ruth in a poised, cool manner. "My own code calls for openness and kindness but my parents have a 'Let's not talk about it' policy. I'm going to spend a year in Europe after high school, before I go to college, because I think travel broadens a person."

Ruth was on course developmentally as she planned her future and developed her own moral standards. I was very taken with this attractive girl and, while appreciating her mother's anxieties, I thought Ruth was a level-headed youngster who was absolutely on track. As often happens in families where children are protected, she was moving slowly into adolescence. It was time.

When I saw her eighteen months later, however, things had taken an unexpected turn. Ruth was prim as she talked endlessly about her mother. Hands folded in her lap, she said, "Dr. Wallerstein, I'm worried about my mom, my brother, and my sister. I try to protect Mom. I don't tell her things that might upset her. She needs as much help as she can get." Ruth clasped her hands more tightly. "Mom wrote me into her will," she said nervously. "In case anything happens, I'd be legal guardian to Sammy and Denise."

As we talked, Ruth revealed that she had taken a strong stance against her father and had moved away from him emotionally, although they had been close before the divorce.

I was interested in what seemed to be a nascent turnabout in this girl. She appeared to be abandoning her adolescent rebellion. In fact, she had moved in the opposite direction, becoming her mother's right arm, helping to raise the younger children, and helping to make major decisions, including which house to purchase after the divorce. Ruth believed it was very important that her sister and brother "grow up right," and she actively enforced household rules and oversaw completion of chores. Ruth was very sweet and loving to her mother, becoming in fact her mother's best friend. Denise and Sammy recognized the situation, going so far as to say, "Ruthie and Mom brought us up." To my mounting concern, Ruth had little to say about friends or school.

Five years later, when Ruth was eighteen, she very much identified with her mother's role. "I have to provide a good role model for Sammy and Denise," she said in explaining why she gave up an opportunity to travel in Europe for two months with a group of unchaperoned teenagers. "I take this very seriously and am careful about who I bring home. I abide by all the rules and regulations so my brother and sister can see I'm setting a good example."

Once again, I was troubled by her insufficient moves toward independence and by too little talk about friends, school, and extracurricular activities. Although Ruth did talk about boys and her relationships with them, she had not been involved in an important relationship, sexually or emotionally.

I am curious, therefore, to see what Ruth is doing with her life a full ten years after the divorce, when her mother no longer needs her help at home. Ruth is delighted to hear from me and responds to my telephone call as if no time has passed at all. "Oh, hello, Dr. Wallerstein," she says warmly. "I'd love to see you." And so begins a reunion that we both enjoy. When Ruth enters my office, I am struck by how pretty she is and, with her blond beauty and tall, lanky build, how much she looks like her mother. Her twenty-fourth birthday is next month.

Ruth describes the years since high school as a slow but progressive move out of her mother's orbit. She has slowly come to realize that living around her mother and father has given her a narrow view of life and that she needs to move out into a more heterogeneous world. Unable to decide what to do with her life after completing her bachelor of science degree, she is living with a much older man who has three children. In her love life, she has moved laterally, into a relationship where she is still the parent to children living in her home.

Ruth is talking animatedly about her mother, whom she still visits twice a week. "I had to help my mom raise the kids," she says in a tone suggesting that she had no choice. "I wanted to help because I am very close to her. But it's been a burden, Judy, and it's taken a lot of my life away. In fact, I'm not at all sure that I want to have children of my own. There's a lot of pain in raising children." She looks tired just thinking about it. "In fact, it's a full-time job and you have to give up so much. I'm not sure I'm willing to make that sacrifice."

Noting that she and her mother stand in the same shoes, I comment, "You've been very close to your mom."

"We started close and we're much closer," Ruth says with warmth in her voice. "She doesn't have a second adult around, so I help her. We spend a lot of time talking together. She still needs my advice. You know, my mom is an ideal parent. She is always there whenever we need her. But I don't think she's that happy. Anyway, both Mom and I look ahead" — again I note to myself that Ruth and her mother are standing in the same shoes — "but I'm looking into adulthood and she's looking at all of us leaving her."

"You're worried about leaving her, Ruth."

"Very," she says, as her tone grows more serious. "I'm very different because of their divorce. Being oldest, I had much more responsibility and sometimes it was hard. I'm not that eager to rely on anybody." Then, revealing a vulnerability that I never suspected, she says, "I've always been prepared for the possibility that I'd come home and find the house locked and all my belongings parked next to my car."

This is an amazing admission. With all her independence and savoir-faire, there is a core of vulnerability in this young woman. In some deep part of her, Ruth clearly expects the worst — that she will be rejected and abandoned in her own relationship. Contrary to what people say, they really believe that lightning strikes twice in the same place; people who have suffered one catastrophe almost inevitably expect and fear a second. Like other children of divorce, Ruth lives with the anxiety of sudden abandonment. And, because she is competent, she prepares for this eventuality so she won't be taken by surprise a second time.

By the end of the interview, I view Ruth as a young woman struggling with many issues regarding her father and men in general, unresolved issues of adolescence, and her feelings toward her mother. While not depressed, she has strong reservations about how her life will work out, and she's apprehensive about finding out.

Mother-child relationships are profoundly altered by divorce, giving rise to new family forms. The single parent and the child have expanded opportunities for love and compassion and mutual dependence, but human psychology being as complex and paradoxical as it is, they also have expanded opportunities for feelings of hurt and rejection. Eager to please their parents, children, especially girls, may rush into the breach, taking upon themselves a wide range of family responsibilities and household chores.

In our study, we see close relationships between mothers and daughters of all ages, the latter ranging from tiny preschoolers through adolescents. Mothers speak lovingly of daughters who respond wordlessly to their moods and needs. "She knows without my saying anything just when to put her arm around me," says one mother.

While mothers can develop close friendships with both sons and daughters in the years after divorce, girls tend to take more responsibility for their mothers' well-being. The daughter may advise and guide her mother in myriad ways, so that the older leans heavily on the younger, leading many a mother to say in all honesty, "My daughter is my best friend." Such relationships are far more intimate than mother-daughter relationships within an intact family. Over half the mothers and daughters in our study maintain a significant degree of mutual emotional dependency during the girls' adolescence. When mothers do not lean too heavily or too long on their daughters, this new parent-child relationship can be very beneficial to both parties, and girls may emerge stronger for their part in it. Ten years after divorce, some of the best-adjusted girls were those who took on a degree of responsibility in the mothers' households. It is good for children to feel that their parents need them — *up to a point.*

Children of divorce acquire practical knowledge and skills not usually found in middle-class children, and girls feel very proud of the help that they give to their mothers as they pitch in around the house, assume responsibilities, and even share in making important decisions. Ruth, for instance, helped her mother decide what house to buy and set rules for her younger sister and brother. When mothers depend on daughters to the point of shutting out other adult relationships, however, the mutuality turns problematic. Some mothers in our study relied on their daughters to help with decisions that children could not possibly make, such as selecting sexual partners or changing jobs. They became emotionally and intellectually dependent on a growing girl, rather than reinvesting themselves appropriately in the adult world.

From the girl's point of view, this stickiness binds her — in a web of love and guilt — to her mother. She has trouble moving out into the world of her own peers and in making a life plan separate from her mother's. Some girls are unable to feel and express the healthy anger that is necessary to separate at adolescence and, as we will see, others are caught in the psychological trap of being afraid to surpass their mothers.

Leaving home is inevitably more difficult without an intact family to help lay the road for the child's departure. In divorced families, it is very often the oldest daughter who assumes the task of helping her mother, taking on two sets of challenges. The first set is external — helping out around the house, taking care of younger children, and enforcing routines and schedules. In the interaction, the mother gets a helper and the daughter develops pride, self-confidence, and real life skills.

The other challenges are internal. The girl wants to help her mother, yet she also wants to grow up and leave the family. Developmentally, she is on the horns of a dilemma. If she grows too close to her mother, she does not address the central issue of adolescence — developing the emotional independence that allows her to separate and establish her own identity.

For many of the girls from divorced families whom we see in our psychiatric clinics today, the most pressing issues concern separation. Mothers have trouble letting go; daughters have trouble growing up and leaving home. Such problems are found in intact families, but they take on a specific cast in divorced families.[1]

When Ruth's parents separated, she had just begun moving away from her family. The divorce cut smack across her developmental road. Instead of continuing on her way, Ruth made a 90-degree and then a 180-degree turn, away from her adolescent rebellion. She took on the role of a second mother in the household. Because she is bright, she did everything well; there were no complaints. But in taking on her mother's external tasks, she left some of the major issues of her own adolescence unresolved.

I wonder, for example, how much pleasure Ruth permitted herself over the years and how heavily her responsibilities must have weighed on her throughout high school and college. She took on the mothering role to the point where she forfeited fantasies about her own future and her own children. Ruth's sacrifice is particularly important because there was no economic necessity for her role as parent helper. The family was well-off, and Ruth was not obligated to work so that her family could survive financially. The weight of her obligations was tallied on a psychological scale, calibrated by her mother's growing dependence on her.

When Ruth left for college, she left in body but not in spirit, for emotionally she was tied to her still-needy mother. After college, she moved right back, to be near Mom, and now she has hooked up with a man twice her age who has children, further casting her into a maternal role.

All the while, she has disrupted what had been a very positive relationship with her father. Though he has remained faithful to her through the years, she has rebuffed him out of loyalty to her mother/herself.

It is no surprise, therefore, that Ruth is having a difficult time a full decade after the divorce, for her identification with her mother goes above and beyond the usual mother-daughter identification. All of Ruth's life experiences are different, yet she acts as if she were inside her mother's skin. She virtually merges with her mother, in violation of traditionally maintained generational boundaries.

A major theme for adolescent girls like Ruth is that they are not given the support they need for gradually detaching from the family. In attending to their mothers' needs, they find later that they have lost their own adolescence — an irreplaceable loss. For children of divorce, independence is like a two-faced coin, with everything that they have done for others on one side and everything that was *not* done for them on the other. It is worth repeating the fact, which seems largely underestimated by the American public, that children need an enormous amount of support during adolescence. The children of divorce say it over and over again. We should listen to them.

I have seen a number of mother-daughter relationships similar to Christina and Ruth's with a variety of consequences to the young women involved.

Very soon after walking through the door for our ten-year interview, Mary, a twenty-five-year-old social worker, asks if I will give her the name of a sex therapist. I say yes, surely, but I'll need more information to help make the right choice.

Although she has been living with Jim for four years, Mary says that she and her boyfriend are mostly incompatible, with different backgrounds and interests. As her story unfolds, it becomes clear to me that their relationship is fundamentally unhappy. Mary feels restricted and demeaned in ways that she cannot articulate to Jim and can hardly express to herself.

"What feels good about your relationship with Jim?" I ask as an opener. "Tell me what you really like. What's good?"

She pauses. "It's hard for me to answer that."

"It's hard to talk about him," I say, hoping to get her going.

But Mary changes the subject. After folding her hands tightly in her lap, she says, "I remember the day my dad left, my mom stayed up all night in the red rocking chair crying. I stayed up with her, and I cried too. Did I ever tell you that?"

I nod.

"Well, not long ago I took this family course at school. The professor told us to close our eyes and think of someone in the family. So I closed my eyes and thought of my mother standing there alone as the sad, repressed woman that she is. And I cried and I cried and I felt I would never stop crying."

"Mary, we were talking about Jim, and now we're talking about how unhappy your mom is. Is there a connection?"

Mary sits stunned for a few moments and then whispers, "I could never do to anybody what happened to my mom."

Soon Mary is crying as she says, "I've thought about leaving. But I could never do that to him."

"Even though you don't feel happy?"

"Yes, even though I have some very serious concerns. In some important part of me I believe I can change him. I feel compelled to keep trying."

Instead of a sex therapist, I recommend counseling for Mary and possibly Jim, so she can make a decision whether to stay involved. I advise her to set a time limit within which to decide whether this is a relationship that warrants work.

I had anticipated that Mary might have some problems separating from her mother, but it did not occur to me before our ten-year interview that these same separation issues would be reinstalled in her relations with men.

Mary's inability to break up or go forward in her relationship with Jim illustrates another dilemma in the queen of hearts game, in Mary's case one that is dominated by the ghost of her relationship with her mother. It is a complex problem with many strands.

On one level, Mary does not want Jim to feel the pain of the rejection that she saw her mother experience. And she certainly does not want to be the agent of his suffering.

And at another level, Mary is fearful of surpassing her mother, of doing better in the world of love and marriage. This is a major issue underlying the fear of success that we see in many young women. It has its roots in Mary's continued strong identification with her mother, whose feelings of hurt and rejection have persisted. Mary feels unable to leave her mother behind, and it is no accident that when asked to close her eyes and conjure up any family figure, Mary thinks of her sad mother and begins to sob uncontrollably.

Finally, Mary feels driven by a need to rescue her mother. She wants to restore her mother, to help her be the happy woman Mary would like her to be, which would then permit Mary herself to be happy. This rescue fantasy soon permeates all of Mary's relationships and may be installed in her career choice in social work. With Jim, she has committed herself to a rescue operation rather than to a love affair. Such efforts are unlikely to succeed and will only perpetuate repeated failures.

As they take up their second chances and enter relationships of their own, all young people are haunted by earlier experiences within their families. The relationship they had with each parent and the relationship they witnessed between their parents are like insistent ghosts that threaten to make the children of divorce repeat their parents' mistakes. These ghosts, reflecting what the children of divorce have witnessed in their lifetimes, have their source in the nature of identification and attachment, the two major strands of all relationships.

Identification is a developmental process that fundamentally shapes human character. Beginning at infancy, it involves the child's embodiment of characteristics gleaned from important figures in his or her life. The parents are the primary identification figures, and children take on characteristics from both parents in complex ways. The object of identification is usually thought of as a person who is loved and highly esteemed. When that is the case, the identification is a positive one. A child can also make negative identifications with people or aspects of a person that the child consciously fears and even rejects. The child identifies with these negative behaviors and attitudes despite himself or herself. Positive and negative identifications have a great deal to do with how children respond to divorce, especially with how they behave as they enter young adulthood.

Identification is not conscious imitation, although imitation may play a particular part, nor is it an inevitable result of living close to someone. Rather, it is a complex internal process borne out of the perceptions, feelings, and interactions between a child and the adults who surround him or her during all the growing-up years. Such identifications, once established within the personality, are likely to remain in place unless modified by extensive psychological treatment. They are part of the unconscious mind and are therefore not accessible to change by admonition, advice, or even a conscious wish to change.

Many identifications stem from positive, loving relationships. For example, a little girl rocks her baby doll just as she was rocked by her mother. As she imitates her mother's motions, she also embodies ideals attached to motherhood: inner feelings of tenderness and compassion along with external caretaking behavior. As she rocks the doll, the child conceptualizes herself as the mother she loves — she becomes in her own eyes a person who is lovable and caring, just like her mother. As she grows up, she incorporates within herself the idea that she, in being a mother, will become lovable and capable of caring. She also incorporates the sexual identity of her mother, including her mother's definition of womanhood and view of the opposite sex.

Similarly, the little boy identifies with his mother's love and caring. He learns to treat himself, and eventually his possessions and other people, with the care that he has experienced from her, and he identifies with her tenderness and compassion. He becomes, like the mother he loves, a person who is loving and caring, incorporating that identity within himself as an ideal.

The little girl, loving and admiring her father for the way he nurtures and protects her, identifies with his values, his style, and most of all the way he relates to other members of the family. She watches her father when he embraces her mother and identifies with his tenderness and caring. The way that he expresses himself — whether it be with kindness, cruelty, gentleness, or selfishness — becomes internalized within her.

Similarly, the little boy identifies with the relationship that he experiences with his father and incorporates this into his own self-image. He also incorporates his father's sexual identity and definition of manhood. He watches the way his father treats his mother and other members of the family; he watches what his father rewards and punishes, and he incorporates many of these attitudes as well.

Just as children identify with parents as individuals, they also identify with the relationship between them, so that the parents' marriage becomes a template for the child's later expectations. Because they carry this experience with them into adulthood, the way the parents related to one another during the marriage, the way they separated, and the kind of relationship they maintained after divorce are critical to the child's development.

Throughout their early years, children encounter many identification figures — parents, grandparents, stepparents, teachers, employers, peers, siblings, and lovers. They are influenced and shaped by all these relationships and more. As they become adults, they are not carbon copies of the figures around them, for in following their inner consciences, they accept some characteristics and reject others. In time, they integrate a range of separate identifications into new combinations, taking on many, but not all, of the characteristics and attitudes of the people with whom they grew up. Out of numerous identifications, they shape their own identities, their views of relationships, their own moral standards, their self-image, and their expectations of the opposite sex, of their friends, of the world, and ultimately of their own second chances. Their self-esteem will forever be dependent on the extent to which they meet the expectations that they have incorporated within themselves as a result of these many identifications.

All children look to their parents or guardians as primary identification figures. Children of divorce, being no exception, look to adults who happen to be experiencing a major life crisis. These youngsters often draw unhappy conclusions from what they perceive around them, especially when one parent seems happy and the other does not. Whether it is true or not, they may perceive that one parent has cruelly abandoned the other. Afraid to identify with the victim out of fear that they might someday suffer the same unhappy fate, they are nevertheless drawn, out of love and compassion, to identify with the parent who is tragically rejected.

Many of the girls in our study find themselves facing just this dilemma as these identifications come to the fore at adolescence. Afraid to identify with a rejected mother, they still want — out of love and admiration — to be like her. Like Mary, many of them are keenly aware throughout childhood and adolescence that their fathers rejected their mothers for other women. Now, as they enter young adulthood, they are terrified of being abandoned and betrayed in their own adult relationships, a fear that is rooted in identifications with their mothers. When Mary closes her eyes and sees her sad, rejected mother sitting alone, she cries because she is deeply afraid of being like her mother; if she is like her mother, she faces abandonment. At the same time, Mary wants to be like her mother — good, gentle, kind, and caring. How can she commit to a relationship when a relationship was denied to her mother? How can she permit herself to commit to a man when her mother — who had been a perfect mom — was rejected and cast away? To take a chance on someone, knowing in one's heart that the relationship could fail, requires more courage than most people realize. It is no wonder that many young people founder.

At the end of our interview, I ask Mary if there is anything she wants to ask me.

"Yes," she says with a frown. "Is there anything I've told you so far today that might help my mom? Should I encourage Mom to go out and have a social life or to get a job, or do you think that would just upset her more?"

Given the opportunity to ask questions of a psychologist who knows her well, Mary chooses to ask about her mother's future. She is preoccupied with the figure of her mother, whom she loves dearly, as the failed woman, a woman whom she can't use as a positive object of identification and whom she cannot surpass without intense guilt. Mary wants to rescue her mother before giving herself permission to move into a happy adult relationship with a man.

Young women follow a variety of courses in their attempts to avoid being in their mothers' position. Some rush into early marriage to avoid being alone. "I've lived with my mom, away from my dad, as long as I can remember," says Leigh, age nineteen. "And I really don't know any other kind of family. All my friends are from divorced families. I want to get married young, to find the right man, and chain him up so he won't go away." She confesses, "I read women's magazines with articles about how to seduce a man. I worry very much that I'll be thirty and still dating. I don't want to be middle-aged and alone. I'm real clear about this. I look at my mom, and she's in a rut. All she does is get up early, clean, go to work, come home alone by herself — I don't want to end up that way."

"Have you come close to getting married, Leigh?"

"Yeah, well, there are a few guys I've dated, that if they asked me to marry them, I would."

In another variation, girls whose faithful mothers are rejected can take an even more destructive path in the postdivorce years. Impelled by the notion that good is weak and likely to lead to betrayal, the young woman makes an all-out attempt to break the rules, engaging in drugs, freewheeling sex, and other destructive behavior. The anxiety of being like her betrayed mother — "I don't want to be nice like you" — is accompanied by anger at both parents: anger at one for betrayal and infidelity, anger at the other for being exploited and weak. The girl also feels angry at both parents for not being parents.

This anger adds to the usual rebellious anger of adolescence, and the result is anger magnified many times — and a young person who feels that there is "no reason not to listen to the voices of the streets." After all, the streets offer excitement, escape, and great pleasure in the present.

Although I cannot predict how these young women will cope with the sticky issues of separation and identifications, I am heartened by a turnaround in Ruth during her late twenties. After our last meeting, she sought therapy for some of the issues we discussed.

"I realized how unhappy I was," she says at our fifteen-year interview, "and that after the divorce I took all the responsibility and worry for everyone. My adolescence shattered when I was fourteen, and I didn't pick up the pieces again until I was twenty-two. Therapy helped me unravel *my* wishes and needs from those of my mom and the other kids. I volunteered to help Mom bring up the kids but never got a chance to separate from the family and do things for me. Therapy also gave me a realistic view of Dad. He is such a dominant person, and the divorce caught me just as I was beginning to rebel against him. I never asserted myself but was instead the good girl, because after all, Judy, Mom did need my help. I also learned to have a more realistic view of men. The last time I left your office I realized how unhappy I was with Len and how ridiculous it was for me to be raising more kids." Ruth sighs, as if relieved that the past is past.

"I also decided what I wanted to do with my life. I've always been interested in health issues and, Judy, I've decided to go into health education. I've finished my master's and I'm in a doctoral program in public health." She smiles. "I'm going to answer one of your questions before you ask it. I'm married."

"What happened to all the misgivings you told me about?"

"I finally realized I have to take a chance on life."

"Well, come on, tell me about him."

"It's realistic," she says with a smile that lights up her face. "I love him, he loves me, and we have a lot of fun together. He's an electronic engineer and I don't understand half of what he does. But Judy" — she smiles — "he's really smart. I used to like older men but he's exactly my age. Now I like men who don't overpower me, and it's very important that we be equal. I plan to work full-time and if we ever get divorced I'll be able to support myself. Of course I've kept my maiden name."

Like so many of her contemporaries, but in striking contrast to many of the young women in this group who were unable to use their mothers' experiences as the basis for their own constructive planning, Ruth is hedging her bets.

I am very proud of Ruth at this juncture in her life. She has caught up and is clearly back on course. She has learned from her parents' experience that relationships might not last, but that does not hold her back from falling in love. In choosing a husband and a career, Ruth maintains a core of independence and a fallback position should her marriage not work.

Fifteen years after their parents divorced, close to 40 percent of the young adults whom we interviewed have been in therapy at various times to work through issues concerning relationships. Generally, men seek therapy less often than women, but the male and female children of divorce in this study have gone for help in equal numbers. When their love affairs or early marriages broke up, men and women alike sought help. Some sought but were unable to locate support groups composed of children of divorce. Most benefitted from individual therapy once a week for one to two years. I am encouraged by the many positive changes that they have reported to me and by how quickly some of them were helped.

The Dreamer

Just before her parents separated, Tina, age fifteen, had a dream. As can happen in dreams, both parents had died and yet remained alive, standing together in a darkened room before a man who was writing at a brightly lit desk surrounded by total darkness. Behind them were two dark hallways and, as the dream ended, each parent walked alone, slowly, away from the other, down the long, dark corridors until both disappeared.

Tina's dream conveyed her loneliness and fear of being isolated as, unconsciously, she equated her parents' divorce with death. Kafkaesque in its featureless landscape, cavernous doors, and lonely figures, Tina's dream accurately represents the mood of many adolescents at the time their families break apart. Tina felt alone. Her parents left her before she was ready, before she had time to become an adult.

The first time I met Tina — a tall, willowy sixteen-year-old with

brown hair and striking blue eyes — she had just had a fight with her
mother on the way to my office. "She almost wouldn't drive me
here," she said, wiping away a tear. "Now it's her back that hurts,
but I told her what I think — what a great trick she's pulling on us.
She's not sick and I told her to get out of bed."

"Are you all right, Tina?"

"Thank you, I'm fine," she said, running fingers through her pixie
haircut. "I just get so emotional. I guess I could have used help a long
time ago, but now I don't need it that much because I've talked a lot
of this out with my grandparents and my brothers. Now I want to
forget it." Tina was laughing and crying at the same time.

"It's not so easy to forget things that hurt you," I said.

"I'm too emotional," Tina said, "just like my dad. He's a lawyer,
you know." I had already heard a great deal about Tina's father from
her mother and the other children in the family, all of whom had told
me that he yelled at everyone around him.

"My dad and I are alike," Tina went on. "I can talk to him. Sure,
he's not perfect and he says terrible things to Mom — that she's a
parasite, a taker — but the truth is, there are probably a lot of weaknesses on both sides. Sometimes I feel like I'm the parent. My folks
should be more mature."

When I asked about her mother, Tina surprised me with her insight
when she said, "I worry that Mom is never going to get her act together, even though she's always been there for us kids, has always
tried her best. She's always going to be looking for something she
can't find. She's got more hangups than you could name. I really
worry about her, and I still feel responsible. She's really been down
on herself lately. I don't want to make it worse and I don't want her
to know how I worry about her. I guess the thing I resent most about
their divorce is not knowing the truth. Mom says one thing and Dad
says another, and it's unreal, just like a damn soap opera with Dad
on one end of the couch and Mom on the other."

When I saw Tina a few weeks later, we talked about her plans for
her future. "I will not be like my mother," she said emphatically. "I
want to have a career and do well at school, and maybe I'll be a lawyer, or maybe I'll marry a lawyer, or maybe I'll be a legal aide. Maybe
I'll go onstage, but I'm not going to marry young." In the meantime,
Tina had decided to live with her mother. "Dad is unbearable," she
said, holding her arms out as if balancing a weight in each hand.
"Mom needs me." Indeed, Tina listened sympathetically to her moth-

er's complaints, assuring her that she would never be abandoned.

For our five-year interview, I drove to Sacramento, where Tina was getting ready to enter law school at the University of California in nearby Davis. "You're seeing me at the most hectic time in my life," she announced. "Dad was here last week and you wouldn't recognize him. Can you believe it, he ran the Boston Marathon last month! He looks fabulous. His new girlfriend runs an art gallery in San Francisco and, boy oh boy, she's really made a difference in his life." Tina explained that, after the divorce, she and her father began to meet frequently in restaurants, where he could not scream at her; hence they got to know each other better. "I've always said exactly what's on my mind," said Tina, "and you learn pretty soon that you just don't talk back to my dad. But I did. He and I have grown very close and, in fact, he is going to help me through law school."

"I thought you had decided against that, Tina."

She smiled. "I did, but then I changed my mind. For my last two years of college, I spent a lot of time with my philosophy professor and his wife. He encouraged me to go to graduate school and pointed out that I think like a lawyer, that I shouldn't waste my talent. So in large part I'm following their advice."

Now, at our ten-year interview, Tina at twenty-six has grown into a lovely, lively young woman whose warm smile and open manner make her a pleasure to be with. Her hair is still cut short, and she wears large horn-rimmed glasses that make her look scholarly. Although we are sitting in a crowded cafeteria, she has no compunctions about telling me deeply personal facts about her life. She has just started to practice law at a prestigious firm, and I can imagine her in a courtroom — brash, competent, intelligent, and fast on the verbal draw.

I ask about her family.

"Mom is okay," she says with a hint of a sigh. "She's still looking for something she can't find. I've gotten used to it. I used to feel guilty and thought I should stay with her and help her out all the time. I still worry about her, but I'm not as frightened as I used to be. She's not working or anything." Tina taps her fingers on the Formica tabletop for a moment, as if to nudge her memory. "I remember Mom getting more and more depressed and not being able to cope. I tried to stay home all I could. Gee, I remember at home we used to hide under the covers and shake when they were fighting."

And her father?

"I admire him. He's bright and he has a sense of humor, but he's a real Dr. Jekyll and Mr. Hyde. When he's bad, he's terrible. On the other hand, I find his approval very important. But I can't work in the same city with him. My law firm is in Sacramento and his is in San Francisco. That's well and good." Tina reflects more carefully for a moment and adds, "I'm glad that my drive to achieve comes from my dad, but he could have been a lot nicer to Mom. Most people have at least a semblance of civility. If it weren't for my grandparents, I don't think I could have made it past sixteen."

Tina warms to the subject of her grandparents. "When my mom and dad were acting like babies, my grandparents became my parents. They still are. Going home for me is going to their house in Sonoma. I worry about them a lot. Grandma is seventy-six and Grandpa is seventy-nine. It's hard to see them getting older, but watching them together is wonderful. One couldn't survive without the other. It's been important for me to see that. I still look to them in times of crisis. They've been a rock for all of us kids. I couldn't have made it through college without their help, financial and emotional."

And her younger brothers?

"My brothers and I have an incredible relationship. We adore each other. The truth is, I don't know what we would have done without each other after the divorce. They've been like a port in a storm to me." As Tina tells me about her youngest brother's recent brush with death in a European train accident, tears stream down her face. "He could have been killed," she whispers.

"I'm a leaner," she says finally. "I lean on my brothers. I lean on my grandparents. And I lean on my friends and teachers."

Like many children her age, Tina had established the beginnings of independence from her parents when their divorce occurred. Nevertheless, she was profoundly threatened by it and, as her dream shows, felt she could not survive without a family.

Several factors protected her, though. First, Tina has a realistic, balanced view of both her parents. Aware of their limitations, she takes from each just what she needs for her own healthy development, rejecting neither. Tina avoids taking sides in their battles, maintaining a compassionate stance toward both her ailing mother and her overbearing father.

Second, both her parents are committed to Tina. Although they were not ideal parents and were certainly not nice to one another, separately they have remained devoted to their daughter, respecting her individuality and independence. Tina's father was pleased that she followed him into law, but he never insisted on it.

Tina's experience with her parents illustrates a fundamental truth about children of divorce. Although there are right ways and wrong ways to bring children up after divorce, what counts most is that children perceive that their parents are committed and give them priority. Tina's parents did this and she knew it.

Tina is also protected by support and affection from the rest of her family. Her grandparents maintained close contact after the divorce and helped her, including financial support during college and law school. Many youngsters turn to family members when their parents' marriages collapse. These relationships work best when family members do not take sides in the divorce and make their primary commitment to the children.

Grandparents can play a particular role, especially if their marriages are intact: symbolic generational continuity and living proof to children that relationships can be lasting, reliable, and dependable. Grandparents also convey a sense of tradition and a special commitment to the young that extends beyond and over the parents' heads. Their encouragement, friendship, and affection has special meaning for children of divorce; it specifically counteracts the children's sense that all relationships are unhappy and transient.

For the fortunate children in our study who could rely on their extended families, the world seemed a more stable, predictable place. What matters most is that these relationships continue well beyond the crucial years immediately following divorce. Although geographical proximity helps, it is not essential. Grandparents can provide a continuing sense of stability from a distance, but they must strike a fine balance of involvement without intrusiveness, of availability and concern without interference. Where these relationships worked, the children always benefited enormously and were eternally grateful.

Like Tina, many young people speak eloquently about their brothers and sisters in the years after divorce. In some families the siblings side with different parents — "his child" and "her child" — and hate each other. But we saw close sibling relationships in many more of the families, with children drawing together after divorce. An older child may bear the brunt, buffering younger children, but all the children learn to depend on one another, to turn to one another with love and compassion. We see this phenomenon among children in war-torn societies, and we see it in divorced families.

"My relationship with my brothers has been the saving of our emotional and physical selves," Tina says. "We have always been close. Without the others our chances of turning out as we are would have been very different. If I'd been an only child, I might have lost my sanity. We have always been faithful to each other. Always."

Finally, Tina benefits from a mentor relationship, partly because she is talented enough to attract a mentor and partly because she reaches out. Mentors have existed ever since the sorcerer had an apprentice. They can be grandparents, uncles or aunts, employers, teachers, or strangers who become friends. When families collapse at divorce, demands on children and adults are enormously increased, and change becomes a way of life. Children of divorce, who need help most of all, may find it even harder than other children to find mentors. So many have parents who are unavailable because they are working full-time or have their own agendas to follow. More profoundly, children of divorce are often fearful of identifying with parents because they are afraid of experiencing similar failures. There aren't many mentors in the shopping mall. Where are modern youngsters going to find them? Of all the children in our study, only very few found and made use of mentors.

And yet each and every one of these children, who feel that they have less priority in their parents' eyes, deeply need adults who will bolster their self-esteem and affirm their potential.

7

The Legacy of Violence

DIVORCE IS A SOCIAL REMEDY designed to bring an end to unhappy marriages and to protect children from growing up in strife-ridden homes. Much of the time, it does indeed rescue parents and children from destructive relationships and gives them second chances in life. There is, however, a glaring exception to this finding. It shows up dramatically in our ten- and fifteen-year study of families who, unlike the Moores, engaged in uncivilized behavior. In families where children witnessed physical violence between parents, the children were not necessarily rescued by divorce, even though their parents often were.

The Abuser

On the day I visit the Litrovski family in Monterey for our ten-year interviews, ice plant is in full bloom on the hills and promontories along the seacoast. The family has lived in this historic California town since Sasha, who learned four languages from his parents, came here to teach Russian at the Monterey Language Institute. His ex-wife, Pat, teaches Spanish at the public high school, and today the three children, Melissa, Janice, and Larry, live with their mother in a clean but ramshackle house near the center of town. While no one in this family is doing well in the decade after divorce, Larry, who is seventeen, is the most severely disturbed. Our interview leaves me chilled and uncomfortable.

As he sits across the kitchen table in his mother's house, Larry makes it abundantly clear that he does not want to talk to me. Smoking cigarettes and staring into space, he gives brief answers and won't meet my eyes. As he talks about his parents' divorce of ten years ago, he uses the present tense, as if it all happened yesterday. "My mom is responsible for driving my father out of my life," he says, scowling. Actually, Larry's parents divorced when his mother finally got up enough courage to leave a husband who beat and humiliated her at every opportunity. An anxious, tense, and modest woman who devoted her life to her children while playing the martyr, she was unable to protect herself from her husband or to protect her children from witnessing abuse and violence in the home. At age seven, Larry was a sad and angry little boy who had grown accustomed to violence. Nevertheless, Larry looked up to his father. After all, his father never laid a hand on him.

Larry now says that the last five years have been a "total bummer," that his life will "never improve," and that he has "every right to be angry."

"I've been saving up money to buy a car," he says, "but it doesn't matter because she isn't going to sign for my license. I think she's fucked. She's such a prissy-teacher type. She wants me to prove I'm responsible."

"What would make her think you are more responsible?"

He laughs and proceeds to tell me a succession of stories in which he was "so bombed, I couldn't, like, even talk."

I decide to take a chance. "Larry, how much do you feel in control of your life?"

My question stops him cold. Looking directly at me, he says wistfully, "About three-quarters." He pauses to gather his thoughts. "My mom is good at getting on my nerves. Most of my friends, you see, have two parents. They get the kinds of things they want. Do you know that when my dad got remarried, I didn't find out for four months! When I talk to him, it's always by phone. Sometimes when he calls me, I'm really bombed. He threatens to come over and kick my rear end off." Larry chuckles, as if this would be welcome attention from his father. "After he screams at me in English, he bawls me out in Russian.

"My dad really does have a drinking problem, and I worry about that," he says more seriously. "But I drink more than my dad did when he was a kid. Except for all that language crap, I think I'm going to live a lot of my life just like my dad. It helps me solve my problems to drink. When I broke up with my girlfriend, I went out and got totally bombed."

"Are there any other parts of your dad that you see in yourself?"

"Yeah, in my relationships with girls, when I get mad," he admits, still scowling. "I slap them, and a couple of weeks ago I hit my girl-friend in the face."

I am staring at him, trying to think of what to say next, when Larry, without blinking, continues. "Look, it's her fault. My mom is respon-sible. My life's been a lot worse since Dad left, and it's her fault."

My concerns about Larry increase when I talk to his mother the next day. "Every time the kids were unhappy about how I disciplined them," she says, "they would call their father at the institute, and he would put me down. He'd start telling them that they could come live with him and that it was my fault that they weren't. He said he was going to court to change custody, but then he wouldn't do any-thing, he'd just drop it."

"Did the children know what he was doing?"

"Yes," she says, "but they blamed me. I'm especially concerned about Larry's drinking lately. Last year he got drunk and threatened me. I couldn't control him, so I asked his father to let Larry live with him. When he refused, Larry attacked me."

"He hit you?"

"Yes. He really hit me hard. I can't control him."

As Larry moves through adolescence and into young adulthood, his relationships with women are crippled by his experiences as a young child. Larry was never a victim of violence or a perpetrator of violence when he was a little boy — he merely witnessed the violent relationship between his father and mother. Yet he hits the women he is now involved with, even though he has not witnessed violence in his home for ten years. Larry prides himself on his influence over women and admits he is imitating his father's behavior. This is not behavior that Larry rejects or turns away from in shock or shame, nor is it behavior that he totally embraces.

Larry's story shows that not all identifications have their roots in love and esteem. While children reject many unhappy characteristics from people around them, some of the most powerful identifications have their roots in anger, pain, and loss. Children of divorce know this all too well. Time after time we see children identify with a parent who is perceived as powerful, especially if that parent has hurt the child's feelings, physically abused the child, or demeaned the other parent. This may seem paradoxical — one would expect a child to reject an aggressor as being cruel and unworthy of identification. But a closer look reveals the child's logic. By identifying with the powerful figure, the child defends himself or herself against the pain of feeling helpless. By being like the aggressor, the child embodies the power to do unto others what he or she experienced as a helpless victim. We see this most simply in the behavior of the frightened young child who gets an injection at the doctor's office. Upon returning home, the child administers the shot — which is perceived as painful — to a teddy bear or to a baby brother or sister. By temporarily identifying with the aggressor/physician, the child masters the pain of having received the shock as a passive recipient. The process of identifying with an aggressor can thus play a positive role in helping children cope with the inevitable pains and frustrations of growing up. It can also have negative consequences, as we saw so clearly at our ten- and fifteen-year interviews.

In mastering his anger and fear of a violent father, a boy can also become an oppressor. By all accounts, Larry's father drank heavily and hit his wife. Larry's mother seemed to accept her husband's view that she was incompetent and could do nothing right. To Larry at age seven, his father was omnipotent. When he found himself left behind with his demeaned mother and sisters, he was miserable and frightened. By identifying with his father, Larry bolstered his self-esteem and separated himself from his mother and sisters.

In a good parent-child relationship, the child's desire to be like the mother or father stems from love and attachment. The danger of a bad parent-child relationship is that identification can proceed without positive forces; the wish to be like the powerful father is irresistible. Without something or someone to counterbalance the father, there is nothing to stop the child from attaching to him. As one young man tells us fifteen years after his parents' divorce, "I confess that I hit my wife. I'm exactly like what I hate in my dad."

It is a tragic irony when divorce allows a mother to escape an abusive husband, while her children are trapped by their identification with him, an identification that is reinforced by their fears of becoming like the victim mother. In fact, the more capricious and rejecting the father, the more intense is the children's admiration and the more powerful are their efforts to be like Dad. At the time of the divorce,

some of the boys at age six or seven donned articles of clothing belonging to their fathers who had just left home and, in full identification with the paternal role, hurled insults at their distressed
mothers. Now, in adolescence, the identification reemerges in the
queen of hearts dilemma. The boys are driven to demean and hurt
their girlfriends, whom they also find appealing and attractive. Violence is more likely to erupt in a relationship with a woman if the
young man has been exposed to violence followed by sex offstage in
his parents' relationship, so that he comes to associate eroticism and
violence. Sometimes the violence may show up later, when the man
has children of his own. He may find a way to justify brutality, or he
may be horrified at his sadistic impulses, which emerge without
warning and seem to be beyond his control.

Nearly a quarter of the families in our study reported violence in the
marriage. Of the thirty-two boys and girls in these families, almost
half became involved in abusive relationships themselves in their late
adolescence and early adulthood. In only three families did all of the
children escape from re-creating the abusive relationships they had
witnessed ten and fifteen years earlier.

In addition, a few of the children in the study whose parents had
not been violent also formed abusive relationships in late adolescence. In other words, violence may reflect issues other than direct
early experience. But it is always associated with low self-esteem and
intense feelings of rejection.

Three-fourths of the young women involved in violent relationships were victims, while the others were perpetrators — that is, they
hit their boyfriends. All of the boys were perpetrators. Very few of
these children were abused themselves. In only five families was
even one of the children beaten by the abusive parent.

Most of the children who later took up violent behavior were very
young when their parents divorced. One has to wonder how they
could remember violence from such an early time in their lives. We
have found, however, that the youngest children of divorce have unconscious memories of it, a point made abundantly clear by Laura's
dream. In her dream, many years after her parents' divorce, Laura's
father threatens her mother with a gun. The police are summoned to
disarm him. Laura's "sister" then takes her across the street where
she watches the violent scene from a window.

Laura recounts this dream at age fourteen, but our records from ten years ago show that the dream recapitulates reality. Laura had been present at just such a violent scene. Her father had threatened to kill her mother. He pulled a gun. Police came. But Laura has "no recollection" of those events, even though she was there. She did not witness the scene from a house across the street; she was in the room. We know because we have a full record of what transpired. She does not have a sister; no one protected her at the time. When I pointed out to Laura that she had been present at this scene, she said, "Yes, I know. My mom told me after I told her the dream. But I honestly don't remember anything."

The dream portrays the traumatic event as well as the distance and protection afforded by Laura's selective forgetting. The older sister in the dream is an older version of Laura herself who removes the vulnerable little girl from the immediate danger of being shot by an enraged father. Meanwhile, Laura herself is "protected" from the memory only in that she does not have conscious recall of it. The memory nevertheless may affect her adult feelings and behavior many years later. She has told us many times during her adolescence that she is afraid she will marry someone violent like her dad, even though she has had only one visit with him over the years.

It is painful to report — and astounding to find — that even children who were quite young when their parents divorced and who have not lived with an abusive parent for ten or fifteen years became directly involved in abusive relationships themselves as they reached late adolescence and young adulthood. Their mothers, on the other hand, who initiated divorce to escape the violence, did not choose abusive men in their subsequent relationships and marriages. We have less information about men who were abusive in their first marriages. Although many described problems in subsequent relationships, they were understandably reluctant to discuss violence in their interviews. Ten and fifteen years later, mothers had escaped the violence, while their children had not. In a particularly sad twist, several women married second husbands who did not beat them but who did beat their children.

The children are a different story. For them, the early experience of bearing witness to violence continues to shape their later relationships. The young men and women in our study who have reinstalled the violence of their parents' marriages into their own current relationships recognize the connection and feel helpless to control their behavior. Perhaps repeating the abusive relationship restores the fantasy of the lost intact family.

The Victim

Deborah's first memories are of her parents' fighting. She was five when they finally divorced, not long after her father beat up her mother. "He always made us feel that it was Mom's fault that he hit her," she said later, "but I still didn't want them to get divorced."

Ten years after the divorce, she says, "I remember that I missed him a lot when he moved out of the house. He never hit us, only Mom, so I know why she divorced him, but I've never understood why he acted the way he did."

"How is he now?" I ask.

"Fine, but I can't condone what he did," she says. "He's still working over at the U.S. Geological Survey in Menlo Park. Actually, I never felt that I needed my dad until this year," she says with a smile. "Now that I'm going to high school, I have time to see him only about once a week. But it's neat."

Deborah says she is worried about her brothers, however, because "they are angry, violent, and they lose control. They got it from my dad." Her mother, a production assistant at *Sunset* magazine, is doing much better. "When I was thirteen," Deborah says, "Mom married a guy I didn't like, and I wanted to run away. But lately I've grown to accept him more."

I am encouraged by Deborah's achievements at school and among her peers. A petite redhead who gets straight A's, is president of the senior class, and has aspirations to go into politics, she seems one of the more successful children in our study. She is close to her mother and brothers, is getting along better with her stepfather, and has a realistic view of her father. She wants to get married and have children and "give the kids the best that they deserve from their parents." As we part, she says, "I think my mom was right to leave because my dad is a cruel and violent person. But I do worry constantly that I'll marry someone like my dad, and that's the last thing I want, the worst thing that could happen. I really hope I marry someone from a solid family."

By the time we meet for our fifteen-year interview, in a Seattle restaurant, Deborah's worst fears have come true: Her boyfriends are just like her father. In an animated, sometimes overanimated, manner she tells me about the last few years. Still a top student, she is studying political science at the University of Washington, but this is the only reassuring thing about Deborah.

"I'm always attracted to these jerks who treat me real bad," she says in an oddly happy tone. "Good guys are boring to me, and I'm always drawn to men with problems. John gave me bruises and a black eye, although he never put me in the hospital. I find him exciting. I think, like, if I can fix my men, then I can fix my dad. There was this one guy — I supported him completely even though he slept all day. I paid for everything. It was control, control over him, so he wouldn't leave my like my dad did. I felt, like, as long as I could control everything in my life, it would be okay. It was very sick."

"How do you explain this 'sick' behavior?"

"I felt abandoned," she says. "I lacked good role models on my father's end and my relationships with men are definitely a problem. I felt like an outcast early on." Deborah sighs. "But my boyfriend really loves me. I know he cares about me because he hits me."

I am stunned by the direct connection Deborah makes between feeling loved and being hurt and by her recognition that the roots of this go back to the relationship between her parents before she was five years old. She understands that while the divorce freed her mother, it did not free her; her adult relationships are sadly governed by her early childhood experiences. I am also stunned at how helpless and unmotivated she is to bring about change. When young people are in this kind of trouble, I feel it is appropriate to offer them help in finding competent therapists. Deborah needs help, and I discuss it with her, but in my own mind I am not optimistic that she will follow through, partly because she finds pleasure and excitement in her violent relationships.

Twenty percent of the young women in our study are in abusive relationships with their boyfriends or husbands ten and fifteen years after their parents divorced. Like Deborah, they identify with the violent relationship that existed between their parents, and they choose these relationships: "I know he cares about me because he hits me." During our fifteen-year interviews, we hear story after terrible story of physical and verbal abuse among these daughters of divorce, chilling stories about broken jaws, bruised eyes, and body welts. Such relationships, the young women say, combine sexuality with violence in an exciting, even pleasurable way. As the young women speak, I remember them as frightened little girls who mutely watched the violence at home. Now they are allowing it to be repeated in their own lives. Surely this is one of the saddest legacies of family violence.

Not all children identify with their parents' behavior, and brothers and sisters often follow different paths in this regard; one may adopt an abusive relationship while the other builds strong barriers against it. But an alarmingly high number of the children of divorce who witnessed family violence — two in five — repeated abuse in their own relationships.

Child abuse has generated widespread concern here and abroad in recent years, but there has been extraordinarily little recognition given to a corollary issue. Children who witness violence between their parents, especially when reinforced in a sexually stimulating atmosphere, are no less victimized than children who are direct victims of abuse. All our findings show that children from violent homes retain searing memories of violence between their parents; if there is just one violent episode leading up to divorce, a child will remember it.

Courts and the law evade the issue. A judge will remove from the household a child who is being physically beaten, but if the mother is beaten the law does not consider that the child is at risk. But our work shows that children who witness family violence are psychologically imperiled. Unfortunately, our laws are not designed to protect children psychologically. I recognize the complexity of this problem. Family life should remain private; we do not want a policeman in every bedroom to safeguard children. But as we have seen, removing youngsters from violence does not necessarily save them. A sexually charged atmosphere alone is detrimental to a child. Violence alone is detrimental. The combination can be disastrous.

Breaking the Cycle

Philip, age seven, was the family clown. As the third child in a family of four children, he found that preposterous antics and play-acting gained him much-wanted attention. Overshadowed by his older brother and sister and outmaneuvered by his little sister as Daddy's favorite, Philip turned to his mother for emotional support. Indeed, she felt sorry for her younger son, treating him with special compassion and kindness. "He seems to repel other children," she said not long after the divorce. "He can't sit still and he's constantly seeking attention."

The children were furious at their mother for demanding the divorce. Their father was an admirable man, the vice-president of a large San Francisco bank. Even though he drank too much and became violent, they felt he was a good father. After the divorce, their mother went to work in the design department of the Levi Strauss Company. Although she supported them well enough, the children continued to feel that she had betrayed them.

In those early years after the divorce, Philip was a hyperactive child who did poorly in school. I remember playing a game of checkers with him at our center and the look of surprise that crossed his face when he won. He was clearly a child who expected to lose.

When he and I sit down together for our ten-year interview, however, I am mightily impressed by how much he has changed. Although he is no more than five feet nine inches tall, Philip seems much larger, from several muscle-building years on the high school wrestling team. His straight black hair is long, tied back in a ponytail, and he wears a gold stud in one ear. "Lots of guys are having it done," he says with a smile. "I did mine on my seventeenth birthday." It is the summer before his senior year of high school.

Diffident at first, Philip opens up when we begin to talk about his hobby as a ham radio operator. "It's my life," he says. "I love it." For ten minutes, he regales me with details about his participation in a voluntary ham radio network that will be activated after a major earthquake in California. And he describes how he has wired the roof of his mother's house with special antennas.

"I didn't use to like school," he says at one point. "I couldn't concentrate. But that was before I found out about ham radio."

"What kind of student are you?"

"Average," he says. "All I ever wanted to do was pass with decent grades. I flunked math in my freshman year but otherwise I've been getting B's and C's. But now things have changed. I like school and can't wait to get back and see my friends. I may go for an A if it looks like I can."

"What else are you looking forward to, Philip?"

"I'd really like to move out of the house," he says with conviction. "I think about that when I get mad at Mom and my stepdad. I've already saved up some from my summer jobs."

I ask Philip about his memories of the divorce.

In a flash, he says, "Dad beating up Mom, trying to get between them, Dad pushing me away." Then, without seeming to notice the total contradiction of what he is saying, Philip adds, "I resented Dad leaving home. It hurt not to see him anymore except a couple of times a week. The worst part of the divorce was not seeing my dad."

Trying to keep amazement out of my voice, I ask, "What was good about the divorce, in your own mind?"

"Well, it was good for my mom. He used to fight with her so much and he'd beat her up pretty bad. But if I was in a marriage and I was henpecked all the time, I wouldn't stand for it. But then I wouldn't beat my wife, either."

"Are you planning to marry?"

"Oh yes, for sure," says Philip. "But I don't ever want a divorce. Divorce hurts other people."

I ask about his mom.

"Things are pretty good," he says. "She enjoys sitting in on my radio conversations. We got Buenos Aires the other night."

About girlfriends, he says jokingly, "There's usually one or two around." As we talk, however, Philip makes it clear that he is not sexually active and has no plans for that now.

Philip says he usually has good feelings about his stepfather. "He's a really loving guy. We have a good relationship, but if we don't obey him, we all get the belt."

"The belt? Tell me, how do you feel about that?"

Again, without seeming to register the contradiction in what he is saying, Philip tells me, "He likes me the best, but he's pretty vicious with that belt."

Obviously in Philip's world, physical abuse is a normal state of affairs, so much so that it doesn't seem to affect his view of relationships. He is staunchly protective of his stepfather and his father.

"Dad doesn't like my hobby," says Philip, "because he thinks it costs too much and puts me in contact with weirdos and night people. My dad still threatens me every now and then."

For the first time in our interview, Philip's body language hints at deeper feelings. He is tapping his foot and flexing his hands as we talk. "I used to be afraid of him," he says, "but not anymore. I still see him once or twice a week. We're both film addicts and go to lots of festivals together."

"You see a lot of him, then?" I say with some surprise.

"Oh, yeah. All the time." He clenches his fists. "About a month ago Dad came to the house and threatened to wring my neck." Philip snorts. "I told him go ahead, just try it, have a good time. I can take care of myself." A pause. "We're a pretty angry family if you haven't noticed, Dr. Wallerstein. My brother hits. My sister hits. But I don't."

"How did that happen?"

"I don't know. I guess I just decided to be different."

"How much did your father hit you when you were little?"

Philip thinks for a moment and says, "The only time my dad really spanked me was when I used the *F*-word when I was seven."

Noting the self-censorship for my benefit, I go on to say, "You mean that was the worst but there were other times?"

"Oh yes. He's jerked me around a lot. He always thinks the worst of everything."

Ten years after his parents' divorce, Philip is a young man at a crossroads. In talking with him and watching his behavior, I have absolutely no idea which way he will go in his relationships. Will he repeat his father's behavior toward women or, as he hopes, "be different"? As he presents confusing images of a father who is cruel and loving, of a stepfather who is vicious but likes him best, I sense only that here is a young man struggling with demons, trying to not be like his father, but not certain of his own inner strength.

I am looking forward, therefore, to seeing Philip at the fifteen-year mark and especially to finding out how he's resolved these conflicting pulls. He walks into my office looking hale and happy. At twenty-two, he is still muscular and has grown a full beard. He has just earned an engineering degree in telecommunications and is looking for a job.

"I'm engaged," he says, pleased with his news. "It was love at first sight. She's dynamite. I really want you to meet her."

After congratulating him and catching up on other news, I ask about his mother and father and ask Philip about his relationship with his fiancée and with women before her. "Do you ever find yourself lashing out or hitting?"

"I never hit," he says, as if I have offended him by merely suggesting the possibility. "I never have. I never will. I want to bust heads when I find that someone is beating up on a lady. That's death penalty time. I handle my anger other ways. I would never hit a woman."

"Have you ever hit anyone else?"

"No one except my dad," says Philip. "Because he messed up big, and he still lies about it. I got into a big fight with him four years ago."

"Tell me about it."

Philip begins, "I was at his house for dinner when I said something he didn't like. I don't remember what it was. He asked me to leave the table. I said no. There was a silence. Then he got up and walked over to my chair. I stood up so I wouldn't look up to him, and he slapped me. I can't remember if it was before or after I called him a bastard and a son of a bitch. I hit him and he went down."

"Then what happened?"

"We talked for three hours. Both of us cried, but him more than me."

"And now?"

"Even today I feel really comfortable getting into a fight with him," says Philip. "I almost feel like it again because I didn't get to kick his butt." He pauses. "I believe my mom a thousand percent more than I believe him. But I want you to know, Judy, that I value my relationship with my dad. We've kept together over the years and he means a lot to me."

Philip is an exception in his, as he calls it, "angry family." Unlike his brother and sisters, who are now caught in abusive relationships, he has been able to avoid repeating the violent behavior with which he was raised. Somehow, Philip is able to maintain a close relationship with his father along with an intense anger at him, a duality that helps him reject identification with a wife-beater. This is a gallant achievement, drawn in part from Philip's love for his mother. But it is mainly rooted in the boy's conscious decision to be different, to be moral, and in his ability to control his aggression by continuing to direct it only at his father. By holding on to intense anger, Philip rejects only a part of his father, but it is a critical part.

We still don't know what enables one youngster to escape being caught in an identification with violent behavior when his siblings do not escape, nor can we predict whether these will be temporary or lasting identifications. Philip provides as close a portrait as I've ever seen — truly an extraordinary portrait — of a boy who was at the crossroads and was able, out of his own inner, continuing resolve, to take the proper turn — and win.

PART 3

Heroic Efforts
and
Broken Hearts

8

Betty and Dale Burrelle

GETTING OFF THE PLANE in Albuquerque, I am apprehensive about what lies ahead. I have come to see Betty Burrelle and her three children. The pressures on this family are enormous. Betty is a single mother who is raising her children without adequate financial or emotional support. Impressed by her courage over the years, I have begun to describe her as "the heroine" in our study. My staff teases me about this — "Judy is off to see the heroine next week" — but they also know and appreciate Betty's sacrifices and accomplishments.

Although it was never entirely clear to me what caused the divorce between Betty and Dale Burrelle, she opposed it with all her heart. "It came without warning," she said the first time we met. "I thought we were happily married, but maybe we weren't. Everything sort of fell apart in November, not long after I built a retaining wall in the back of the house. We had a gigantic rain storm that washed out the wall and I guess I got pretty upset. After that, Dale got a big promotion and started coming home later and later every night. I felt completely marooned in that big house with three little kids. I felt like I was going crazy. Once I kicked a hole in the side door to the garage. I'd find myself suddenly crying. Or suddenly screaming. It just got to be too much. But even then, at my worst period, I never thought about divorce. I think what happened is that he thought I didn't love him or want him. Then I took the kids to visit my sister for a week and he decided he really liked living alone, without all the commotion. That was the beginning of the end. Maybe if the retaining wall hadn't let go, maybe things could have held up better."

Betty was thirty-three when she recounted these facts and had been married ten years. An attractive woman with Irish features — curly black hair, freckles, and green eyes — she never once smiled during our first meeting, for she was clearly distraught. Before the separation she had been experiencing a deep depression, the source of which she did not completely understand — although several months before her marriage broke up, her mother's death in an automobile accident had left her extremely distressed. She had been unable to cry and had been sleepless. Her dreams, when she did sleep, had been disturbing, with images of her mother standing at the foot of her bed. Now she was even more restive with foreboding about what lay ahead. Her children, Steve, Tanya, and Kyle, were seven, five, and three.

At the separation, Betty seemed unable to defend her own interests. Although her attorney advised against it, she signed a paper that permitted immediate sale of her house. The divorce settlement provided $1 a year for alimony and $450 a month for child support. There was no provision for increases to accommodate the greater needs of the children as they got older. Dale eventually earned a good income as assistant director of a hospital in New York. Nevertheless, within a few years he returned to court claiming his payments were too high. His obligation was reduced to $360 a month for the three children.

Betty and Dale grew increasingly angry and bitter as their marriage ended. She accused him of infidelity. He hotly denied it. I never was able to find out the truth. Whatever it was, the anger between them mounted to the point that Dale demanded — screaming and fuming — that Betty get a job, any job, a waitress job, to support herself immediately, despite having three small children at home. Betty could not control her anger in front of the children. She was overwhelmed by daily responsibilities and by no longer having another adult to help, even just in the evenings and on weekends. As I gradually learned, Dale had been a good father who liked to read bedtime stories and settle his children down for the night.

I could see that Betty was holding on to a wisp of hope that when her husband saw how much she and the children loved him and needed him, he would come back. If he were to find out how upset they were to lose him, maybe he would return.

The children were in despair and Steve, the oldest, badly needed treatment. None of them could believe what was happening. There was no warning — Daddy was there one day, gone the next.

None of their hopes or prayers changed Dale Burrelle's mind. He pressed for divorce.

Five years later, I flew to Albuquerque, where Betty and her children had moved to make a new start. I was shocked at their living conditions. Their white stucco house, in a working-class neighborhood, was crumbling and cracked, and it had a small, badly cluttered yard. The children were clean but their clothes were worn and patched. The house was clean but shabby. One wall of the living room was covered with books. Creative toys were scattered over the floor and under the piano. The overall impression was one of genteel poverty.

Everything had changed for this family. "First of all let me tell you that I still don't know what happened," said Betty, running her fingers through her curly hair. "The more I've thought about it, the less I understand. I've given up. I know I was upset, but he left so quickly. And he's been so uninvolved with us since. I think he wants to hurt me. He sends so little money to the kids. The strange thing is, I thought we had a good marriage. I thought he thought so, too."

Betty showed me a shoebox with the few letters they had received from Dale since moving to New Mexico. Most were four years old. There had been little contact and few phone calls since.

"How is it that he doesn't get in touch with us at Christmas," asked Betty, "or on their birthdays?"

Betty used her earlier training to get a job as a speech therapist in the local school district. But because of her low seniority and the district's funding problems, she earned only about $600 a month and got no medical benefits. When child support checks came, they were for $250. Dale was $5,000 behind in payments. Betty worked playground duty after school for extra money. She was not making ends meet.

"I worry about the children," she said. "But they help keep me going. They give me the strength to do what I have to do."

I asked if she had dates, a social life.

Betty looked at me and laughed. "I can't manage to run my home now, let alone other things. I dream of getting a job where I could work eight hours a day. I came to Albuquerque because my father and sister are here, and I hoped they could help with some babysitting. But that hasn't worked out. Dad hasn't been well and my sister has her hands full. As for dating or sex, I don't know how to tell you this, except to tell it straight. The divorce left me numb. I lost those feelings."

On my second visit to Albuquerque, at the ten-year mark, Betty is happy to see me. She looks very much the same except that her black hair is flecked with gray. "Despite all my problems with divorce, I have good memories of California," she says. "My biggest problem today is money. I'm working two jobs. I do speech therapy during the day and work as a watchman at night. I have to go out on catwalks without railings, high up in the air." I must look shocked because Betty says quickly, "Yeah, I know it sounds dangerous, but I like it. I like high places. The job goes fast. There aren't any breaks."

Betty's schedule is daunting. She works from eleven at night to seven in the morning as a nightwatch, goes home for one hour to shower and get ready to report to school at eight o'clock. She works with students and does paperwork until school is over at three in the afternoon. She goes to bed at four o'clock and gets up at ten o'clock at night.

"How much sleep are you getting?" There is disbelief in my voice.

"I do well on six hours," she says jauntily. "Any more and I'm groggy."

"But when do you see the kids?"

She laughs. "That's my whole weekend."

Betty has no medical insurance and no savings. Two years ago she had to pay $1,200 to rule out a diagnosis of cervical cancer. "I've come close to a breakdown," she says. "But you know, I've landed on my feet. I've taken some summer courses in computer programming that would make me more money. I also took courses in graphic arts, plumbing for dummies, and a graduate course in speech pathology. It turns out that I don't have enough training to get into the computer business, at least not yet. and I'd have to go back to school for a Ph.D. to get a teaching job at the university in speech pathology. I guess you could say I'm open to new ideas and will try just about anything."

What an extraordinary woman this is. She takes me outside to show off the new addition to the house and the carport that she designed and built with her own hands. Inside she has polished all the woodwork and built new bookshelves. The house looks good.

"How is your social life, Betty?"

Her answer is crisp, no-nonsense. "I have no social life. I don't go out. I dated a physicist for three months but it got to be too much trouble. I can't handle it. I don't like to get dressed up and go out. I have my children, I have my work, I love working with my hands. A friend gave me her old kiln and I'm going to set it up in back of the house next weekend. And I belong to a hiking club where we go on long weekend trips into the Santo Cristos."

About her former husband she says, "We have no contact. There's absolutely nothing to talk about. He's been sending the $360 he owes us every month for the last couple of years, so that's a blessing, I suppose. But the kids are big now." She looks at me knowingly. "You can count all the phone calls he made on one hand. He's seen the kids three times. I don't know how much money he's making, but Steve says it's between fifty and sixty thousand dollars a year."

Betty now attributes her emotional upset ten years ago to her feeling trapped. "I don't know what happened to me," she says. "I was just sad for a whole year. But do you know what Dale gave me for our tenth wedding anniversary?" She pauses for effect. "Divorce papers. I really took it hard. Now, in retrospect, I'd have to say cruel is the word for what he did. It was the most painful event in my life. But I don't feel responsible anymore for what happened. The hardest part was setting up a new home for the kids. I was very sad that they would lose the benefit of having two parents, but there is no way I can marry again. I know that two parents set a better example for children, of a working model of relationships. I worry that my kids won't have that model. But maybe they'll learn something positive from me. Who knows?"

Betty Burrelle presents us with a paradox in terms of winners and losers after divorce. There is no question that her life has become incredibly more difficult as she works two jobs and raises her children from dawn to dawn. Indeed, she feels so depleted by her circumstances that she has no inclinations even to think about a sexual relationship. "Those feelings are gone," she says, as she struggles to raise three children with very little help from others. Although she has a college degree, it is in a field that does not command enough money to support her family, nor does it allow her a job with medical and other insurance that she needs. Despite her education, full employment, and heroic efforts, Betty's quality of life has deteriorated in the postdivorce decade, although the last few years have been a little easier.

At the same time, the very hardship that she experiences catalyzes in Betty a psychological response that is gallant and successful. Relying on her own resources and strengthening her own capacities, Betty emerges with an increased sense of pride and higher self-esteem. She is no martyr. She rises to the challenges before her, showing enormous psychological growth and change during her adult years. Betty is perhaps the new frontier woman of modern America, winning some and losing some, as she keeps herself and her children above the poverty line — but with incalculable cost to her own happiness.

While I am still not sure what made Betty's marriage fail, her mother's sudden death in an automobile accident was undoubtedly a contributing factor.

A family tragedy has the potential for bringing people together, to hold hands, to lean on one another, and to cement relationships; but tragedy is just as likely to drive people apart. In our study, several divorces followed the untimely death of an important parent. When people cannot acknowledge the loss — and, like Betty, cannot cry, mourn, or react appropriately — they often become very angry at their spouse. In addition, many feelings — anger, abandonment, guilt as a survivor, and anguish over not having done something theoretically useful to prevent the death — ricochet into the marital relationship. The bereaved person erupts with unexpected tantrums, demands, and criticism that the spouse finds incomprehensible. If the spouse does not make a connection between the parent's death and the erratic behavior — and many do not — the marriage can fall apart amid seemingly irrational accusations and counteraccusations.

This phenomenon is also present in families experiencing an acute crisis, such as the diagnosis of a fatal disease in a child. Adults may turn on each other as if to say, "You failed to protect me from this horrible thing." Many marriages fall apart at these critical times when, ironically, people most need one another.

Oddly enough, the planned birth of a baby can also trigger difficulties that lead to divorce. In one common scenario, the husband feels hurt and excluded as his wife turns most of her attention to the newborn. Envious of the close mother-infant bond, he feels that he is asked to participate only in the less rewarding aspects of infant care. On top of that, his sex life deteriorates because his wife is tired and says that intercourse is uncomfortable for the time being. As the

father's disappointment and anger mount, he turns elsewhere —
usually not seriously — for sexual intimacy. But he finds a response
beyond his expectations when his wife discovers his affair, as many
women in this situation do. Her hurt and outrage are boundless, and
the marriage heads on a downward course that is very, very difficult
to reverse past a certain stage. The point of no return undoubtedly
varies among people, but I do know that this scenario can occur even
following a wanted and long-awaited pregnancy and birth.

Common sense and clinical wisdom tell us that people should get
over being angry at one another, but our study shows that we may
be wrong. Betty Burrelle has stayed angry at Dale throughout the
postdivorce decade. In the years after divorce, anger can last, anger
can intensify, anger can be refueled. Anger can also be walled off so
it cannot spill into the present. And anger can be diminished and it
can be resolved.

Half of the women and one-third of the men are still intensely angry at their former partner ten years later. In comparing these figures
with the amount of anger at the time of the divorce, I am surprised
to find how little the anger has changed. After all, one of the purposes of divorce is to clear the air. We assume that once people are
allowed to live apart, they will get past their conflict. But many do
not.

Anger falls into two general categories, old and new. Old anger
may take the form of memories — memories of humiliation and hurt
at the time of the separation, of angry and violent scenes. Such memories last and last, sometimes recurring as unbidden flashbacks. In
talking with many people ten years after divorce, I sometimes get the
feeling that I am wandering into the same play, where the same characters are using the same lines to tell the same story with the same
intensity of feeling to the same audience. They do not seem to remember telling me — the audience — the same stories many times
before. They do not seem to care about audience reaction. One particular scene sticks in my mind. Ten years after their divorce, a man
approaches his former wife, who is getting into her car, intending to
thank her for the excellent job she has done in raising their only child.
Not giving him a chance to speak, she glares at him, rolls up the
window, and drives off. This behavior would not be odd if they were
just going through the divorce, but this incident takes place ten years
later.

New or refueled anger often stems from ways in which people continue to influence one another in the postdivorce family, particularly over issues of child support. When an ex-husband is living the good life while his ex-wife and children are struggling for survival, anger burns steadily. When fathers fail to pay child support, anger flares. When a man feels that his ex-wife is using his child support money for her own selfish or frivolous purposes, he feels resentment. New babies, new spouses, new jobs, and other changed circumstances can provoke anger among former spouses.

Child support is a continuing sore spot in most coparenting relationships, as mothers often feel — and the data substantiate — that child support is inadequate, and fathers often feel that they are contributing more than their fair share. In general, men earning $30,000 a year are ordered to pay about 10 percent of their gross income for child support. Of the millions of women who are entitled to child support, fewer than half receive payments as ordered, about one-third are paid a fraction of what they have been promised, and one-fourth of the women get nothing.[1] Wealthier men do not have a better record of child support. Several men in our study unilaterally cut child support when their ex-wives began to earn good salaries or married well-to-do second husbands. Others reduced child support when they themselves remarried, especially if they acquired stepchildren or had more children with the second wife. Not one father in our study voluntarily raised child support because his ex-wife was physically or psychologically not well.

Compared with younger women, those who are in their mid to late thirties at divorce do not have the sense of second chances opening before them. Because they usually have been married longer and may have preadolescent children, it is generally much harder for them to detach from the marriage and restart their lives. Many are immobilized for the first few years after divorce, held back by anger, depression, and helplessness. These women know their job skills are rusty and are frightened about reentering the work world. Some, like Betty Burrelle, reenter immediately but find little reward for their heroic efforts and much that is both backbreaking and heartbreaking.

For many women, the second purpose of divorce — to build a new life — is therefore delayed several years, sometimes indefinitely, while they cope with a variety of overwhelming external and internal issues. Women trained as schoolteachers, as social workers, or in other so-called women's work find that they cannot earn enough money and thus must rethink earlier career decisions. A whole group in our study entered business or professional careers in which the higher monetary rewards could support the whole family. But in today's economy, most families need two incomes.

These women enter a world in which there is a high potential for failure, if not disaster. Should Betty Burrelle lose one of her jobs, she would not be able to feed and shelter her children. With welfare her only safety net and homelessness a step away, she walks a psychological tightrope as well as a catwalk at work. Many women find that they can get only low-paying jobs, so that divorce has the effect of reinforcing their sense of low self-esteem, depression, and discouragement. The consequences for the women and their children can be as serious and enduring as the divorce itself.

Although some of the women had jobs before marriage, they say that working as the sole provider for a family is a different experience. The stakes are higher, the game is survival. The psychological sense of responsibility for a family forges a different identity for women, one rich with both excitement and anxiety. This role as working woman is not equivalent to that of the working wife in a dual-career couple. For divorced women there is no backup, no help in the wings. It is the very life-and-death reality of this new woman's role that galvanizes change. Several women, asked to give advice to others, said, "For God's sake, be sure you have medical and dental benefits for the kids."

Divorced women work extremely hard and under incredible stress, as Betty Burrelle attests, especially in keeping up with the physical and emotional demands of raising small children. And when their children reach adolescence, single mothers encounter a barrage of powerful emotional demands on top of their other responsibilities. Those who succeed master a whole new way of life, achieving a higher level of self-confidence than they had in the marriage.

Despite their greater self-esteem, most have a chronic, gnawing sense that they are not available enough for their children. Worried about food and shelter, their resentment mounts. Even many with good educations find themselves in jobs with no security, benefits, advancement ladder, or perks.

Some of the women in our study who divorced while in their late thirties have developed interesting careers ten years later, but few have combined those careers with a happy second marriage or a stable relationship. Most got one and not the other. "A lot of men don't want to be serious," one woman says with a candor that was never part of her earlier personality, "and I don't want to break up somebody else's marriage." Concerned that her success makes men anxious, she notes, "Some get scared off." But she closes our interview with a grin, saying, "If I had a choice of being successful or having a relationship, I'd take the success and worry about the relationship later."

Women in this age group frequently complain that eligible men are hard to find. Betty Burrelle ultimately decides that her social, sexual self will not be satisfied and she gives up trying, accepting as permanent a grievous loss in the quality of her life. This sense of "being dead inside" is a rarely acknowledged, but very serious, consequence of divorce. I've seen it mostly in women who truly feel that they have lost forever interest in sex along with the capacity to reach out in a loving way to a man.

On the other hand, women who divorce in their thirties tend to seek out new groups and activities, determined to reach out to others for support. They join cooking classes, aerobic classes, drama clubs, tennis clubs, and women's groups; they take courses at the local college in antiques, art history, jewelry making, theology, and ceramics. They go out of their way to reestablish connections with extended family members and old friends and to pursue new friendships. By avoiding social isolation, many achieve psychological growth. This does not guarantee happiness, but it helps ease the pain.

Dale Burrelle is an impressive man to behold. Standing six feet four inches tall, with broad shoulders and longish blond hair, he looks more like a Viking than a hospital administrator. He was thirty-three when he and Betty separated in 1972 and seemed anxious to get our initial interview out of the way. "Betty was upset for no reason," he said, looking at his watch. "I guess I just got sick and tired of her constant nagging and complaining. It's been going on for eight endless months."

"Has anything happened within the last year?"

He shrugged and said, "I don't enjoy being berated and accused of things. I think it'll be better for all of us when I'm out of the picture."

Dale warmed up a bit when we talked about his career, his busy travel schedule, and his children. I remember his saying over and over how much he enjoyed playing with them, reading them bedtime stories, and horsing around in the living room after dinner. At one point, when we talked about Betty, he said defiantly, "If she can't manage the kids, then I'll take them to live with me." More gently, he added, "She's a pretty good mom, and I wouldn't want to deprive her."

As I tried to get Dale to talk about his plans for the future, he blocked me again and again with the phrase "Everything will work out fine." As we parted he said, "I'm a happy-go-lucky guy. The future will take care of itself. You see, I was sort of raised not to look at the negative."

One year later, Dale seemed unchanged. "I've been seeing the kids a lot," he said, leaning his huge frame into an easy chair, "but it's catch as catch can because I've been traveling so much. Looks like I'm going to get transferred to New York, which is a real opportunity for me." Dale was enthusiastic about the prospect.

"That's a long way from the kids," I said.

"Yeah, well, Betty is talking about moving to New Mexico to be near her sister and her old man." He folded his hands behind his head and said, without convincing me, "I'm really sorry."

"It might be hard to have the kids that far away."

"I might split my vacations," Dale replied, offering a potential solution to the problem. "I could take a bunch of four-day weekends and see them more often."

It was hard for me to gauge if this was Dale's plan or simply a wish. According to Betty, he was not visiting the children much at all. Her oldest boy, Steve, was extremely upset and had said he wanted to go to live with his daddy in New York. I understood Betty to say that she was willing to let Steve go, but Dale didn't seem to encourage the idea.

"I'll miss being able to drop in," Dale was saying. Once again I tried unsuccessfully to get him to spell out how he planned to stay in contact with his three young children. Again, he evaded a direct answer and said, "I'll miss them, but what's to do?"

It seemed to me that Dale did not recognize the importance of this pending separation from his children, even though the children told me often how much they loved him and wanted to be near him. In fact, the children seemed to have realistically evaluated the situation:

Dale was either denying the impact of the separation or was feeling its effects much less than his children did.

"As you know," I said, "the school is very worried about Steve. His teacher called me last week and says he seems depressed to the point where he can't learn."

Dale nodded. "I talked to her last week, too. I felt better because she said it probably wasn't my fault and that Steve maybe has a pre-disposition for learning difficulties that the divorce just brought out. I'm of a mind to let matters take their course."

I could not see Dale in person for a five-year follow-up but I did speak to him on the telephone. He was receptive and seemed open to talking about his children. "I saw them last summer," he said, "and they're looking good. They weren't depressed or anything, but it was hard on them when I left. I just told them my philosophy, that pain and hurt are our own standards."

I asked about Steve, who was still having trouble with his school-work, but found to my astonishment that Dale had a hard time talk-ing about his children individually. Instead, he referred to the "older, middle, and younger" child, as if they were subunits in a single en-tity. "I enjoy them vicariously," he said at one point. "Betty is doing a great job bringing them up."

Dale was remarried and his wife was expecting a baby. "Things maybe could have been different between me and Betty, but that's the way the cards tumbled," he said. "I'm adapting."

Once again Dale was courteous, but it was hard for me to know what he was feeling. Clearly, the relationship with his children had become distant and disjointed and he was no longer a parent in their lives. But I was not sure that he realized it.

I decide that it is important to meet face to face with Dale for our ten-year interview and so I fly to New York and see him at his office. Large photographs of Steve, Tanya, and Kyle hang on the wall beside his desk. At age forty-three, he is assistant director of a hospital.

After telling me about the details of his job, Dale reveals that his second marriage is on the brink. "I was surprised when Inara asked for a divorce," he says with a genuinely perplexed look. "I couldn't see that anything was out of line. We went to a marriage counselor and that was okay, but nothing got any better. I felt that I had to make more money and that I'd never be happy unless I got richer and richer. I guess that's been my thinking in both marriages. I've always been a hundred percent devoted to my work and believed that if I was a good provider, everything would work out." Dale looks away for a moment as he says, "I guess there's more to a relationship than cash." He looks back at me and adds, "I think it probably was a bad relationship from the start."

"Which one?"

"Both my marriages," he says with a half-smile. "I think I made the same mistake twice."

"In what way, Dale?"

"I wasn't what they wanted. The truth is, Judy, I was less unhappy than both my wives in both marriages."

I ask about his youngest son, Noah, in New York and about the three children in New Mexico.

"Noah is four," says Dale. "He's okay — he'll have a broader perspective on life." (It occurs to me that this is a strange way to talk about a four-year-old.) "You know," Dale continues, "I stayed in this marriage longer than I might have because of my previous divorce. I really wanted this one to work. Steve came and lived with us last year — it was his idea to come — which was fine with me, but it was also his idea to go back. I think things haven't worked out for him. But he was a great asset to us, as a built-in babysitter."

I ask again about the other children.

"I saw Tanya and Kyle three times in the past two years," he says. "Whenever I'm traveling near the Southwest, I stop by for a visit. In 1979 to 1980 I saw them all four or five times."

"Did that amount of contact feel good to the kids?"

"I think they felt pretty good," he says blandly. "I don't think they'd want a lot more. They're more interested in their friends at this age."

Once again I have the feeling that it is hard for Dale to talk about his children separately or about his separate relationships with them.

"I have a theory about fathers and kids," he says. "Me, I have four kids and each represents a fantasy of mine. Steve is doing the same thing I did after high school. He's working in a bowling alley while he figures out his next move. Tanya is into art. Kyle is into music. Noah will get all the love in the world." Then he startles me, saying, "I don't influence those guys at all other than being who I am on a day-to-day basis."

There is now no question in my mind that Dale feels he has been very available to his children through the years. Several times he says, "If they need anything, they can get it." Later he says, "And if Betty needs anything, I'll help. She still has some animosity about the divorce, but it's not as bad as it was. We spent a weekend together before I got married again, went out for dinner and dancing. She said I had grown and was amazed at how much. I don't know what made the difference but it was nice of her to say so. I don't have any regret, Judy, I've never had regrets." Dale is reflective as he says, "My mom and dad gave me a good foundation for life. They've never been critical of anything I've done. Mom always says, 'Be sweet and don't hurt anyone unnecessarily.' That's been my motto."

Dale has absolutely no conflicts about his relationship with his children. From his perspective, all is well. From theirs, the past ten years have been a disaster. Dale keeps huge photographs of his children on his office wall, reinforcing my sense that this man and his children have phantom relationships from both sides. Dale's relationships with his children are in large measure his own inventions, bearing little resemblance to what really goes on between them. Similarly, the children attribute things to Dale that have little to do with reality. This father and each of his children are projecting their own needs on one another, each believing what he or she wishes to believe. While the relationships are not real, the feelings are powerfully real.

At our fifteen-year interview, Dale is again unchanged. He is married for a third time, has lots of friends, and sails a small sloop in Manhasset Bay every weekend. "One of the best things that's ever happened to me was meeting Wendy," he says. "I'm real happy."

"Have you talked to Betty lately?"

"Sure have," he says merrily, "and she's still trying to ice me over a couple of things. She wanted some money so Steve could take a special course. So I called Steve and he said for me not to worry, that he was saving money and could probably get it together. So I decided it would probably be better to let him handle it."

"How is Steve doing?" I ask, knowing full well the troubled life that the boy has been leading.

"I'd like to see him succeed," says Dale. "I'm not worried about him. Once he gets more experience, he'll do fine. Tanya's okay and Kyle is going to college. It's like I told you, they're going to be fine. Except that I get the feeling Betty still wants to control me."

"How?"

"It's her tone of voice. She freaks out and overreacts when anything happens to the kids."

Many adults, like Dale Burrelle, have trouble achieving a major dimension of adulthood that psychoanalyst Erik Erikson calls generativity. Generativity means taking an interest in guiding the next generation, a concern that can be funneled through one's children or through other forms of creativity and altruism. Erikson argues that generativity is the opposite of stagnation and that unless an adult achieves this stage, he or she becomes emotionally stuck in place, with a sense of impoverishment.

Removed from regular contact with their children after divorce, many men stagnate in just this way. They seem unable to maintain their perspective as fathers or to hold in view the needs of their children. Young fathers in particular seem to have their development blocked, and a whole part of their lives may remain forever unfulfilled. Some men, like Dale Burrelle, turn their backs on the loss and ignore it, saying, "I can't be responsible for anybody, just me." Women may also turn their backs on children, invoking the same argument, saying, "I've got to take care of me. I'm no good to anybody unless I get my life together." But this attitude toward one's life and one's children, when it lasts, more often than not has the opposite effect. Instead of growing, these adults stagnate. Instead of gaining a foothold in life, they forfeit a tremendously valuable aspect of adulthood.

There is no evidence that Dale is aware of how much he has disappointed his children. If he understood, he might have done things differently so as not to hurt them, for he was a good, caring father before the divorce. What his children see as painfully intolerable rejection represents his way of defending himself, of shutting out potentially disturbing stimuli, of maintaining his own equilibrium. He says, "Things will work out. I have no regrets. Everything is fine." Divorce is much more difficult for his family than it is for him. In our catalog of winners and losers, therefore, Dale is neither. He is almost unchanged ten and fifteen years after divorce, not only in the quality of his life but in the kind of person he is. While Dale claims to be attached to his children, keeping their portraits on his wall, to them he is a phantom father.

Dale Burrelle does not understand how other people feel. His wife becomes depressed after her mother dies, and he thinks she is intemperate. His boy gets into an emotional crisis, and he says time will solve it. He can function as husband and father only within the confined structure of an intact marriage, where people meet him more than halfway. Lacking day-to-day contact and family structure to bolster his role, he feels far removed from his children. So increasingly abstract have they become that, he says, "Each represents a fantasy of mine." The kinds of relationships of which he is capable cannot and do not endure in the divorced family, where people have to take initiative, set up plans, judge things realistically, and empathize. The tragedy of the Burrelle family is that Dale wants to be a father, tries to be a father, but cannot do it outside the marriage. This is a common pattern in our society. Some men cannot find within themselves the resources to span geographical and emotional distances to recognize the needs of their children and to keep up with them. For these fathers, out of sight is often out of mind, reflecting a passivity that defines their relationships in the years after divorce.

9

Steve Burrelle

LONGING AND LOSS

LIKE MOST TEENAGERS, Steve Burrelle is possessed of a "bottomless pit." Today he has arranged a long lunch break from work, and he takes me to a small café where we can talk undisturbed for several hours, after he wolfs down four huge tacos. Tall and thin, with a genuinely friendly and appealing manner, Steve has an aura of gentleness that I find moving. Underneath the readiness to smile, however, I sense an underlying sadness that every so often rises to the surface, interrupting his thoughts and our conversations. At several points he asks me whether I have seen any sad movies. Have I read any sad books? It soon becomes clear that this bright young man is suffering from the intrusion of bleak thoughts and memories.

Steve has no plans. He is living at home and works at a bowling alley in town where he accurately feels he is marking time. In more bitter moods, he says he is wasting time. Having graduated from high school almost two years ago, Steve feels his interests in poetry, fiction writing, and music are also at a standstill. He tells me shamefacedly, "I only made a C average, Dr. Wallerstein. And it isn't that I didn't work. I liked school a lot, and I worked hard. But I had trouble in class keeping my mind on the work, even though I liked it and I wanted to." Steve takes a swig of his Pepsi. "Mostly I haven't been able to figure out what I can do. As you know, it's been real rough for my mom. I worry about her a lot. Before I was eighteen, Dad sent her $360 a month. That's $120 for each of us. After my birthday, he stopped sending money for me. But that's when I really could have used it. For going to school."

"You've been discouraged."

He nods.

"For a long time?"

"Yes, for a very long time. The only happy time in my life that I remember, and I think about it a lot, was when I was six and a half . . ."

Steve vividly remembers life before the divorce, when his family lived in a large house with a big back yard. His father came home every night and always read the children a bedtime story; if Dale was late coming home, they were allowed to wait up.

The divorce was a shock to Steve. He remembers, as I do, our first meeting, when he could not believe that his father had moved out and would not accept the idea that everything had changed. When Steve came into the playroom at our center, he was a very attractive little boy, with dark hair in a bowl cut, who played and talked happily about the zoo. Placing the mother doll and father doll in bed together, he said, "The mommy and daddy have to sleep together." When I asked him to draw a picture, he said, "I'm an artist. I can make different things." Indeed, his drawings were advanced for his age, for he had mastered perspective by making train tracks that met in the distance. He was a happy child who had no way of understanding the storm that was engulfing his parents, himself, and his brother and sister.

A year later the reality of divorce had sunk in, and Steve was a different little boy. Although he then saw his father once a week, he cried himself to sleep each night, such was the pain of his loss. His mother was agitated and disorganized, life was uprooted, and the family house was for sale. His teacher — who had earlier raved about his "adjustment" to the divorce — sent a distress signal to the parents advising immediate psychological help for Steve. The teacher's report was unusually clear, reflecting the alarming change in this child. The school record described Steve as having "difficulty in learning, frequently forgetting and relating poorly to peers."

The teacher said Steve's ability to learn had been seriously disrupted by the divorce; his ability to read would come and go as he struggled to distinguish fantasy from reality. This pattern was surely ominous if it could not be interrupted.

Steve's early response to the divorce, while severe, was not surprising. Because the marriage had seemed happy, with no history of fighting or discord, Betty was genuinely disbelieving when Dale filed divorce papers, and the children could not imagine what was wrong. Steve was reacting to the breakup of his family and to the inescapable fact that the world can suddenly become an unreliable, unpredictable, frightening place. After Dale moved to New York, he rarely visited, sometimes missed Christmas, and often forgot birthdays. What with four or five long-distance telephone calls each year, Steve's contact with his father was neither totally ended nor maintained.

Steve eventually did well in elementary school but was a loner. As the oldest child, he helped his mother all he could and worried about her constantly. As we sit in the café, he says, "I get along with her. There are no barriers between us, but if I could change anything in the world I would try to make things happy for her again. She was happier when she was married."

When Steve was sixteen he took the initiative of calling his dad in New York to ask if he could come and stay a year. The answer was yes. Steve left with high hopes of reestablishing the relationship that he craved. But, as he tells it, the year was a disaster. Dale and his second wife were in the midst of their own marital breakup, and each grabbed on to Steve as audience and adviser. "I was caught in the middle," he says. "They talked about divorce all the time. I could feel the hate between them and pressure building that had to be released. They each asked me how I had felt about divorce. I have a little half-brother, Dr. Wallerstein. He was about the same age that I was when my folks got divorced. My stepmother kept asking me" — Steve's voice rises to a nasal falsetto — "'What was it like for you, Steve?'" — and then resumed an even tone — "so she could know what it would be like for Noah."

"I guess they didn't realize the sad memories that they were bringing up for you," I say, aware of my own impulse to reach out and touch his arm. "How terribly difficult it must have been for you."

"They didn't understand anything," Steve says. "It's like I wasn't a person. It was like I didn't have feelings."

As Steve talks more about his father, he fights to control his emotions. With moist eyes, he says, "What I've realized is that my dad is selfish. It's like he's in quicksand. The more he struggles to have fun, the more selfish he becomes. Like, he doesn't realize that I came to

spend the year with him. He was away so much of the time. I try to
understand him, but, you see, he has a problem. He can't keep a
relationship for very long. I've never said this to him because I don't
want to hurt his feelings. He just gets tired of people who don't conform to what he wants them to be. But he doesn't understand that
you can really hurt other people. To divorce is to leave them
stranded."

Steve looks at me and says, "You know, this is the first time I've
thought about this." His hands are trembling. "My dad loves life. But
he has no heart for others."

I ask Steve how he might use his understanding to guide his own
future. Can he begin to move ahead on his own?

He shakes his head. "I don't know. I can't help hoping I'll get something from him. I can't help thinking that he's my dad and that I can
count on him."

"Steve, with all that you've told me, you still love your father and
miss him very much."

He looks up and nods a yes. He cannot speak.

An hour later, I leave Steve with a heavy heart. This is a deeply
depressed young man. His ability to move forward, to develop his
many talents, to choose a direction befitting his high intelligence, is
blocked by his powerful, continuing psychological tie to his father —
he cannot let go. Indeed, he is so overwhelmed by feelings of rejection that he simply cannot accept them or deal with the present realistically.

I am deeply impressed by Steve's sensitivity, gentleness, and judgment, but he is unable to make use of his insights to free himself from
a lifelong yearning to rewrite the history of his relationship with his
father. His keen, even eloquent observations are not enough to save
him. Here is a promising, intelligent youth — with high integrity, a
real vision of what relationships should be, a capacity for love and
compassion — who is going nowhere. What a pity for the boy. What
a waste for society. I can only hope that his brother and sister, whom
I will see later in the afternoon, are leading less troubled lives.

Over a third of the young men and women between the ages of nineteen and twenty-nine have little or no ambition ten years after their
parents' divorce. They are drifting through life with no set goals, limited educations, and a sense of helplessness. Some stay home well

into their twenties; others leave and wander without purpose. Many feel discouraged and rejected and, like Steve, cannot close the door to the past, cannot give up the fantasy that history can be changed.

Although only a few dropped out of high school, most have not seriously pursued higher education. They tend to drop out after one or two years of college to take up unskilled jobs — as messenger, delivery truck driver, waitress, physical fitness instructor, video store clerk. They don't make long-term plans and are aiming below the intellectual and educational achievements of their fathers and mothers. This discrepancy between life goals and talents is defined as underachievement.

Like most teenagers, they have experimented with drugs and alcohol but are not dangerous or violent. Rather, they are inhibited and unable to plan beyond the immediate present. Many have distant plans but no practical sense of how to put those plans into action. Of course, plenty of children from intact families show similar patterns; no adolescent is immune to feelings of rejection and low self-esteem. Our sample of divorced families, however, shows an exceptionally high number of these children.

Low self-esteem in late adolescence is often related to unresolved psychological issues between divorced fathers and their children, in which the major strand is that the young people feel rejected, unloved, and undervalued. Children long for their fathers in the years after divorce, and those who are close to their fathers beforehand are especially preoccupied with the notion of restoring the closeness that they remember or fantasize. One of the saddest realities of the divorced family is the difficulty (although not the impossibility) of continuing earlier relationships. And one of our major discoveries ten years after divorce is that this longing is infused with new intensity at adolescence. For girls, the intensity rises during early adolescence. For boys, the need for the father crests somewhat later — at age sixteen, seventeen, or eighteen. Some young people physically search for their fathers, while others psychologically search for some explanation of why their fathers let them down. In so doing, they often interpret their fathers' neutral indifference, passivity, or insensitivity as outright rejection. Just as they are forming a separate identity in adolescence, just when they most need support and approval their self-esteem is injured by someone they love. With wings clipped, it is no wonder they cannot fly.

Although important differences exist between boys and girls in this relationship, their thinking follows an identical line: "My father is not closer to me because I am not good enough. If I were a better person, he would pay more attention to me." Boys and girls turn on themselves as being unworthy of love and support, incapable of achievement. In their own eyes they become identified with the unloved and unlovable child — the child whom they think their fathers recognize and avoid.

One of the great tragedies of divorce is that many fathers have absolutely no idea that their children feel rejected. Although the fathers seem indifferent or uncaring, this may not be the case at all. I have talked with many fathers who genuinely think that they have good relationships with their children, while the children feel rejected and miserable. I am convinced that Dale Burrelle never intended to hurt his son Steve. He thought he was doing his best, and he would be very surprised to hear about Steve's pain and yearning. It is surely a love story of modern times.

Unfortunately, all too many fathers do fail their children, especially those who never manage to put their lives back together after divorce. As one adolescent boy describes it, "My father does what he can." Others lose interest in their children immediately after the divorce or gradually over the years. Then the rejection is real.

Interestingly, many of the young men in our study have devoted mothers — competent, dynamic women — but the mother-son relationship in divorced families is often insufficient to compensate for the lack of a father in their lives. While the boys often identify with their mothers' sense of morality, integrity, and work ethic, mothers have difficulty providing that essential male acknowledgment that allows boys to move forward in an organized way, to shape their own lives as young adults. Without the continued support of their fathers, these boys lack self-confidence and pride in their own masculinity. The issue, although different, is just as serious for girls. Afflicted with a sense of longing and rejection, they too feel hurt, unsure of their femininity, and insecure in their relationships with men.

The situation may be especially painful when the father appears, say, once a year, suggesting that the rejection is not absolute. With one foot in the door and one foot out, the father by his occasional visits constantly reawakens hope and reopens the fantasy door. This is a relationship that breaks children's hearts.

Many young people, especially boys, cannot express the anger they feel toward the parent who is rejecting them. Clinging instead to fantasies that the world will change, they fail to turn their backs on the hurtful relationships. They do not rebel.

Adolescent rebellion is one of the terrors of life for parents, but it is a stage that serves an important psychological purpose for children. The rebellion permits them to loosen ties with parents and to move outward, to begin to use aggression constructively on their own behalf. But adolescence is psychologically and socially a different experience in the divorced family. While most teenagers are rebelling against their parents, the children of divorce may hold back. As Steve knows so well, it is hard to fight with a parent the child sees episodically or to defy a parent when the child worries whether he will visit or send child support money on time or to stand up to a custodial parent who is clearly worn to a frazzle.

The secure haven needed in adolescence is not available for many children of divorce. The healthy aggression that adolescents will need to enter a competitive world, to aim high in life, is inhibited because it is tied to the incomplete resolution of love and hate toward the rejecting parent. This inhibition of anger and healthy aggression is one of the serious long-term effects of divorce. Some young people overcome it. Many cannot.

The Delinquent

Kevin was twelve when his parents brought their stormy marriage to an end. For as long as the boy could remember, his mother and father yelled, screamed, and hit one another amid mutual accusations, probably justified, of infidelity.

Kevin's mother, a local television producer, and his father, a prominent attorney, were well-educated, well-connected people who stayed married, as they told me, "for Kevin's sake." One day, however, as part of a fight, the father filed for divorce and then became committed irrevocably to that course.

Seemingly unfazed by his parents' fights, Kevin worshiped his father and spoke of his big hands, resonant voice, and knowledge of everything, from deep-sea diving to racing cars. When his father moved out, Kevin was incredulous. Virtually overnight, he was transformed from model, insightful, intelligent student to problem student. A year after the divorce, Kevin's teacher said he was "the most irresponsible child I've ever seen, restless to the point of hyperactivity." Refusing to complete or hand in school assignments, Kevin spent his time beating up other children. He became the bully who antagonized everyone in the school with his compulsive punching, lying, and destructive behavior.

Unlike many children of divorce, however, Kevin's symptoms, which developed in the acute stage of divorce, did not subside after a year or two. He got worse. His mother threw herself into work and was rarely home; she had persuaded her mother to come live with her and Kevin, to "keep an eye on things." Although Kevin's father never remarried, preferring to play the field, he rarely visited his son but instead made promises — to take him to Disneyland, buy him a bicycle, let him come live with him next summer — but these were promises he never kept. Nor did he ever apologize for breaking his promises.

Despite this treatment, Kevin remained loyal to his father, inventing conversations between them to ease his pain. "My dad told me to get my booster shot in my left arm so that it doesn't hurt my pitching arm," he told me a year after the divorce. When I asked the father about this a few days later, he was puzzled; he had never said any such thing.

Kevin defended his father bravely, except for one moment when his feelings of having been betrayed slipped out. Tears rolled down his cheeks as he said, "A week before he left home, Dad kept telling me to be good, be good, be good, but all that time he was planning to leave." At age thirteen, Kevin felt a mounting sense that the man he worshiped had betrayed him and lied to him.

Nothing improved in high school. At the five-year follow-up, I learned that Kevin regularly drank and smoked pot, had been caught breaking and entering, and had even forged one of his grandmother's checks. He refused to go to school, ignored chores, and never flushed the toilet. His mother said she was afraid that Kevin, now a strapping seventeen-year-old, would attack her and that she always kept telling him, "Don't treat women the way your dad treats women."

Kevin had all the body language and vocabulary of a young delinquent. Amid the swagger and anger, however, he allowed one glimpse into his internal world when he said, "I wish I didn't have to keep real feelings inside."

At the ten-year follow-up, I cannot locate Kevin. Along with a group of other young people in our study, he is in trouble with the law and his parents do not have his phone number or address. Kevin has been in jail three times — for drunk driving, dealing dope, and beating up his girlfriend. The only time he calls his father is to ask for help getting out of trouble. In a way, it is a continuing relationship, but surely not what Kevin hoped for as a little boy.

Unlike Steve, who turns his anger inward, Kevin turns his anger outward — smack against the world that let him down. One of the hallmarks of depression is anger turned inward; delinquents turn their anger outward.

In our study, one out of three of the young men and one in ten of the young women between ages nineteen and twenty-three at the ten-year mark are delinquent, meaning they act out their anger in a range of illegal activities including assault, burglary, arson, drug dealing, theft, drunk driving, and prostitution. Many of these children got involved in one episode of breaking the law before age eighteen, but a disturbing number of them continue this delinquency pattern into their early twenties.

Unlike many juvenile delinquents, who tend to be brutalized by poverty and crime in childhood, these young delinquents are saddened. Made wretched by the experience of divorce, most feel rejected and abandoned by both parents. After the family structure collapses in adolescence, they do not recover. These young people are not generally engaged in crimes of violence. They steal cash to buy drugs or alcohol but do not use knives, guns, or other weapons. The only incidents resulting in serious injury are related to driving while intoxicated. When their driver's licenses are suspended, they continue to drive. Their gangs are ad hoc gangs organized around particular missions. In fact, most of these adolescents are incompetent criminals — they move around frequently but do not cover their tracks; they usually get caught.

At our fifteen-year follow-up, Kevin and the boys like him are still nowhere to be found. Although they are repeatedly in touch with their families, they don't have addresses and are reluctant to answer our requests for interviews.

People often ask whether children of divorce become delinquent. In our work with primarily middle-class families, serious delinquency has not loomed as a major long-term consequence of divorce, although it does show up in a significant number of young men in a highly self-destructive way.

The kind of misbehavior that we see — abuse of drugs and alcohol, petty vandalism, and the like — is widespread in our society, divorce or no divorce. Although such misbehavior emerges in children of divorce, the more frequent pattern in their lives is one of underachievement, low self-esteem, and inhibition of anger related to feelings of rejection.

At the fifteen-year follow-up, we do begin to notice a surprisingly high incidence of alcoholism in the children of divorce. Twenty percent of all the children in our study are now drinking heavily. Out of this group, a third come from homes in which neither the parents nor stepparents have ever abused alcohol.

Several of the children admit they have a problem only when it is under control. Now twenty-three and no longer drinking, Kristin says, "I'd get drunk at least twice a week in high school and go to class drunk, I mean really drunk."

"How drunk?"

"Staggering," she says.

"I had no idea you were drinking so much in high school," I say.

"I'd never have admitted it back then," she says. "But things got worse. I've been charged with drinking in public, got busted for driving under the influence, and passed out in bars."

In looking over our records, I discover that very few parents sought help for their teenage children in dealing with drinking problems. Should we count ourselves lucky that only one of the children in our study was killed an an automobile accident because he was driving while drunk?

The Bucks Stop at Eighteen

Jarrett is twenty-two years old at our ten-year interview. I remember him as a highly intelligent youngster — the eldest son of a distinguished college professor — who was full of plans the last time we met. He is quiet for the first half-hour of our interview, but then he opens up, spilling forth his personal saga of the last five years. Life has not gone the way he expected.

"I've been working in a Crown bookstore at the shopping mall for three years," he says with a tinge of bitterness in his voice.

"But Jarrett," I say in surprise, "I thought you had plans to go to college to study English. Your grades were excellent."

"They were," he says, "but my father let me down. Mom can barely pay the bills at home. She works real hard and does the best she can, but she can't help me, I know that. I guess you could say that I don't really have a father, not someone I can count on. All through high school I saw him once a month. But it doesn't matter. Once I went to his house to visit him and found him sitting in the living room. He looked up at me and didn't say anything. Then I realized that he thought I was one of Helen's friends — Helen is his stepdaughter — and that I wasn't there to see him. Finally I had to say, 'Hi, Dad. Hey, I'm here to see you.' He put his glasses on and when he recognized me he was so embarrassed he laughed. I cried all the way home."

"I'm not surprised," I say.

"There are times when I really want to go to Dad and tell him how I feel," says Jarrett. "But every time I decide to confront him, I think it's not worth it."

"What would you say to him?"

"I'd say, 'You're a real cop-out. You're a college professor, a respected archaeologist, and you wouldn't even come to my high school graduation. You don't care about my future. You got a good education, but what about me? You care more about your stepchildren than you care about me. You were so anxious to get rid of me that you prorated my last child support check to end on the tenth of the month that I turned eighteen.'" Jarrett looks ready to cry. "I never say it to him, though. I never could say it to him."

After a moment, Jarrett delivers the coup de grâce of hurtful memories. "My dad used to take me bird watching. He has a pair of lightweight binoculars that I just love, and they were supposed to be mine someday. But guess who got them? Dad gave them to my stepsister Helen for Christmas last year. I didn't expect how much that would hurt. Jesus, it hurt." Jarrett sighs. "There's nothing I can do about it, Judy. I'm coping the best I can. I'm saving up to go back to school next quarter. I'll have enough units next year to be a junior and then I can finally declare my major. Sometimes I think I'll never finish."

"Have you looked into scholarships?"

"Sure," says Jarrett. "But I don't qualify. Dad's income is too high. If he had died I would have qualified. I'm going to be twenty-five and a half years old by the time I finish getting my degree, and what can I do with just my B.A.?"

Like Jarrett, most of the youngsters in our study are from middle-class families where one or both parents have college degrees. Most of the children graduate from local high schools where 85 percent of the students routinely go on to college. And yet barely half of these boys and girls are attending or have completed a two-year or four-year college. One third, including many very bright youngsters, dropped out of high school or college. Of those who *are* attending college, only one in ten is receiving full financial support from one or both parents. Others are receiving limited financial help — even from well-to-do fathers who could afford much more — or no help at all. Among fathers in our study who could afford to help with tuition, just over one-third helped their children, while two-thirds offered no assistance whatsoever. One successful engineer tells us point-blank, "I don't care whether my son goes to college. I couldn't care less. My responsibility is to get my life together." Nor did stepfathers come to the rescue. In our study, only one stepfather substantially helped his stepchild with college tuition.

This is not the way the world is supposed to work for these children, who are, after all, offspring of well-educated middle-class parents. Middle-class families are supposed to encourage their children to go to college. Such parents traditionally make sacrifices to help pay for their children's higher education, opening special savings accounts, earmarking sources of income, and sometimes taking on extra jobs to pay the high costs of tuition, room and board, and living expenses.

As their children grow up, middle-class parents send out none too subtle messages concerning higher education. "When you go to college, Justin, you can study more about computer graphics and find out how those video games you like so much are put together." Or "I can't wait, Jill, for you to go to Columbia. I'll bet the dorms haven't changed much since I went there." It is a form of parental propaganda. The message is phrased "when you go," not "if you go." The question is "What studies will you pursue?" not "Will you pursue your studies?"

Parents identify strongly with their adolescent children, saying in myriad ways, "I want you to follow in my footsteps. I want you to be more successful than I have been." These lines of identification are very clear: The parent says to the child, in effect, "I see you as representing me. I see you as conquering mortality for me."

Such attitudes and expectations do not necessarily survive divorce. Many children of divorce do not feel encouraged in the same way that children from intact middle-class families do. Children raised by a financially strapped single parent do not receive constant propaganda about the future. Instead they frequently hear, "How are you going to pay for your car insurance? How are we going to make ends meet?" Not surprisingly, then, many children of divorce seem less future-oriented than peers whose parents talk endlessly of plans and career opportunities. Few divorce settlements make any arrangements for college education. Among all the children who are over eighteen at the ten-year mark, *60 percent are on a downward educational course compared with their fathers and 45 percent are on a similarly downward course compared with their mothers.*

In most divorced families, it is not clear who will pay for higher education. The mother's income plus child support does not generally provide savings for college tuition. Since fathers are usually financially more secure than mothers, it is fathers who can most afford to pay the bulk of college tuition. Many fathers provide child support payments, with more or less regularity, when their children are young, but the support does not rise when the children become teenagers and expenses go up steeply. And it usually stops abruptly at age eighteen — just when the child is ready to enter college. Children of divorce feel less protected economically; unlike children from intact families, whose parents usually continue to support them through college and sometimes even beyond, the children of divorce face an abrupt, premature end to an important aspect of their childhood. That is, their fathers and mothers are no longer — in the eyes of the law — obligated to support them after age eighteen. At this so-called age of majority, the clock stops ticking, childhood is over, and economic support stops. Nowhere is it writ that psychological or emotional support stops at age eighteen, but many children of divorce cannot help but feel that when child support stops, something else stops in the social contract between parent and child.

From an early age, these children are aware of money: It is scarce. Growing up, they know full well when their court-ordered child support payments will stop. If they have college plans, they face losing financial support when they most need it, and many adolescents seem to lower their ambitions in the face of this loss. At the ten-year mark, only one in ten children in high school said they knew there would be enough money for them to go to college. But even those raised by well-to-do parents feel more vulnerable than peers from equally well-to-do intact families. When fathers in our study do help children with college, they are twice as likely to help boys as girls.

In accord with their low self-esteem, many children of divorce do not make strong demands on their fathers — they neither exploit Dad's bank account nor make excessive demands on his earning power. They tend to hold down jobs themselves, save money, and work hard to help support the household. Many students alternate school semesters with work, or they carry several part-time jobs along with a full academic schedule.

I am continually surprised at how passive these young people are in the face of disappointment from their fathers. Instead of getting angry, they conclude that they are powerless and undeserving. Not feeling the right or power to get angry, they do not complain.

As we have seen, a father's attitudes and feelings about his children can become blunted by divorce — a finding that took me by surprise and one that is hard to understand. Psychologists, lawyers, and judges used to think that a father's relationship with his children during marriage would, within reasonable limits, predict his attitude toward them after divorce. If he was an attentive, loving, and sensitive father before divorce, those attributes of fathering would continue long after the breakup. It was assumed that his connection to immortality via his biological children would hold. But we are finding otherwise. In following our families over the years, we have seen that a father's commitment to his children does not necessarily carry over into the postdivorce years.

For reasons I don't understand, many fathers who pay all their child support over the years and maintain close contact with their children draw the line with college. While they can afford it, value education, and have cordial relations with their children, they do not offer even partial support through college. One-quarter of these men hold advanced degrees in medicine, law, or business administration, and the majority have college educations. But when I ask about college for their children, they don't want to discuss it. They don't plead poverty. Rather, they tend to say, "I paid my child support through the years. I met all my obligations. I've given my wife thousands of dollars, and now it's up to her." They do not say, "I am worried about my boy's future and how he's going to make it through college." On the contrary, these fathers seem strangely at peace about not helping their biological children with higher education and content to avoid the sacrifices that parents in intact families expect of themselves. A middle-class father living with his children does not question his moral obligation to set aside college savings. A middle-class father who only visits his children may see his obligations differently. Since he sees the child only occasionally, there is a distancing — both physical and psychological — between himself and his child. He sees paying for college as a voluntary act, one that is not very compelling in most cases.

The psychological connection between father and child is weakened. Sometimes a remarriage introduces new attachments that, for the father, emotionally replace the former family. For the child of divorce, this represents a grave injustice and a personal tragedy.

Unfortunately, society is not helping children from divorced families get the educations that they need, want, and deserve. Many people think that eighteen-year-olds are full-fledged adults and that a youngster who puts himself or herself through college is all the stronger for the struggle. I disagree. Working three jobs or taking alternate semesters makes for poorer learning. It is nearly impossible to follow a scientific or other challenging curriculum and simultaneously hold down a full-time job. Of course, college students can, should, and do work at various jobs during their educations, but should they bear the full financial responsibility? Should parents who can afford to help feel obligated to do so? Should fathers who meet all child support payments until age eighteen feel free to withdraw from the child's life course because the "obligation" is met? A handful of states permit the court to order a father to pay toward college if circumstances and family values warrant, but should this be a national policy?

For their part, colleges are well aware of these problems but generally avoid the issue. Several major universities have held meetings about the subject but have not been able to decide what to do. Most require financial aid information from both parents in considering scholarship awards, and they do not acknowledge one parent's refusal to help pay for tuition. Most make scholarship awards based on the combined income of both parents, even if only one is willing to pay. Colleges argue that it is not their job to enforce morality issues between parents and children. If fathers refuse to help pay for their children's higher education, it is not an issue for the scholarship office to adjudicate.

These three young people — Steve, Kevin, and Jarrett — represent the plight of many adolescents and young adults from divorced families. Although they respond differently, each is reacting to a profound sense of loss. While others his age are planning the future, Steve is overwhelmed by feelings of longing, powerlessness, and depression; he hits a dead end. Feeling betrayed by the father he worshiped and neglected by his mother, Kevin directs his anger randomly at the adult world and back onto himself. For Jarrett, the economic doors to a middle-class adulthood are needlessly barred, reinforcing his sense of not having the same rights as other children, of not being valued or even recognized as an heir. In countless ways that combine psychological and economic issues, divorce exerts a chilling effect on the hopes, aspirations, and achievements of our children.

10

Tanya Burrelle

LONELY GIRLS

I AM VERY DISAPPOINTED when Tanya Burrelle, Steve's younger sister, makes herself unavailable during my two-day stay in Albuquerque. When I go to the house after my long lunch with Steve, I expect to find her ready for a three o'clock appointment, but she does not show. Betty Burrelle is extremely upset because she especially wants me to spend time with Tanya. As the two of us sit at the kitchen table, waiting for her, Betty tells me how distressed she is with her fifteen-year-old daughter's recent behavior. Like Steve, Tanya is bright and manages to keep up her grades, apparently without doing any homework. An aspiring artist, she works as a "go-fer" for a local designer who creates window displays in several department stores around the city. But Betty is worried that Tanya is, in her words, "out of control" because of an ongoing pattern of promiscuity. Tanya has had at least one abortion that her mother knows about. "Tanya is pleasure-driven," says Betty. "I think she started sleeping with boys at the end of eighth grade, not long before her fourteenth birthday. I might not mind so much if she were involved with one steady boyfriend. You know how kids are these days. But, Judy, Tanya is sleeping with one boy after another. I'm really worried about her getting venereal disease or an unsafe abortion."

"You've talked with her about this?"

"Yes," says Betty, "but I don't think she listens to me. Tanya has no sense of control over her life." Betty stammers, "God knows, I've tried to do my best for her, but I seem to have lost her somehow."

Before leaving Albuquerque, I write Tanya a note, inviting her to call collect, anytime. Since she and I had a good relationship earlier, I respect her feelings and hope that she will change her mind and visit when she is ready to talk to me.

I am delighted, therefore, when Tanya comes to see me three years later while on vacation in San Francisco. Now eighteen, with dark curly hair like her mother's, she has finished high school, has a job with the designer back in Albuquerque, and wants to save money for further education in art and design. She is ready to get on with her life.

"I'm a few years late," says Tanya as she walks through the door, "but I'm here! I want to see my records."

I am taken aback. No one has ever asked for his or her records like this.

"I want to know why I've been unable to be by myself, meaning without a guy, without sex, since junior high school. I want to know in detail how I reacted back then so I can understand why I am so driven today."

Tanya is an attractive young woman with clear eyes, a trendy haircut, and a vibrant curiosity about issues related to divorce. I want to help her as much as possible, so I skip the issue of records, which I take to be peripheral, and ask her a direct question, "Tanya, what is it you really want to know?"

"I used to be mad at my mom," she says, "but I stopped being angry at her when I was sixteen, when I suddenly realized that all of the kids who lived in tract houses with picket fences were not any happier than I was. It took me a long time to stop blaming her for not being in one of those houses." She pauses, as if to emphasize this insight.

"But my real problem is that I never had a reliable man in my life," she says in a tone suggesting that she has given this issue interminable thought. "Mom works all the time and Dad never comes to see us, so I just began to have lots of relationships, lots of boys. There isn't a time since junior high that I haven't had a steady guy. Then there was a whole period of my life when I was a Grateful Dead fanatic. All the time I just wanted to be with somebody. I realize it was a way of keeping some pretty intense feelings from coming out."

"It's been hard."

"Yes, it has. I've had two abortions. That really makes me feel sad. I just wish I could relate to people in a healthy way. You see, I don't like to be dependent on anybody, and I don't want them to be dependent on me. I was so disappointed by my dad. He let me down a lot. I think I'm trying to get back at him," says Tanya, "by having so many guys. If my parents had paid more attention to me, I wouldn't have been so driven to find attention by sleeping around in high school."

Despite her problems, Tanya is on course with much of her life, has done well academically, and is thinking of a career in accord with her talents. In terms of her personal achievements, she shows high self-esteem.

In contrast with the rest of her life, though, Tanya's relationships with men are driven by her anger at her father and, as she says, by an intense fear of being alone. Tanya is frightened because an hour, a day, or a night alone is linked in her psyche with the fear of abandonment, fear of loneliness, and a profound sense of rejection. As much as she wants to understand herself, Tanya is only dimly aware that she uses sex to resolve these issues and to satisfy hungers that have little to do with sexual appetites. Indeed, many of the youngsters in the study use sex to shut out anxiety and to ward off a sense of emptiness and depression, and they started early. Over a quarter of the girls became sexually active in junior high school and have continued their sexual activity ever since.

When Tanya impulsively undertakes a rapid succession of relationships to try to assuage loneliness, her reasoning is clear, the tactics old hat: If you have a lot of men around and you lose one, it doesn't matter, someone will take his place. If you rush headlong into that which is feared, you will overcome your fear, like the claustrophobe who takes up deep-sea diving. If you are afraid of being rejected, it may make sense to plunge into relationships, one after the other. Such counterphobic behavior is common among young women in our study. Thirty percent of the young women have had five or more relationships in the last five years. "Don't get too attached," says one twenty-five-year-old. "If you don't build up a relationship, you don't fall so hard. I'm on a roller coaster. I fall in and out of love and in and out of relationships."

By virtue of her looks, charm, and intelligence, Tanya should be able to attract and hold a young man appropriate to her emotional and companionship needs. But she follows another course. Her habit of taking many lovers expresses her internal need for the quick change and inhibits her ability to choose.

Acknowledging that her liaisons with men reflect anger and disappointment in both her mother and her father, Tanya says, "I really felt abandoned by my folks when I was a teenager and then I began to have many relationships." She also tells me that she wishes to belong to somebody, anybody, but fears that if she depends on or belongs to someone, "he will let me down. Like my dad let me down." Tanya lives a self-fulfilling prophecy marked by disappointment and misery.

Tanya's greater tragedy is that she understands herself, recognizes her vulnerability, and has insight into why she is driven into sexual experiences that give her little pleasure. And yet her understanding in no way rescues her from continuing the pattern.

In the same way that her brother Steve grew up with a continued sense of longing and sadness, Tanya throws herself into relationships to undo feelings of longing, loneliness, and rejection. As she goes from lover to lover, she also repeats feelings of being abandoned and alone, but she does so in reverse — *she* abandons, *she* leaves. Tanya appropriately feels that although the behavior keeps her unhappiness at bay, it does not help her to resolve the feeling that she cannot count on a sustaining relationship, either in another person or in herself.

I find Tanya's request to see her records very interesting. As we talk, it gradually becomes clear that what she wants, in a sense, is to hear some good news about her parents' relationship with each other. She specifically asks, "Did they ever love each other? Did they ever hug and make up after they fought?" It seems terribly important for her to have access to good memories about her parents' marriage. Lacking a good memory of parents who could love each other, she feels greatly handicapped in her own capacity to believe in a loving relationship with a man.

I have seen many instances of Tanya's dilemma. Younger children of divorce in particular used interviews at one or another of our follow-ups to go back to a parent and request a more positive retelling of the marriage. One young woman in her twenties calls her mother after a fifteen-year follow-up to say, "Mom, I want to talk to you about Dad, but this time I only want to hear something good." She later reports with excitement, "And do you know? They loved each other once." The children of divorce seem driven by this need to know that their parents once loved each other, in order to confirm a sense of inner goodness in themselves and their origins.

At the fifteen-year interviews, we ask all the youngsters, especially those who have been promiscuous, about how AIDS has affected their behavior and relationships. For the most part, like many young adults, they are very concerned about AIDS. As a result, their sexual activities have diminished and their anxieties about finding lasting relationships have greatly increased. "I worry about it quite a lot," says a twenty-four-year-old woman. "In fact, I'm real scared about it. It's one more reason for me to step back and think about relationships. Just recently I went to the drugstore to buy condoms and that night I had an anxiety dream about AIDS. The worst part is, I wouldn't be able to track down who might have given it to me, I've been with so many guys. I guess I'm getting tired of relationships that don't work out."

Most young adults say that they are still having sex, but it is less casual. "It's sure put a damper on my style," says a young man, also twenty-four. "I used to go out to pick up girls and try to get them in bed. Now I do have an eye out for relationships, but I'm not hunting down at the bar."

The Throwaway

I have always been concerned about Becky. She was raised in a house filled with violence, sex, and accusations and counteraccusations of infidelity. The first time I saw her, at age ten, I was impressed by how well she was holding up in a home that would undo most youngsters. She had a steely, resilient quality; despite her home life, she was able to get good grades and have many friends. She was on course developmentally in a family that fit every measure of pathology.

As I wait for her to come to our ten-year interview, I remember with some amusement the play she wrote about an ideal family, just as her own family was falling apart. She staged it for the entire school and invited her parents. They did not come.

I also remember her Jonathan Swift–like fantasy of magic animals. Whenever things got difficult, Becky went into her room and talked to her collection of stuffed animals, all of whom talked back in her imagination. "They live in families," Becky said. "Some are married and some have children. In one family, one is called Virgin, another is called Bachelor, and they have a child called Marriage." She described how the animal families came alive under her watchful eyes and had adventures in strange lands, including run-ins with bad people who would try to catch and destroy them. She then showed me a book in which she had carefully recorded her animals' genealogies.

Becky spotted some stuffed animals in the playroom at the center. She took the mother lion and the child lion and put them together, noting how well they looked.

"They do go well together," I agreed. "Lionesses and cubs don't fight."

"Of course not," she said with great indignation. "Even if they wanted to, no mother lion would hurts its child."

I was touched by her confidence and by her bitter view of humans who are selfish, lose their tempers, and hurt children.

Now, on a stormy day that befits her life story, Becky the nineteen-year-old is catching me up on recent events in her still disorganized family. With her jet black hair pulled tight in a bun, her olive skin, and her long dangly earrings, Becky reminds me of a gypsy girl whose world is untamed and dangerous. Whatever minimal structure and care she received before the divorce has long since vanished. The amount of sexual stimulation has increased in both parents' homes. Although the violence has disappeared, anger continues at full pitch.

Becky describes a life that is pure Fanny Hill. At thirteen, she began sleeping with boys, and at fifteen she joined a high-class prostitution ring at the local high school. For two months — until she got bored with the scene — she had sex with married men, for five hundred dollars a trick. She was supposed to live with her mother one year and with her father the next, but there was no supervision in either home. Her father, who owned an Italian restaurant and enjoyed flirting with customers and his young waitresses, worked long hours, rarely getting home before midnight on any night of the week.

A few years ago, after Becky moved in with her father, the days became a blur of drugs, alcohol, and sex. She did not go to school. "No one stopped me," she says slowly. "Until I was seventeen, my life was one big instant gratification." Becky laughs easily. "I screwed everybody. All my money went into dope and clothes. Oh, yeah, and a couple of abortions."

"What happened when you were seventeen?"

"Well, I moved in with Freddy. It was a big mistake, I gotta tell you. He got pretty violent most of the time, but so do lots of other guys I've been with. I keep swearing I won't let anyone hit me again, but I keep doing these things." Becky will not look at me.

I ask Becky if she still sees her parents.

"I've always been Daddy's little girl," she says in total contradiction of her experiences. "I'm real proud of him and he likes to show me off to his friends in the restaurant. It's okay." When Becky looks up at me now, she can see that I do not believe that everything is okay. Before I can speak she says, "Yeah, well, I guess I don't have much control over anything that happens in my life. I'm prepared for anything. I don't expect a lot out of life. I can handle anything that happens. I'm just happy to be alive and go through my days." She squeezes a stray lock of hair tightly around her fingers. "Life is a chess game. I'm a pawn and my dad's the king. I've always been a pawn."

"It sounds like a crazy game, Becky, and not such a great one for the pawn."

"Look, the way you learn right from wrong is when you experience something yourself," she says, shifting her weight. "I sure have experienced a lot of things. I sure have learned right from wrong. If my parents hadn't divorced, I wouldn't be so wild. I wouldn't be smoking cigarettes here with you. I'd be going to college and living at home. When you're a kid, you really need your mom and dad. It's okay if your parents get a divorce after you're fifteen, but it really crushes kids if they're younger than that. But you can't blame divorce on anybody. It's really nobody's fault. Nothing is anybody's fault."

Before the divorce, Becky had a home. Despite episodic fighting and violence, there was an established dinnertime, a bedtime, and a getting-up time. After the divorce, the family structure disintegrated and no one was in charge. Becky's mother began having affairs in a desperate attempt to make herself happy, while Becky's father sought the fountain of youth in his own affairs. At age ten, Becky had to take care of herself, and she knew it. By developing her rich and nurturing animal fantasies, she called upon an inner core of integrity, creativity, and capacity for relationships. These fantasies held her together, but only through preadolescence.

Then, against a rising press of sexual and aggressive impulses, Becky's world fell apart. Standing on the verge of adolescence, she had been exposed to an enormous amount of sexual stimulation and brutality. No one tried to show her how a man and woman can mutually love and respect one another. "I can't trust my parents one bit," she said. "I rely on my friends." By the time she was fifteen, Becky was what we call a throwaway child.

Although their stories may be less dramatic, there are many children like Becky, for whom divorce means the end of care and stability. As violence and infidelity continue or escalate, parents chronically neglect their children, with terrible consequences. In these families, instead of bringing an improvement, divorce ushers in a much greater disruption of childrearing — no one is in charge.

If there is a sexually charged atmosphere in the home, children will experience very high anxiety. They are unable to concentrate in school and feel physically on edge. As one ten-year-old girl told us after attending one of her mother's orgiastic parties, "I almost feel like I could swallow my tongue."

Girls seem to have a particularly strong need for family structure during adolescence. Starved for rules or even for a person who will say something nice to them, they may find comfort in promiscuity. In many cases, this is a short-lived phenomenon, peaking around age fourteen. But other girls, like Becky, continue to be promiscuous throughout adolescence. Their sexual activity is characteristically combined with drug and alcohol use.

Becky is correct in saying that her parents' divorce came at a bad time in her life. Girls are especially vulnerable to divorce when they are on the verge of adolescence and are feeling helpless in the press of their own rising sexuality. At this very time, their parents' sexuality may come out from behind closed bedroom doors. Becky finds her mother making love to strange men on the living room couch; the door to her father's apartment is opened by strange women wearing bathrobes. Becky's parents, who are certainly entitled to a private sex life, fail to protect her from being a vicarious part of it. By being too open about their sexuality, they stop acting as parents and start acting as older friends, not realizing that Becky needs parents more than older friends. Unprotected from her own impulses, Becky is overstimulated and vulnerable. If sex comes along, why not try it? If the household is disorganized, who's to stop her?

Throwaway girls say they feel empty inside. Their inability to postpone gratification is in keeping with their low self-esteem and high impulsivity. In referring to herself as a "pawn, always a pawn," Becky exactly captures the sense of life out of control, of herself as the most expendable piece on the board.

Adolescents are more vulnerable than most people realize. Young teenagers need a family structure, a sense that they are being valued and protected. We all know without thinking that a three-year-old needs care and attention, that someone has to be present for that child because of his or her physical and emotional needs. But certainly a thirteen-year-old can open the refrigerator and make an after-school snack. Or dinner. Or breakfast if need be. But are we confusing the ability of thirteen-year-olds to care for themselves physically with the ability to care for themselves psychologically? Certainly children can fend for themselves on days when parents are tied up. But can they be expected to do so over the long haul? As one fourteen-year-old girl says, "The worst thing about divorce was that my mom wasn't home. There was no discipline, no rules — just an empty feeling. That's how I got into drugs and sex."

Locked In by the Court

Dora's parents were in their late thirties when she was born. They hovered over her — a miracle child. Dora's father had emigrated from Israel and ran a successful carpentry business; her American-born mother worked in a bakery. Dora was a quiet, obedient little girl. There was little laughter or joy in the strictly Orthodox household.

When the marriage ended after twelve years, Dora stayed with her mother. "Mama needs me," she said. "She can't lift anything heavy. I don't know what she would do without me." One day Dora flatly refused to visit her father; when begging failed to work, she went into a severe rage. Sweet, shy Dora tore at a chair and literally ripped the arms off. Her father took her mother to court. As the mother and daughter told us, he told the judge, "My ex-wife is brainwashing my daughter. Dora is not spending time with me. I demand my rights." The court listened. Despite protests from Dora and her mother, the child was ordered to spend every other weekend with her father from 9:00 A.M. Saturday morning until 7:00 P.M. Sunday evening. After her one desperate and heroic effort to resist, Dora surrendered. Every other weekend during her adolescence she went submissively to her father's apartment. She cried in the privacy of her bedroom — the one in her mother's house.

Her father's apartment was spacious, decorated with Oriental rugs, Menorahs, and lots of silver that Dora had to polish. Her father expected her to dress modestly. When she menstruated, she wrapped her underwear and soiled napkins in a special pouch to take back to her mother's.

As Dora told us, the routine was set early on. On Saturday, they walked to the synagogue. Later she would wait for evening to turn on the stove and prepare his meals for the next week. On Sunday

Dora did his laundry and cleaned the house. "We never see anyone else. I'm always alone with my father," she said when we met one year after the divorce.

"What have you said to your dad?" I asked.

"I told him I wanted to go on a day bike ride on Sunday with my girlfriends. He yelled at me for two days. Always he says, 'You've forgotten all the things I've done for you.' He mentions hundreds of things I can't even remember. I can't stand his 'I did so much for you' speech."

Five years later, Dora was bitter about the court order. I agreed it was constricting her social and emotional development during her teens and was very concerned about her unhappiness. At sixteen, she wrote poetry and played her guitar at a favorite rock in a nearby park. "I've learned that I like to be alone," she said in an unsure voice. "But things have been hard. Father pays ninety-five dollars a month for my support. But I guess you could say I work for it."

I could feel Dora's sense of powerlessness, but it is not until we meet at the ten-year mark, when she is twenty-two, that some of the consequences of her parents' divorce and the court-ordered visiting become clear. A month before she was to leave for college, eighteen-year-old Dora met a twenty-nine-year-old electrician. After three weeks, she called off college and married him. "It was strange from the first," she now says. "He was my first relationship. During our marriage he did the yelling. I did the crying." It was the same submissive relationship that she had described with her father and that had been reinforced by the court order.

Given such pressures, girls like Dora often take a time-honored escape route: They marry the first man who comes along. By the ten-year interview, Dora has divorced her husband but nevertheless says, "I get mad at all these programs about how bad divorce is for children. They should tell both sides of the story. I felt pretty happy after the divorce. At least my mom and dad wouldn't be fighting anymore. The divorce changed my life for the better because I got away a little bit from my dad." She pauses to reflect. "But I don't think the effect was very good for me. I could have been more of a person. Some people after divorce become more careful in their relationships with men. I became careless. Anyone who gets married when she is eighteen years old and goes out with the guy for only three weeks deserves to be divorced."

All but one of the young women in our study who married early, before age twenty, are now divorced. Like Dora, they married men they hardly knew, and most of their marriages were violent. (A handful of young men married early; at the ten-year mark, their marriages are intact.)

Early marriage is one pathway taken by young women with low self-esteem and little capacity to maintain themselves. In the effort to escape from home situations that they feel are difficult, they ironically, tragically, but not surprisingly end up in situations that fail to rescue them. These poor early marriages reinforce their unhappiness and their economic vulnerability.

Dora faced another issue, the court-ordered visiting schedule that she so strongly opposed. I'm sure the judge did not expect it to last throughout her adolescence, probably assuming that once the order was made the parents and child would renegotiate the matter in accord with the wishes and changing developmental needs of the youngster. Courts certainly assume that adolescents will struggle on their own behalf. But according to my observations, this is not true. Whenever I raise this issue with judges, they refuse to believe that some teenagers cannot and do not act vigorously on their own behalf or that one parent will not act for them. In Dora's case, the court order was carried out to the letter. The child grew up understanding that it was impossible to fight on her own behalf. I have seen many cases where the court order reinforces the children's sense of powerlessness and strengthens their sense that no one of any importance, no one with any power, is on their side. Society, in its institutions, does not seem to care. With little room to maneuver or to change things by their own efforts, children's self-esteem is further eroded, and they become discouraged at even trying to help themselves. Their sad expectations translate into self-fulfilling prophecy.

As Tanya, Becky, Dora, and so many other children of divorce — boys as well as girls — have taught us, adolescence is a perilous time. Unfortunately, we do little to help. In fact, our society does much to hinder children's growth.

Adolescence is characterized by the biological rise in sexual and aggressive impulses. At first, children are bewildered by these impulses. They are afraid of being overwhelmed and feel vulnerable. In our culture, this rise in impulses is accompanied by a great deal of stimulation. Sex and violence are commercially exploited to sell virtually every product and service in the American economy. In our affluent society, young adolescents are targeted by many adults as ready consumers of drugs and alcohol — and there is a fortune to be made on their willingness to experiment with forbidden adult "pleasures." As our teenagers confront their own sexuality, aggression, and rebelliousness, they meet with heightened stimulation from the media and the voices of the street — promises of instant gratification, guarantees of the quick fix. Children are pushed into sexuality and pseudoadulthood too early and are exposed to violence from many sources. In the face of these impulses and stimulations, all young people require several types of support.

Teenagers need a strong family structure and a clear belief system. They need rules, agreed-upon curfews, and an understanding that parents care about their children and that children, in turn, are expected to care about others, including their parents. Parenting is never more needed, nor more challenged, than with adolescents. As youngsters deal with the impulses of increasing sexual maturity, they need to know that the world has stability, that there is right and wrong, give and take. Moreover, it is critically important for adolescents to have a home that is a safe haven when the world gets too competitive, too hurtful, or too frightening. The teenager's prized possession is his or her own room, even if it is no more than a cubbyhole, because it represents stability. It is a safe mooring.

These supports are often undermined during and after divorce, with tragic results. As the divorce unfolds, the family structure unravels, and adolescents feel adrift psychologically. They are thrown prematurely into being dependent on peers for emotional and physical support, and they are cast into serious competition in an outside world without a home oasis. Issues of right and wrong are open to question.

Few adults realize how much adolescents have to accomplish before they can move on into young adulthood. It is tempting to think of adolescence as a period "to get through, to survive." But the adolescent years serve a purpose on the developmental ladder to adulthood — to gradually detach from the family and establish greater independence while remaining connected with that family. Adolescence is not a total breaking away; it brings to an end the earlier parent-child framework and engenders new relationships with parents and with peers. Divorce poses a serious threat to this complicated developmental process, which is already very delicately balanced.

11

Kyle Burrelle

THE YOUNGEST CHILD

As THE YOUNGEST of three children, Kyle Burrelle was given special protection by his mother, Betty, who drew him closer during the storm of divorce. Unlike Steve and Tanya, Kyle — who was going on three when Dale moved out — does not remember his father reading bedtime stories, wrestling with him on the living room floor, and taking him to the ice cream parlor. Like many very young children, he was confused about time and space, about where his daddy went, and about how long he had to wait between visits. In our playroom at the time of the breakup, his play was about dinosaurs, toy lions, and lurking monsters. He was struggling with aggression and a sense that the world is not a safe place, but he was not overwhelmed with anxiety.

At my ten-year interview with Kyle, we sit in his back yard and talk about his life and what he enjoys — school, recess, football, basketball, playing the drums, his newspaper delivery route — and about his best friend who lives two blocks away. Thirteen-year-old Kyle talks freely and easily without prompting. He is calm and at ease with an unfamiliar adult. Having just entered a growth spurt, he is thin and angular, with the hint of an Adam's apple at his throat.

"Me and my mom get along pretty good," he says in answer to a question. "We belong to the same hiking club, but lots of times we just go off for a couple of hours walking, just the two of us. When I come home late, I get grounded. She doesn't like me to fight with

Steve and Tanya. I can talk to her about everything. She's good to talk to. She understands stuff better than most people."

And his father?

"My dad calls me sometimes. He talks to us all. He's proud of me for going out for football. I like to talk about that stuff with Dad. He likes sports."

I ask Kyle to describe visits with his father.

"Well, when I saw him last year, we got three or four hours together," he says evenly. "My dad had to go somewhere, so we couldn't spend more time. I don't expect him to call, but when he does it's sort of nice. I think he'd sort of like to be back with us. I would like that, but it's okay now. I don't worry about it. I can get along without him. But I'd like to see him more. I'd like to visit him two times a year for a couple of weeks each visit. But he's usually working and doesn't have much time to spend. And I don't get along that great with my stepmom. My stepbrother cries when he doesn't get what he wants. It's a real pain. Dad is always getting married and divorced."

I ask Kyle why he thinks the divorce happened in the first place.

"I don't know what caused it," he says. "He walked out, I guess. I can't understand why. I tried to think what happened. He must not like her anymore. It's been hard on Mom. She's had to bring us up alone."

"You've done so well," I say. "What helped you?"

He grins. "Well, I just tried to take it as best I could. Mom's around if I really need her. And I talk to my best friend and stuff."

I ask about his plans for the future.

"I want to get married when I'm thirty. I'd like to be on my own for a while, get a good job, save some money. You shouldn't get married unless you love someone. You have to be able to talk about your problems. I have a girlfriend. She's nice, with a good personality, and we talk about stuff."

After our interview, Kyle goes upstairs and beats on his drums for a long time. I think to myself that drum playing is not a bad way for a child to express the host of feelings — anger, sorrow, and longing — associated with all that he has been brave enough to tell me.

I was impressed by Kyle's poise and pragmatism. When he says, "I tried to take it as best I could," he is being realistic about what he can expect from himself and from others. Unlike many boys his age,

Kyle is able to talk about feelings, future plans, relationships, and memories.

Indeed, Kyle is doing well in school, makes excellent grades, has close friends including a girlfriend, and has a close, very trusting relationship with his mother. He tries to paint his father in a positive light, keeping in check feelings of hurt and anger without denying them. Keenly realistic about his life and relationships, Kyle plans to work hard to meet appropriate goals. Compared with his brother, Steve, who is drifting, and his sister, Tanya, who is caught in a web of promiscuity, Kyle is a stunning success.

When people ask me what spares children from the traumas of divorce, I cannot give them easy formulas or simple answers. I can say, however, that the age of the child when the marriage comes apart strongly affects his or her reaction at the time as well as his or her behavior and feelings over the subsequent decade. In general, preschoolers are the most frightened and show the most dramatic symptoms when marriages break up. Many are afraid that they will be abandoned by both parents and so have trouble sleeping or staying by themselves.

It is therefore surprising to find that the same children ten years later seem better adjusted than their older siblings. Now, in early adolescence, they score better on a wide range of psychological measures than the older children. Sixty-eight percent are doing well, compared with less than 40 percent of older children.

Kyle and his older brother, Steve, are good examples of this phenomenon. Steve, at age seven, reacted strongly to the breakup, prompting teachers to recommend professional help. Many boys this age continue to be preoccupied or obsessed with their fathers if the fathers do not maintain reliable, ongoing relationships. Steve never recovered from the disruption of his relationship with his father.

But Kyle was just turning three when Dale left, and the father-son relationship was not central, as it was for Steve. Kyle's need for a close, masculine identification figure was not at its peak, as it was for his older brother. Kyle was still primarily in his mother's care, physically and emotionally. Therefore, the loss of his father, while painful, was not experienced at the core of his being and was not perceived as an overwhelming blow.

As the youngest child, Kyle had the advantage of a privileged relationship with his mother. Naturally drawn to protect the baby and worn to a frazzle by single parenting, many mothers — including some as exhausted as Betty — often give what little energy is left over at day's end to the youngest child in the family. In general, the younger siblings in divorced families are buffered as the older children bear the brunt of their parents' distress. First-born children have traditionally been found to hold an advantaged position among siblings, often demonstrating higher intelligence and greater achievement.[1] This native advantage is usually attributed to the fact that first-borns are nearer and sometimes dearer to their parents. With divorce, this natural advantage may be reversed.

When divorced mothers give their youngest child extra protection, developing a close and loving relationship, the children benefit enormously, spending nearly all of their growing-up years in a stable, albeit postdivorce environment. They expect the world to treat them well and are considerably more optimistic than older siblings. Unlike Steve, Kyle expects people to be kind to him, and he has some sense of control over his life and feels confident about setting plans and following through.

Moreover, these very young children are not haunted by memories of the intact family. They feel less nostalgia for what was lost and have fewer memories of turmoil and conflict stemming from the separation. "It's funny," says Kyle. "The whole period of time is blocked. I can't remember it. I was three."

Kyle is also able to reach out for help when he needs it, whereas Steve holds back. Steve is afraid to ask his father for money because he is sure he will be rejected, again. But Kyle is not tormented by such fears, and so he simply reaches out. At the fifteen-year mark, Kyle is attending the University of New Mexico on a scholarship. When school started, he called Dale to ask for money, and Dale responded by sending Kyle $100 a month.

Whether being young at the time of divorce will continue to protect children as they enter young adulthood and search for the queen of hearts is still an open question.

The Girl with Two Homes

Dana, age four, pushed an unruly lock of red hair out of her eyes and reached for a papa doll. Withdrawn and silent, she would not smile on her first hour-long visit to our playroom but concentrated intensely on her fantasy, a game of togetherness. First she created a scene in which the mother and father dolls lay in bed together while the children dolls played happily in the next room and the tiny baby doll slept peacefully in a crib. As the hour ended, all the dolls arose finally to enjoy a bountiful breakfast.

A week later, Dana again arranged the dolls into a happy family scene where they all watched television together. The father doll held his little girl on his lap, and after the show they all had dinner together. The father continued to hold his little girl tenderly on his lap during the meal. All the sounds that children usually make while playing dollhouse games were eerily absent in Dana's play. We tried to engage her in conversation, but all she would say was "Daddy is in the city and Mommy is unhappy." Her play belied her words, for in the dollhouse no one had left home; it was paradise.

On her third visit to our playroom, the togetherness theme of Dana's dollhouse world took on new and rising intensity. Soberly and wordlessly, she placed the mother, father, and children in the bathtub together. Then she moved the entire family to the roof, with the father, mother, and children all piled on top of one another. Suddenly, the dolls, the puppets lying nearby, and Dana herself all began to bite one another. Dana bit the crocodile and pummeled it with her fists and then moved on to bite another object. Her loss of control continued, unabated, in the complete absence of any sound. One needs no special training to read in Dana's play her inexpressible grief over not being able to restore the family she had lost. Tenderness, togetherness, and mutuality gave way to attack, anger, and destruction. Paradise was lost to Armageddon.

Although all our preschool-age children reacted strongly to divorce, Dana's reaction was particularly powerful. In the first weeks after divorce, she alternated between screaming temper tantrums and extended periods of silent withdrawals. Dana showed symptoms of depression along with severe sleep disturbances, including night terrors, for about six months after her parents' divorce. She was almost inconsolable and angrily rejected or sorrowfully withdrew from her parents' efforts to reach out to her. But gradually, as she visited her father regularly and her mother calmed down, Dana improved. At our one-year interview she was in a better mood, was doing well at school, and told us that she liked having two homes. At age five, she enacted a hopeful scene in the playroom where the father and mother dolls carried the children on their shoulders.

When it is time to see Dana for the ten-year follow-up, I call her house to ask who wants to come first, Dana or her brother, and Dana volunteers. When she strides into my office, it takes me a moment to recognize her now that she is a striking fourteen-year-old with dangling earrings. The freckles are gone, but her hair remains red and unruly. Dressed in designer jeans and a rugby shirt, Dana seems very unlike the petite little girl in frocked pinafores who played so intensely in our playroom long ago. The diffidence is gone as she takes charge of the interview.

"Dr. Wallerstein," she says, "I'd like you to know that I'm a normal child with a normal childhood from a normal family."

I say I am very glad to hear that and ask her to tell me about her life. With very little prompting, Dana says, "My friends ask whether divorce is hard on me, and I tell them, nope, I have two different lives. I go on trips with my dad in the summer and I fly down to see him once a month during the school year, but I live with my mom. There are still big differences between the two homes," she says, pushing her hair off her forehead. "Mom mostly lets us do what we want, but Dad expects more, especially about school. But Mom understands us more and we do work hard."

"Are there other differences, Dana?"

"Lots," she says. "Mostly about rules, table manners, and yelling. But I really like having two lives and I like my stepmom a lot. There is more family at my dad's house. I like it all. Sometimes, though, I have something happening at school and I get mad that I have to go to Dad's. He calls three times a week and we arrange our trips. I really feel bad when I have to tell Dad that I can't come for one of the visits. In fact, I usually go, even when I've got other things I want to do real bad. I hate to hurt his feelings."

"How do your mother and father get along these days?"

"Okay, I guess," says Dana. Then, more honestly, she continues, "Really they don't get along so well, but at least they don't fight. Sometimes my stepmom wonders what my mom thinks about her, and sometimes she isn't sure how much we like her, but I like her a lot. My mom and stepmom just don't understand each other, but it passes over."

Later I ask Dana about her plans for the future.

"I want to go to college, maybe study math, engineering, or computer science, get a good job, get married, and have kids," she says in one breath. "Marriage is a good thing if you love someone. But if you want a divorce, you should get that."

"Do you think you ever will?"

"I like to think not," says Dana. "But you never can tell."

I ask Dana to tell me about her mother.

"Oh, Mom's fine and I'm proud of her," says Dana. "My mom and I are very close, and I'm Mom's best friend. I'm real proud of her. You should see her in action in court — she's real strong. There's just one problem, though. Her boyfriends drive me up the wall. I feel sorry for her sometimes because I want her to be happy and I wish she could find someone nice. Sometimes she's sad and depressed and I feel bummed out. But I think she's happy most of the time."

I ask Dana, as I ask all the children, what advice she has for other children of divorce and for their parents. Her advice for children: "Don't try to fight it and don't try to get your parents back together. If it's a little fight, try to talk them out of it, but if it isn't, don't try or you'll get yourself in the way. Children shouldn't hate their parents for divorcing; they should give their parents a chance."

Dana's advice to parents: "Be patient. Explain that it's the best. Understand that it's hard for the kids as well as for the parents."

Although Dana reacted seriously to the divorce, she was considerably recovered one year later and, after ten years, she is one of the best-adjusted children in the study.

People sometimes think that the way in which a child deals with and survives a crisis will affect his or her later strength or resiliency in other crises, as if early strengths translate into later invulnerabilities. Undoubtedly Dana has many personal strengths, but the severity of her reaction at the time of divorce reflected her enormous vulnerability and sensitivity to the changes in her family. She was not particularly strong during the crisis, yet she has done better than most children over the long term.

What helped or protected her? There is no single thread running through the lives of all children who do well in the decade after divorce. Each child puts together a unique mix of internal and external factors in coping with the inevitable stresses of the postdivorce years. There are, however, some common factors.

The first is absence of open conflict. Dana benefited from continued good relations with both her parents and from her parents' ability to cooperate with one another for the sake of the children. With their major concern focused on the children, the parents maintained conditions conducive to the children's healthy psychological development. Both parents gave priority to the children's needs and refrained from disrupting the schedules the children had established with the other parent. This involved a lot of planning, flexibility, and continued talking. The achievement is especially striking because we saw no evidence that Dana's parents were any less angry at each other than any other divorced couple. Dana's mother was furious at the time of divorce and was still furious five, ten, and fifteen years after the fact. Nevertheless, she was able, without dishonesty or hypocrisy, to keep her anger within bounds that protected her children from becoming innocent victims. Among all the things that people can do to protect their children in the wake of divorce, this is one of the hardest and one of the most important. It is, unfortunately, one of the least common. It seems all too easy for parents to use their children, lawyers, new spouses, or old friends as a Greek chorus to echo the sins of the former spouse. With the background chorus, anger does not diminish; it is refueled with each incantation of sins. Forty percent of the children spent the first ten years after their parents' divorce in an atmosphere of conflict and anger.

It is profoundly distressing for children to grow up in an atmosphere from which they can only conclude that the divorce and all its dislocations have failed to produce a remedy. Such children are inevitably disappointed in their parents.

Dana also benefited from the fact that her parents, except for one screaming episode at their separation, did not physically or verbally attack one another. They tried from the start to limit the open conflict between them. Dana has no memories of unhappy encounters that would haunt her in young adulthood. It is to her parents' credit that they not only contained their anger in the postdivorce years but did not let it get out of control at any time. The child was protected by their restraint and concern for her well-being.

A second major factor is continued good relations with each parent individually, whether or not they continue to fight. Dana did not lose her father after divorce. Her relationship with him, although confined to a visiting framework, was not pro forma. Dana's father continued to be her father, not a Dutch uncle or playground director. He took an active interest in her upbringing, her studies, and her everyday life. He had standards to be enforced and values to be upheld, he was available when she was sick, and he supported her economically. She

counted on him to help her with her college education and he had no
intentions of letting her down. In all important respects, he was her
father, a good father, a moral, protective, and concerned father.

Dana shows high self-esteem and the confidence of a youngster
who is valued by her parents, particularly by her father, a need that
all adolescent girls have. Research has shown that women who aspire
to high intellectual or professional achievement have often been in-
spired by their fathers' encouragement. Dana exhibits this support as
she talks about possible careers in engineering or computer science.

A third protective factor is that Dana clearly benefited from a close
mother-daughter relationship. Although her mother was devastated
by an unexpected request for divorce, she quickly resumed parenting
as she successfully combined the role of professional career woman
with the role of mother and homemaker. This, too, is no small
achievement. After divorce, Dana's mother went back to school for a
law degree. She has been practicing environmental law in Sacramento without the help of a nanny, housekeeper, or other storybook
supports. Although not making a lot of money, Dana's mother is
proud of her achievements and her children are proud of their
mother. Dana, like all children of divorce, is deeply concerned about
her mother's welfare and well aware of the sacrifices that her mother
has made over the years, but this concern, in an important way, contributes to Dana's moral integrity and understanding of other people.

Fourth, Dana benefited from the fact that her life was organized
and well planned. I cannot repeat often enough that adolescent girls
especially need home lives that are structured and organized. (Surprisingly, adolescent boys are not as strongly affected by household
disorganization.) For Dana, life was organized, but not rigidly so. All
along, she has visited her father's house once a month, but he is flexible and considerate of her wishes, and as a result she extends herself
to oblige him. Meals are on time, and the family has dinner together
in both households.

Each of the two homes is organized somewhat differently, around
somewhat different values. In the mother's home, for example, children are encouraged to express themselves freely and can have
friends over without notice; at the father's home, the children must
listen to the parents and plan social engagements days ahead of time.
The differences themselves do not interfere with Dana's adjustment
because she feels valued and loved in both households.

A fifth factor is Dana's good relationship with her stepmother, who does not attempt to replace Dana's mother, and from her sense that her father and stepmother have an enduring commitment to one another. Dana perceives the tension between the two women but is quick to realize that the competition is not over her, which is reassuring. In general, the adults in Dana's life behave in responsible ways, providing her with rational but not saintlike models.

Finally, as we learn from her parents, Dana benefited from having three sets of grandparents, all of whom were faithful to her, continuing over the years to reinforce her vision of a stable world.

When I meet Dana's mother for our fifteen-year meeting, I tell her how pleased I am about her children and how well they have turned out. Since I am aware that her life has not been without suffering all these years, I ask her what she thinks has made a difference for her children.

Taking my question very seriously, she leans forward and, in rapid succession, ticks off points by raising her fingers one at a time. "One, my former husband and I have tried very hard from the beginning to keep our animosities in check. Two, the children have had excellent support over the years. I worked very hard at maintaining the social group that my husband and I belonged to when we were married. We visit these families and their children several times a year, even though we left the neighborhood fifteen years ago. I did it on purpose because I thought it would be important for the children to maintain their early friendships." She raises another finger. "Three, my parents, my former husband's parents, and his second wife's parents are all very interested in the children. The children visit their grandparents and are invited on trips with them. Four, I've been very honest with the children, and I am convinced that that has helped a lot. Whenever I had a man over, I didn't lie about it. They might object, or they might not like him, but I wasn't furtive or deceptive. I was always straightforward and open, which has helped them be the kind of people they are." With the next point, her hand is wide open like a fan. "Five, I encourage them to make their own decisions whenever I can and let them live with the consequences. I try not to stand in their way because I have great confidence in them. And it's paid off. I think they're proud of me, of my going back to school, and they're proud when I go into court to argue a case. Certainly, I am proud of them."

At the fifteen-year mark, Dana is still doing well. Enrolled in a fine liberal arts college more than a thousand miles from home, she is making good grades, has a wide circle of friends, and is being courted by a young man. I do not see in Dana the intense anxiety evident in other children of divorce, and I suspect she will have easy access to her queen of hearts. She tells me that she is worried about divorce and wants to be sure of the young man she eventually marries, but in this moderate anxiety she shares the concerns of most in her generation. I can't help but agree with her first words to me: "I'm a normal girl in a normal family."

12

The Overburdened Child

ONE OF THE TRAGEDIES of divorce is that the breaking of the marriage bond reverberates into the parent-child relationship. Children are almost inevitably burdened by greater responsibilities and feel less cared for.

Many youngsters, like Ruth Moore and Steve Burrelle, feel burdened for almost a decade. In caring for her mother and younger siblings, Ruth was forced to put her development on hold. But she eventually broke free and caught up — by dint of her own efforts and her mother's strengths. Steve, while feeling abandoned by his father, was protected by the heroic efforts of his mother on his behalf and by her example. Although burdened by depression and longing for his father, he was not pressed into taking responsibilities beyond his capacities.

Unfortunately, many youngsters confront far greater problems and pressures than do Ruth Moore or Steve Burrelle. Within such families, the needs of chronically troubled parents override the developmental needs of the children — and the children have nowhere to turn for help. After divorce, the burden of caring for a disorganized, alcoholic, intensely dependent, physically ill, or chronically enraged parent falls almost entirely on the child. There is no other adult to buffer the pain or to take charge. In some families the child picks up the vacated role of the departed parent; then, what begins as a temporary caretaking role can go on to last for years, as the parent fails to recover from the divorce.

These pressures can overburden children to the point that they become psychologically depleted and their own emotional and social progress is crippled. Instead of gathering strength from their childhood and adolescent experiences to facilitate the move into young adulthood, these young people are seriously weakened by the demands made on them within the divorced family. In their efforts to help needy and distressed parents, children can and do assume a wide variety of unfamiliar roles, including arbiter, protector, adviser, nurturer, sibling, battle ally, confidant, and concubine. A child can become the key figure who wards off a parent's depression and allays a parent's fear that the world is falling apart. Others become instruments of their parents' rage. Still others, like Becky, take full responsibility at a very young age for bringing themselves up.

It is clear that when a marriage fails, especially when it ends in angry conflict, parents can experience an erosion of empathy for their children. In the same way that men and women in happy, fulfilled marriages have an expanded capacity to welcome and embrace the children born into that marriage, the ending of the marriage can erode the deep feelings parents have for children and the extent to which they voluntarily undertake responsibilities for the children. Children are undoubtedly a greater economic and social burden following divorce; at the same time, they may be more needed than ever as a source of comfort, of joy, and of meaning in the life of the parent. The commitment of the parents may careen back and forth between these two extremes. It is almost as if the swing of the pendulum is set into motion by the shattering of the marital contract. Sometimes these changes in parenting are temporary. Too often, they are lasting.

Debbie was an attractive young wife, devoted to her baby girl. As her marriage floundered, she grew closer to the child, nursing her well past her second birthday. Although the marriage was sterile and unfulfilling and Debbie's husband cheated on her, the couple did not fight openly. Nevertheless, as Debbie approached her thirty-fifth birthday, she suddenly decided to end the marriage. Within the space of a few months, she filed for divorce, threw her reluctant husband out of the house, weaned her daughter, who was then two and a half, placed the little girl in day care for the entire day, and looked for a full-time job. Motivated neither by economic need nor career interest, Debbie was in full flight from her marriage and, to all appearances, from motherhood as well.

The consequences to the child were devastating. Accustomed to being with her mother twenty-four hours a day, the little girl had never had a babysitter and was still breastfeeding. Suddenly she was weaned and placed in day care, simultaneously losing her mother and her father. The child went out of control. Although she was previously well cared for, she could not handle this kind of neglect. Debbie, in wanting to wipe out her marriage, also wiped out the supports her daughter had previously depended on.

It is a fact of life that during the early stages of separation and divorce, children find that their mothers and fathers are much less available as parents; the adults' attention is focused elsewhere. They spend less time with their children, drop routines, let controls fall away, are less sensitive, and have trouble separating their own adult needs from their children's needs. I call it the diminished capacity to parent.

After divorce, a mother is caught between two newly powerful urges regarding her children. She experiences conflicting wishes — she needs them more, she needs them less — that set up a dynamic tension in her psyche. On the one hand, she is worried about them, fearing that they will be angry with her for letting the divorce occur. She watches for signs of distress or anguish and, perhaps out of her own guilt, may bow to unreasonable pressures and demands. She wants her children to be loyal to her and close to her, to approve of her, and perhaps to represent her in battle. She may have trouble saying no, and this difficulty may result in a general lack of order and discipline, if not chaos, in the household. At a more profound level, she may become overdependent on her children, turning to them to fulfill a wide range of her own pressing psychological and social needs. Indeed, her needs may become paramount over the children's needs.

On the other hand, she wants to have a good time, reevaluate her choices, rejoin the adult world, and live her own life. A deep, unspoken part of her may wish to abandon her children because they are, after all, living reminders of the marriage that failed. Although this wish is usually only a symbolic fantasy, she cannot help but feel how much easier it would be if they were not around, so that she might restore her wasted years. While she does not abandon her children, she does give them less talk, less play, less attention, and less protection. I've noticed that children of divorce have more serious accidents at this time — and this may be because there is less supervision in their lives or because they are distraught.

Fathers also experience a diminished capacity to parent and are pulled by powerful urges similar to mothers' — they are eager to stay close and embrace the children and eager to let go of them. Social attitudes favoring the mother's custody after divorce have tended to push many fathers into following the urge to let go and run away. At the ten-year mark, over two-thirds of the children in our study have poor relationships with their fathers, including fathers who were estranged and those who visited regularly. Only recently has society permitted and encouraged men to express their feelings for and strong attachment to their children. Now, instead of running away, more fathers than ever are experiencing the full range of the dilemma and facing the same internal conflicts as women. Fathers' help will surely be welcome because divorce places an extraordinary if not terrifying burden on mothers.

I have found that the quality of the mother-child relationship is the single most critical factor in determining how children feel about themselves in the postdivorce decade and how well they function in the various domains of their lives. As we have seen, mothers and their children are often closer in divorced than in nondivorced families. When the mother is psychologically stable and can maintain closeness and separation simultaneously, this relationship is very helpful to the child's development. When the mother is in poor shape, depressed or preoccupied, the same closeness can intrude on the child's development and cripple the child's capacity to move forward. When a mother can restore a nurturing, maternal relationship, her children blossom as a direct consequence. But when she cannot, her children suffer.

Unfortunately, many women in unhappy marriages assume that divorce will enable them to become happier, better mothers. But I find little evidence of that. Mothering does not improve by virtue of divorce. In only a few families did the mother-child relationship in the postdivorce family surpass the quality of the relationship in the failing marriage. As a matter of record, the opposite occurred more frequently. At the ten-year mark, over a third of the good mother-child relationships have deteriorated, with mothers emotionally or physically less available to their children. More than half of the good father-child relationships deteriorated over the same period. This erosion of parenting is a serious issue in divorce and one that merits wide attention.

*

In every well-functioning intact family countless conflicts get battled out on friendly turf. Parents and children line up on different sides of minor issues — how late the children stay out, how much television they watch, whose turn it is to do the dishes, and so forth — and on serious issues — whether the family should move to another city, what the proper values are in a given situation. And while family members agree on many things, no one is surprised when differences of opinion crop up. Fights erupt, tears may be shed, and feelings can be hurt in the normal course of family life. At the same time, the fighting is constrained by the bounds of family unity and mutual love. People get angry but then they kiss and make up.

In the divorced family, these constraints are broken. People get angry but they have lost the framework in which to kiss and make up. Instead, parents and children are dragged onto new, unfriendly turf where the fighting never seems to stop. More often than not, children are handed a hunting license by one parent to go out and take shots at the other. This phenomenon is so common that it hardly shocks us anymore, but it should. Parents shamelessly and openly coopt children as battle allies, with a nakedness of purpose that can only cause harm to all parties involved. Parents overburden children by casting them into a great many roles in these marital battles, ranging from that of audience to that of committed, fully positioned soldiers. The children range in their participation from astonished, frightened observers to, in some cases, a full force aligned with one parent against the other. Such anger-driven parent-child relationships are new to all parties involved.

When children willingly play an active role in the battle between parents, they see themselves as fighting to restore family unity, to right perceived wrongs, or to soothe the injured parent. They are driven by loyalty to the marriage that was or by a quixotic impulse to rescue the parent who is identified — sometimes mistakenly by the child — as the victim. Children may sometimes take the part of the parent who is not present, actively representing his or her interests. In this, the child becomes in his own mind guardian of the family honor, a gallant Horatio standing at the bridge. For example, waking up at 3:00 A.M. shortly after the marital separation, Karla saw a man's car parked outside her home. In tears the next morning, she said to her mother, "It's too soon. It's too soon. He's not my dad." She began staying up until morning to keep an eye on her mother and her mother's boyfriend to prevent them from going to bed together.

As we have seen in numerous cases in our study, when marriages break up, it is not uncommon for men and women who have never raised a hand to one another to engage in physical violence. Again, half the children in the study saw such violence; most were badly shaken by it and felt completely helpless to intervene either to control the violence or to protect one parent against the other.

Many children, especially from age nine into adolescence, join the battle themselves, either by engaging in activities that they do not personally condone or by accepting the accusations of a distressed parent. For example, Mary, who was eleven years old when her parents separated, was enraged to learn of her father's new girlfriend. Siding with her angry mother, Mary regularly listened in on the telephone arguments between her parents. She took the initiative in calling her father frequently to shout accusations at him, telling him that he was immoral and that he was letting his children starve. Mary denounced her father to neighbors, friends, and teachers at school, telling them all, "I hate my father!" By all accounts we heard, she and her father had been close before.

Some parents encourage their children, or a selected child, to provide information about the other parent's activities. They want to know about that parent's sex life, social activities, or financial condition. Children are requested or ordered to open bureau drawers in the other parent's house, to open closets, to search for signs that a lover has been present in the house, to report who was present during the visit, and to provide a wide range of information that has no practical use for the inquisitive parent. Children pressed into these espionage services are enjoined from telling the other parent about their activity, and they are debriefed after each visit.

And children cooperate with these requests. In fact, more than half of the eight-to-twelve-year-olds in our study regularly rendered such reports to one parent during the first year or more after divorce. Their motivations were rooted in pity and worry for the suffering parent, in fear of punishment if they denied the request, in a wish to keep the peace, in a need to placate the parent, in the child's sense of powerlessness to say no, and sometimes simply in the excitement of spying. These dynamics are especially evident in families where the children develop a united front against parental pressures. As often happens, one child breaks ranks. Then, in complying with the adult's requests, the spy is dubbed a "traitor" by the siblings.

When children are asked to carry messages back and forth between feuding parents, they generally find the task painful, burdensome, and humiliating. Even when the message itself is completely innocuous, they feel caught in an awkward role. They fear that the message might anger the receiver or that they might incur the wrath of the sender if they forget to deliver the message. Either way, they feel as if they can only lose. They are especially humiliated when asked to remind a parent to pay a tardy bill for child support. Both parents often seem totally oblivious to a child's utter misery at having to beg a parent to pay for a pair of trousers or dental work. Such requests are categorically different for children of divorce.

Rita, at age ten, wrote a school composition titled "What I Wish For the Most": "I wish that my mom and dad would get back together so that we could be a happy family. Or if they don't do this, I wish that they wouldn't fight about buying me clothes, like 'you get her pants' and 'you get her blouses.' I hate that!"

Sometimes parents and children join in a close, enduring alliance to do continual battle against the other parent. Although this happens in countless intact families in which people are unhappily married, the interactions take place behind closed doors. Divorce, however, flings those doors wide open, giving us an unprecedented opportunity to see these dynamics in full play. In divorced families these powerful alignments happen most often between the preadolescent child and the parent who opposed divorce. The adult is driven by a sense of moral outrage combined with boundless anger at having been cruelly exploited for so many years. For example, a woman who supported her husband through higher education, only to watch him leave for a younger woman, turns to her children as allies. Or a man whose wife takes a lover to cuckold him seeks his children's help to inflict punishment on the wife. The avowed agenda is to restore the marriage. The unspoken agenda is almost always revenge.

It is difficult to discuss these matters with the participants. Adults tend to deny their role, insisting that the children are acting on their own. One mother pressured her son to report the father's drug use to her attorney. Her goal, of course, was to nail the father legally as a drug abuser. When urged to stop using her son in this way, she denied her role in the mischief. "I'm a good Christian woman," she said. "I never get angry. But my son will never forgive or forget."

The children are equally protective of alignments. They speak like little adults, using language that is often stilted and moralistic. It is almost impossible to talk to them, for they strongly identify with the aggrieved parent and remain tight-lipped.

These alliances and shared identifications, forged in anger, are in one sense psychologically useful for both parent and child. It is lonely after divorce and the partnership fills a vacuum. Children fear abandonment after divorce and the alliance makes them feel safe and connected. By directing anger outward at the opposite parent, parent and child create a powerful antidote to intolerably painful feelings of rejection and helplessness. Moreover, they feel buoyed up by the heady feeling of power that the alliance with the parent brings with it. It is no accident that many children turn against a parent they earlier loved and cherished. Children feel better because they are able to create convenient, clear repositories of virtue and villainy.

Not surprisingly, though, our study indicates that children and adults who play these games are psychologically less stable than those who do not. Those youngsters who get caught up are the ones who seem most distressed and frightened at the time of separation. They feel vulnerable to parental blandishments. Some emotionally hungry children find the one parent's attention dazzling and irresistible. They enjoy their role in the alliance and are loyal, resourceful, and valuable in their capacity to carry out the parent's strategy. They can also inflict considerable psychological suffering on the parent under attack.

When Jan filed for divorce, her husband did not object until he heard that she had a boyfriend. Enraged, he began enlisting his children in an all-out assault against their mother. It lasted nearly a year. Under their father's coaching, the children — ages twelve, eleven, nine, and eight — called her a "whore acting like a teenager, wearing her skirts too short." The children yelled, "She has fallen. She doesn't care about her children." They insisted they wanted to stay with the father and would have nothing to do with the mother. Needless to say, Jan was astonished and heartsick. Eventually she was awarded custody of the children largely because her ex-husband was unable to sustain his claims in court. The children protested bitterly at the time, saying they did not want to live with their mother because she exerted a corrupt influence on their lives.

Five years later, we interviewed one of the girls, who had just turned sixteen. Looking back, she expressed profound appreciation of her mother's devotion, recognizing that her mother had raised the children single-handedly after many years of struggle and poverty. Like other children who participated in revenge-driven alliances, she also talked about her guilt and her shame at having turned against a parent whom she had known to be loving and trustworthy. The girl vividly recalled her alignment with her father, saying, "I don't want to make my dad sound rotten, but he was very persuasive. I'm really ashamed to tell you how my father brainwashed us. We were terrible to my mom. I'm still surprised that she was so willing to keep us after all that we said and did to her."

Medea

Kirk remembers hearing stories as a little boy about how his mother and father met on a romantic mountain trail. As outdoor enthusiasts and active Sierra Club members, his parents shared conservationist values, setting out to work for their beliefs. For many years, his mother worked as a lab technician to fully support her husband through a Ph.D. program in ecology and land management, telling friends that she loved wide open spaces because she herself had been born on crowded Taiwan. When her family emigrated to San Francisco, she said, she fell in love with the wilderness and with a man who would protect it for her.

Soon after Kirk's father earned his graduate degree, however, he demanded a divorce without warning, saying that he no longer loved his wife and that she should keep their three children. He was moving to Washington, D.C., he said, to begin a job at the Department of the Interior, where he would continue the valuable research he had been doing in graduate school. Kirk's mother was understandably outraged. She loved her husband, had paid for his education, and had worked hard for him. But when he no longer needed her, he cast her off. Although she eventually got back on her feet, she could never help but believe that he had exploited her intentionally. This thought consumed her night and day.

For years, this obsessed mother coached her children to say that they hated their father, that he was not welcome, that he was evil and mean. When he flew to San Francisco to visit them, they would not come to the door or answer his phone calls. Although their father kept up his child support payments, the children joined their mother in an alliance against him, saying whatever she told them to say. When Kirk was sixteen, he opted to live with his father for one year, but the two of them could not get along. The year was a bitter disappointment and whatever Kirk was looking for, he did not find.

At our ten-year interview, Kirk is a tall, good-looking eighteen-year-old who wears a bandana around his neck, cowboy style. With his half-Chinese, half-American background, he looks exotic in his western outfit and I think to myself that he must be popular with the girls. As soon as we begin talking, however, I realize that Kirk is a very troubled young man. More than any other teenager I have talked to at this follow-up, he seems reticent to talk about his family and is almost secretive about his relationships.

One of the first things he says confirms this view. Remembering our first meeting ten years ago, when he was eight, Kirk recalls that he wanted to disappear into the blocks so that I wouldn't ask him anything.

About his father, he says only that he was stunned when the divorce came along and is still confused by what happened. His mother told him that his father had turned his back on her and on all the children. "My mom is still recovering from the grudge she's had all these years," he says. "It's too bad that Mom has always been poor when Dad is well-off. She still gets carried away and I have to tell her, 'C'mon, Mom, let's not go back ten years again.'" Kirk says that he is very close to his mother but that he is not comfortable always attacking his father. "And I have to wonder if what she says is true. I remember I hurt my dad over and over again. He'd drive out from the city and then I'd tell him I changed my mind and wouldn't spend time with him. I think I did it to hurt my dad because Mom filled me with so many ideas that he was a bad person. I feel sorry about that now."

Kirk says his somewhat vague goal, if his father will help him, is to work on government land in some capacity. "My dad bugs me," he says finally. "He says I'm a know-it-all and just an average student, who can't even handle a full load at college. But I'm going to solve my problems without either of my parents."

It is at our fifteen-year interview, however, that the legacy of Kirk's childhood hits home. As we talk, Kirk begins to condemn his mother, blaming her for everything that has gone wrong in his life. His voice has a whiny, singsong quality that sounds very odd coming from a twenty-four-year-old man. His expression is sullen and at times he looks ready to cry. I am very disturbed by what I see.

He begins our interview by saying, "My mom taught me how to lie. She did a real number on me, kept telling me that Dad had abandoned us, but I was too little to understand what really happened." I have rarely seen a grown child turn so vehemently on a parent.

"Kirk, what really happened?"

"I drove my dad away. I lied to him. Mom told me I didn't want to see him and I did what she said." Kirk folds his arms tightly across his abdomen, as if in pain.

I ask gently, "Have you talked with your mom about any of this?"

"My mom loves me a lot," he says, "and my dad never comes to help when I get into trouble. I've been in a lot of trouble all my life and she's there for me." Then Kirk repeats, several times, "My dad loves me, my mom loves me. They both love me." This young man speaks in an almost hopeless, childlike tone. "They both love me. But all my life I've been wanting to show my dad that I didn't mean to drive him away. My dad thinks of me as a black sheep."

"And what do you think?"

"I probably am a black sheep," he says. "But I'm waiting, waiting forever, for my dad to say to me, 'Life is hard, Kirk, we all make mistakes. You have my support and I believe you're going to make it.' But he never says that. He says, 'You're in big trouble, you're a bum.' He doesn't say, 'I love you.' He doesn't say, 'I forgive you.'"

"And what if he never says any of these?"

But Kirk doesn't hear my question and cannot consider its meaning. He is completely caught up in the fantasy that his father will forgive him for what he regards as his heinous crime, of having been his mother's henchman in driving him away with lies. Kirk has a threadbare, depressed, sad quality about him and exudes the sense that he has been depreciated and corrupted.

His mother, who has symbolically destroyed much of her son's spirit, today regrets her actions. "If I knew then what I know now," she tells me at our fifteen-year interview, "I would not have taught him to lie, and I wouldn't have lied to him."

Ironically, her strategy of using the son to avenge her, whether or not it was based on the mother's accurate perception that she had been ruthlessly used and then discarded by the father, fails in every way. Kirk is haunted by guilt for having driven his father away and by shame at having done his mother's bidding. He is preoccupied by the need to be forgiven for crimes that his father is probably unaware of. Kirk's longing for his father has been reinforced by all the years of coached lying. His strong dependence on his mother is almost unmodified by his adolescence. He remains tied to her by his many years of obedience to her wishes, by the dependence that has been fostered in their alliance against the father, and by his continued anger at her. It is as if there is no distinction between past and present. Both are fused as he stands at young adulthood feeling ill equipped, morally and emotionally, to move forward.

There are many children like Kirk who are burdened by a pernicious and persistent anger between their parents. Rooted in feelings of betrayal, exploitation, rage, revenge, and sexual jealousy, this is the kind of anger depicted in the classical Greek myth of Medea, who in modern times can be either a man or a woman.

Widely known for her witchcraft, Medea betrays her father and homeland for Jason, who is searching for the Golden Fleece. Medea helps Jason in his quest and then travels to his country, where they are married and she bears his two children. With time, however, Jason rejects his wife for a younger woman. Medea is enraged as she feels exploited and betrayed by the man for whom she betrayed her own father and country. Her anger has no bounds; she feels that there is no course of action that can save her pride and no course that can rescue her from humiliation. Carried away by a psychotic rage, Medea murders her children.

Surely this is one of the most heinous acts imaginable. And yet the power of her anger is such that, although the story is horrible, it is comprehensible and plausible to the audience. We understand that Medea has few choices. She cannot kill Jason because he is too powerful. She must not kill herself because that would remove Jason's dilemma. Her psychotic killing of her children is based on the rational perception that the only way she can hurt Jason now is through his children, and she destroys them despite the fact that, as the Greeks tell us, she was a good mother. The children come to her willingly, and she embraces them before murdering them. In killing her children, Medea destroys the symbols of the marriage, and in so doing she symbolically destroys herself. Medea did not want to kill her children; she wanted to destroy Jason. Likewise, modern Medeas do not want to kill their children, but they do want revenge on their former wives or husbands — and they exact it by destroying the relationship between the other parent and the child. In so doing, they severely damage and sometimes destroy the child's psyche as well.

The myth captures the powerful feelings that many people have at the time of divorce, specifically the kind of anger that does not change over time and that is based on a sense of being profoundly hurt, rejected, abandoned, betrayed, and outraged to the core of one's being.

Medea-like anger spills into American courtrooms every day as people litigate over issues of who gets, controls, or pays for children after the divorce. Although such battles do not murder the children outright, I have seen a great deal of evidence that Medea-like anger severely injures children at every age. An estimated 10 to 12 percent of divorcing families engage in protracted and bitter litigation over children. Judges and attorneys are amazed at the enormity of the passions played out before them, for which no part of their law school curriculum ever prepared them.

Whether one or both parents act the Medea role, children are affected for years to come. Some grow up with warped consciences, having learned how to manipulate people as the result of their parents' behavior. Some grow up with enormous rage, having understood that they were used as weapons. Some grow up guilty, with low self-esteem and recurrent depression, while others desperately wish to rescue a parent and feel anguish when they realize they cannot. Many acquire disdain for both parents. All of Medea's modern-day children sense that no one has any real regard for their needs; they know that they have become extensions of their parents' anger. Kirk tragically shows many of these features.

The Medea syndrome has its beginnings in the failing marriage and separation, when parents sometimes lose sight of the fact that their children have separate needs. At this time, a mother or father can begin to think of the child as being an extension of the self. The thoughts "he left me" and "he left me and my child" become synonymous, until the lines separating parent and child are blurred. A parent's natural empathy for the child's separateness is eroded by the injury of divorce. When the pattern is long-lasting, we find Medea-like relationships.

A child may be used as an agent of revenge against the other parent, as in Kirk's case, or the anger can lead to child stealing. An estimated one hundred thousand children each year are abducted by one parent, primarily to hurt the other parent. There is no evidence that parents who kidnap their children are good or loving parents or that their act is based on a genuine wish to rescue the child. Few children who have been restored to their homes after being kidnapped by a Medea-like father or mother appear better off; more often they are in terrible shape — abused, neglected, and poorly raised.

Most parents who steal children do so not out of love but for their own selfish needs. Such parents, having sustained a succession of unmourned losses in their lives, cannot abide another loss, and hence cannot yield or share the child. They rationalize, "If my child is not with me at all times, I have sustained another loss and the only way to undo this loss is to fight for the child or, if necessary, steal the child." Disputes rooted in such beliefs are not likely to diminish because a judge makes a ruling.

Court-ordered visiting can also be entangled with Medea-like rage. A woman betrayed by her husband is deeply opposed to the fact that her children must visit him every other weekend. Her jealousy of the husband's new lover can also include the child in its orbit, and she may be jealous because the father comes to visit the child and not to see her. She cannot stop the visits, but she can plant seeds of doubt — "Do not trust your father" — in the children's minds and thus punish her ex-husband via the children. She does this consciously or unconsciously, casting the seeds of doubt by the way she acts and the questions she asks. For example, she may ask her daughter, in a worried tone, "Where will you sleep at your father's house? What kind of nightgown will you wear?" The daughter senses her mother's anxiety and, especially if she is a young adolescent, may get frightened over suggestions of potential sexual abuse. Fathers in similar circumstances make use of techniques congenial to them, often conveying to the boy or girl that the mother is depraved and dangerous.

In some families, parents become so angry that they can't stand to be in the same room with one another. The rage goes both ways. The mother's behavior conveys to the child the sense that "your father is a dangerous man." Some fathers who have had close, loving relationships with their children before divorce suddenly find themselves cut off, distrusted, and accused of sexual molestation. In turn, they feel enraged as their own self-esteem is attacked. The father's behavior then conveys the sense that "your mother is out of control, crazy." The mother feels destroyed.

The irony is that, like Medea and Jason, many of the parents who do this to their children can function adequately or even well in other aspects of their lives. They appear rational, intelligent, well educated, and well dressed in court. It is only in this one area that they are as mad as Medea, for it is a form of madness that drives their behaviors.

Linda's parents were both strong, handsome people from Swedish backgrounds, which they parlayed into the workplace: Her mother worked as a Swedish masseuse at the Fairmont Hotel in San Francisco; her father was a chef at a Scandinavian restaurant. When they divorced, Linda's mother said she would be killed by or she would kill her husband, and she meant it. The end came amid guns and threats.

When we first saw Linda she was a sweet five-year-old child who clearly felt that she was her father's favorite. Indeed, she was the only person in the family he never hit. Preoccupied with being good and helping to calm both parents, Linda opposed the divorce because she knew it would take her daddy away from her. As it turned out, she also lost her mother who, soon after the divorce, drowned her sorrows in schnapps and sex, a combination that left little time for mothering.

A year after the divorce, Linda was getting herself dressed, making her own meals, and putting herself to bed. A teacher noticed the dark circles under Linda's eyes and asked why she looked so tired. "We have a new baby at home," explained Linda. "Every night we have to get up to take care of the baby." The teacher believed the story until, very worried about Linda, she visited the household and discovered there was no baby. Linda's story was designed to explain her own fatigue and enabled her to fantasize endlessly about a caring, loving mother — the kind of mother Linda wanted.

Linda's father moved to Minneapolis not long after this episode to work in another restaurant. When we saw her four years later, she pulled out a packet of tear-stained letters from her father. Evidently, he sent one or two a year, and these were Linda's treasures. She explained how much she thought about him, how concerned she was that she hadn't seen him, and how worried she was that he might get in trouble. Knowing her father had the kind of temper that could land him in a serious fix, she behaved as if she were the parent and he the child who had left home.

"I always knew he was okay if he drew pictures on the letters," she said. "The last two really worried me because he stopped drawing. I thought something was wrong. You know, I've always worried about my dad. I never knew when he was in trouble. I know he's real violent. And I always worry about his hurting other people."

"Did you worry about his hurting you?"

"No. I knew he wouldn't hurt me."

Linda is one of the few children in our study who was literally deserted. She knows which city her father lives in, but he stopped writing letters when she was ten.

Now fifteen years old, Linda describes how she has taken care of her mother for the past ten years. "I felt it was my responsibility to make sure that Mom was okay," she says. "She was drinking a lot. So I would go out with her or I would stay home with her instead of playing or going to school. I tried to stay close. When she got mad, I'd let her take it out on me instead of breaking something in the apartment."

"How did she take it out on you?"

"She'd hit me or scream. It scared me more when she screamed. I'd rather be hit. She always seemed so much bigger when she screamed. Once Mom got drunk and passed out on the street. I knew I had to get her home so I called my brothers, but they hung up. So I did it. I've done a lot of things I've never told anyone."

In such families with two troubled parents, divorce does little to help the children — unless at least one of the adults uses his or her second chance to improve the family's circumstances and resume parenting the children. Divorce for Linda was no improvement over her previous situation. Abandoned by her father, she gave up much of her life to become her mother's keeper. Although her family structure collapsed when she was five, Linda held on to the semblance of a normal childhood for several years, keeping up her schoolwork, making friends, and taking responsibility for an alcoholic mother, trying to absorb her mother's aggression in ways wise beyond her years, and willingly accepting the role of target. Despite a total lack of parenting, after divorce she was sweet, caring, and compassionate.

Linda's story exemplifies a situation in which the child is present but the parents are absent, in body or spirit. While this pattern is familiar in war-torn or impoverished societies, it is a fast-growing phenomenon in middle-class America. In our study, about 10 percent of the children had poor relationships with both parents during the marriage. This number jumped to a shocking 35 percent of children at the ten-year mark. These children were essentially unparented in the postdivorce decade, and in fact many of them were called upon to take care of their parents.

I have seen many children, from toddlers to adolescents, who are rearing themselves. While we are more familiar with this pattern in teenagers (like Becky, the "throwaway" girl who took to the streets), it affects all ages. Small children come home to empty houses, make their own supper, put themselves to bed, get themselves up in the morning — or fail to do so. Jimmy, age six, taped a slightly mis-spelled sign at the foot of his bed: "Go to sleep, Jimmy. Don't be afraid." Studies show that children from divorced families have more school absences than children from nondivorced families. Kin-dergarteners being raised by single parents show significantly lower academic and social readiness at school, regardless of socioeconomic status.

For some children, their early fears that divorce will lead to a par-entless world are realized. Bobbie was ten when her parents sepa-rated. Both were successful businesspeople who took good care of her before the divorce. A few years after the divorce, though, Bob-bie's mother went to New Orleans for nine months to live with her lover. Bobbie refused to move in with her father, believing that if she stayed in her mother's house, her mother would be sure to return. As a result, Bobbie lived alone in a large house, without adult super-vision, playing video games, eating candy bars, getting herself to school much of the time, and coming home every day to watch tele-vision alone. When we found her in this situation, Bobbie was clini-cally depressed and painfully lonely and was having great difficulty in distinguishing reality from her vivid fantasy life. Her parents had completely failed to protect her.

When their parents divorce, many young children are afraid that both parents will abandon them. The logic is simple. If one parent can leave, why can't the other? After a time, of course, most children realize that they are not completely abandoned. But others are not protected. One mother in our study abruptly sent her "naughty" ad-olescent son one thousand miles away to live with his father. Although the boy had not lived with his dad in eight years, the mother simply sent a telegram: "Jack is coming."

Some children feel that they do not have a home of their own after divorce. One mother locked her thirteen-year-old son out of the house. She left a note: "Go live with your father." But the child had not lived with his father in seven years. In turn, the father refused to accept the boy because he was "not comfortable" raising a child. In despair, the youngster turned to a distant relative who had once said, "If someone were to drop him on my doorstep, I would not refuse him." This is what happened, but the arrangement lasted only one year, whereupon other temporary arrangements for his care were improvised.

Other youngsters after divorce feel that there is no one in charge, no adult to make or enforce rules, no one to insist on proper conduct, and, perhaps most of all, no one to take over in an emergency. This sense that no one was in charge in their lives comes up repeatedly in our ten-year follow-up interviews. Children speak of empty homes, of needing adult guidance in protecting them from their own impulses, and of having too much responsibility for themselves and for younger children. Harry, who at sixteen had dropped out of school and had been in trouble with the law, explains that he has a friend who also dropped out of school, but *his* dad had made him go right back.

Ethan was sixteen when his younger sister was seriously hurt and needed to be taken to a nearby hospital. Frantically he telephoned his mother and father, each of whom worked nearby. Each parent told him, "You drive her to the emergency room." In despair, Ethan cried that he could not legally sign the child in; he was too young. But this moved neither parent to come to the aid of their two frightened children. Both parents had been reasonably responsible during their marriage, but their commitments had changed.

Gail's father, a politician, drank heavily and took his seven-year-old daughter to adult parties, including political meetings, and made the child his constant companion. When they arrived at parties well past midnight, Gail was placed on any available empty bed. When her father was feeling lonely, Gail was kept home from school. When her father wanted to stay up late watching television, Gail was kept awake to keep him company. Gail occasionally shared her father's bed when he needed someone to hold, and she was ordered out of it when her father brought home a female companion. At times, she became her father's drinking companion and, on several occasions, suffered hangovers.

Gail, in turn, devoted all her attention to her father, withdrawing from her interests in school and from her friends. She advised her father whom to date, what to wear, and sometimes how to make decisions about political affairs. To the extent that Gail was called upon to serve her father's pleasure and needs, it is accurate to think of her as a concubine — even though I do not suspect that there was any sexual involvement between them.

The last time I saw Gail, she was twelve, although I could hardly believe it. She looked much older, almost as if she were moving into adulthood rather than adolescence. She gave the impression of someone who has seen and heard too much, ever wary and careful in talking about herself and very circumspect in discussing her father. It was only in prompting her to talk about a "nameless friend" that I was able to get a glimpse of her inner world. She told me about a girl who feels "weird," an "oddball who has no friends" and worries that other people are not going to like her. She talked about how this child has to rely on herself and how hard it is to tell what is real from what is fantasy.

At the end of our time together, she allowed herself to speak more directly: "Divorce is hard, because it messes up people's lives and nobody helps children," she said. "When people divorce, one person gets a normal life and the other person gets trouble."

A quarter of the mothers and a fifth of the fathers have not gotten their lives back on track a full ten years after the divorce. They are chronically disorganized and, unable to meet the challenges of being a parent, they lean very heavily on their children. Simply put, the child's role is to ward off the serious depression that threatens the parent's psychological functioning and to keep the parent from feeling that he or she is coming apart.

The result for the child is continued suffering and serious derailment of his or her psychological development. The situation causes severe disturbances of the parent-child relationship, with long-term deleterious effects. Like battered and sexually abused children, overburdened children are found in every social class, and their predicament is not temporary. It affects their entire growing up and certainly their attitudes as young adults toward themselves and toward the adult world. Since most children live with their mothers after divorce, women overburden their children more often than men. But men who are awarded custody of their children or who visit their children regularly may also make similar demands. Several children in our study who were visited several times weekly by their fathers over the ten-year period fell into this role of maintaining the psychological functioning of a man who was intensely dependent on them.

These are not role reversals, as some people have claimed. The child does not take on the role of parent. Rather, these new roles played by the children of divorce are complex and unfamiliar. They merit our careful examination, for they affect many youngsters in our society.

Children who end up playing these roles are often those who naturally feel a great deal of empathy. They pity the adults around them and are frightened about losing their parents. Feeling vulnerable, they tend to yield to the parent's wishes and threats. Their sensitivity becomes their undoing, as they assume multiple roles to support the parent's neurotic needs, often over many years.

Children can, and do, provide the needy parent with a magical looking glass in which flaws, wrinkles, and cracks are erased. Paradoxically, and tragically for their development, young children have an extraordinary capacity to fulfill this role. They are able to bolster a parent's self-esteem, to assure the parent that he or she is a good person, to grant indulgences, to forgive.

Unfortunately for the overburdened child, the price is very high. Under the facade of her competency, for example, Gail was preoccupied with fears of abandonment and she suffered night terrors, chronic constipation, social isolation, and poor learning. Because her role in life was to stave off her father's psychological problems, she had no permission to be a separate person with her own identity and feelings. Many such youngsters are under the terrifying impression that their ministrations and their very presence are keeping their parents alive. Within this fantasy, the children alternate between feeling pleasure and excitement at their own power and despair at their own helplessness. To survive, they often become profoundly defensive and emotionally constricted. Or they become adept at manipulating the vulnerability of others to their own ends. They feel separate from their peers — as Gail says, "weird, an oddball who has no friends." They feel less fortunate and are envious of others. As time goes on, these youngsters have trouble sorting out reality. Although they are keen observers, they do not necessarily make accurate sense of what they observe. The empathy they show to a troubled parent does not necessarily extend to others.

In truth, few children can really rescue a troubled parent. Many become angry at being trapped by the parent's demands, at being robbed of their separate identity and denied their childhood. And they are saddened, sometimes beyond repair, at seeing so few of their own needs gratified.

PART 4

New Ties
and
Old Ties

13

Rosemary and Bob Catalano

MARRIED AT EIGHTEEN and divorced at twenty-four, Rosemary Catalano packed a wallop of experiences into her young adulthood years. When I saw her after the divorce, she came straight to the point.

"It was a bad marriage from the start," she said. "I was too young. If I hadn't been pregnant I'd be in a different place today."

"How bad was it?"

"Within two months it was bad. He didn't like the way I kept house, but I had no interest in it. I'd never kept a home. Hell, I'd never been in a Safeway before. I was not the most cooperative teenager. If we had any extra money, Bob would go out and buy another camera lens. I hated cameras. Still do."

"Did pregnancy and childbirth complicate things?"

Rosemary hooted. "There was nothing more to complicate. It was already complicated. That marriage could have been knocked over with a feather."

"Was there physical violence?" I asked, wanting to know what the children, Billy and Kelly, might have witnessed. "I know how excitable you and Bob can get."

"Yes," said Rosemary. "But only a few times. We got so disgusted at ourselves for being so animalistic. It didn't happen often, but we both did it. Look, I was a kid. And a pretty wild kid. You might say we were both pretty self-centered." Rosemary punctuated her speech with dramatic gestures. "We tried everything. The counseling lasted six months, and it helped me, but not our marriage. The last few months of our marriage, Dr. Wallerstein, we were ready mentally and physically to kill each other. We agreed to separate, to see if we would miss each other, and he did miss me, wanted to come back. He promised to overlook all my faults. Ha! We tried for five months. That was it. He still doesn't want to divorce, but I need it. I've got no choice. I have to get on with my life. I feel like I've wasted six years."

Rosemary and Bob were separated for nearly two years before she pressed for the divorce. I asked about their relationship now.

"His visits are haphazard," she said, "like, now and then. He comes a half-hour once or twice a week. He stops by in the driveway where the kids go out to talk to him, and then, when they're all excited about seeing him, he drives off, just like that" — Rosemary snapped her fingers — "and they stand there crying their heads off. But he does send payments, regularly and on time. I know it's not easy for him. As for me," she said, "I've started to change things. I'm going to college full-time to get a degree in business administration. I'm pretty good at that. Bob is right that I'm a lousy housekeeper, but I have a head for figures. I hated high school, but I like school now. I guess you could say I was hardly in high school enough to know what it was like."

"You've changed since then?"

"Man, have I ever." She laughed. "Nothing makes you change so much as being home with two small kids and a husband who never stops nagging, telling you you're good for nothing. I don't know about other women, but I feel a fire being lit under me."

There was nothing gradual about the changes in Rosemary. I asked her how she managed going to college and taking care of the children.

"It's a terrible scene," she admitted. "I rage at them, they rage at me. 'Uptight' understates it. I scream, they cry, sometimes I cry. I have them in school full-time, just like me, only they hate it. Billy cries all the time. He doesn't like it, doesn't let me hug him. He tells me that he loves me but always from across the room. The truth is, the kids have lost their dad and mom. I should also tell you, my problem with Billy is that he's too much like Bob. Maybe that's why it's easier for me to spend time with Kelly. My parents help out. They like the kids, but they're too far away to pitch in every day. So it's mainly me and the kids. I'm determined to get my degree. I've changed and matured a lot since the separation.

"I've been thrown into a cold, cruel world," Rosemary went on. "I am determined to swim and not sink. Now I'm at school, I got a part-time job, I got a divorce, I got me and my kids. But I've learned a lot. I never worked for anything before. I never had any responsibility. I never had to think before I acted. I do now."

Rosemary wished that her former husband would be more helpful. "All he does is criticize me. He says I'm lagging, that I'm not policing the kids enough. He still berates me in front of them. He even makes me feel like a kid. He still picks on me about housekeeping. *Pigsty* is his favorite word. But now I don't have to count on him except for the money he sends. It's not enough, but we need it desperately."

One year later, Rosemary was transformed. She had lost twenty-five pounds, had cut her dark hair into a short bob, was stylishly dressed in a white linen suit and black patent leather pumps, and walked with a determined step. She was direct and spontaneous in that appealing manner of hers. I made a note: a personable and attractive young woman.

Rosemary was still studying for her degree in business while working part-time in an office. She had been living with a new boyfriend for six months and they were planning to be married. "It's a great thing," she said. "I can't believe it. I mean, I thought I'd never meet a guy I could love, live with, and still want to marry. It's not only good for me, it's great for my kids. Charlie loves them."

I asked her to tell me about him.

"He's ten years older than me and he's never been married. He owns a tree nursery that's doing real good. At last I'm going to get some financial security. We won't be affluent, but I've sure joined a different world when it comes to money. That end of the month freak-out won't happen."

"How do Billy and Kelly feel about Charlie?"

"I think they like him very much, but I hope that a stronger bond develops on both sides. Kelly climbs into his lap and curls his mustache. Charlie really tries to be nice to the kids. When we first started dating, he always brought them little toys to play with after the babysitter came. They liked that. And sometimes we'd all go out for ice cream sundaes. We do less of that now, but the kids like having Charlie around the house. He's not the kind of man who likes to rough-house with them. It's more that he likes to teach them things. He said he's going to teach them horticulture when they're older. I really hope it works out. Billy needs a man. He daydreams a lot. Sometimes

I think he's out in left field. If I had the time, I'd worry about him a lot."

Rosemary was reminded of her husband. "My ex stops by one afternoon every two weeks. He's real involved with another woman. But the kids still get very excited when he visits, and they still cry when he drives off. They beg him to stay longer. We aren't very civil to each other. He doesn't pay me alimony anymore, and he wouldn't have to pay child support if he'd let Charlie adopt the kids. But Bob doesn't go for that. He's got too much pride."

Life was looking up for Rosemary. She was happy and optimistic, enjoyed her schoolwork, and was talking to employers about job possibilities. With improved self-esteem, she looked back at her adolescence and first marriage as an unhappy rite of passage. But it was not an experience that threw a shadow over her life.

Five years later, Rosemary still looked great and had been married to Charlie for two years. "We have a good, sound relationship," she said. "But he puts up with a lot from me. Probably more than I do with him."

Rosemary had suffered a brief depression a year into the marriage. She found a therapist and was treated for three or four months. As she understood it, the therapy had to do "with becoming an adult. It helped me a lot. I feel fine."

Rosemary finished school and opened a fresh pasta shop with a woman associate. "It's taking a lot of my time," she said, "but we own the business. I can set my own hours and be my own boss. We may open a second store early next year if things keep going this good."

Bob reduced his child care payments to $65 a month per child. "I got mad," said Rosemary. "But then he doesn't have as much money as we do. What annoys me the most is how little he sees the kids. I really can't believe it. I know his new wife doesn't like it when Bob spends time over here. And she doesn't like it when he takes Billy and Kelly over to their house. I don't think she likes my kids. But I don't think Bob understands what he's doing to them. I guess he never understands how terrible it is for them, how much grief they have, when he pulls out of the driveway. In the past six weeks he's come over twice and stayed ten minutes each time. The kids are out there hanging all over him. He's so cold to them."

I remembered Bob telling me a few years earlier that he got "all soft inside" when he was around his children, that he comforted himself with the thought that "at least they know I love them."

"He treats them like little dogs," said Rosemary. "He can't relate to them. They feel ignored and hurt real bad." The only bright spot seemed to be Billy's shared interest in photography. Bob had bought his son a special camera for Christmas.

I asked how the children got along with their stepfather.

"Well," she said, "what the kids wish for is an honest-to-goodness, start-from-scratch daddy. But they don't get that from Charlie or Bob. They like him okay, but the truth is, Judy, there's no love. We stopped spanking the kids because of what my therapist told me, and I try not to yell at them. I'm not as good at that as I should be. I guess the big problem is that we're still a new couple. We need privacy. We go into the bedroom and close the door in the evenings, but sometimes I think we should be down in the living room, as one family. But this is the only time we have to be together. We try to go away weekends, and we try to have the honeymoon that other people get. But it's hard with the kids around all the time. Maybe that explains part of my depression. I felt torn in two directions, and I didn't know what to do. What I got out of the therapy is a more realistic recognition that life is not perfect. You can't please everyone. Charlie is a good man, a responsible man. He treats Kelly differently than he treats Billy. He's tough on Billy and much more affectionate and forgiving with Kelly. I don't know if that's because she's a girl — she sure knows how to twist him around her little finger — or because she's so little. I'm a much better housekeeper for Charlie and I'm a hell of a cook. He likes me to dress in nice clothes. And I like to look nice for him."

Ten years. Rosemary comes into my office bearing the aura of success. She is thirty-five and co-owner of three successful fresh pasta and Italian specialty stores. Most of her profits are plowed back into her business. Rosemary, it seems, is a smart businesswoman. She says Charlie and the children are all in excellent health. They just bought a cabin at Lake Tahoe for snow skiing in winter and water skiing in summer.

Getting down to problems, Rosemary says, "My main concern is Billy. He's almost fifteen and he's just not trying in school. I know he can do better work, but he doesn't seem to want to try. Maybe I should get him some counseling."

Rosemary fidgets with her purse for a moment and goes on, "Billy still loves photography and has his own darkroom. He doesn't have many friends, and I suspect he's starting to drink. Kelly, on the other hand, is doing well at school. She's into everything that twelve-year-olds like — rock stars, TV, telephone calls, and animals.

"I'm not worried about Kelly," says Rosemary. "Charlie is concerned about the way she's dressing and won't let her use makeup. He doesn't like it. But I hope he doesn't make too much of a fuss. Kelly's pretty stubborn."

I ask about her relationship with Bob.

"It's gotten better," she says. "It used to be more bitter. I was amazed at how angry I'd get just to see his car in the driveway and how long that anger lasted. I think Charlie helped me. He said I couldn't let my anger get in the way, for the sake of the kids. He let me use him as a sounding board. I was really burned up about those visits. It's been ten years but I'm getting used to the way Bob is. It's funny. The kids still adore him. To them, he's some kind of hero. Kelly spent a weekend with him recently. She talked like she'd gone to see Jesus Christ. It was the first weekend she's ever spent with him. As far as Billy is concerned, Bob can do no wrong." She pauses. "You know, every now and then I think he's really screwed up his life. I feel bad about his second divorce.

"I'm still not crazy about Billy's relationship with Charlie," she continues. "I think it's better, but I'm not sure. I think they worked out an arrangement. But I'd be telling you a lie if I said there was real affection or friendship between them. There's no question that Charlie gets along better with Kelly. Always has. She makes it easy to love her. Sometimes she and Charlie share a joke. She's real interested in plants and is learning a lot about horticulture. Who knows? Maybe she'll inherit his business. Anyway, Charlie still comes down pretty hard on Billy. He has a tendency to make snap decisions and then stands by them. I think he tries very hard but he demands a lot of chores. He has strict ideas about how teenage boys should work. Billy feels the demands made on him are unfair."

"Would you have wanted anything differently, Rosemary?"

"I wish I would have been in a better place," she says. "I have a tendency to pick up loose guilt that lies around. In the beginning I was into myself and my situation when I was married to Bob. I was really afraid because I'd never been on my own. I delayed getting a divorce because I was afraid, and he had this unending sense of obligation, that we should stay in the marriage for the sake of the kids. I was very me-oriented in that marriage and I was very angry at him. But it was the best thing that ever happened to me, to get that divorce. I grew up. I learned I won't ever have to be afraid again. If for some unknown reason something happens to Charlie or our marriage, I wouldn't fall apart. I know I could handle it."

I ask if she has any concerns about this second marriage.

"Not really," she says. "Except that I wish he wouldn't be so hard-nosed with the kids, especially with Billy. I wish he could be more sensitive. I wish he'd listen more and weigh what they say. All they want is attention and love. It wasn't easy for Charlie to take on two children."

"Was the divorce good for the children, in retrospect?"

"As difficult as it's been for them," she says, weighing her words, "yes, it was a good thing. You can survive anything as long as you know people care about you and love you. I know the kids know that Charlie and I care about them. They care about us. My parents are behind us. I think I put the kids through an awful lot as I drag them through my life, but I think they're neat. I credit Charlie for a lot of it. I'm proud of them."

"You have very good reason to be proud of *you*, Rosemary."

"I think we're all survivors," she says.

Rosemary is a winner in the decade after divorce. From being a discontented, sullen teenager caught in a marriage that was unsatisfactory from the start, she has grown into a mature, confident, and responsible person who is proud of her accomplishments, and rightly so. Nothing has been easy for Rosemary; her life course took many zigs and zags. For the first couple of years after divorce, she ran from college campus to schoolyard to babysitter to job to home and around the course again. She has told me that she felt overwhelmed and depressed by all these demands and that the first two years of her second marriage were strained by tensions between her children and new husband. Nevertheless, Rosemary comes out on top after ten years. She is married to a man whom she respects and likes; their sex life is good, and she fully expects the marriage to continue happily. With all her achievements, Rosemary remains a committed mother, tempering her earlier impulsive outbursts at the children with her greater maturity. She remains concerned that her second husband is not playing the hoped-for role in her son's life, and she is disappointed and angry with Bob for what she regards as his poor relationship with the children. At the same time, however, she feels concern and compassion for him, recognizing his attempts to keep up his economic obligations to the family. At age thirty-five, she is a clear-eyed, competent, energetic person for whom the first marriage was a sorry rite of passage and for whom divorce was a wise and mature decision. That whole period in her life is a closed chapter, except for continuing concerns over her children in relation to her first and second husbands. Rosemary is an entirely different person.

As a group, women who divorce while still in their twenties or early thirties are significantly happier and better off financially a decade later than women who divorce in their late thirties or over forty. Many younger women are literally energized by divorce, throwing themselves into backbreaking routines designed to make the best use of their second chances.

Divorce brings many changes and new challenges for these young women. They move households, find jobs, go back to school part-time, pay their share of debts carried over from the marriage, and usually take full responsibility for their young children. Few in our study are helped by their families. Since the youngest children of divorce show the most symptoms at the outset — crying, refusing to go to bed, waking up at night, bedwetting, night terrors, and so on — younger women are exhausted by the demands made on them. When they rise successfully to these challenges, they inevitably grow. For those like Rosemary who marry right out of school, divorce provides their first opportunity to live independently. Such women may never have had full responsibility for themselves, much less for an entire family. Then they suddenly become head of the household, making a full spectrum of decisions, including where to live, which schools to attend, how to budget their finances, and so on. Even if they shared in such decision making before divorce, the task of doing it all alone is a new ballgame.

Single parenting involves different responsibilities and skills than does parenting as part of an intact couple. There is no one to lean on when times are rough. The parent who raises children alone must be able to live with a great deal of day-to-day anxiety. He or she must take a stand and hold to it, without backup, often in the face of vociferous opposition. He or she must be responsible for children when they are sick, injured, or emotionally upset. Remarriage also makes new demands on women who are single parents. They must decide who will discipline the children — the natural father, the stepfather, herself alone? All of these decisions regarding children represent growth-promoting challenges to women after divorce.

The internal pressures young women face are equally daunting. Divorce offers a second chance to rectify a major mistake in their lives — which usually was to marry impulsively, before they were ready. Many of the younger women in our study got married on the spur of the moment; one recalls saying to her boyfriend, "Hey, it's my birthday, let's get married!" Others, like Rosemary, married because of an unplanned pregnancy. She thought, "Why not?" The more adult response would have been "Why?"

Married before age twenty-one and divorced five or six years later, most of the younger women in our study wanted to recapture their lost years and choices, to get on with life and grow up immediately. Leaving a marriage is easier for them than for older women; they are anxious to shed their role in the marriage, and by the time of separation or divorce they have detached themselves from the relationship and from identities within it. There is little depression with divorce for them because the depression occurred within the marriage. While they may be very angry at their husbands, they do not have an intense sense of betrayal or outrage at divorce; they do not mourn the loss so deeply, for they have not sacrificed the best years of their lives. Some feel a bittersweet compassion for their ex-husbands, an anger tinged by sadness that the relationship didn't make it.

Most of all, young women feel a powerful drive to catch up, to compress their second chances into a brief period of time. Those who succeed look, talk, and act differently in the years after divorce, becoming new people with new careers, new images, new lives. In working hard, they develop a new sense of confidence and self-esteem and are proud of their achievements and independence. Divorce helps them grow up, set realistic goals, and achieve them. At the same time, some end up feeling that they have sacrificed their children and the gratifications of mothering to the heavy pressures of building a career and social life.

Because they are younger, these women tend to have less trouble finding eligible men to date or take as friends. Seventy percent of our study remarried, usually within the first four years after divorce.

When this happens, they face yet another major reorganization of their lives, adapting to another new household, routines, values, and expectations. In other words, a new marriage rarely subtracts from the complexities of their lives; it adds new problems and stresses along with satisfactions and stabilities.

Through all this, children often feel pushed to the periphery. Rosemary acknowledges that she neglected her children in the first few years after divorce. She also admits that her parenting dipped at the time of the remarriage and that she later took Charlie's side in many family disagreements. Younger mothers do not mean to neglect their children, but often, inevitably, the children suffer — they feel rejected at the time of the divorce, during the hectic years that follow, and again at the time of the remarriage. In trying to rescue themselves, these mothers mean to rescue the children. It is no surprise that Rosemary, even with all her energy, feels overwhelmed and gets depressed.

Obviously, not all young women attempt, or are able, to reorganize and establish their lives as successfully as Rosemary. Some marry impulsively for a second and a third time. Some define their second chances in a more limited way, specifically to escape stress in the first marriage. Whereas Rosemary used divorce as a springboard for change in every part of her life, others were overwhelmed and immobilized. Others go quickly into second marriages, more out of the need for economic security than for love. Another group put marriage on a back burner, investing all their energies in advancing their careers and enjoying an active social life.

Bob Catalano married Rosemary, a girl from his hometown of Fresno, when he was twenty-one. Rosemary had just finished high school when Bob went out of town for summer session at junior college. She called him after two weeks to tell him she was pregnant.

Both are from closely knit Italian families and, given their background, there was only one choice. "I liked the idea of being a father and husband," said Bob. "We got hitched right away."

Six years later, Bob was in my office discussing why his marriage broke up. He was tall and good-looking, with black curly hair and an aquiline nose. Yet underneath his appealing exterior, I could sense an inner core of sensitivity coupled with self-doubt. I asked him when things started going downhill.

"Well, I'm not much for words," he said, launching into a lengthy monologue. "We fought from the beginning. I would jump all over her when I came home from work, but she didn't understand about the house. I'm not an ultra-fanatic. But I wasn't raised in a chicken coop. She never pulled her share of the work." Bob's young face seemed open, honest. "Now, I admit I wasn't always the best. And she was only eighteen when we got married, so it was probably a mistake. We really didn't have time to get to know each other. We were too busy worrying about food and a roof over our heads. I got a job repairing TVs at Meyerson's TV and radio shop in town. Some nights I was real exhausted when I got home, and it just didn't seem fair. A man's home is supposed to be his castle. And a woman should keep it neat and clean for him. Rosemary didn't take care of herself or the house. When I got home, her hair was a mess. She's a real pretty girl, but she looks like hell. Our sex life went down the tubes." He sounded worn out. "Anyway, we separated. I wasn't thinking of divorce. I have a lot of good feelings for her. Divorce isn't something we do easily in my family. My folks didn't approve of the marriage, but they sure don't approve of the divorce, especially with the two kids."

"Then it's really very sad for you."

"Very sad. If I were a man of words I could tell you. But seeing the kids and leaving — it breaks my heart."

"Tell me about your children."

"My boy, Billy, is like me. He's sensitive like me. And he's slow like me. I get mad at him, and I don't want to. I get mad at him a lot sooner than I get mad at Kelly. And she's the terrible two-year-old. Billy is five."

"What makes you get mad at Billy?"

"When he asks me a lot of questions," said Bob, "something happens inside me."

"What could that be?"

Bob stopped to think. He obviously had a real capacity for reflection and concern for his children, and he identified strongly with Billy. "When he asks questions," said Bob, "it feels to me that maybe he's insecure. I think he's going to be hurt. I say to myself, 'Damn it, it's a cold, cruel world, and Billy had better learn to cope with it.'"

"You want to protect Billy," I said, noting that Bob used the same metaphor as his wife did in describing herself. "You want so much for him to make it."

Bob put his head on my desk and was quiet for several seconds.

As he looked up he said, "Do you know what it's like for a man to lose his son?"

"Does the divorce mean you have to lose your son?" I asked. "Can you imagine, in your mind, that you might continue to be the father that you want to be?"

He shook his head. "Rosemary is twenty-four. She used to be a real pretty girl. There are going to be other men. One of them is going to be in my shoes. What chances do I have?"

"I understand what you're saying about Rosemary," I said. "But does that also have to include the children?"

Bob shook his head in a gesture of surrender.

We talked briefly about little Kelly. "I don't know her all that well," said Bob. "But she sure is independent. Stubborn and smart."

I thought to myself, This contrasts oddly with the boy. He seems to think the girl is stronger.

"Kelly treats me like a stranger," he continued, "even though I see her a lot. She was never a cuddler. I took care of her a lot even during the separation. I'd come over and see how she changed."

I asked Bob about his work and he said, "I like what I do, but I still want to get a college degree. I quit when we got married. But I want to better myself. My dad learned electronics in the navy — he worked radar out of the Presidio military base in San Francisco — and taught me most of what I know. Someday I'd like to do more than fix broken TVs, but for now the work is okay. It doesn't pay the best, but it's good work. One of my problems is getting along with people. I'm on a short fuse. But I'm thinking about it and working on what I should do. I moonlight on the side, you know. I'm a pretty good tile setter. I get a lot of odd jobs. Sometimes I work through the weekends."

"That doesn't give you much time for visiting your children," I noted.

He smiled and said, "If I give her two hundred twenty-five dollars and I have to live, I don't have much time or money for anything else. I could give her less, and no one would touch me. My buddy told me that. But then I'd be up at night worrying about the kids getting enough to eat." Bob spoke movingly about his wife. "I asked her to give it another try. This will surprise you, Dr. Wallerstein. But my attorney told me to go to her and beg her to let me back. Because divorce costs too much. I did that. But she said no. I think she knew better than me that we just can't make it. She's right. She'd be the right wife for the right guy. I can't give her what she needs. I can't change enough to accept what she does. But I know she has suffered. She's up against it. She's bitten off more than she can chew in getting the divorce, running the family, and going back to school. She'll sink or swim. I just hope she makes it. We're uptight with each other. Every time we talk, we bang heads. We wanted to be friendly after the divorce but it hasn't worked."

I was very moved by this young man, by his sense of the "cold" world in which one "sinks or swims." I was also concerned about his economic burdens and the emotional cost of starting over. Bob seemed ill equipped to reestablish his life and all too ready to relinquish his fatherhood role. The most mature aspect of this young man seemed to be the strong feelings he had for his children.

One year later Bob had acquired a girlfriend with two boys, and they were planning to get married. Still working in a television repair center, Bob was disappointed that he had not received a hoped-for promotion to assistant manager. After catching up on his life, I asked him about his children.

"I see them on and off," said Bob. "We don't have any set schedule. Nothing is fixed. I guess it's every couple of weeks."

"What happened?"

"We've just grown further apart," he answered. "It could be closer." He seemed upset. "Look, I'll be honest. I've let myself grow away. Rosemary's new guy is their dad. He's doing a pretty good job. The kids don't seem to miss me that much."

"How does that feel for you?"

"I've accepted the fact that I won't be their full-time father. I've got my own life now. It's just a new ballgame. If they're happy and she's happy, that's what counts. If she could be as happy as I've been these last three months, it'd be nice."

Bob seemed detached from his children. In truth, it was harder and harder for him to maintain interest in having a direct influence on them, in imprinting his ideas on them about how to behave and how the world works. With some intensity, he held on to the comforting thought that as long as he loved his children, they would turn out all right, yet at the same time he seemed relieved to have his responsibilities taken over by another man. He was sad about it but the sadness was buried. Sensing this, I asked, "How hard is it for you to visit?"

He didn't answer. Then, "I don't like to think about that." Finally he said, "Kelly really slays me. She's such a charmer."

"And Billy?"

He looked down, and said, "I guess Billy needs me."

Five years after the divorce, Bob came a considerable distance to my office, despite his busy schedule. Remarried and struggling to make ends meet, he worked three jobs — television repairman, tile setter, and tree trimmer. "I do all the *T*-jobs," he said jokingly. Except for a much shorter haircut, he looked the same. By his own account, Bob was bogged down and depressed in his second marriage. While he paid regular child support to Rosemary, it was done at considerable sacrifice to himself and his new family. Much of the friction between Bob and his second wife stemmed from money matters. "I love her very much," said Bob. "She's a terrific painter and one of these days her work is really going to take off. In fact, she was mentioned in the *Pacific Sun* last week. But we've got our problems," he said, lowering his voice. "It's real hard. To be a dad to her children, especially. Maybe I overplay it as disciplinarian. I just can't keep my temper when they get obnoxious. You know, my dad never would have taken that guff. But my wife and I have always agreed. The older boy was in with a bad crowd. I had to try to straighten him out."

Bob's stepsons were almost teenagers by now. I thought it must be difficult for him, at thirty-two, to relate to adolescent boys as a father. He certainly would not want them to repeat his somewhat wild adolescence. Maybe he was bending over backward to keep them in line. I suggested this gently, but Bob was quickly on the defensive. I thought to myself it would be easy for him to antagonize them.

When I asked about his own children, he said, "I don't know, Judy. I'm ashamed to tell you, I haven't seen them, even though I live only a few blocks away. I haven't taken the time to see them. But I doubt that they miss me. They're in a good situation with Rosemary's remarriage. Maybe you should talk to her. Tell me what she says. There are still bad vibes between us."

He went on to talk about the conflict in his second marriage. "It sticks in her craw — all this money I pay out for my kids. The main thing is, she feels that every time Rosemary snaps her fingers, I jump. It's too much." He shook his head sadly. "It's too much strain about the money, too much strain about the children, too much stress. Maybe if I lived far away it would be okay."

As he said this, he became very sad, and I felt that only his pride kept him from breaking into sobs. "Look, Judy," he said. "I'm so ashamed. I see my kids only five or ten minutes every couple of weeks. I got my own marriage. I got my own life. I want to do what's right. I've got to make choices." Our interview ended on a note of his utter helplessness to change what was wrong in his life.

Ten years after his divorce from Rosemary, Bob is living in southern California. Now in his late thirties and gray at the temples, he is still a very good-looking man. The outdoor climate seems to agree with him, although he chain-smokes unfiltered Camels. As Bob welcomes me into his sparsely furnished apartment, a Verdi opera is playing in the background. An opera buff, Bob tells me that he saw Pavarotti sing last month and still feels "high from the experience." We chat about opera for a while before getting into the many changes in Bob's life over the last five years. His second marriage failed and he felt he needed a major change, so he quit his job and moved south to pursue his long-time interest in photography. Bob is studying under a well-known teacher while working as a salesman in a Radio Shack store.

"I gave up all my job seniority at the repair center and went back to something I've always wanted," he says with boyish enthusiasm. "You know, I always messed around with photography. I just bottomed out on my two marriages and was afraid for a while I was going to bottom out on everything. I had to get a job immediately down here, to keep up with the payments to Rosemary." He glances around the nearly empty apartment to emphasize the truth of his statement. "It's a funny thing. I haven't seen my kids hardly, even during my marriage to Oona. But it's funny, Judy. I still care about Rosemary, but I wouldn't want us to get back together or anything. I still care about my kids a lot, even though I hardly see them. Actually I only did things with them when it was convenient or when the mood struck me. Rosemary gave me a lot of heat about those drop-in visits." He pulls on a cigarette. "To tell you the God's honest truth, I don't think I ever once went down to take them anywhere. The only thing was that Billy likes photography like me. I could talk to him about shutter speeds and f-stops, and every now and then I'd lay a few rolls of film on him. I could feel badly about not seeing them enough, about not seeing them at all these days because I'm so far away. But what is, is. I've been pretty inconsistent over the last ten years — sporadic, you might say. I comfort myself by telling myself they don't need me much, but Rosemary would rip that to shreds, I know. I hope they know their dad loves them and would do anything for them if they asked. I'm probably not going to do anything different than I have." He laughs halfheartedly. "Their dad is still chasing rainbows."

"What are the rainbows, Bob?"

"Coming here was part of it," he says. "I'm earning so little it's ridiculous, but I'm managing. At least I'm doing something for the first time that I like. Though I don't think it's got a future. I guess I'm just kidding myself."

Bob's plans for his future are loose. "I may move to Hawaii," he says. "I wish I knew what to do. Most guys my age know what they want. Me, I keep starting over."

I was shaken by what I learned from Bob and other young men like him in our study. Of all the subgroups, I expected that younger men would have the best chance to undo their mistakes, establish better second marriages, lay the foundations for a new start on life, and find fresh opportunities to set out on careers.

Quite the reverse is true. Ten years later, most of the men who divorced while in their twenties are seriously derailed. Forty percent are struggling financially. During the preceding five years, nearly half lost ground economically.

Following their first divorce, every one of the young men in the study remarried, half of them within one to two years. Ten years later, nine in ten of these second marriages have failed. Half of the younger men have been unable to establish stable careers, and as a group they are less successful than the other men in our study. Many have not arrived at an integrated view of themselves as competent people and instead seem sad, bewildered, and unfocused, as if saying, "Look at me, I'm a failure."

Their record of child support is dismal. Seventy percent pay irregular and partial child support or none at all. In many cases, these fathers have second families to support and jobs that don't pay enough to meet all their economic and moral obligations, but that does not explain all the failure to pay.

Their stories have elements in common. All married very young and their children were born soon afterward, when they were barely into their twenties. In most cases, the divorce was initiated by their wives. The women often say that their husbands were childish, that they had surpassed their husbands in maturity, that they wanted a different kind of relationship with an economically and emotionally stable, more mature man. The younger men, as a group, also fought valiantly to make their second marriages work, but most failed.

Divorce does not free these young men and promote a developmental spurt as it does in many young women. On the contrary, divorce seems to exert a negative influence on their self-confidence and their subsequent psychological, social, and economic development, impeding their ability to develop goals, careers, relationships, and even important aspects of their identities as adult men. What could account for such a difference between young men and young women?

One possible explanation is that the third decade of life holds particular importance in a young man's adult development. Until his thirties, a young man is in many respects less mature, less formed, than his female counterpart. Young women come to grips far earlier with issues of relationships and intimacy. Since childhood they have been preparing themselves, unconsciously, for marriage and parenthood. Young men prepare for these same roles in a different way. According to psychologist Daniel J. Levinson, they formulate "a dream" when they are between the ages of twenty-two and twenty-eight that projects a tentative life structure, including a vision of themselves in the world.[1] Much of the dream involves choosing an occupation — which for males in our society is a wellspring of identity, pride, and self-esteem. Along with choosing a realistic occupation, the young man puts together a realistic image of himself as a husband and a father. Unfortunately, as our study tragically shows, these images are still fragile while men are in their twenties and may be vulnerable to disruption within a failing marriage and divorce.

Psychologically, the men face another disadvantage. Many newly divorced young men are unable to build comfortable homes for themselves, to create their own lives in a self-designed space. Some move from apartment to apartment, desperately seeking something. The instability of their place of residence is mirrored in the instability of their relationships. Unlike the older men, they date many women, leading active social and sexual lives. But unlike their older counterparts, they tend not to establish stable live-in relationships or stable marriages, despite the availability of many women.

The younger men in our study have fewer supports than the women, are not joiners, do not have a close group of male friends, and are not involved in community activities. In general, their chief social network is based on male peers, girlfriends, and their weakening ties to their children and former wives. These relationships are not enough to undo a chronic, gnawing sense of loneliness, of which they speak poignantly.

"Sometimes it scares me that I could go through my whole life without committing to anyone or anything," says a thirty-three-year-old man who has lived alone for three years. "My drinking buddies are great, but if the right woman came along, I'd share my life with her in an instant."

The visiting relationship can be frustrating and difficult, especially for men who did not welcome the divorce. One of the saddest consequences of divorce is that the visiting father does not have the kind of relationship with his children that encourages and promotes his continuing pleasure as a parent and his pride and competence in this important role. In our study, every family but one was headed by a woman at the outset of divorce. The only man to raise his two small children single-handedly developed great maturity and sensitivity in a very short time. He was, in fact, the fastest learner we have ever seen in communicating with his children. When he first came to us, he was confused about how to soothe the fears of his boy and girl, ages two and three and a half, who had been frightened by an earthquake and thought that their mother had been swallowed up. He learned to say, "Daddy is going to stay with you. Daddy will put you to bed. Daddy will be here in the morning." He took the children to visit their mother, to show them that she was safe. When the children improved rapidly, this young father was elated. In the years that followed, he raised his children as a single parent, giving them every bit as much love and nurturing as any woman. His children adore him.

Ten years after divorce, one-fifth of the fathers in our study have children living with them. In several instances, the children speak proudly of how they have influenced their fathers and how important their fathers are to them. Most young fathers in our study — those in their mid to late thirties at the ten-year mark — have not had sole or shared custody of their children at any point in the ten years, nor have they wished to have it. Instead, they visit with their children and their images of themselves as fathers are seriously impaired. They feel that they are no longer centrally important to their children's lives and, more than any other group of fathers, seem unable to maintain relationships with them. At the decade mark, all but one of these men have children under age sixteen, yet they visit them much less frequently than do older fathers. In a pattern established early after the divorce, three-fourths see their young children only two times a year or not at all — they seem to have divorced their children as well as their spouses. But divorced young men need their children more than they seem to know. Bob longs for his children but feels usurped by Rosemary's second husband. He says, "My children don't need me anymore." With his fragile identity as father and husband, Bob is vulnerable to displacement by the person who is, in his view, the "real man." Intimidated by the psychological stresses attached to visiting his children, he is also overcome by financial burdens in the postdivorce period. He feels unimportant, not needed, and unloved as a father and a husband.

Fatherhood is, in part, a challenge to take up adult responsibilities. With divorce, many young men turn away from that challenge. As fathers in an intact family, they could be expected to grow and mature, but without the family structure, many are less able to grow up. Several of the young men are aware of this problem, speaking vaguely and abstractly about their love for their children. Bob repeatedly says, "I hope that they know I love them, even though I don't see them." Some young men never seem to regain their footing — they lose direction, feel alienated, and have a diminished sense of mission in life. They feel weighed down by economic responsibilities they cannot carry and morally guilty about not being able to do so.

In a final sad note, we find that these men are most likely to take the blame for their failed marriages. Of all groups, they are least angry at their former wives ten years later and many speak of them with respect and affection, as former sweethearts. "It's a funny thing," says Bob. "I still care about Rosemary, but I wouldn't want us to get back together or anything." It is as if an important chapter in the lives of these young men came to an untimely end and, unfortunately, they were not able to use the experience for psychological growth. Instead, their marriages remain unhappy memories associated with nostalgia and lost opportunity.

Remarriage

Nothing restores adult self-esteem and happiness after divorce as quickly and as thoroughly as a love affair or a successful second marriage. No matter how badly the men and women in our study were burned by their first marriages, not one turned his or her back on the possibility of a new relationship. All who could do so actively sought a new mate.

More than two-thirds of the men and a little over half of the women in this study remarried during the decade. Those who managed to make these second marriages work — and many did not — felt that their divorces were worthwhile and that the quality of their lives had vastly improved. Those who remained single throughout the decade — 50 percent of the women and 30 percent of the men — say they are lonely and would welcome a second marriage but have not had the opportunity.

Although folklore has it that people are fated to make the same mistakes in their second marriages, most of those in our study did not. With a few exceptions, women who had left abusive husbands did not marry wife-beaters the second time around. By and large, those who had been divorced from alcoholics avoided new partners who drank heavily. Men who had left sexually inhibited women found new wives who were more responsive. It was less true, however, that women who had been married to men who were unfaithful were able to avoid infidelity in their second marriages.

Men and women say that they looked for different kinds of people in their second marriages. Women seek men who are more stable, economically dependable, and affectionate. They often turned out to be divorced men with children, who were a decade or so older than the women. Sex is openly acknowledged as important to the marriage, while economic security is an unspoken but undoubtedly significant consideration. Saying that they have willingly made concessions in these second marriages and generally consider them "good enough," the women do not try to change their husbands into something they are not, and they are willing to meet them more than halfway. It is very important to them to make these marriages work; the thought of a second divorce is intolerable to most.

Since the women in our study bring children into their second marriages, they carry their share of the workload. Most work outside the home and assume the major responsibility for housework and child-rearing. The women state clearly that they do not want to make too many demands on their second husbands. If the needs of the children and the second husband come into conflict, many women tacitly admit that they take the husband's side. Some women, to save their second marriages, sent their children to live with the fathers.

As a group, men remarried more quickly than the women. They, too, were eager to make their second marriages work, and many found women who were more flexible and more accommodating to their needs than their first wives. Sex was an important, openly discussed issue. Many men married women they had been involved with during the marriage. Several married much younger women who eventually insisted on having children of their own. Although the men initially objected to this, most eventually went along, becoming fathers again in their forties and fifties. Indeed, in general they enjoyed the role and grew very attached to their new children.

In what may be a widespread social phenomenon, we are also finding that many divorced men and women choose to live together rather than to marry a second time. Ten percent of the men and women in our study are in long-term cohabitation relationships. Outspoken about their motives, some men say that having come through an unhappy divorce, they never want to marry again. They resent paying alimony and feel that their first wives are punishing them financially. One man tells me that "marriage kills love." Some women say that they are afraid to remarry because the institution itself might destroy the relationship. Jenny, for instance, continues to live with Max by choice. She had her name legally changed to his last name, but there is no marriage certificate. "We look at our friends as examples," she says, "and we see many living together who then get married and end up getting divorced six months later. When this happened to one of our best friends, we asked what happened. She said that they stopped trying to please each other." Jenny looks sage as she adds, "We're more married than most couples. We talk out our problems and give each other space and freedom. We've given each other a real commitment."

In interviews, we learn that it is usually one of the partners in a long-term cohabitation who does not want marriage. The other often does but is powerless to force the issue.

When second marriages fail, men and women are devastated and often sink into severe depression. "I've always thought I should work hard and live for the other person," says one man. "Now I'm trying to learn to be more selfish. It's not easy to live for myself these days." As he describes how his house and yard have deteriorated since his second wife left, I can't help thinking he is really talking about his inner self. "I can't rejuvenate it," he says, "can't replace anything. It was a showplace when my second wife lived there."

"What happened to her? What ended the marriage?"

"In my first marriage, I wasn't sure who was to blame. But in the second marriage I turned every rock, tried everything." It is clear that his wife sought the divorce. "With my first wife I was so confused that by the time we split up I didn't care. But this second time has taken everything out of me. I can't seem to get back on my feet. The first divorce was a physical relocation, with loss of property, an empire destroyed. I hardly see the kids anymore. But my second divorce was total emotional destruction. In both I had financial losses, but the second time around I was oblivious to them. In the first divorce, I was angry and worried about my children. In the second, I'm sorry for what could have been."

"You feel regret?"

"No, my dear," he says. "Just sorrow."

Half of the men in our study who remarried were divorced a second time. It is an astounding failure rate, with serious implications for the men involved. In most instances, the second wives asked for divorce. There was no evidence that any of these marriages failed because of the man's attachment to his former wife. The men tell us that they worked hard to make their second marriages work, yet they failed. A quarter of remarried women in our study also experienced a second divorce, often prompted by conflict over adolescent children, his or hers. Considering how both men and women suffered after their first marriages broke up, the number of second divorces is startling. The consequences of two divorces are inevitably traumatic. But when men and women — especially later in life — are twice rejected, the emotional blow is enough to make them feel as if their lives are over. They feel that life holds no more chances.

14

Billy Catalano

SONS AND FATHERS

WHEN BOB CATALANO moved out, five-year-old Billy went to his room, shut the door, pulled down the shades, and refused to come out for three days except to eat and use the bathroom.

When we first saw Billy at our center, he did not explore the colorful playroom like most children did but rather sat in one corner, near the dollhouse, repeating the same play. Time and again he carefully put the mother and father doll into a toy bed together and took them out. He seemed to take no pleasure in the game and would not smile. When I asked him the questions I ask other children — what is going on in your family, can you tell me about the divorce, what do you understand about it — he was too sad to talk. Anytime I mentioned his father, especially what the two of them did together, Billy looked out the window. Finally it was too much; he burst into tears.

When Billy did eventually talk, he spoke of broken images. He showed me a spot on his finger and said, "I bleed here." He talked about broken toys, broken furniture, broken fingernails, and bleeding. His dog was sick and the cat in trouble. Everything he said evoked a landscape littered with casualties and wounds. By all clinical standards, this was a depressed child.

At the five-year interview, Billy was a handsome nine-year-old with black curly hair who looked remarkably like his father. Before he came, Rosemary had told me, "Billy is doing better in school, has some friends, especially in the scouts, and one reason he seems happier is that Bob is coming over more often. The only trouble is that Bob tends to pull into the driveway and stays only ten minutes. The kids hang all over him and then cry when he leaves." Nevertheless, she said, "Billy thinks his father can do no wrong."

Billy fidgeted in his chair as he talked about his stepfather, Charlie, who was too strict, his love of photography, his Cub Scout troop, his teacher, and his sister. He answered my questions in a cooperative, economical way — he was a child clearly aiming to please — until I asked about his father. Suddenly Billy grew vague and disconnected, as if we had entered an entirely different realm. This was something that Billy had a hard time thinking about, much less talking about. He lapsed into silence, which gave way to a full thirty-five minutes of uncontrollable sobbing. All I had asked him was "How much are you seeing your dad?"

When I see him again five years later, Billy is tall and muscular — a "hunk" to his female peers. According to his mother, he is getting low grades and is not trying hard in school.

Remembering his earlier sorrow, I approach the subject of his father with trepidation and decide to begin by asking him about photography, an interest shared by father and son.

"I love photography. Cameras turn me on," he says happily. "I want to base my life on photography. My dad is going to work as a photographer full-time someday."

I then venture, "How often do you see your father now that he's moved to Los Angeles?"

Billy's face clouds over, but this time he is able to go on. "Dad is squeezed for time," he says. "When I found out he was moving, I didn't say anything, I just walked up to my room." Tears well in his eyes and Billy never recovers his composure for the rest of our conversation this day. "I'm sorry," he says. "I get so emotional."

"Have you thought about living with your father?"

"Yeah, well, I told Mom I wanted to and she said, 'Go ahead and ask him.' Then when I went down there, I realized she's right. There's no way, no stability there. He lives alone in one room and eats out most of the time."

"How do you get along with your mom?"

Billy shakes his head as if it is not the easiest topic. "It's fine most of the time. Sometimes we yell, but" — he shrugs — "that's family living, I guess." Billy says he is expected to do most of the heavy chores. Little sister Kelly "gets away with murder. She's pretty close to my mom, and Charlie likes her the best. I feel kind of farther out."

Billy says he mostly talks to his friend Justin, who also loves taking pictures. Justin's parents recently got a divorce "and he didn't even tell me," Billy exclaims. "I read it in the newspaper, for crying out loud." But Billy says that his friend is lucky. "He gets to see his father two to four times a week. He's not having any problems."

I ask Billy to describe his girlfriend.

"She's quiet," he says, "your stereotype of sweet and quiet but friendly when you get to know her. I've had lots of girlfriends but this one is the longest." He got caught cheating on her last summer — "fooling around with someone else" — but all is now forgiven. "I got off the hook that time," he says laughing.

I ask about drugs.

Billy says, "I'm not into drugs or anything. I've never tried a drug. Is alcohol a drug? I've been loaded a few times. Well, I have tried grass too." I begin to get a very different picture. Billy tells how his mother caught him smoking pot last year. "She was mad. I was also cutting school that day and I really caught it. Now I only smoke at parties. But at the beginning of school this year, me and some others would toke up before school started. I know that was wrong. It was making me so weird. I couldn't think." The binge lasted three weeks. Billy says he does not use cocaine. But alcohol? "I like that. I still do that all the time. I like to feel totally relaxed. This summer I went overboard drinking Seagram's. This was the best summer I've had. All my friends were there. I don't drink to get out of problems. I just relax and feel good. I can never sleep, so alcohol feels good."

Billy has a job at a local camera shop where he is learning film developing techniques from the store owner. But when his grades began to slide even lower than before, Charlie insisted he quit. Billy was mad but acquiesced. He says his relationship with Charlie is not too good. "We argue a lot. It's up and down. Mostly down. He never admits he's wrong about anything. He never backs down." Rosemary sometimes steps in and takes Billy's side, but not often. "I can't count on her," he says.

Billy says he thinks his mother and stepfather get along pretty well. Does he ever worry about their getting a divorce? "Well, I do," he says. "But I don't think they would." When I ask why he thinks that, tears well up in his eyes once again. "I just don't want to go through that again."

I ask why he thinks his parents divorced.

"I don't know. I suppose they couldn't get along."

He nods tearfully when I say he has lost something. "What would you like to change if you could?"

"I'd like to trying living with my dad," he answers. "I don't know if it would work. Just starting over."

"Starting over from where?"

"From the beginning."

"From six or seven years old?"

"No, Judy, from before I was born."

New Family Forms

The divorced and remarried family is not a leftover or warmed-over version of the intact family. It is a new family form, and each family is distinct, with a different history, starting at different points in the life cycle of each family member and having different turning points, stresses, and implications for the psychological development of men, women, and children.

As long as the intact family is held up as the primary model for parent-child interactions, we won't be able to decipher the distinctly different interactions within divorced families. There is no counterpart in the intact family for the visiting parent relationship or the joint custody relationship. Nor is the two-career couple, with the mother rushing off to work each morning, the same as the single-parent family. As we have seen, when a marriage ends, parents and children are cast into new, unfamiliar roles that may be in sharp contrast to those they played before the separation and divorce.

We need to look at these new family forms and relationships with fresh eyes if we are to understand their specific qualities and master their intricacies. Only then can we move psychological and social theory ahead to accommodate the reality around us. When we began our study in 1971, psychological theory had led us to expect certain continuities in the years after divorce. For example, we thought that core parent-child relationships would survive and that a parent's emotional investment in a child would not change. If a parent was loving and concerned during marriage, we believed, the love and concern would endure the vicissitudes of the postdivorce years. Good parents would continue to be good parents, no matter what their marital status.

But experience is teaching us otherwise. The entire patterning of psychological needs, wishes, and expectations between parents and children is radically modified by the breakdown of marriage and the process of divorce. Parent-child relationships are caught up in a web of angers, and children's needs are put on hold as parents struggle to rebuild their own lives. We have seen loving fathers turn their backs on very young children and watched loving, competent mothers grow to neglect their children. We have seen children track their parents' every move with the gnawing question "Do you love me?" and adolescents anguish over issues of closeness and separateness as they struggle to leave home. Parent-child relationships are permanently altered by divorce in ways that our society has not anticipated.

Adults and children navigate through divorce and later enter new families with a greater sense of anxiety and apprehensiveness about the reliability of human relationships. They bring to the new families a sense of having been aggrieved, of having lost out on a first and critical step. Parents and children are more vulnerable to failure, more needy of success and approval.

In a reasonably happy intact family, the child gravitates first to one parent and then to the other, using a combination of skills and attributes from each in climbing the developmental ladder. With access to both parents, children intuitively create their own recipes for growing up based on a rich mixture of what they value and respect. The parents complement one another, so that when one is unavailable, the other steps in to meet the child's needs.

In a divorced family, these parental resources are greatly diminished; relationships that are taken for granted in the intact family seem more fragile, less permanent, and less reliable. The problem for children of divorce is that it is so much harder to find the needed parent at needed times. The little boy entering elementary school may have a father who lives three hundred miles away. The adolescent girl who turns to her father may find that, without her mother present, greater closeness to her father seems frighteningly erotic. When children are in important developmental transitions and cannot make use of the parent they need, their recipes for growing up are missing essential ingredients.

As Billy and Bob Catalano demonstrate, the new relationship between visiting father and visited son may be rife with misunderstanding and disappointment on both sides. Amazing as it may seem, developmental psychology has only recently become aware of the vital role that fathers play in the lives of their children. For many years, child psychology was preoccupied with the mother-child relationship, as if fathers were secondary figures whose primary role psychologically was to help their sons consolidate a sexual identity.

Our research is part of a growing body of knowledge that puts this lopsided view of child development back into perspective. Fathers exert a critical influence on their sons and daughters throughout childhood and adolescence, helping to shape their characters, values, relationships with other people, and career choices. Divorced fathers continue to exert such influences — in what they do and don't do, both in the reality and in the fantasies that children weave around them — even though they may move away, take a new wife, or visit their children infrequently. Exactly how their influence differs from that of fathers who remain at home or from stepfathers, we have not known, and that is part of what we're learning from this ten-year study. Children do not dismiss their fathers just because there has been a divorce. Indeed, it is the children of divorce who taught us very early that to be separated from their father was intolerable. The poignancy of their reactions is astounding, especially among the six-, seven-, and eight-year-olds. They cry for their daddies — be they good, bad, or indifferent daddies. I have been deeply struck by the distress children of every age suffer at losing their fathers.

Whether living three blocks away and visiting regularly or absent and visiting erratically, fathers remain a significant psychological presence in the lives of children after divorce. The father is part of the child's emotional life, a factor in the child's self-esteem, self-image, aspirations, and relationships with the opposite sex. In our study, only one child — who was an infant at the time of divorce, whose mother remarried soon thereafter, and who had no contact with her father — fully substituted her stepfather for her father, and even she talked about getting to know her real father during adolescence. Most children do not give up on their biological fathers, even if they are ne'er-do-wells who have abandoned them without a backward glance. As we saw with Carl Patton, children turn around and construct a credible image of the father they never knew from any scraps of information that they can collect and tend to idealize him in the process.

Few people realize how difficult it is to transplant the father-child relationship from the rich soil of family life to the impoverished ground of the visiting relationship. At its core, the visiting relationship is ambiguous and therefore stressful. What *is* the visiting father's role? Lacking a clear definition of his responsibility and authority, he often feels unneeded and cut off from day-to-day issues that are embodied in the intact father-child relationship. The pattern of visiting is established at the most trying time for all, within the first year after divorce, so that visits are crammed into "convenient" time slots, punctuated by frequent leave-taking, at a time when feelings about divorce are running high. Children encounter new adults in the father's home and no one knows how to act. Adults and children are thrust into new social roles unsupported by social convention, generating a changing mix of frustration, anxiety, and gratification.

Courts assume that any father who loves his children will visit them. Mothers and children assume the same. These assumptions completely fail to appreciate how hard it is to retain the subtle, multifaceted father-child relationship after the family has come apart. People do not understand how vulnerable the visiting relationship is to the passions of the divorce and the father's complex feelings. Men like Bob Catalano, who desperately love their children, can fail to visit; although they want to remain close and committed, they may also want to escape the painful feelings associated with the failed marriage. Each visit may ignite lingering hurt, anger, shame, loss, pain, guilt, and nostalgia. For many men, the urge to take flight is irresistible. For Bob, the situation is more than he can stand, and he solves it by visiting on the run. He pulls into the driveway and stays for ten minutes. The result for his children is emotional havoc.

Visits require frequent separations that can lead to depression and sorrow in men who love their children. As they watch their children grow up, seeing them every so often, men may feel a terrible guilt over having left them — and visits only seem to emphasize the discontinuity of the relationship. The father realizes, with each visit, that he is not part of the children's lives. He feels both sorrow and relief at having been replaced by another man.

The logistics of the visiting relationship are extremely complicated. Where to take the children? What to do every other Sunday with a ten-year-old and a three-year-old? Intact families do not plan every outing in advance but do many things together spontaneously. The visiting relationship, on the other hand, is often transformed into a recreational relationship. Fathers take children to zoos, ballgames, video arcades, and other places of amusement in lieu of more complex, personal interactions. The visiting father does not, unless he makes a special effort to find out, know when his child's next term paper is due, which math problems are giving the child trouble, or whose turn it is to drive home from school next Thursday. Unlike fathers who live with their children full-time, the visiting father is removed from the daily flow of routines and is not involved in a rich mixture of parenting functions.

People have the illusion that the visiting relationship is often sabotaged by jealous wives. But we did not see a lot of that in our study; only a few men did not visit their children because they were consistently blocked by their former wives. Some children are occasionally coached by angry mothers to lie or refuse to visit, and in one family the children were forbidden to mention their father's name, as if he no longer existed. But almost half of the women saw real value in visits and encouraged their ex-husbands to continue them.

In any case, as time goes on, the mother's influence about visiting tends to diminish steeply. As everyone gets used to the visiting and as the children grow up, mothers intervene less. Ten years after divorce, visiting is no longer related to the mother's feelings; a growing number of children take full responsibility for visiting arrangements.

Within an ideal intact family, parents grow psychologically as their children grow. As each youngster reaches a new developmental stage, the parents respond appropriately to that child, expanding their own perceptions and understanding and drawing on their memories, resources, and backgrounds in different ways. Each tries, in conjunction with the other parent, to arrive at solutions that are uniquely tailored to the needs of each child and that are in harmony with his or her own values.

A father outside the family structure has a much narrower arena in which to maneuver. Deprived of day-to-day, year-to-year, and stage-to-stage contact with his children, he has less understanding of his children and of himself. The fully interactive parenting role is cut off as a wellspring of psychological growth. At the same time, the visiting father may not keep up with developmental changes in his children and may therefore behave inappropriately. One of the fathers in our study, before his divorce, held his four-year-old daughter in his lap at the dinner table. He continued this practice years later when she was eight, although it was certainly not in tune with her developmental changes. The stepmother realized the inappropriateness of his behavior but felt constrained to say anything, lest it be taken as an attempt to drive a wedge between her husband and his child. Many stepmothers who are visited do not feel comfortable in taking on the woman's historic and sometimes critical role of interpreting developmental changes in children. The father thus loses important input from the female point of view and is therefore more likely to continue inappropriate behavior.

Although a national study tells us a very large number of children are not visited by their fathers — 40 percent in one national study[1] — most of the children in our study were visited on a fairly regular basis. More than a third of the boys and girls saw their fathers at least once a month or more at the ten-year mark. Considering that the children were older and that teenagers can be very busy, this is an unexpectedly high number. More than 10 percent of boys and girls saw their fathers at least once or twice a week at the ten-year point, while only 10 percent were visited less than once a year. Few fathers dropped out completely over the decade.

From the child's point of view, the visiting relationship is equally complicated. Children almost always want to be visited and wait anxiously and restlessly for the visiting parent to arrive. Many regard the visit as a high point of their week or month and worry that their father might not appear at the appointed time. Some are on their best behavior to ensure that the father will come. The father thinks, Will I be welcome? Will she like the ballgame? The child thinks, Will he come? Will he be offended if I don't want to go to the ballgame? These kinds of uncertain interactions take place within an intact family but are exaggerated by the visiting relationship.

Visiting is different, of course, if the father and child are separated by great distances, as are Steve and Dale Burrelle. Children, I find, make liberal allowances for these real obstacles and have surprisingly realistic expectations if they are confident that they are important to their fathers. There is no question that the father who lives close by and fails to visit, like Bob Catalano, creates much more hurt. The child can interpret this failure in only one way — disinterest and rejection.

In our experience, the visiting relationship is often experienced differently by children and by their fathers. For example, the father tells us, "My door is always open. My son is welcome to come visit me anytime, and I'll give him anything he needs." The son tells us, "I'm not welcome in his house. I feel awkward and uncomfortable there. All I do is watch television while he talks to his friends." Most commonly, the father thinks he is doing his best while the child feels he or she is starving. The father thinks he is meeting his obligation, the child feels pushed to the periphery. The father thinks he is loving, the child feels rejected. The father feels he is being neutral and honest, the child thinks he is lying. On the other hand, if the father feels shame, the child feels forgiveness. The net result: Most fathers in our study thought they had done reasonably well in fulfilling their obligations whereas three out of four of the children felt rejected by their fathers; they felt that their fathers were present in body but not in spirit. Most fathers would have been very surprised and upset if they had realized the connection between their children's feelings of rejection and the profound consequences.

I find it startling that the sense of loss the children experience is unrelated to how often they are visited. Most of the young people regularly visit their fathers, yet most feel that they have lost them. Contrary to what many parents expect, frequency of visiting is not related to outcome; the few children in our study who have been visited by their fathers once or twice a week over the ten-year period still feel rejected.

What counts is not the quantity of time but the extent to which the father and child have been able to maintain a relationship in which the child feels valued. Our study clearly finds that the overall psychological adjustment of boys is strongly linked to father-son relationships, whether or not the mother has remarried. The frequency of visits is not the important thing. Rather, the relationship and the kind of person the father is make the difference. When the father-son relationship is poor, the boy may suffer low self-esteem, poor grades, weak aspirations, and rejection. When the father-son relationship is good, where the father is regarded as moral and competent and the boy feels wanted and accepted by his father, then the boy's psychological health is likely to be good. The psychological adjustment of teenage boys within divorced families is greatly eased by the perception that "my dad is a good man, my dad cares for me, encourages me, respects me." Boys who spend summers or blocks of time with their fathers seem to benefit very much from the relationship.

*

Billy identifies with his father, feels unloved by his stepfather, and feels alienated from the family. Although he is very much aware of his father's failings, Billy does not reject him as a role model, loves him anyway, forgives him everything. Bob's many failings as a father infuriate Rosemary. She is genuinely mystified when Billy says he worships his father. (Rosemary is not the only bewildered mother in this situation.) Billy looks to his father passionately for all the things he has not had over the years. In Billy's eyes, his father is a kinder, gentler man than his stepfather, and Billy cannot give up hope, in part because he feels he has nowhere else to turn.

Billy's longing for his father, a problem he regards as the major tragedy of his life, is not lessened by time. Billy knows he cannot live with his father, so he cries for the fantasy father he never had, for the father he needs, and for the real father he misses, loves, and pities. He cries knowing full well that his longing can never be satisfied.

It is hard to know how much Billy's longing is fueled by his feeling that his mother is not as available to him as he would like. He talks about how busy she is and understands that she works, takes care of the family, and runs the household. At the same time, he does not speak of any real pleasure or shared experiences with his mother, stepfather, and sister. Nothing helps to offset the longing for his father or his sense of not belonging anywhere.

Ironically, Billy's father loves his son but cannot translate his love into a relationship that might be useful to the boy. Billy turns to his mother but feels she is much more available to her new husband than to him; and she does not reach out and sympathize with Billy's sense of loss. It's very doubtful that she even realizes the enormity of Billy's neediness. He is doubly alone because he does not feel his father's love from a distance and does not feel his mother's love and commitment up close.

If Billy had felt closer to his mother and stepfather — or even to his mother alone — the visiting relationship with his father might have taken on less importance in his life. Billy's longing for his father is more powerful because he feels — correctly or not — that Rosemary and Charlie are not behind him one hundred percent. One of our sadder findings is that half the children whose mothers remarried said that they do not feel welcome in the new family. And in a quarter of these families, one child felt excluded while another felt included. Many of the children who felt excluded spoke poignantly and sadly of their experience, as if they were onlookers at a feast that they acknowledged was good for their mothers but to which they had not been invited.

Thus Billy Catalano describes a common pattern in the relationship between himself and his stepfather, Charlie. As Billy and Rosemary both told us, Charlie quickly asserted himself as master of the household and tried to discipline Billy at every turn. Billy has never accepted Charlie in this role. "He's not my father," he says over and over. "He's Mom's husband. All he wants is conformity and obedience. All he wants from me is yard work."

Billy avoids loyalty conflicts regarding his father and stepfather because, in his mind, his stepfather is not a candidate for his affection. Like many boys, Billy remains primarily attached to his father. In general, older boys who know their fathers find it harder to attach to stepfathers without considerable inner conflict. Sometimes these triangles are complicated by the fact that the son resembles — or is thought to resemble, or just thinks he resembles — his father and therefore represents his father in the new family. Rosemary told us early on that Billy is just like Bob, and Billy's interest in photography is an attempt to identify with his father, a factor that may have added to Charlie's inability to develop closeness with Billy.

Billy continues to feel like an outsider in a marriage that began when he was six years old. Even though he has spent most of his life in the remarried family, he says he never feels welcome. His younger sister, however, does feel included, as we will see.

15

Kelly Catalano

MODERN LOVE TRIANGLES

KELLY CATALANO is a sturdy, very sassy almost-twelve-year-old at our ten-year interview. After talking to her brother, I am particularly curious to hear what she will say about her relationship with her father, whom she rarely sees, and her stepfather, whom she has lived with since age four.

After going to a nearby restaurant for lunch, we walk across the street to sit on a park bench. Kelly, wearing a colorful print skirt and high-heel clogs, pulls her knees up under her chin, tucks her skirt under her feet, and continues talking in her stream of consciousness style. A loquacious child, she holds nothing back.

"I don't remember anything about the divorce," she says. "I was just two. I know that it was Mom who left Dad, but it took me a long time to accept the fact. But I also know that if my folks hadn't gotten divorced, if they'd stayed together, they would be happy now, because my dad has really gotten himself together."

"That's wonderful, Kelly," I say. "You must be very pleased."

"Yeah," she says with conviction. "I saw my dad a lot until I was six or seven — I think it must have been twice a month — but I know it was a lot. He only lived a few blocks away. But then he got married to Oona." She frowns. "I hated her. She was like Cinderella's stepmom — mean."

"That sounds awful, Kelly."

She nods and continues in her rapid-fire speech, "After they got divorced, Dad didn't get a promotion at the TV shop where he works and he was real disappointed. You see, he didn't have time to come and see me a lot, and he didn't have a lot of money to send child support either, but I know he wanted to. He worked all day and all night and only got three hours sleep." Kelly's tone is urgent, as she strives to make me understand how hard it was for Bob to spend more time with her. "I wrote him notes all the time," she says, "even though he lived only three and a half blocks away. But I didn't send the notes because he only had a few minutes to see me and wouldn't have time to answer all my questions." Kelly looks at me to see if I have followed her reasoning, but before I can say anything she continues her train of thought. "Once he went away for a few months and I was angry because he didn't let me know, he didn't write me or tell me that he was going away. He didn't even tell me when he moved to Los Angeles." She draws her skirt more tightly around her legs. "But things aren't all bad. Once, a couple of years ago, after he got divorced again, he invited me to spend a weekend. I had the best time of my life, because I love him more than anyone in the world."

"How is he now?"

"I saw him a month ago, and he looks great. Actually, he likes living in Los Angeles and says that I can come down someday and visit him. We spent three hours together." It was the first time Kelly had spent any time with her father in two years.

"I miss him. I miss him so much," says Kelly. "My girlfriend says he's probably just a hippie, a bum, and a no-gooder, because he doesn't visit me a whole lot."

"What do you think?" I ask gently.

"I think he used to be, but he's shaped up now. He cares about people, and he really cares about me." Her eyes are tearing up. "He told me he's going to make up for all the times he didn't come. On my last birthday he didn't send me a card or anything, but he was so confused he didn't know what time it was or even what day it was. He never really forgets. My dad used to live three blocks from here when I was little," she says, "but it's now that I want to be close to him."

Kelly and her father had a close, loving relationship during her very early childhood that has deteriorated over the years to almost no contact. But in Kelly's inner world, the relationship with her father remains powerful and may well be even more important now that she is entering adolescence. Unlike Billy, who is depressed, Kelly buoys up her spirits and self-esteem with a vision of a loving parent who is just over the brow of the hill, on his way but never quite making it.

Kelly does not deny the record of Bob's failures. Indeed, she keeps the dates in her head along with a running tab of promises kept and promises broken. At the same time, she maintains a benign, idyllic image of her father. When Bob does not respond to her overtures, Kelly speaks of his confusion, his fatigue, and his three jobs, invoking a range of explanations in which she holds on to the hopeful idea that he is improving and getting his life back on track. Despite loyalty to her mother and stepfather, Kelly maintains the undimmed hope that she and her father will someday enjoy a closer relationship and that he will be the father of her dreams.

It oversimplifies matters to say that children idealize their absent fathers. I have found a more complicated phenomenon, a kind of double imaging. Like little detectives, the children of divorce know their fathers' real records, their good and bad sides. But they do not, as a rule, draw the conclusions that an objective observer would make from those records. Instead, they have a powerful need to create a protective, loving father, one who would never intentionally let them down. Coming to their generous conclusions through a prism of compassion and willingness to forgive, they express undying love for the man who has let them down as provider, as role model, and as a loving, interested parent. Without any sense of contradiction, they are able to maintain a benign image of the loving father side by side with a history of repeated rejections and failures.

As boys and girls feel a rising internal need for their fathers in adolescence, they go out of their way to gather scraps of information to construct an image that suits those needs. If the mother is too strict, the invented father is compassionate, a Prince Charming who will come to the rescue if necessary. If the mother is brusque and distracted, the idealized father is gentle and attentive. Indeed, the younger the children are at divorce, the less bogged down by facts and the more inventive they can be in later years at weaving elaborate fantasies about their fathers and in explaining their fathers' lapses in parenting.

Beyond a fantasy father, however, children of divorce need real fathers to encourage them at particular points in their lives. This is true for girls in early adolescence, around the ages thirteen and fourteen. Many of the girls in our study do reach out for their fathers at this time. As Kelly tells me, "It's now that I want to be close to him."

One girl in our study, who hardly knew her father, wrote a letter the summer she turned thirteen: "Dear Dad, Remember me? Here I am, your daughter." She was elated when he wrote back, but the correspondence did not last.

When another girl reached thirteen, she sent her father her diary, which she had labeled "Bleeding Writing" because it revealed all of her hurts, anger, and sadness — all of her most secret feelings about herself and the world. She needed to share her feelings with her father, who lived three thousand miles away, she said, "because he will understand me." The father, who had seen his daughter only during summer vacations, was completely taken aback and had little appreciation of what this correspondence meant to his pubescent offspring. Leafing through the passionate poetry, fragments of songs, and confessions, he failed to recognize the great honor she had bestowed upon him and the profound need she was expressing.

Such outpourings are astonishing. In intact families, children go to great lengths to make certain that no adult reads an intimate diary or personal letter. As most parents know, this is forbidden territory. But children of divorce, especially girls, do not share this need for secrecy, at least at the dawn of adolescence. The young teenage girl endows her absent father with magical capacities to understand and support her at this time in her life.

The idealized father that the young adolescent girl imagines is the exact opposite of the image that later becomes prominent in their minds as they grow older — namely, the father as betrayer. Both images block the real picture of the father. And because daughters of divorce often have a hard time finding out what their fathers are really like, they often experience great difficulty in establishing a realistic view of men in general, in developing realistic expectations, and in exercising good judgment in their choice of partner and in their relationships with men.

After Kelly finishes telling me about her father, we turn to the subject of Charlie, her stepfather. "What is he like and how do you get along?" I ask.

"My step," Kelly says with a giggle. "I call him my step. My step wants me to learn the piano. We listen to music together and he plays the trumpet, banjo, and guitar." Obviously in awe of her stepfather's talents, Kelly adds, "I don't remember my dad ever playing a musical instrument."

"Tell me about Charlie."

"I met him when I was real young," she says, unfolding herself so that her legs stretch in front of her. "He's always treated me like a real father would, and he really tried to make me forget the divorce. I guess most people don't like their stepparents, but we get along fine." Kelly dangles an arm over the side of the bench. "He's a kind person, nice and warm, never in a bad mood at me, and he cares about me, never even yells at me. He's just the kind of father you always want to have, the kind you daydream about in school."

"You really like him a lot."

"The kind of husband I want to marry is the kind my stepdad is," says Kelly happily. "Mom and Charlie have a real good relationship, no relationship could be better. They have a one hundred percent marriage." She pauses for a second. "I guess I'm a daddy's girl with my step. Daughters go better with dads."

While there have always been remarriages, the modern remarried family is far more complicated and ambiguous than earlier versions. In previous generations, people remarried primarily because their husbands or wives died from accidents, disease, or childbirth. When a stepmother or stepfather arrived on the scene, he or she was expected to step into the shoes of the departed parent in every way possible. But now most people remarry after divorce. The child's departed mother or father is not dead, and the stepparent's role is very much changed.

Of the 113 children in our study at the ten-year mark, 55 had lived with stepfathers at some time in the decade after divorce. From the youngsters' lengthy discussions about these relationships, one thing became crystal clear: It is far more difficult to create a second marriage than a first marriage when children are involved — and it is more important to succeed. The stakes are higher. The risks are greater. And everybody involved knows it.

From the child's point of view, a stepfather is like a main character in a play who arrives in the middle of the second act. He sweeps onstage, like a masked intruder, into an ongoing story. He may be welcomed as rescuer, rejected as alien, loved as potential provider and source of love and affection, resented as an object of envy, or hated as a potential rival, but in any event he does not arrive until the middle of the play — as an unknown but powerful quantity, someone late on the scene who has the tremendous power to influence other characters and maybe even to determine how the play comes out in the end.

One thing is certain. The foreboding that children have about acquiring a stepparent, as reflected in favorite fairy tales, is psychologically accurate. From the child's point of view, it is terrifying to meet a man who is not related to you and who has not shared many years of your life but who expects you to accept him as a parent. While it is true that children are hungry for role models and identification figures, it does not follow that they will identify with or model themselves after their stepfathers or that they will love or be loved by the stepfathers. Children are anxious when mothers remarry because they know deep inside that their agendas differ from those of their mothers and that parent-child relationships are not automatic but are hard-won and complicated.

The world is suddenly full of anxious questions: What will this new man do for me? Will he threaten my position in the family? Will he interfere with my relationship with Mom and Dad? Since children closely identify with their mothers' welfare, they ask: Is he good for my mom? Will she be in a better mood? Will she treat me better? And since they worry about their fathers, they ask: Will my dad be angry? Will having a stepfather around make Dad want to visit me more or less? Will he fade out of the picture? Will Mom be nicer to Dad now? Will Mom and Dad ever get remarried now that someone else is in the picture?

All children come to second marriages shaped by the earlier marriage and burdened by its failure. Children of divorce are more eager to be loved and more frightened of being rejected and pushed outside. Unfortunately, one ready-made source of rejection stems from newlyweds' need for privacy. Children often view this need as blocking their access to their mother; their fear that she will be less available seems to be borne out. In our study, we were told about children who congregate at the bedroom door, which their parents would lock behind them every evening after dinner. In other homes, children and adults began to dine separately, although it had not been customary to do so before the remarriage. I have found that adults with the best intentions can make their children feel that the central meaning of the remarriage is the loss of the mother.

From the child's point of view, stepfathers rarely become full sub-stitutes for biological fathers. The stepfather relationship is not, nor can it ever be, the same relationship that a child has with his or her natural father. When a stepfather becomes preoccupied with stepping into the shoes of the absent biological father, he is bound to fail. Of course he can be a good and wonderful man. He can be that and more — including friend, mentor, and role model — for his stepchildren. Some children prefer their stepfathers because they think of them as more honest and more loving than their natural fathers, but the distinction between the two fathers is not lost. In the child's mind, there can be only one biological father in this world. Even children who are very young at divorce clearly differentiate stepfather and father as they grow older. When a parent remarries, the child adds a parent but does not subtract the one that was there before. The added parent goes into a new slot, and eventually there may be a slot for mother, a slot for father, a slot for stepmother, and a slot for stepfather.

Children have different expectations of and fantasies about stepfathers and biological fathers. One twenty-two-year-old explained it very well. I pointed out, trying to draw him out about his sadness, that he had a wonderful relationship with his stepfather. "How is it," I asked, "that despite all your stepdad's help and encouragement, you still get so hurt and intensely angry about your father? The relationship with your father still occupies so much of your emotional life."

He replied patiently, "You don't understand. My stepfather could be Saint Benedict or Saint Francis. He could walk on water, and it would not change the hurt I feel about my dad." This is very evident with Kelly. She loves Charlie, respects him, thinks he's preferable in many ways to Bob; she says that when she grows up, she's going to marry someone like Charlie. But these feelings in no way diminish her yearning for Bob and the fantasies that she weaves about him.

A child's age at remarriage strongly influences the stepfather-stepchild relationship. As a rule of thumb, younger children, like Kelly, are more apt to get along with their stepfathers than are older children. Of the younger children in our study whose mothers remarried, nine in ten feel that their lives have been substantially enhanced by their stepfathers. Two-thirds feel they are able to love their stepfathers and fathers at the same time, while only a third are struggling with loyalty conflicts.

It is also easier for a stepfather to bond with a younger child because little ones are more responsive to adult overtures. A stepfather naturally feels more protective and paternal toward a five-year-old than a fifteen-year-old, and rewards for both parent and child come faster when the child is young. The child benefits enormously.

Even though Kelly maintains a separate relationship with Bob, Charlie arguably exerts the greater influence on her development. Because Kelly sees her mother's second marriage as successful and happy, she is able to visualize her own future with confidence. Kelly admires the relationship between Rosemary and Charlie, embracing it as an internal vision of a good marriage, and she hopes someday to marry someone like Charlie. This triangle of daughter, mother, and stepfather forms a template for Kelly's future relationships. Her self-esteem is enhanced by her conviction that Charlie loves her, and she loves him in return. She puts it all succinctly when she says he's just the kind of husband a person wants to have. She explains her difference from Billy when she says daughters go better with dads.

Older children — those who were well along in elementary school when their parents divorced — tell a different story ten years later. Like Billy, more than half of them resent their stepfathers and 90 percent feel that their lives have not been enhanced by their having a stepfather. Because they are older, these children had closer relationships with their biological fathers before the divorce and tend to feel intense loyalty conflicts. Very few older children, age nine and over at divorce, developed good relationships with their stepfathers, with some important exceptions. From the adolescent's point of view, the stepfather is a man who is moving into the center of the mother's life and bed. Although he is a main character in the play, he arrives at exactly the wrong time to be acceptable as an authority figure. As we have seen, the adolescent is engaged in one of the central tasks of growing up — separating from the adults in his family and beginning to carve out an independent identity. The teenager inevitably challenges adult authority, which becomes embodied in the stepfather who has just entered the scene. As the internal drama of the adolescent is worked out on the family stage, the stepfather — through no fault of his own — becomes an antagonist or perhaps even a villain, just by virtue of being there. From the start, the stepfather also stimulates excitement and anxiety around sexual issues, again by his presence and by his relationship with the mother. In addition to all this, the adolescent struggles with questions of loyalty: How does this stepfather affect my relationship with my father? How can I stay loyal to my father and get along with my stepfather?

Boys and girls also react differently to the stepfather. Girls are much more likely to welcome the stepfather's participation in the family after the initial period of worry, distrust, and testing of each other is behind them. Many girls and very few boys told us they preferred their stepfathers over their fathers. Moreover, girls were much more willing than boys to accept the stepfather as a parent rather than as a friend. By and large, the girls did not share the loyalty conflicts that burdened the boys. Kelly's affectionate relationship with Charlie is very much in accord with that of other girls in this study.

There are some hazards, though. From the adolescent daughter's standpoint, the presence of a stepfather can raise the difficult issue of a thinner incest barrier. Fathers and daughters from intact families have heavy, built-in barriers against the temptation to think of one another sexually. Typically when a father looks at his young daughter in a bikini, he is constrained from thinking of her sexually because he helped change her diapers, wiped her snotty nose, and forced her to eat her vegetables. This history, plus powerful social taboos and the knowledge that he is her biological father, acts as a powerful constraint against incest. The father's role is to protect his daughter, an impulse that is normally more powerful than any excitement he experiences.

These impulses are part of the normal tensions in family life as mother and father share responsibility in helping their daughter control any exhibitionist tendencies and come to terms with her sexuality. But in a remarried family, adults seem less prepared to cope with an adolescent girl's sexual development. In the first place, the stepfather does not have the long history of having cared for the daughter from birth. Second, from the girl's point of view, he is a new man and, as the mother's lover, he clearly performs a sexual role. The stepfather is not the biological father and the girl knows it. In their mutual perceptions, then, there is a higher potential for generating sexual interest and excitement. This is not to say that these impulses are inevitably acted out, for that is not the case. But they undoubtedly add to tensions in the remarried family, and they may lead to overload that destabilizes the marital relationship. In my work I have seen more instances of high tension leading to marital breakdown than of actual incest. Some stepfathers lay rigid rules on their stepdaughters as a way of coping with their own sexual excitement in response to the girls' burgeoning sexuality. This, too, can destabilize the second marriage.

From the mother's point of view, a second marriage carries great expectations. Rosemary hoped that Charlie would very quickly take on a parenting role and help her by exerting moral, social, and psychological influences on Billy and Kelly. She particularly hoped that Charlie would provide a positive identification figure and male role model that would help Billy grow successfully into young manhood. But that was not to be.

Unfortunately, when introducing her husband-to-be, many a mother fails to recognize her children's mixed feelings and their sense that both welcome and unwelcome changes are about to occur within the family. In her eagerness to cement the new family relationship, a woman may forget that trust, acceptance, and affection take time to develop and that any new relationship requires an overture. Her second husband and her children will need time to get to know and trust one another. Sometimes, in the face of her own better judgment, the mother expects her children instantly to respect and approve of her choice and to feel, or at least show, immediate affection for the new person. She wants them to accept his right to take over household discipline and routines and to become the new center of power in a home that — from the children's point of view — may have been entirely satisfactory without his presence. Very rarely does the mother recognize that the children may feel displaced or pushed to the periphery and might be concerned about losing the one parent who has been central to their lives. These anxieties may not be brought to her attention until, as often happens, there is open friction between her second husband and one or more of her children. Or she may never find out, as her children retreat emotionally, going through the motions of cooperation but feeling excluded from the new family. Time and again, we find that mothers who *are* aware of conflicts between their new husband and children can be generally less protective of their children. In an extreme example, one mother, anxious to maintain her second marriage, allowed her new husband to beat her teenage daughter, although the mother had divorced her first husband because he beat her.

The role of the stepfather is probably the most difficult of all, and there can be lost opportunities all along the way. As the stepfather moves into the family, he has many choices. He can move in with seven-league boots, taking on the role of disciplinarian and expecting instant obedience. Or he can take time to get to know the children and stay out of a commanding role until he and the children have constructed a scaffolding of affection and respect. I find it amazing that in dealing with children, adults often overlook everything they know about beginning a friendship. In part, this may be related to the fact that the stepfather's role is highly ambiguous, especially when the children continue to visit their biological father. There are few experiences that the stepfather can draw on in his own life to provide guidance for his new role, and this ambiguity makes for uncertainty and anxiety at the outset. Even so, I have often asked myself why stepfathers so often make the mistake of moving too quickly into the disciplinarian role. As he enters the household, a stepfather can't help but ask himself, "How do I compare — as a lover, provider, and father? Will the children accept me? What will they expect of me? Will I fulfill their expectations? Will they love me?" Perhaps to allay his own anxieties and to help himself feel more comfortable with another man's children — even perhaps to make a good impression on his new wife — he assumes an authoritarian role to protect himself from hearing his own doubts.

For the same reason, many stepfathers want to believe that the family history begins with them. It is a romantic fantasy that may or may not be shared by his new wife, but the children never accept it. To the contrary, children are the self-appointed guardians of family history. They do not want to forget act one of the play, and they are suspicious of the new character in act two. Because so much of their identity is wrapped up in act one, their strongest wish is to bridge the acts, not to erase one.

It is often very difficult for stepfathers to understand the children's point of view, in part because they don't know the family history at first hand. They cannot know the children's experience and it is not easy to learn it from what the mother tells them, for usually the children's viewpoint is very different from the mother's. It is hard for many people to understand that children can feel very attached to a man whom their mother perceives as a scoundrel. Stepfathers can't help but be confused by the different perceptions among family members.

Any new parent-child relationship requires hard work. It takes more than "having fun together" to develop a good relationship with a stepchild. It requires tact, a sense of humor, and intelligence as well as time and patience so that trust can develop gradually and feelings can grow naturally rather than being forced. Children are responsive beings. An independent relationship between a stepparent and stepchild is made of countless transactions and responses through which the child learns, hey, this person cares about me. This adult belongs to me. I have a claim separate from my mom. When a stepparent brings this feeling about, it is a magical moment — created by sweat and tears.

There are some striking examples of a stepfather's ability, through his relationship with a child, to turn the youngster's life around 180 degrees.

Rina was a disheveled little girl with long bangs covering her face. At age twelve when her parents divorced, she was doing poorly in all areas of her life — with friends, at school, and at home. She hated being interviewed and answered my questions in a surly tone. Rina was preoccupied with a fantasy of living by herself on a mountaintop and seeing her parents maybe once a fortnight. She said that her mother was selfish and her father was mean and that they were never home except when they fought. I was very concerned about her at the time; she was among the neediest children that I saw and I was especially worried about her moving into adolescence with so much anger, feeling so estranged from her parents.

Five years later, I was dismayed but not surprised to find Rina, now living in Portland, in much worse condition. I learned from her mother that she was hanging out with a tough gang, was involved in a wide range of petty delinquencies, and attended school maybe once a week. Her mother had little influence or control over her. I interviewed Rina in her home at the five-year follow-up, in part because I was concerned that she would not keep an appointment elsewhere. Dressed in a tight leather halter and jeans and chain-smoking Marlboros, she expressed anger at the world and everyone in it. She was clearly bored with me and my questions. Looking for an opening to engage her, I asked, "Rina, is there any grown-up that you like?"

"I like one," she replied. "The lady who cleans the bathrooms in high school because she lets me smoke."

"Is there anyone else?"

Yes, she admitted. There was one teacher that she liked because he gave the class an assignment to rewrite "Little Red Riding Hood" from the point of view of the wolf. This appealed to her. It was easy for her to identify with the wolf.

Suddenly, with no particular point of reference, Rina said, "I've decided to tell the truth. Not to lie about anything. Adults lie. I'm not going to." I was very taken with her remark, and it occurred to me that there might well be an inner core of integrity hidden beneath the leather and the heavy makeup, if one could only reach it. I also thought that this was a very bright youngster who actually had responded rather quickly to my interest. But I was concerned about her self-destructive behavior and the fact that she recognized no adult figure as important in her life. I found myself liking her very much, although, as we parted, I was not hopeful. I decided to talk to several people at Rina's high school and learned that she turned people off. Teachers and counselors had all given up on her, declaring her aggressive and unmanageable.

I am therefore absolutely startled to meet a transformed Rina at our ten-year interview. When she walks up to me dressed in a tailored business suit and introduces herself, I blurt out, "Rina, I didn't recognize you. It's a good thing you recognized me."

She smiles, and the hardness is gone. "Well," she says, "I'll bring you up to date. I'm in my senior year at Chico State College in computer programming." She gives me an impish grin. "I bet you're wondering what happened to me."

"Please, go on," I say with incredulity.

"My mom married this wonderful man when I was sixteen and a half," she says, smiling. "I was spending all my time with that rat of a boyfriend and all his cronies. But after Mom married Jeff, he took me aside and talked to me like no one had ever talked to me before. He said I was going nowhere with my friends. He talked to me a bunch more times, asking me where I was going in my life and where I would be in a few years. Then Jeff made me an incredible offer. He said if I wanted a new start, he'd help me. If I wanted to go to college, he'd help me." She pauses dramatically.

"Judy. He put his money where his mouth was." She sighs. "So I went to junior college and got good grades. He was so proud of me. My mom was so proud of me."

Rina reaches across the table and touches my hand. "I want you to know this. Before I turned eighteen I went to Jeff and asked him to adopt me. I knew I was going to be an adult, but I wanted to have his name. I talked to Mom first and she said to go ask him. He said he'd be honored. So then I asked my real dad. He said he was hurt but he'd do it if it was what I wanted. I knew it was just symbolic, but I wanted it."

When I speak with Rina's stepfather, he says proudly, "I got her at just the right time. Also, I'm half Irish and half Jewish, which my wife tells me makes for the best parents. When I went to her graduation, that was my daughter standing there."

There's no question that Rina's stepfather turned her life around at a time when both her parents had already given up. He put love and commitment into his relationship, which she tested and found to be real. Rina was fully aware of the central role that he has played in her life and wanted to acknowledge its importance, in love and gratitude, by her request to be his adopted daughter, although she was within six months of adulthood when she undertook this symbolic step.

Although sixty-eight of the children in our study had a stepmother at some time during the decade, very few children lived with their stepmothers while growing up. During adolescence, many children spent a year or so in their fathers' homes and got to know their stepmothers better. But in general the stepmothers in our study played a limited role as parents in the emotional lives of the children — although it was certainly beneficial psychologically for the children to see their fathers happily remarried. And since I did not get to meet most of the stepmothers, I cannot evaluate the family from their point of view. But I can report what the children told me.

In general, stepmothers engender fewer loyalty conflicts in children because they simply are not serious rivals for the mother's love and devotion. When children compare mothers and stepmothers, the mother is almost always the winner. Less than 10 percent of the children in our study grew close to their stepmothers. Even so, many stepmothers took their role seriously, wanted the children to like them, and were disappointed at not receiving the affection that they would have enjoyed. One stepmother, who was never accepted by her husband's children because they never forgave his infidelity during the marriage, says after ten years, "If I had known then what I know now about how difficult it would be for me and his kids to get along, I might not have married him."

Most fathers hoped very much that their children would love their new wives or at least become close friends. But for most of the children, the stepmother was a pleasant person valued mainly for her contribution to the father's happiness. "If Diana left Dad, he'd be nothing," says Terry. "It's astonishing how much he idolizes her. I've never seen him look at anyone like that. He's so afraid of losing her. But I really do see a solidarity. They are probably forever."

Some of the adolescent girls were drawn to a stepmother, especially a young stepmother, as friend and ally. A teenage girl may be able to tell her stepmother about her sexual relationships more easily than she can tell her mother. She can also complain about her mother's strictness or insensitivity to her needs. Real friendships can develop, with stepmother and stepdaughter both keen on the relationship. And when stepmothers have babies, the older children often take great pleasure in participating in the care of the infant, as long as they don't feel exploited in this role. In several such instances, the stepmother served as an important role model for both sexes, but especially for the girls.

From the children's perspective, stepmothers are generally not the wicked stepmothers in fairy tales. There was not much anger between the children and stepmothers in the study, except when children felt — usually with real justification — that they were unwelcome in their father and stepmother's home. In some families, stepmothers were angry about their husbands' paying child support and let their frustration spill onto the stepchildren. Others felt that their stepchildren intruded on their space or were untidy when they visited. The children also felt that, although the stepmother was pleasant, she was not an ally. They complained, "She rarely takes my side." In general, the children regard their stepmothers more realistically than other parental figures. Expectations are not as high, and disappointments not as great. Children want a stepmother to be nice to their father, to welcome them, and to not make them feel like intruders. Many children whose fathers redivorced were sad at losing a relationship that they valued, and they perceived accurately that their relationship with the stepmother was unlikely to survive outside the remarriage.

16

Joint Custody

THE NEWEST FAMILY FORM

WHEN WE BEGAN our studies in 1971, joint custody was hardly known. Today, amid a movement to make it public policy throughout the nation, at least thirty-three states make joint custody a preference or allow it as an option. The movement has grown faster than our knowledge of what this new family form means for men, women, and children.

The term *joint custody* has several definitions that are sometimes confused. Joint legal custody refers to an arrangement in which parents share responsibility and major decisions about their children, including education, religious instruction, health issues, and sometimes place of residence. Day-to-day decisions are left to the parent who has physical custody. Some states require parents, at the time of separation, to clearly state which areas require mutual consultation or agreement.

Joint physical custody, or shared custody, is a new family form in which divorced parents share parenting in separate homes or, put another way, where children literally have two residences, spending substantial amounts of time alternately with the mother and the father. The core of the joint custody arrangement reflects the parents' commitment to maintain two homes for their children and to continue cooperating with each other in decision making. In one variation of this arrangement, called *birdnesting*, parents take turns moving into the home where the children are living. In other words, the parents move in and out while the children stay put. Because such arrangements are so difficult to sustain, they usually do not last more than a year or two after separation and divorce. In this chapter I use the term *joint custody* to refer to joint physical custody.

There is no set pattern for joint custody, and in most cases, parents decide on the formula they want. A common schedule calls for children to spend three days with one parent, four days with the other, and so on. Other children alternate visits to parents' homes by the week, and still others alternate by year. Sometimes the custody arrangement is day to day. Some infants and very young children spend Monday with Mommy, Tuesday with Daddy, Wednesday with Mommy, Thursday with Daddy, and so on through the weeks and months.

The rationale for joint custody is drawn from a body of research, including my own, that characterizes the divorce experience as a series of losses for the child. In divorce, children lose the family they have always known and very often lose contact with one of their parents, usually their father. Joint custody is an attempt to soften those losses; the child benefits from knowing that he or she has two committed parents despite the breakup of the marriage. The central psychological argument for joint custody therefore rests on the importance of maintaining two parents in the postdivorce family. My work consistently shows that good father-child relationships can be critically important to the psychological well-being and self-esteem of children of divorce. Our ten- and fifteen-year studies reveal new evidence that adolescents are particularly vulnerable when deprived of relationships with their fathers. Unfortunately, many fathers drift away from their children if visiting arrangements do not meet mutual parent and child needs, as so often happens. Failure to pay child support can be linked to the infrequency of visiting and the subsequent blunting of a father's feelings for his children. Joint custody is designed to maintain fathers in their crucial childrearing roles.

The movement for joint custody also reflects the growing interchangeability of men's and women's roles in the workplace and in the family. Women are not ordained to be better parents than men, just as men are not ordained to be better career professionals than women. Nowadays, more men want to remain deeply involved in their children's lives and are less willing to cede full custody to an ex-wife. More women want to pursue or resume their careers along with childrearing and may welcome the opportunity that joint custody arrangements provide.

A third boost for joint custody relates to the unspoken agenda of child support. Many courts adjust payments according to how much time a child spends in each home. In California, if a child spends 30 percent of his time with the father, the father gives proportionately less money to the mother. Such formulas ignore the fact that it inevitably costs more to raise a child within the realm of joint custody than in sole custody.

Parents tell me that each home has to be fully equipped to raise children. This often means two tricycles, two sets of clothes, two separate bedrooms, and so on, as well as adequate space in each house for the child's everyday activities, including having friends stay overnight. When joint custody children change homes frequently, as many do, it costs money to shuttle them back and forth.

The court's formulas do not consider these additional expenses but are essentially based on dividing up the child's daily living expenses, such as food and entertainment. But this so-called hotel bill approach to child support fails to capture the true costs of raising children in two separate homes.

As more states adopt joint custody legislation every year, widespread interest in it increases. Many groups in the national debate on divorce have been quick to jump on the bandwagon in favor of joint custody. And yet there has been very little research into how these arrangements actually affect children over the short and long term. We hear that fathers get depressed when their children are taken away and that mothers need more time to pursue careers while raising children without husbands. But all too little is known about the psychological effects of joint custody on the children themselves. Is it good for them? What is it like to shuttle between two homes? How does the children's experience differ from those of the adults? We want to know how parent-child relationships are sustained in joint custody. How are they changed? What are the effects on a child's development, on social skills and academic learning? Most of all, we know nothing about the long-term effects, as our joint custody parents are intensely aware. There is no way that the little knowledge we have should be regarded by legislators as sufficient for a public policy that makes shared custody a preference or presumption under the law.

In 1985, in an effort to begin to find out how these new family forms are evolving, we asked twenty-five couples with joint custody of their children to join a pilot study. We had no idea how the children, who were between eight months and five years old, would adjust to moving back and forth between two homes. The group of parents — a mix of career professionals and blue-collar or unskilled workers — shared the idea that both parents should remain committed to their children; they voluntarily chose joint custody, hoping it would help their children become better adjusted in the long run. The most common custody pattern was three days with one parent and four days with the other. Some alternated weekdays and split the weekend. Most of the families had only one child. Many of the parents met in a group once a month for six months at our center to discuss their experiences and the experiences of their children. In addition, we saw individual children and parents every three to six months for several more years.

"Well, first you decide on joint custody and then you find out what it's all about," says a young father, throwing up his hands. Everyone around the conference table laughs.

"We're probably pioneers," says a mother. "You know, as much as we've been through, I would feel very good about passing on what I've learned to other people."

Another woman says, "I didn't want joint custody, but he said to me that if I didn't go along he'd take me to court and I didn't want that."

We do not know what motivates parents to choose joint custody of their children. Many people assume that parents always do it out of love for their children and because they want to continue a close relationship. Others, despite misgivings, are convinced that a child needs both parents while growing up.

"I wanted to go off to Siberia or someplace with her, where her father could never find her," explains one mother when asked why she finally opted for joint custody. "I'd protect her and in some way shield her from what I could only imagine at the time was going to be a very painful period. And yet, at the same time, in the back of my mind, was a voice that said, 'But how can you deny the fact that she has a father? Sure, you can take her away and her father may not see her and might not play an active role in her life, but at some point he is going to have to become integrated into her life and how do you do that?' I now think, 'Did we do the best thing by deciding on joint custody?' I just don't know because it's such a hard decision. I would feel so much better if someone could say, 'Yes, you did the right thing because when she's eighteen she's going to be a totally well adjusted teenager because of what you did.' It's been so hard for us. There was no question about the divorce. That had to happen. I hope that by letting her father share in her life she'll be enriched."

When she finishes, a man says, "I know what you mean. I have three sons and as far as I'm concerned they're the greatest. When my youngest was three, my wife upped and left, just walked out. She was gone for a year and then showed up, saying she wanted the kids back. I wouldn't go for that, but I had already seen how devastated they were to lose one parent. So I said we could try joint custody. I think it's important for the boys to be with their mother. Sometimes she's still kind of flaky, and they get upset. But I think they'll figure her out for themselves as they get older."

At the same time, we see other motives for parents' choice of joint custody. Parents can use the arrangement to accommodate work schedules. A flight attendant, for example, can schedule work on days when the children are living with the other parent. Such scheduling is especially convenient and perhaps necessary for parents in a wide range of occupations, such as restaurant work, medicine, and the entertainment industry, although it is useful as well for people who work nine to five.

In some cases, joint custody reflects the unwillingness of both parents to take full responsibility for the children, and the arrangement is a compromise. We find many cases where both parents say, in effect, "Take her, she's yours." Each bargains for less time.

In some instances, when a woman initiates the divorce knowing that her husband loves her and is suffering, she may use joint custody as a way to soften the blow of her unilateral decision. By inviting her ex-husband to share the children, she feels less guilty. I have even seen the same thing happen when a battered woman leaves her husband and chooses joint custody as a way to alleviate her own guilt. Other parents choose and use joint custody as a way to maintain frequent contact with an ex-wife or ex-husband. The children become a symbol of the marriage and a means for keeping a foothold in the marriage that came undone. These motives affect how children and parents relate to one another throughout the joint custody years.

Parents tell us they feel a continuing anxiety about doing something new and untried. "What will it mean for our children?" asks a father. "Is my son acting this way or that because he's developing normally or because he's in a new school or because of something having to do with joint custody?" Such comments reflect a gnawing anxiety about conducting an experiment with the lives of one's own children. "You have to believe your kid is resilient," says one man, "and hope that he adapts well. There's no one out there who can tell you when you're making a mistake and no one to give you a pat on the back when things go right."

Parents tell us that they worry all the time about "monkeying around" with fundamental aspects of their children's upbringing. Everyone knows that these custody experiments profoundly affect a child's life, but I believe that parents understand this better than judges and lawyers. Joint custody fundamentally transforms the experience of growing up, and it is to the parents' credit that they realize they are venturing with their most precious possession. Mental health professionals have differing theories about the effects of joint custody and can offer few concrete guidelines for what works best in the long run.

All the parents agree that their children encounter real problems in going from one household to the other — an event they have dubbed "changeover day." "We have a three-year-old and we're on an every-other-day routine, and this kid is going back and forth maybe fourteen times a week," says a woman with a worried look. "Last week he said, 'Mommy, I don't like being divorced because there are too many things to think about.' Going back and forth is so incredibly hard."

"Fran comes into the apartment and checks to see if everything is in its place," says the mother of a four-year-old. "If I've moved one stick of furniture, she notices right away. When it's changeover from my house, we get up and I say, 'It's Saturday morning. Your dad will be here at ten o'clock.' We have breakfast and then we pack her stuff. I ask, 'Is there anything you want to take?' I check with her father beforehand to see if they are going to do anything special. I discovered that if he arrived and announced something unexpected, Fran would get upset, so I prepare her in advance. When we first started the changeovers, I had to go to work and would drop her off at the babysitter to wait for her dad, but that never worked. My daughter needs a direct transition between us. School is not good as an in-between either. She wants me there and her dad there, and we have to have an interaction. It doesn't work with a third party.

"When she comes home from her dad's, it's an entirely different story," Fran's mother continues. "She's a different person. For an hour and a half she's agitated, and it is hard for her to settle in. She's often belligerent and cold. You know, kind of on guard, like something is going to jump out of the wall at her. After an hour and a half, she calms down, and by the time she leaves a few days later, she's affectionate and gives me hugs and kisses. I always walk her out to the car."

Another mother nods sympathetically. "I used to try to be real affectionate when my daughter came home, and I'd ask about the weekend with her dad. I learned that that made her angry and that she really needed time to walk around, check out her toys, go into her room, and play. She seems to need time to unwind from being with her dad, and if I give her space she gets comfortable."

Each parent has a story about how anxious the children feel on returning home, how they look to see that nothing has been changed, and how they settle into small routines to comfort themselves. Some children seem to need several hours to make the transition, and each parent has learned to recognize the process.

A father adds, "At each changeover day, my son kind of goes through a big separation all over again, like running an old movie on fast forward to bring it up to the part you haven't seen yet. He's asking me to give him space."

Changeover days are difficult for adults as well as children. Preschool children, as every parent knows, demand the kind of constant attention that has to be experienced to be believed. When the child departs, the parent's mindset that goes with caring for a young child is disrupted. Parents report intense feelings of missing their small children at changeover. Then, after three days or a week of readjusting to the freedom of being an adult in an adult world, the parent gets the child back. This constant shifting takes an emotional toll on parents but, as hard as it is, they say it is worth it.

"I want to be with my daughter twenty-four hours a day all the time," says one mother. "I can't tell you how many Friday nights I've sat and cried because she was gone, because it was his turn to take care of her. She was only two and a half, and I ached because she wasn't there. I was afraid he wouldn't take good care of her. I would think, 'Oh, no, he's not going to brush her teeth, put clean pajamas on her.' It was such a hard decision to share custody."

Joint custody of very young children requires an extraordinary degree of cooperation and communication between estranged parents. They must be able to discuss daily details of naptime, runny noses, toilet training, teething, diaper rash, and so on. Each parent must set up routines and schedules to coincide with day care arrangements. Children must learn the telephone numbers of both parents in case of emergency. Every little detail — lost toys, missed naps, doctor appointments, and so on — must be shared regularly and openly if joint custody is going to work.

"It's really the little things that matter, like the baths," says one mother. "I could compromise and let her be dirty, and it would make it a lot easier for Pammy. But he doesn't give her a bath every day, and she goes three days without one at his house, while I bathe her every night at my house. Or it's bedtime that's a mess. She goes to bed at eleven at her dad's and at seven-thirty at my house. It's a fight all the time."

As the parents talk, we learn that bedtime seems to be the most nonnegotiable and probably the most upsetting subject between households. Many children seem to go to bed at seven o'clock in one home and at midnight in the other. For one parent bedtime is a major part of the child's health regimen, while the other feels that bedtime is of no consequence. For their part, children have a hard time adjusting to two very different bedtimes. They come home tired and red-eyed from one home and cannot fall asleep in the other. While they can adjust readily to white bread in one home versus whole wheat in the other, wildly disparate bedtimes take a heavier toll.

Another thorny issue revolves around children who sleep with one parent at one home but sleep in a separate bed at the other home. Parents who take their children into their beds generally do not want to discuss the issue and are not willing to give the practice up. Nevertheless, the child experiences a great deal of difficulty in sleeping if he or she is expected to sleep alone in one household and in the parent's bed at the other. My feeling is that if the parent-child relationship is not eroticized, occasionally sharing a bed is not dangerous; but it is certainly not recommended to last for all of childhood.

"Then there's television," continues another woman. "I found out from Kent that he's allowed to watch television in the afternoon at his dad's house. This is upsetting me. I don't want him sitting there watching TV. I want him playing outside. Now I have to figure out how I'm going to bring this up. His father writes me letters when he has something to say, but I'm no good at that. I could call him up or talk to his wife, but I probably won't have any success at all."

"I know what you mean," says a woman across the table. "My kid was into Smurfs and Rainbow Brite. I said, 'Are you watching this junk at your dad's?' When she said yes, I suggested we never turn it on and have each other for company instead."

A man next to her jumps into the discussion. "I told my daughter that kids who watch the least television do better in their studies, so now at my house there's no television. But I know she watches a lot at her mom's house." Everyone around the table is familiar with this subject and has strong feelings about it.

While joint custody increases cooperation, it does not necessarily diminish anger. This is a surprise to many people, who are under the impression that communication diminishes anger. It was very clear that many of the parents who telephoned each other frequently continued to be very angry and that their anger rose every time they met face to face. As one woman says, "My ex-husband and I can't be together five minutes without getting into an argument. I bite my tongue a lot these days. You have to if you're going to make it work."

Others are less restrained. "Sure," says another woman. "First you bite your tongue. Then you haul off and let him have it with all the ammunition you've got."

According to their parents, joint custody children are literally leading double lives. A father volunteers, "I'll tell you what I worry about. My son has two lives, then he has school and that's another life, and then day care. I'm beginning to think we're creating a multiple personality."

"One day, when Wendy was with her father," says one mother, "she ran into my best friend, Helen, on the street. Wendy has known Helen all her life and has probably spent more time with her than with anyone except her dad and myself. But Wendy acted like she didn't recognize Helen. She didn't show any signs of recognition. And not long after that a friend of mine was at Wendy's dad's house and she heard another little kid ask Wendy, 'Do you have a mom?' Wendy said yes but the other little girl didn't believe her. 'Are you sure you have a mom. I never see her.' Then my ex-husband and I realized how awkward it must be for Wendy to have two separate lives that don't overlap."

A father adds, "Yes, that happened to me, too. A mutual friend saw my son and said hi, but my son didn't answer. He was living his other life."

A mother says, "Talk about schizophrenic life. When my son goes to his dad's house, he jumps on the furniture, hangs from the chandeliers, and stays up till ten or eleven when boom, his dad reaches his limit. At my house, he's got lots of limits and his life is very compartmentalized. It's two different worlds."

As these problems are discussed, I am surprised to learn how inflexible most parents are about time-related arrangements. Evidently the parents' work schedules and the structure of child care settings make change almost impossible, as children are tied to work and school schedules and are written into the margins of the calendars their parents carry around in their briefcases. I had expected that the joint custody arrangement would be fine-tuned or changed once it got under way. If every other day wasn't good for the children, it would be modified in their best interests. But this is not how things are working out. Once the schedule is made, it seems to become inflexible. Some of the rigidity, of course, may have its roots in a parent's intransigence. In any case, people entering joint custody do not realize beforehand how rigid these arrangements will be.

On the other hand, parents say it is easier to start new relationships within the highly prescribed structure of joint custody. Women are especially pleased to be able to enjoy a more spontaneous social life — to bring a date home or stay out late on nights the children are at the father's home. On the down side, parents continue to be more closely involved with each other, and there is more room for jealousy and animosity between them. When one parent is having a fun-filled social life while the other is not, the one who stays home may accuse the other of being a bad parent, of having lovers who mistreat the child, and so on. This can add new friction to the coparenting relationship.

When joint custody works well, we find that men and women develop a genuine regard for their former partners in their roles as mothers and fathers. They realize they have to trust each other as parents.

"He's a decent guy and a loving father," one woman says of her ex-husband.

"You have to decide at some point you're going to trust his parenting skills," says another woman, laying her hands flat on the table. "You've got to make a commitment and to realize there is no good solution. This is the best you've got."

"It's real important to separate out your perception of your spouse as a person and as a parent," says a man. "I don't think my ex-wife is a good person but I have come to conclude that she is a good parent. I still don't trust her as a person, but she at least has learned to trust me as a parent, so as far as our son is concerned, we both can focus on his welfare."

"Okay, we didn't trust each other and we divorced," another man says. "But I would wish to be trusted as a father. I mean, as a husband, okay, I'm lousy, forget it. But as a father, I'd like to be trusted."

Many parents become convinced that helping their children become accustomed to change prepares the children for the twenty-first century. "Well, my views on this are very much influenced by the way I grew up, in a small town and in a neighborhood where all the kids went to the same school, played together after school, you know, that type of thing," says one father. "That's what I think is the best way to grow up. Same friends all the time, same house, same neighborhood. And I find myself thinking about my son. I wish he could have the same house to live in like I did for twenty years, the same everything I had — just a plain, ordinary, conventional life, with everything and everyone around you that you know, all the years of your childhood. But I guess it's not going to be that way for him, and maybe in this day and age he's better off getting used to changes right away. Because he's going to have a lot of them, you can bet on that."

In addition to meeting with parents, we saw each child individually, in our playroom, every few months for up to four years, to assess independently how they fared over time. We also talked periodically with caregivers or nursery school teachers to get their observations. Children tend to behave differently in different settings, so that a child who plays quietly at home can be a terror on the playground at school. We wanted to know if our impressions, the caregivers' impressions, and the parents' comments about their children would all match up.

Overall, the joint custody children resemble not so much children from intact families but rather children raised in traditional sole custody households. About half are developmentally on target, happy and spontaneous at home and at school, while an equal number are anxious, having difficulty with peers and showing symptoms such as insomnia, phobias, and withdrawal, not unlike children this age in sole custody. Joint custody does not undo the child's distress. The central worry for young children in both custodial arrangements remains the same: fear of abandonment. The creation of two homes, from the child's perspective, still adds up to less stability than the one home where mother and father live together with the children under one roof. Moreover, the transitions between the two homes can easily reinforce anxiety about constancy and reliability of people and places.

Overall, the children in this study turn to adults, rather than to themselves or peers, to solve their problems. In some instances, they cling to adults at school and seem less independent than other children their age. At the same time, they seem to trust that adults' help will be forthcoming.

The children's adjustment is not related to any particular formula of joint custody but very much reflects the quality of parenting in each home, the amount of conflict and cooperation between parents, and the situations the child has to face outside the home at a given time.

We have been surprised to observe that children entering nursery school and kindergarten (the three-, four-, and five-year-olds) show more troubled behavior than the one- and two-year-olds. Some four- and five-year-olds have chronic nightmares and seem upset by the many changes in their lives.

One reason four- and five-year-olds do less well may be that children at this age face complex developmental challenges. They are in a major transition, moving away from mother and out on their own. They have a lot more to master — beginning group play, sharing, taking turns, riding bikes, and taking chances different from those faced by the toddler. Some children seem overwhelmed by the combination of changeover days, school demands, new adults brought home by parents, and many different caretaking arrangements — all in addition to the normal developmental demands of early childhood.

There is evidence from other research[1] and from my own observations that children in elementary school may be better equipped to adapt to joint custody arrangements. For one thing, they can speak for themselves. They may adjust to having different relationships with different people, coping with changes in routines more easily than preschoolers. Children in elementary school are more likely to adapt to the changeovers, whereas younger children sometimes regard the changeovers as a form of punishment, as if they are being sent away because they have been naughty. School-age children are more likely to feel wanted by the other parent and to cope with leaving one parent to visit the other. They can feel pride in mastering the changeover that poses such problems to younger children. Six-to-ten-year-olds may even enjoy the sense of being courted by two parents, of dividing their favors and holidays. Having outgrown Hansel and Gretel–like fears of getting lost in the woods, older children do not worry so much about the transitions, for they usually have mastered the concepts of time, distance, and alternating schedules. In addition, with older children, parents must continue to be vigilant and sensitive to all the childrearing issues, but they do not need to keep up the intensive, detailed communication required in raising preschoolers.

Many elementary school children tell us that they prefer joint custody to single custody. Admitting that it is often difficult, they say they feel better off, luckier than their peers in single custody homes. Nevertheless, in a recent joint custody study, one-third of the elementary school–age children were troubled and unhappy.

Every now and then, though, we are fooled. One eight-year-old boy, who we thought was content, had spent half his life going from state to state between two homes. When I asked him the usual question that we ask all children of divorce — if you had three wishes, what would they be? — he said, "I want to die."

Startled at this unexpected response, I said, "Why? What would happen if you died?"

"If I were dead," the little boy said in a somber tone, "I'd be in heaven. My dad would be there. My mom would be there. And we'd live in the same house."

We lack detailed information about how younger or older adolescents feel about joint custody. Most adolescents that I have seen, with some exceptions, prefer to live at one house and have one telephone number. This seems more compatible with their social lives. Many teenagers say that they prefer to spend vacations with the other parent rather than to carry on a full-fledged joint custody lifestyle. They find it somewhat insulting to have to move between parents at a time when parents are not at the center of their lives. Some adolescents prefer joint custody when one or both parents are remarried.

The group in our joint custody study is very small, but it represents, at this writing, the only reported study of very young children in joint custody arrangements. We conclude that young children are not necessarily protected from the deleterious effects of divorce simply because of joint custody. Nor is there any evidence that good joint custody better serves these children than good single custody when the noncustodial parent stays involved. It is important that the fathers be more involved in their children's upbringing, but joint custody arrangements do not guarantee more happiness for children.

Voluntary joint custody is not easy. It requires two parents who are able to maintain a commitment over time and who are able to carve out a conflict-free zone for their children. Such parents live with a high degree of ambiguity and tension, learning to compromise their differences in the children's best interests. In my experience, the courts tend to worry about "big" family issues such as religious training, education, and moral influence. But joint custody succeeds or fails on the bedrock of "little" issues. Coparenting requires large amounts of cooperation, communication, sensitivity, and flexibility and also the ability to allow the ex-partner to enjoy a separate life including love affairs.

In addition to making special demands on parents, joint custody makes new demands on children. Not all children have the flexibility to go back and forth between homes and to adjust to two different environments. Indeed, a child's basic temperament is a major contributing factor to his or her adjustment. Children who succeed in a joint custody arrangement have an elusive characteristic that we are not used to considering in psychological assessments — flexibility, an important factor in how well this new family form works. Psychological tests measure many characteristics, but flexibility is not one. Children who are relatively calm and easygoing from birth are more likely to adapt well to joint custody arrangements, as they are more likely to adapt to many other changing circumstances. Children who are cranky and irritable from the start and who have trouble mastering simple routines seem to have more trouble with joint custody, as they do with other changes. Basic temperament therefore plays a role in how well this family form works.

At its best, joint custody enables children to maintain a close relationship with both parents and to enrich their lives with membership in two functioning households. At its worst, joint custody can lock children into a destructive relationship with a violent or otherwise inadequate parent or into a continuing, bitter struggle between angry parents, so that the child runs the gauntlet in both homes — and feels that he or she has no home anywhere.

Worse, perhaps, joint custody exposes the children of divorce to a potential but devastating psychological blow: If and when a parent pulls out of joint custody, there is absolutely no way the child can attribute his or her loss to the parents' rejection of the marriage. The child can only perceive in his or her heart that the loss of commitment is really rejection of the child himself or herself.

While small studies such as this provide rich details about the effects of joint custody, larger studies are required to scientifically assess the various custody arrangements. The largest study on joint custody to date, which included careful examination of children over time, was recently completed at our center.[2] In 1981, we enlisted 184 couples with 354 children between the ages of three and fourteen and followed them for several years. Two years after the separation, a third of the children were living in joint custody households while the others were in sole custody households. In comparing the two groups over time, we have had an unprecedented opportunity to compare how children adapt to custody arrangements in the first few years after divorce.

When we examined the children's lives, it soon became clear that the amount of time spent in either household is not the critical issue, but the sheer frequency of transitions between households can be upsetting. For example, a child can spend one week at each parent's house or can switch homes every other day. The amount of time spent with each parent is roughly equal but one child experiences many more transitions or changeover days than the other child. Frequent transitions, we have learned, matter to children, for they introduce disruptions and require many new adaptations in a brief period of time.

When we began this study, our profession was divided into two camps in the joint custody debate. One held that it would hurt children to go back and forth more frequently between two homes because the children would feel insecure and bewildered, as if they had a home nowhere. The other said that the children would be much better off after a few years because they would be less traumatized by divorce. They would have maintained equal access to both parents, more like an intact family.

Our findings will come as a surprise to both camps. Two years after divorce, children raised in joint custody households are no better adjusted than children raised in sole custody homes. Despite more access to both parents, joint custody children show neither less disturbance nor better social adjustment than sole custody children. Unfortunately, joint custody does not minimize the negative impact of divorce on children during the early postdivorce years. The custody arrangement itself exerts but a minor influence on the psychological adjustment of children. Other, more familiar factors weigh more heavily — the mother's anxiety or depression, the parents' emotional functioning at separation, the amount of conflict between the parents a year later, the age and sex of the children, and the children's temperaments. Joint custody *may* have positive psychological effects over the longer haul — we just don't know yet. Since we do know that the first two or three years after divorce are the most stressful and that important differences may show up between the groups, as they do for individuals, five and ten years after divorce, we hope to prepare a long-term follow-up of these families.

On a more encouraging note, we find that the fathers in joint custody families are more committed to their children. None has "dropped out" or stopped the visiting, whereas 7 percent of fathers have stopped visiting their children in sole custody arrangements. As one father of a two-year-old told me, "This has forced me to have a different kind of relationship with my son. When we're together, we're totally together." Many fathers are proud of their new parenting skills and are gratified by new relationships with their children. But the fact that fathers are more involved does not, in itself, improve the psychological outcome of children two years later. The fact that the father feels better about parenting may not be enough to override the trauma of divorce.

All our work has pointed to the fact that many strands influence and compose an individual's psychological adjustment. It is tempting to focus on one aspect or another, but such efforts are misleading; a confluence of factors determines psychological well-being in the years after divorce. Our newer studies indicate that custody and visiting arrangements are but one thread in the tapestry that makes up the family's quality of life after divorce and that relationships in the family and the overall quality of life are what determine a child's well-being.

We know even less about another variation on new family forms — *court-ordered* joint custody. Up to now we have looked only at families who voluntarily enter particular custody arrangements. Both parents were committed to the arrangement and worked to set aside their differences in the interest of coparenting their children. The legal system, however, has at times ordered joint custody over the strong objections of one parent. What is life like for such children? Do their parents come to some sort of accommodation? Or are the children shunted, like weapons, between two warring households?

The first study of such families, directed by Dr. Janet Johnston, research director at our center, does not augur well.[3] Children raised in joint custody arrangements that result from a court order in the wake of bitterly contested divorces seem to fare much worse than children raised in traditional sole custody families also torn by bitter fighting. In the light of our findings that frequent contact with two angry, feuding parents is detrimental for children, this is understandable. In some instances, however, courts have optimistically presumed that joint custody would cool the anger between angry parents and that the cooperation required to bring off joint custody would force angry parents onto common ground. This is not so. The opposite has proved true. Children caught in these situations look more depressed, more withdrawn or aggressive, and more disturbed. Generally, little girls are protected by close mother-daughter relationships that develop after divorce. Forced joint custody, however, can prevent this protective relationship from blossoming. Some mothers in these bitter disputes become irrationally angry at their little girls for going to the father's house and may just as irrationally reject them when they return. Little boys are similarly caught up and used by one or both parents in the continued conflict, as they crisscross the no-man's land between the two homes. The custody arrangement designed by the courts to help these children boomerangs and makes them much worse. Simple solutions do not work in complicated situations like bitterly contested divorces.

These findings are discouraging because many of us who work with divorced families had hopes that bringing fathers back into childrearing roles would help children. But a joint custody arrangement to which both parents do not submit voluntarily may not be the answer; there is no evidence that joint custody is best for all, or even for most, families. We still do not know what kind of arrangement is best for whom and when. Nor do we know how long voluntary joint custody arrangements do or should last. In a brief follow-up with the members of the joint custody study group in the spring of 1987, I discovered that many had changed the arrangements because one or both parents no longer considered the earlier arrangement suitable for the children. At the same time, an equal number had endured and these children and parents seemed very satisfied. Actually, there would have been no way of knowing from the discussions in the group when it first started meeting which of the arrangements were likely to endure or to break down.

Just as there are many kinds of marriages and divorces, there should be many kinds of postdivorce families. The formal arrangements between the parents and children — who spends time with whom and where — does not seem to shape relationships between parents and children in divorced families any more than it does in intact families. Simply spending time together does not ensure a good parent-child relationship any more than placing a man and a woman in the same house, room, or bed creates a good marriage. It is the relationships themselves that matter.

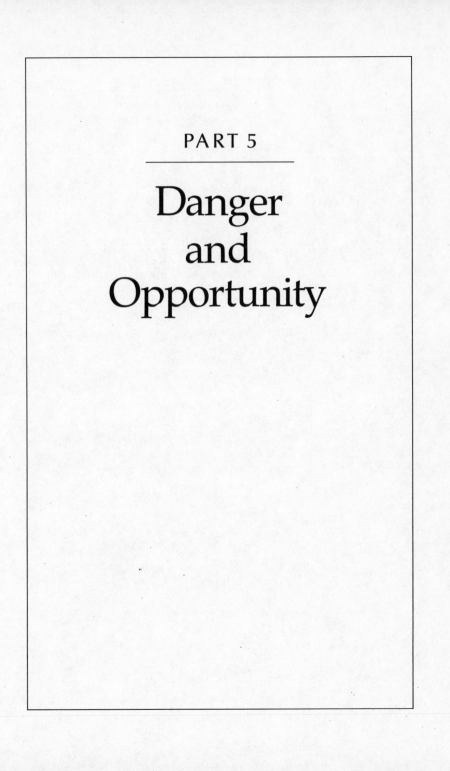

PART 5

Danger
and
Opportunity

17

The Psychological Tasks
of Divorce

IN CHINESE CALLIGRAPHY, the word for crisis is written by joining the symbols for danger and opportunity, capturing the essence of what psychologists have learned in many years of observing people in different kinds of crises. Whereas a severe personal disappointment, bereavement, divorce, community disaster, or other crisis threatens the psychological and physical well-being of individuals and families, the way in which people respond to the crisis is critical in shaping the final outcome. Thus, each crisis presents both a blow *and* a challenge, or more accurately, a set of challenges or tasks.

The danger in every crisis is that people will remain in the same place, continuing through the years to react to the initial impact as if it had just struck. The opportunities in every crisis are for people to rebuild what was destroyed or to create a reasonable substitute; to be able to grow emotionally, establish new competence and pride; and to strengthen intimate relationships far beyond earlier capacities.

Psychological Tasks for Adults

Divorce entails two sets of tasks for the adults involved. The first is to rebuild their lives as adults so as to make good use of the second chances that divorce provides. The second task is to parent the children after the divorce, protecting them from the crossfire between the ex-spouses and nurturing them as they grow up.

Although people may indeed feel overwhelmed, as if everything is happening all at once, the families in our study have taught us that there is an order and sequence to these tasks, a certain logic underlying the chaos. No one person will fully confront and resolve each one of the challenges inherent in divorce. That is not humanly possible. Rather, they represent ideal guideposts that can help mark the way. Negotiating these tasks requires all the strength and pluck, all the dogged persistence that any one person can muster. I have often wondered where people find the energy and courage needed to go through a divorce and reconstruct their lives. My answer came from a woman who, in the face of opposition from her family, husband, and friends, nevertheless pressed for divorce, marshaling extraordinary courage in the act. She said, in words I will never forget, "I felt that I was dying."

TASK: *Ending the Marriage*

The way that a family separates in a divorce (apart from what actually went on in the marriage) can help determine the nature of the post-divorce years for everyone involved. Indeed, the separation becomes an entity in itself, a major marker of divorce that freezes certain images — the goodbye note left on the kitchen table, the child's bedroom emptied out — and forever influences the course of the life that follows. When families continue erratic, mutually destructive behavior for many years after the divorce, the fury is often rooted in and feeds on the way the marriage came apart — one partner suddenly finding the other having an affair with a mutual best friend; one partner leaving a note informing the other, without warning, that the marriage is dead; one parent departing suddenly, taking the children, providing no address, and leaving the abandoned parent to search frantically for word of their safety. When marriages end on such notes, images freeze, fanning enduring rage and crippling second chances.

The first task of divorce, therefore, is to bring the marriage to an end in as civilized a manner as possible, without one partner guiltily giving away his or her rights, taking flight just to get it over with, playing saint or sinner, sadist or masochist, or being controlled by the wish to inflict pain or get revenge. Such feelings and temptations can compete for center stage as the marriage ends. Although it is extraordinarily difficult, adults must negotiate and conclude financial and child custody arrangements with as much reality, morality, emotional stability, and enlightened self-interest as they can muster. This demands the near impossible at the time of greatest stress. The adults need to set aside intense, competing passions, realistically assess the children's needs as separate from their own, and strike the best and fairest overall deal.

When well done, this task has the potential to ease future years for adults and children. Done poorly, it can set the stage for years of continued anger, deprivation, and suffering for everyone involved.

TASK: *Mourning the Loss*

This task begins as the marriage comes apart and lasts well into the postdivorce period. If the marriage has lasted many years, mourning is more difficult and can take longer. But even a brief marriage requires a proper burial, especially if there have been children.

Each ex-partner must first acknowledge the loss and mourn the dreams and hopes that were never fully realized and never will be realized. It is important to cry, for only crying reduces anger to human size. And only by mourning can a person regain or maintain perspective on what was lost. And only by mourning will the adults be able to close the door and move on. Even the most miserable marriage embodied some expectation of a better life, companionship, love, and esteem, and although no tears may be shed for the lost partner, the symbolic meaning of the marriage should be put to rest with gentleness.

An unmourned marriage harbors many dangers. Some people refuse to believe that the marriage is ending and act as if it were not so. They sit night after night by the telephone, hoping that the ex-partner will call. Preoccupied with the former partner's life, others use their children as voyeurs and spies. Still others force continued contact through protracted litigation. An unmourned marriage is one that psychologically continues and in so doing shores up the feelings associated with the separation, keeping them at their most hurtful.

TASK: *Reclaiming Oneself*

This is another step that, along with mourning, signifies detachment from the marriage. It involves reclaiming or establishing a new sense of self, a new sense of identity. In a long-term marriage, a partner's sense of identity is tied to his or her spouse and to the marriage. Most married people carry the same name for reasons beyond convention.

In a multitude of ways, they have become a new "we" that is different from the "you and I" who entered the marriage. Even in this feminist age, many women continue to derive their primary sense of who they are from their marriage. These roles fall away at divorce and a new sense of self needs to be built to replace the old identity.

There are many ways to do this. One is for each partner to reach back into his or her early experience and find other images and roots for independence, for being able to live alone, and for undertaking the second chances provided by divorce.

Most of all, the voice of the former partner — carping or demeaning, petulant or demanding — needs to be exorcised from within, so that the man or woman does not carry the old marital failure into the new relationships and ventures. Expectation of failure can become a self-fulfilling prophecy.

TASK: *Resolving or Containing Passions*

Unlike any other crisis, divorce engenders feelings that can engulf people for years, coming as unbidden flashbacks and bitter memories of exploitation and betrayal. These feelings are often refueled over the years by subsequent events: the remarriage of the ex-partner, the failure of one's own remarriage, financial inequity, or the inevitably different life courses each person follows after divorce. These preoccupying passions have the potential to destroy the person who feels so wronged. The reason to try to resolve them is not to turn the other cheek but to save oneself from being dominated by the trauma of divorce.

Anger or a sense of outrage can erupt into violence of many kinds. Direct physical violence between adults is rare after divorce. But child stealing — a form of displaced violence between parents — is not uncommon. Other, less direct forms of violence include Medea-like efforts to use children as weapons in the ongoing, unremitting conflict and allowing harm to the children as part of the revenge against the ex-spouse.

TASK: *Venturing Forth Again*

To restore a sense of competence and self-esteem, a divorced man or woman has to find the courage to try new relationships, new roles, and new solutions to old problems in both the workplace and the sexual arena. People who divorce often lose confidence in their own judgment; at some point they must venture forth in order to regain that confidence. They think, "How could I have been so stupid?" And they conclude, "How can I ever trust myself again?" Feeling that they have erred, they are afraid to risk again.

Sometimes people come to feel that planning is futile. They sense that life gives hard knocks and is essentially unpredictable; they conclude that the best-laid plans go awry and become discouraged about setting long-range or even short-range goals, much less working toward those goals.

There is no substitute for courage. In trying again and again to move out of the lingering shadow of divorce, people encounter the inescapable fact that failure is always possible, that danger is the flip side of opportunity. Confidence is achieved not in one large step, but in many little steps along the way, and hardly ever in a straight line.

TASK: *Rebuilding*

This is the central psychological and social task of divorce, involving all the foregoing tasks as building blocks. The goal is to create a new, sustained adult relationship that will be better than the one left behind and that will include the children or to establish a gratifying life outside of marriage that includes but does not overburden the children. In finding postdivorce stability, a person must allow the obligations, the memories, and the lessons of the past to coexist peacefully with experiences in the present. This is the true essence of second chances.

*

Although I have spelled out these tasks in sequence, each person necessarily goes back and forth, working on one and then another, or on some simultaneously, over the years. Like all else in life, solutions are relative. I have found that some people forgive and most never forget, nor need they. But it is true that new growth can take root only in prepared soil that is not already overgrown. Similarly, new relationships need space created by a person's detaching from the old and being receptive to the new.

TASK: *Helping the Children*

Above and beyond the tasks of rebuilding adult lives are the equally daunting tasks of helping children through the breakdown of the marriage and all the postdivorce years.

Children of divorce have learned firsthand that relationships can be broken, and they are afraid of being abandoned. Having seen their parents do battle, they are afraid of being caught in the middle. Having seen their parents fail, they fear future failures in their parents' and their own lives. Having seen infidelity in their parents' marriage, they feel that their parents will be unfaithful to them. They therefore need strong assurances that parents will safeguard their growing-up years and will be responsive to their needs and concerns.

Despite their unhappy feelings about each other, both parents need to make long-lasting commitments to their children for as long as the children need them. This involves being able psychologically to separate the child's needs from their own adult needs. It means providing financial support to the extent the child would have expected in the intact marriage and greater emotional support to offset the greater anxiety suffered by the child.

This does not mean that parents can or should always try to be coparents or that all parents should be encouraged to remain close to their children. In the real world, some parents are detrimental to their children. In such situations, it may be in the children's best interests not to have close contact with a parent. On the other hand, occasional contact may prevent children from idealizing an inadequate parent. These are complicated matters that need to be assessed case by case.

Children respond initially to divorce according to their age and development at the time of the breakup. By understanding age-specific reactions and knowing what to expect, parents will be better able to help each child.

Preschool. Because preschool children are dependent on parents for their total physical care, they are most afraid of being abandoned. Because they are young, they do not yet understand time and cause and effect. Their lack of experience generates an obvious logic: If one parent can disappear, certainly the other one can disappear just as easily. Since their concept of time is so limited, it may not help them to be told that "Daddy will come next Monday." Since their concept of distance is equally limited, they can't always be sure when they visit Daddy's house that they will find their way back to Mommy's house. Like Hansel and Gretel, preschoolers constantly worry that they will not find their way home. Given their dependence, fears, limited understanding of family events, and inability to comfort themselves, preschoolers react strongly to divorce.

They may have trouble separating from parents, day and night, and they especially do not want to let the custodial parent out of their sight. Many have trouble settling down or sleeping through the night. They may resume earlier behaviors such as thumb sucking, bedwetting, and Linus-like attachment to a security object. Young children are likely to become increasingly cranky. They may smack a younger baby or clobber their playmates. They often feel that their real or imagined naughtiness caused the divorce, and they can become sad and withdrawn.

Parents have trouble realizing that very young children experience things differently from adults. Often what strikes a child as terrifying — an unfamiliar face or noise — completely escapes adult attention. Because young children don't understand cause and effect, it is no wonder they cannot understand their parents' behavior. It is very hard for adults to realize how big we look to two-year-olds. We really are the giants in the fairy tales.

Early school years, ages five to eight. Children this age are likely to be preoccupied with feelings of loss, rejection, guilt, and loyalty conflicts. They are profoundly worried that they will forever lose the parent, usually the father, who has left home. They are especially afraid of being replaced. "Will Daddy get a new dog? A new mommy? A new little boy?" Little girls weave elaborate fantasies, asserting that the father will return to them "when he grows up."

Their behavior during and after the divorce reflects these fears and fantasies: They may cry, be cranky, feel empty inside, be unable to concentrate. In our study, half the children in this age group suffered a year-long precipitous decline in school performance. Many little boys show an intense longing for their fathers that seems physically painful. They seem very worried about being left in the sole charge of a woman, someone who in their unconscious fantasy drove their father off the turf. Because of their own psychological needs — and not necessarily because of parental coaching — many children this age cast the divorce as a fight in which they feel required to take sides. They are often tormented by these loyalty conflicts.

Later school years, nine to twelve. Children this age rely tremendously on their parents for stability, as if the parents are holding up a stage on which the children act out their lives. The child on stage learns, plays, and acquires social skills. With divorce, children become intensely anxious that the stage will collapse, disrupting their present and future plans.

Their behavior, in turn, reflects this anxiety. Many children this age become intensely angry at their parents for divorcing. They are especially furious at the parent whom they blame for the divorce. They also suffer grief, anxiety, an acute sense of loneliness, and a sense of powerlessness. Their insecurity and tendency to think in terms of black and white make them vulnerable to the blandishments of parents who seek to ally the children in their warfare. In our study, it is mainly children of this age who formed mischievous alignments with one parent designed to humiliate or harass the other parent.

Children also worry very much about their troubled parents and can become adept at helping them. They can provide love, care, and companionship, and they may feel that their parents would fall apart without their constant care. Sometimes they take on very adult roles in relation to the needy parent, a situation that can drain the child emotionally.

Children of this age sometimes complain of somatic symptoms, usually stomachaches and headaches. Peer relationships may suffer; delinquent behavior, such as petty stealing, lying, and manipulations, sometimes appears; and school performance often drops suddenly. These children can be overstimulated by the dating and sexual behavior they observe in their parents.

Adolescence. People are often surprised at the severity of reactions to divorce among adolescents, for they assume that teenagers are old enough to understand and accommodate to what is happening. But people do not realize how frightening divorce is to young people. The collapse of the household is especially upsetting for adolescents because they have a strong need for family structure to help them set limits on their own sexual and aggressive impulses.

Teenagers are also terrified that they will repeat their parents' failures. They worry about the future. Will their own marriages also fail? Many feel rejected by both parents, who are wrapped up in their own problems and have little time for them. Teenagers may also grow acutely anxious as they see the vulnerability of their parents. The normal anxieties of adolescence are heightened. It disturbs teenagers to see their parents as people with sexual problems and impulses, just as they themselves are trying to cope with their own emerging sexuality. They sense that the generation gap has been violated, and in response they may spend more time away from home. Feeling angry at and abandoned by their parents, some teens move quickly into sexual activity; others may respond by assuming more responsibility such as helping out with chores and decisions. In this process they may acquire greater strength and independence or may forfeit important aspects of their adolescent experience.

Every aspect of the children's lives can be made easier by the parents' attitudes at the time of the crisis as well as later. Parents' support is critical in preparing children for the divorce and in seeing them through the turmoil surrounding it. The children of divorce are dependent on adult help to understand what is happening in the family, to master the new, complex relationships during the postdivorce years, to mourn the losses associated with divorce, to master anxiety, to overcome guilt, and to undertake all the psychological tasks that divorce entails.

The first step in helping children occurs at the time of the impending separation, when parents can prepare the children for what lies ahead. Parents should take very seriously what they say to their children and how they say it, for what they say or fail to say will long be remembered. There is no way to prevent children from suffering at the time of divorce, but there are many ways to ameliorate suffering and fear:

If possible, both parents should tell the children together. By representing unity, they convey the sense that a rational, mature decision has been made. If such unity is impossible, one parent should break the news.

It is better to tell all the children at once than each separately. We have found that children in divorced families can genuinely help one another. If there is a wide age difference, it is useful to tell them together and then separately, adapting each explanation to each child's level of understanding.

Children should be told about the divorce when it has become a firm decision. They should know within a few days or a week or two beforehand of one parent's intention to leave the home. It is cruel to tell children after one parent has already left, for it is an experience they never forget.

When it is time to discuss the decision, parents should offer a clear explanation of what is going on in the family. Children need to know what divorce means, although the explanation will vary according to their age. One cannot tell a three-year-old, "Daddy and I are divorcing," for a child that age does not know what marriage is, much less divorce. By the same token, an adolescent should be told about the legal process, what is involved in filing, and how decisions are made.

Children have the right to understand why the divorce is happening because it is a major, if not *the* major, crisis in their lives. Also, children cannot mobilize their energies to cope with a crisis that they do not comprehend. Details of infidelity or sexual deprivation need not be divulged, but parents can say something along these lines: "We married fully hoping and expecting to love each other forever, but we have discovered that one (or both) of us is unhappy. One (or both) does not love the other anymore. We fight with each other. The divorce is going to stop the fighting and restore peace." In essence, the divorce is presented as a solution that the parents have come to reluctantly, only after exploring a range of other options. The decision has been made rationally and reached sadly. In this way, in this best of all possible worlds, the goal is to present the child with models of parents who admit they made a serious mistake, tried to rectify the mistake, and are now embarking on a moral, socially acceptable remedy. The parents are responsible people who remain committed to the family and to the children even though they have decided to go their separate ways.

The expression of sadness is important because it gives children permission to cry and mourn without having to hide their feelings of loss from the adults or from themselves.

Rationality is important because it contributes to the child's moral development. The parents can remain as moral figures in the child's mind.

Clarity is important so that the children will not be encouraged to undertake any efforts at reconciliation. While parents need to assure children that the children are not responsible for the breakup of the marriage, children also need to hear that they cannot rescue or restore the marriage.

Reluctance is important because children need to feel that parents are aware of how profoundly upset the children will be. By apologizing for imposing this disruption on the children's lives, the parents make it clear that it is not their intention to cause hurt. Put simply, parents should tell the children they are sorry for all the hurt they are causing.

If true, parents can say that the children have been one of the greatest pleasures of the marriage. If true, parents should tell children that the marriage has been loving at some time in the past.

Parents need to prepare children for what lies ahead in as much concrete detail as possible. They should admit that in all honesty, things will change. Life will be disorganized, routines disrupted. One parent is moving out of the home. The house may be sold. The family may have to move to a new neighborhood. The mother, if not already employed outside the home, may go back to school or out to find part-time or full-time work.

Courage is a good word to use in explaining divorce to children. Parents should tell children that everyone will have to be brave. It is a crisis that the whole family will need to face together.

Children also need to be assured that they will be told of all major developments. As soon as the parent who is moving out has a new place to live, the children will be taken to see it. They will have a say in setting up the visiting arrangements, which will start as soon as possible. They should be told the visiting schedule in detail.

Children feel powerless at divorce and should be invited to make suggestions that the adults will consider seriously. In this way, they can feel like active instead of passive agents in the crisis. This does not mean that the children should be made to feel responsible for major decisions. The goal is to involve them appropriately so that they can feel that they are participating in negotiating a solution to the family crisis.

Children also need to be told repeatedly that the divorce does not weaken the bond between parent and child, even though they will now live apart. Geographical distance does not translate into emotional distance or less love. Parents may divorce each other but they do not divorce their children. But children should be told realistically that parents and children will have to work harder to maintain the important connections.

Finally, parents need to give the children permission to love both parents. This may be the hardest task of all for the parents, but children need to feel that their individual integrity is respected, that they have a right to their own feelings, and that they are not being asked to ally with one parent against the other. The divorce, it should be emphasized, is a matter between the two adults. The children should not be burdened with having to share one parent's anger against the other.

The foregoing advice, of course, applies to the early stages of the divorce. As we learned from the Moores, the Burrelles, the Catalanos, and others, children and adolescents continue to need the support of their parents during the years that follow. The tasks that the children confront make this very clear.

Psychological Tasks for Children

At each stage in the life cycle, children and adults face predictable and particular issues that represent the coming together of the demands of society and a biological and psychological timetable. Just as we physically learn to sit, crawl, walk, and run, we follow an equivalent progression in our psychological and social development. Each stage presents us with a sequence of tasks we must confront. We can succeed or fail in mastering them, to varying degrees, but everyone encounters the tasks. They begin at birth and end at death.

Children move upward along a common developmental ladder, although each goes it alone at his or her own pace. Gradually, as they pass through the various stages, children consolidate a sense of self. They develop coping skills, conscience, and the capacity to give and receive love.

Children take one step at a time, negotiating the rung they are on before they can move up to the next. They may — and often do — falter in this effort. The climb is not steady under the best of circumstances, and most children briefly stand still in their ascent. They may even at times move backward. Such regressions are not a cause for alarm; rather, they may represent an appropriate response to life's stresses. Children who fail one task are not stalled forever; they will go on to the next stage, although they may be weakened in their climb. Earlier failures will not necessarily imperil their capacity as adults to trust a relationship, make a commitment, hold an appropriate job, or be a parent — to make use of their second chances at each stage of development.

I propose that children who experience divorce face an additional set of tasks specific to divorce in addition to the normal developmental tasks of growing up. Growing up is inevitably harder for children of divorce because they must deal with psychological issues that children from well-functioning intact families do not have to face.

The psychological tasks of children begin as difficulties escalate between the parents during the marriage, continue through the separation and divorce and throughout the postdivorce years.

TASK: *Understanding the Divorce*

The first and most basic task at the time of separation is for the children to understand realistically what the divorce means in their family and what its concrete consequences will be. Children, especially very young children, are thrown back on frightening and vivid fantasies of being abandoned, being placed in foster care, or never seeing a departed parent again, or macabre fantasies such as a mother being destroyed in an earthquake or a father being destroyed by a vengeful mother. All of these fantasies and the feelings that accompany them can be undone only as the children, with the parents' continuing help, begin to understand the reality and begin to adjust to the actual changes that the divorce brings.

The more mature task of understanding what led to the marital failure awaits the perspective of the adolescent and young adult. Early on, most children regard divorce as a serious error, but by adolescence most feel that their parents never should have married. The task of understanding occurs in two stages. The first involves accurately perceiving the immediate changes that divorce brings and differentiating fantasy fears from reality. The second occurs later, when children are able at greater distance and with more mature understanding to evaluate their parents' actions and can draw useful lessons for their own lives.

TASK: *Strategic Withdrawal*

Children and adolescents need to get on with their own lives as soon as possible after the divorce, to resume their normal activities at school and at play, to get back physically and emotionally to the normal tasks of growing up. Especially for adolescents who may have been beginning to spread their wings, the divorce pulls them back into the family orbit, where they may become consumed with care for siblings or a troubled parent. It also intrudes on their academic and social life, causing them to spend class time preoccupied with worry and to pass up social activities because of demands at home. This is not to say that children should ignore the divorce. Their task is to acknowledge their concern and to provide appropriate help to their parents and siblings, but they should strive to remove the divorce from the center of their own thoughts so that they can get back to their own interests, pleasures, problems, and peer relationships. To achieve this task, children need encouragement from their parents to *remain* children.

TASK: *Dealing with Loss*

In the years following divorce, children experience two profound losses. One is the loss of the intact family together with the symbolic and real protection it has provided. The second is the loss of the presence of one parent, usually the father, from their daily lives.

In dealing with these losses, children fall back on many fantasies to mask their unhappiness. As we have seen, they may idealize the father as representative of all that is lacking in their current lives, thinking that if only he were present, everything would be better.

The task of absorbing loss is perhaps the single most difficult task imposed by divorce. At its core, the task requires children to overcome the profound sense of rejection, humiliation, unlovability, and powerlessness they feel with the departure of one parent. When the parent leaves, children of all ages blame themselves. They say, "He left me because I was not lovable. I was not worthy." They conclude that had they been more lovable, worthy, or different, the parent would have stayed. In this way, the loss of the parent and lowered self-esteem become intertwined.

To stave off these intensely painful feelings of rejection, children continually try to undo the divorce scenario, to bring their parents back together, or to somehow win back the affection of the absent parent. The explanation "Had he loved me, he would not have left the family" turns into a new concern. "If he loved me, he would visit more often. He would spend more time with me." With this in mind, the children not only are pained at the outset but remain vulnerable, sometimes increasingly, over the years. Many reach out during adolescence to increase contact with the parent who left, again to undo the sad scenario and to rebuild their self-esteem as well.

This task is easier if parents and children have a good relationship, within the framework of a good visiting or joint custody arrangement.

Some children are able to use a good, close relationship with the visiting parent to promote their growth within the divorced family. Others are able to acknowledge and accept that the visiting parent could never become the kind of parent they need, and they are able to turn away from blaming themselves. Still others are able to reject, on their own, a rejecting parent or to reject a role model that they see as flawed. In so doing, these youngsters are able to effectively master the loss and get on with their lives.

TASK: *Dealing with Anger*

Divorce, unlike death, is always a voluntary decision for at least one of the partners in a marriage. Everyone involved knows this. The child understands that divorce is not a natural disaster like an earthquake or tornado; it is caused by the decision of one or both of the parents to separate. Its true cause lies in the parents' failure to maintain the marriage, and someone is culpable.

Given this knowledge, children face a terrible dilemma. They know that their unhappiness has been caused by the very people charged with their protection and care — their parents are the agents of their distress. Furthermore, the parents undertook this role voluntarily. This realization puts children in a dreadful bind because they know something that they dare not express — out of fear, out of anxiety, out of a wish to protect their parents.

Children get angry at their parents, experiencing divorce as indifference to their needs and perceiving parents sometimes realistically as self-centered and uncaring, as preaching a corrupt morality, and as weak and unable to deal with problems except by running away.

At the same time, children are aware of their parents' neediness, weaknesses, and anxiety about life's difficulties. Although children have little understanding of divorce, except when the fighting has been open and violent, they fully recognize how unhappy and disorganized their parents become, and this frightens them very much.

Caught in a combination of anger and love, the children are frightened and guilty about their anger because they love their parents and perceive them as unhappy people who are trying to improve their lives in the face of severe obstacles. Their concern makes it difficult even to acknowledge their anger.

A major task, then, for children is to work through this anger, to recognize their parents as human beings capable of making mistakes, and to respect them for their real efforts and their real courage.

Cooling of anger and the task of forgiveness go hand in hand with children's growing emotional maturity and capacity to appreciate the various needs of the different family members. As anger diminishes, young people are better able to put the divorce behind them and experience relief. As children forgive their parents, they forgive themselves for feeling anger and guilt and for failing to restore the marriage. In this way, children can free themselves from identification with the angry or violent parent or with the victim.

TASK: *Working Out Guilt*

Young children often feel responsible for divorce, thinking that their misbehavior may have caused one parent to leave. Or, in a more complicated way, they may feel that their fantasy wish to drive a wedge between their mother and father has been magically granted. Many guilty feelings arise at the time of divorce but dissipate naturally as children mature. Others persist, usually with roots in a profound continuing sense of having caused the unthinkable — getting rid of one parent so as to be closer to the other.

Other feelings of guilt are rooted in children's realization that they were indeed a cause of marital difficulty. Many divorces occur after the birth of a child, and the child correctly comprehends that he or she really did drive a wedge between the adults.

We see another kind of guilt in girls who, in identifying with their troubled mothers, become afraid to surpass their mothers. These young women have trouble separating from their mothers, whom they love and feel sorry for, and establishing their own successful relationships with suitable young men. The children of divorce need to separate from guilty ties that bind them too closely to a troubled parent and to go on with their lives with compassion and love.

TASK: *Accepting the Permanence of the Divorce*

At first, children feel a strong and understandable need to deny the divorce. Such early denial may be a first step in the coping process. Like a screen that is alternately lowered and raised, the denial helps children confront the full reality of the divorce, bit by bit. They cannot take it in all at once.

Nevertheless, we have learned that five and even ten years after divorce, some children and adolescents refuse to accept the divorce as a permanent state of affairs. They continue to hope, consciously or unconsciously, that the marriage will be restored, finding omens of reconciliation even in a harmless handshake or a simple friendly nod.

In accepting permanence, the children of divorce face a more difficult task than children of bereavement. Death cannot be undone, but divorce happens between living people who can change their minds. A reconciliation fantasy taps deep into children's psyches. Children need to feel that their parents will still be happy together. They may not overcome this fantasy of reconciliation until they themselves finally separate from their parents and leave home.

TASK: *Taking a Chance on Love*

This is perhaps the most important task for growing children and for society. Despite what life has dealt them, despite lingering fears and anxieties, the children of divorce must grow, become open to the possibility of success or failure, and take a chance on love. They must hold on to a realistic vision that they can both love and be loved.

This is the central task for youngsters during adolescence and at entry into young adulthood. And as we have seen, it is the task on which so many children tragically founder. Children who lose a parent through death must take a chance on loving with the knowledge that all people eventually die and that death can take away our loved ones at any time. Children who lose the intact family through divorce must also take a chance on love, knowing realistically that divorce is always possible but being willing nevertheless to remain open to love, commitment, marriage, and fidelity.

More than the ideology of hoping to fall in love and find commitment, this task involves being able to turn away from the model of parents who could not stay committed to each other. While all the young people in our study were in search of romantic love, a large number of them lived with such a high degree of anxiety over fears of betrayal or of not finding love that they were entirely unable to take the kind of chances necessary for them to move emotionally into successful young adulthood.

This last task, taking a chance on love, involves being able to venture, not just thinking about it, and not thinking one way and behaving another. It involves accepting a morality that truly guides behavior. This is the task that occupies children of divorce throughout their adolescence. It is what makes adolescence such a critical and difficult time for them. The resolution of life's tasks is a relative process that never ends, but this last task, which is built on successfully negotiating all the others, leads to psychological freedom from the past. This is the essence of second chances for children of divorce.

18

On the Brow of the Hill

NEARLY TWENTY YEARS have passed since my daughter's friend
Karen started me thinking about divorce and its consequences for
men, women, and children. Indeed, I have spent almost two decades
of my life interviewing families in transition — separating families,
divorcing families, and remarried families, all kinds of families with
children. It has been a full-time commitment, often running seven
days a week.

Since 1980, when I founded the Center for the Family in Transition,
and in addition to my regular work, I get at least two, sometimes
three, telephone calls on an average day from people asking for help
in the midst of divorce. Mostly these are strangers who have read my
name in a newspaper or heard of my work from a friend. Many of
the calls are from parents. Just the other day a man called from Penn-
sylvania and said, "I'm a teacher. My wife is suing me for divorce."
His voice was strained. "I understand you have written about the
importance of fathers, how much their children need to still see them.
Can you direct me? Can you send me something to help?"

On the same day I got a call from a woman in southern California
who told me that the court had ordered her to send her nursing infant
to spend every other weekend with the child's father, who lives several hundred miles away. The woman, who must express and freeze
extra breast milk to send along with the baby, told me that she was
never married to the baby's father, only lived with him briefly, and
has no idea what kind of parent he is. She asked, "What should I
do?"

Shocked by her story — reflecting an intrusion into the most intimate of human relationships, that between a nursing mother and her child — I could say only that there is no psychological research anywhere to support the court's decision but that I knew of no immediate way that I could help. We are staying in touch.

Every now and then I get a call from one of the children or parents in our study, usually to announce an important change in his or her life. During this same week, Kedric called to say that he has been accepted into a graduate program in aeronautical engineering — a lifelong dream that he is finally pursuing. And not long ago Denise called from Denmark to say that she is getting married, adding, "You know, I still think about my parents' divorce every day." I made a mental note that she said "every day."

The third telephone call on an average day is from a lawyer, usually asking if I will be an expert witness in a custody dispute. Although the practice could be lucrative, I have never accepted any of these invitations because I do not want to compromise my impartiality. My credibility as a researcher might diminish if I became identified with any particular point of view in the courts.

My daily correspondence also reflects how deeply I have become involved in the issues surrounding divorce and how widespread the divorce phenomenon has become in our country and throughout the world. Last week, I was invited to speak at the University of Rome for two days, to help shape a study of divorce in Italy. I was also asked to attend a conference on child custody in Wisconsin that will attempt to develop national guidelines on these issues. My primary task for the week was to write the keynote address for a family law conference in Los Angeles involving judges, mediators, and attorneys from all over the United States and Canada.

All of these activities — combined with my ongoing long-term research, the work on joint custody, and my close supervision of the various counseling programs at the center — have given me a ringside seat at the drama of changing relationships between the men and women, and the parents and children, in our society. I feel that I have been privileged to observe at first hand, close up, what is undoubtedly one of the most important revolutions of modern times. In looking at divorce, we are looking at the flip side of marriage; and we are gaining new insights into basic family values — what people believe is right and how people behave toward one another. We are a society in the process of fundamental change in a direction that is entirely new and uncharted.

In thinking about these changes, I am reminded of a conversation I had with anthropologist Margaret Mead in 1972. Upset over my early findings at how troubled children are after divorce, I arranged to meet her at the San Francisco airport at midnight. She was on her way to what was to be her last trip to New Guinea, and we had several hours together before she had to leave. She, too, was disturbed by the findings and at one point said, "Judy, there is no society in the world where people have stayed married without enormous community pressure to do so. And I don't think anybody can predict what you will find."

Her words continue to impress on me how little we really know about the world we have created in the last twenty years — *a world in which marriage is freely terminable at any time, for the first time in our history.* Perhaps as a clinician and a psychologist I should confess that when we began to look at family changes caused by divorce, we began at ground zero. We lacked, and continue to lack, the psychological theory that we need to understand and to predict the consequences. This is because psychoanalysis, family systems theory, and child development theory have all developed within the context of the two-parent, intact family. Now we are in the awkward position of inventing the theory we need as we discover new facts. So if we've been sashaying back and forth as new findings come to light, it's because that is the state of our knowledge. Only painfully and slowly, essentially since the mid-seventies, have we begun to build a consensus and theory on which we can agree.

From the stories of these children and their parents and all the other people I have spoken with over the years, however, several lessons do emerge. They have taught all of us a great deal that we did not know, that we had no way of knowing:

• Divorce is a wrenching experience for many adults and almost all children. It is almost always more devastating for children than for their parents.

• Divorce is not an event that stands alone in children's or adults' experience. It is a continuum that begins in the unhappy marriage and extends through the separation, the divorce, and any remarriages and second divorces. Divorce is not the culprit; it may be no more than one of the many experiences that occur in this broad continuum.

• The effects of divorce are often long-lasting. Children are especially affected because divorce occurs during their formative years. What they see and experience becomes a part of their inner world, their view of themselves, and their view of society. The early experiences in a failing marriage are not erased by divorce. Children who witnessed violence between their parents often found these early images dominating their own relationships ten and fifteen years later. Therefore, while divorce can rescue a parent from an intolerable situation, it can fail to rescue the children.

• Almost all children of divorce regard their childhood and adolescence as having taken place in the shadow of divorce. Although many agree by adulthood that their parents were wise to part company, they nevertheless feel that they suffered from their parents' mistakes. In many instances, the conditions in the postdivorce family were more stressful and less supportive to the child than the conditions in the failing marriage.

• Children of divorce come to adulthood eager for enduring love and marriage. They do not take divorce lightly.

• For the children in our study, the postdivorce years brought the following:

Half saw their mother or father get a second divorce in the ten-year period after the first divorce.

Half grew up in families where parents stayed angry at each other.

One in four experienced a severe and enduring drop in their standard of living and went on to observe a major, lasting discrepancy between economic conditions in their mothers' and fathers' homes. They grew up with their noses pressed against the glass, looking at a way of life that by all rights should have been theirs.

Three in five felt rejected by at least one of the parents, sensing that they were a piece of psychological or economic baggage left over from a regretted journey.

Very few were helped financially with college educations, even though they continued to visit their fathers regularly. But because their fathers were relatively well-off, they were ineligible for scholarships.

• Many of the children emerged in young adulthood as compassionate, courageous, and competent people. Those who did well were helped along the way by a combination of their own inner resources and supportive relationships with one or both parents, grandparents, stepparents, siblings, or mentors. Some later experienced nurturing love affairs and good marriages of their own making. Some of those who did well were very much helped by the example of parents who had been able to successfully rebuild their lives after divorce. Others did well because they were deliberately able to turn away from the examples set by their parents. A smaller number benefited from the continued relationship with two good parents who — despite their anger and disappointment with each other — were able to cooperate in the tasks of childrearing.

• In this study, however, almost half of the children entered adulthood as worried, underachieving, self-deprecating, and sometimes angry young men and women. Some felt used in a battle that was never their own. Others felt deprived of the parenting and family protection that they always wanted and never got. Those who were troubled at young adulthood were more depleted by early experiences before and after their parents' divorces, had fewer resources, and often had very little help from their parents or from anybody else. Some children literally brought themselves up, while others were responsible for the welfare of a troubled parent as well.

• Although boys had a harder time over the years than girls, suffering a wide range of difficulties in school achievements, peer relationships, and the handling of aggression, this disparity in overall adjustment eventually dissipated. As the young women stood at the developmental threshold of young adulthood, when it was time to seek commitment with a young man, many found themselves struggling with anxiety and guilt. This sudden shock, which I describe as a sleeper effect, led to many maladaptive pathways, including multiple relationships and impulsive marriages that ended in early divorce.

• Adolescence is a period of grave risk for children in divorced families; those who entered adolescence in the immediate wake of their parents' divorces had a particularly hard time. The young people told us time and again how much they needed a family structure, how much they wanted to be protected, and how much they yearned for clear guidelines for moral behavior. They told us they needed more encouragement from parents in the complicated process of growing up and that, failing to get it, they were seduced by the voices of the street. Feeling abandoned at this critical time in their lives, they were haunted by inner doubts and uncertainties about the future. An alarming number of teenagers felt abandoned, physically and emotionally.

• Finally, and perhaps most important for society, the cumulative effect of the failing marriage and divorce rose to a crescendo as each child entered young adulthood. It was here, as these young men and women faced the developmental task of establishing love and intimacy, that they most felt the lack of a template for a loving, enduring, and moral relationship between a man and a woman. It was here that anxiety carried over from divorced family relationships threatened to bar the young people's ability to create new, enduring families of their own. As these anxieties peak in the children of divorce throughout our society, the full legacy of the past twenty years begins to hit home. The new families that are formed appear vulnerable to the effects of divorce. Although many young people in the study eventually were able to move forward and to establish good relationships and good marriages, this is a critical passage for all.

For adults, divorce more often brings an end to an unhappy chapter in their lives. Many of the individuals in our study succeeded in creating a much happier, better way of life for themselves, often but not necessarily within a happy second marriage.

More, however, experienced divorce as essentially the beginning of a long-lasting discrepancy between themselves and their former spouses. As the years went by, one person was able to create a better quality of life while the other felt left behind — economically, psychologically, and socially. These are the winners and losers in this book, the ex-husbands and ex-wives who — relative to one another — made better or worse use of their second chances in the decade after divorce.

In watching adults take up or fail to take up their second chances, we have learned the following:

• Many of the second marriages are in fact happier. These adults learn from their earlier experiences and avoid making the same mistakes.

• Many adults, especially women, show striking growth in competence and self-esteem.

• Recovery is not a given in adult life. The assumption that all people recover psychologically is not based on evidence. On what basis do we make the assumption that after twenty or twenty-five years of marriage people can inevitably pick themselves back up and start over again?

• Feelings, especially angry feelings and feelings of hurt and humiliation, can remain in full force for many years after divorce.

• Some adults are at greater risk than others. Women with young children, especially if they are driven into poverty by divorce, face a Herculean struggle to survive emotionally and physically. The stress of being a single parent with small children, working day shift and night shift without medical insurance or other backup, is unimaginable to people who have not experienced it. No wonder some women told us that they feel dead inside.

• Many older men and women coming out of long-term marriages are alone and unhappy, facing older age with rising anxiety. They lean on their children, with mixed feelings, for support and companionship ten and fifteen years after divorce. Opportunities for work, play, sex, and marriage decline rapidly with age, especially for women.

• Younger men are often adrift. Divorce seems to block them from expanding into their adult roles as husbands and fathers.

• Finally, for adults, the high failure rate of second marriages is serious and, as we discovered, often devastating because it reinforces the first failure many times over.

Many of our more baffling findings have to do with changes in parent-child relationships that occur at the time of divorce and in the years that follow. Because children long remain dependent on parents for economic and emotional support, these changes can have serious consequences. Evidently the relationship between parents and children grows best in the rich soil of a happy, intact family. But without this nurturing growth medium, parent-child relationships can become very fragile and are easily broken. What does this mean for families? What have we learned?

• As in the intact family, the child's continued relationship with good parents who cooperate with each other remains vital to his or her proper development. However, good, cooperative parenting is many times more difficult in the postdivorce family.

• When a marriage breaks down, most men and women experience a diminished capacity to parent. They give less time, provide less discipline, and are less sensitive to their children, being caught up themselves in the personal maelstrom of divorce and its aftermath.

Many parents are temporarily unable to separate their children's needs from their own. In many families parenting is restored within a year or two after divorce. But in a surprising number of families, the diminished parenting continues, permanently disrupting the childrearing functions of the family.

• Since most children live with their mothers after divorce, the single most important protective factor in a child's psychological development and well-being over the years is the mother's mental health and the quality of her parenting.

• We have seen how difficult it is for fathers who have moved out of the house to sustain a close and loving relationship with their children, especially if one or both parents remarry. Yet we have also seen how poignantly the children hold on to an internal image, sometimes a fantasy image, of the absent or even the visiting father and how both fathers and children create phantom relationships with each other.

• We have seen that the children's need for their father continues and that it rises with new intensity at adolescence, especially when it is time for the children to leave home. The nature of the father-child relationship, and not the frequency of visiting, is what most influences the child's psychological development.

• Many a father seems to have lost the sense that his children are part of his own generational continuity, his defense against mortality. This blunting of the father's relationship to his children is a stunning surprise.

• New, unfamiliar parent-child relationships have developed in some families, in which the child is overburdened by responsibility for a parent's psychological welfare or by serving as an instrument of parental rage.

• We have learned that good stepparent-child relationships are not assured. They need to be properly nurtured to take root in the minds and hearts of the children. Many children feel excluded from the remarried family.

• At the same time, we have seen some mothers and fathers, and even some stepparents, undertake heroic measures of loyalty, selflessness, and devotion to their children.

I have asked myself many times if these children and adults who experienced divorce in the early 1970s are different from those who are experiencing divorce today. At the Center for the Family in Transition, we are counseling about thirty new families every month, more than any other agency in the country. Although the divorce rate rose steeply in the 1970s, it reached a plateau in the 1980s, at a level where one in two recent marriages can be expected to end in divorce. Children born in the mid-1980s stand a 38 percent chance of experiencing their parents' divorce before they reach age eighteen.[1]

I see surprisingly little change in how adults or children react emotionally to divorce. Parents still have trouble telling the children. Despite the tremendous proliferation of media attention to divorce, nearly 50 percent of the families that we counsel waited until the day of the separation or afterward to tell their children that their familiar world is coming apart.

The causes of divorce have not changed, nor have men's and women's feelings changed. The amount of suffering is no less. People like to think that because there are so many divorced families, adults and children will find divorce easier or even easy. But neither parents nor children find comfort in numbers. Divorce is not a more "normal" experience simply because so many people have been touched by it. Our findings reveal that all children suffer from divorce, no matter how many of their friends have gone through it. And although the stigma of divorce has been enormously reduced in recent years, the pain that each child feels is not assuaged. Each and every child cries out, "Why me?"

One very worrisome difference between the 1970s and 1980s, based on reports from mental health clinics, is an increase in severe reactions in today's families — more violence, more parental dependence on children, and many more troubled, even suicidal children. I am very worried about the acute depression in many adolescents who functioned well before the divorce. There has been a rise in reports of child abuse and sexual molestation. Although it is sometimes difficult to separate real from fabricated abuse, especially when these are at issue in child custody battles, the problem is alarming. Worse yet, the system set up to deal with the problem is woefully inadequate.

We have seen a major shift in the attitudes of fathers, more of whom are trying to maintain an active parenting role in their children's lives. There is also a greater willingness among women to allow this involvement and a wider expectation that it will occur whatever the custody arrangement. On the other hand, we see a small but significant increase in the number of women who are leaving their children, choosing to place them temporarily or entirely in their ex-husbands' care. There are many motives involved in this decision, including the fact that it has become a more acceptable option in our society.

Economically, the impact of divorce on women and children continues to be a serious problem. As a result of national legislation passed in 1984, states have more tools to enforce child support payment, but it is too soon to tell how much their efforts are helping children. There continues to be little general support for equalizing the standard of living between the fathers' and mothers' homes in the years after divorce. As a result, children continue to be primarily dependent on their mothers' earning power, which is usually less than their fathers'. Despite the women's movement, few mothers in the 1980s are prepared to enter the marketplace with skills that will maintain them and their children at a comparable or a reasonably good standard of living.

One major difference between the 1970s and 1980s has been the rise in joint custody, which can be helpful in families where it has been chosen voluntarily by both parents and is suitable for the child. But there is no evidence to support the notion that "one size fits all" or even most. There is, in fact, a lot of evidence for the idea that different custody models are suitable for different families. The policy job ahead is to find the best match for each family.

Sadly, when joint custody is imposed by the court on families fighting over custody of children, the major consequences of the fighting are shifted onto the least able members of the family — the hapless and helpless children. The children can suffer serious psychological injury when this happens. I am in favor of joint custody in many cases, where parents and children can handle it, but it is no panacea. We still have a great deal to learn.

Another question I have asked myself: Does the experience in California speak for the rest of the nation? It speaks primarily, in my view, to middle-class America and perhaps to middle-class families in other parts of the postindustrial world. We know much less about the divorce experience of families in other social classes and among other ethnic groups. As for middle-class America, however, my findings have held up well in the light of studies conducted in other parts of the country.[2] When I speak at conferences around the country, in

Europe, Latin America, and elsewhere abroad, professionals and parents confirm that the reactions they have observed in children and adults are remarkably in accord with my observations.

Although our overall findings are troubling and serious, we should not point the finger of blame at divorce per se. Indeed, divorce is often the only rational solution to a bad marriage. When people ask whether they should stay married for the sake of the children, I have to say, "Of course not." All our evidence shows that children turn out less well adjusted when exposed to open conflict, where parents terrorize or strike one another, than do children from divorced families. And while we lack systematic studies comparing unhappily married families and divorced families, I do know that it is not useful to provide children with a model of adult behavior that avoids problem solving and that stresses martyrdom, violence, or apathy. A divorce undertaken thoughtfully and realistically can teach children how to confront serious life problems with compassion, wisdom, and appropriate action.

Our findings do not support those who would turn back the clock. As family issues are flung to the center of our political arena, nostalgic voices from the right argue for a return to a time when divorce was difficult to obtain. But they do not offer solutions to the serious problems that have contributed to the rising divorce rate in the first place. From the left we hear counterarguments that relationships have become more honest and more equal between men and women and that the changes we face simply represent "the new family form." But to say that all family forms are equivalent is to semantically camouflage the truth: All families are *not* alike in the protection they extend to children. Moreover, the voices of our children are not represented in the political arena. Although men and women talk *about* children, it is hard for me to believe that they are necessarily talking *for* children.

Like it or not, we are witnessing family changes which are an integral part of the wider changes in our society. We are on a wholly new course, one that gives us unprecedented opportunities for creating better relationships and stronger families — but one that has also brought unprecedented dangers for society, especially for our children.

We have reached the brow of the hill at the end of the 1980s. As I survey the landscape, I am encouraged by signs of change for the better:

• Society is beginning to pay attention to the economic plight of its women and children, to the so-called feminization of poverty. We are less tolerant of the economic injustice promoted by divorce.

• There are strong voices raised in the legislatures and the courts that reflect concern about the unmet needs of all children and families in our society.

• There seems to be growing community awareness about the impact of divorce on families and children. Teachers, psychotherapists, clergy, physicians, judges, family lawyers, and parents are more attuned to the special needs of divorcing families.

• There has been an increase in divorce services, including mediation in the courts and more psychological counseling services in the community.

But these encouraging signs still do not measure up to the magnitude of the problem. Legal, mediation, and mental health services focus almost exclusively on the here and now of the divorce crisis. Child support payment is set in accord with the present and not the changing future needs of the children. Even visiting schedules for the children are established on the basis of current need and age. All of these services assume that if only we can help people settle property, custody, and visitation, all else will follow. This is clearly not the case.

If the goal of the legal system is — and I fully believe that it should be — to minimize the impact of divorce on children and to preserve for children as much as possible of the social, economic, and emotional security that existed while their parents' marriage was intact, then we still have very far to go.[3]

At a minimum, the variety of supports and services for divorcing families needs to be expanded in scope and over time. These families need education at the time of the divorce about the special problems created by their decision. They need help in making decisions about living arrangements, visiting schedules, and sole or joint custody. And they need help in implementing these decisions over many years — and in modifying them as the children grow and the family changes. Divorcing families need universally available mediation services. They also need specialized counseling over the long haul in those cases where the children are at clear risk, where the parents are still locked in bitter disputes, and where there has been family violence. Divorcing men and women must make realistic provision for the economic support of their children, backed up by the government when necessary. These provisions should include health care and college education, where it is appropriate.

Beyond all this, we need to learn much more about divorce. We need to learn how and why things worked out so badly between divorced men and women who have had children together, most of whom tell us that they married for love. We need to learn how to reduce the unhappiness, anger, and disappointment that is so widespread in the relationships between men and women. And we need to learn more about courtship, marriage, and remarriage and about what makes good marriages work.

As a society we have always been quick to respond to individual needs; it was easy and natural for us to rivet our collective attention on the little girl who was recently trapped in an abandoned well. But it is harder for us to face up to the problems affecting our collective selves — and for a very good reason. To echo the immortal words of "Pogo" cartoonist Walt Kelly, "We have met the enemy and he is us." Divorce is not an issue of "we" versus "them." Profound changes have shaken the American family. It is not that we are less virtuous or less concerned for our children and their future, but we have been slow to recognize the magnitude of the needs of children of divorce and their parents. And we have been reluctant to take collective responsibility.

A society that allows divorce on demand inevitably takes on certain responsibilities. It is up to us to protect one another, especially our children, to the extent possible against the psychological and economic suffering that divorce can bring. All children in today's world feel less protected. They sense that the institution of the family is weaker than it has ever been before. Children of divorce grow up with the notion that love can be transient and commitment temporary, but all children — even those raised in happy, intact families — worry that their families may come undone as well. Therefore, the task for society in its true and proper perspective is to support and strengthen the family — all families.

As I bring this book to a close, a biblical phrase I have not thought of for many years keeps running through my head: "Watchman, what of the night?" We are not, I'm afraid, doing very well on our watch — at least not for our children — and, consequently, not for the future of our society. By avoiding our task, we have unintentionally placed the primary burden of coping with family change onto the children. To state it plainly, we are allowing our children to bear the psychological, economic, and moral brunt of divorce.

And from what the children are telling us, they recognize the burdens that have been put on their slender shoulders. When six-year-old John came to our center shortly after his parents' divorce, he would only mumble, "I don't know." He would not answer questions; he played games instead. First John hunted all over the playroom for the baby dolls. When he found a good number of them, he stood the baby dolls firmly on their feet and placed the miniature tables, chairs, beds, and eventually all the playhouse furniture on their heads. John looked at me, satisfied. The babies were supporting a great deal on their heads. Then, wordlessly, he placed all the mother dolls and father dolls in precarious positions on the steep roof of the dollhouse. As a father doll slid off the roof, John caught him and, looking up at me, said, "He might die." Soon all the mother and father dolls began sliding off the roof. John caught them gently, one by one, saving each from falling to the ground.

"Are the babies the strongest?" I asked.

"Yes," John shouted excitedly. "The babies are holding up the world."

AFTERWORD
TO THE PAPERBACK EDITION

APPENDIX
METHOD AND SAMPLE

ACKNOWLEDGMENTS

NOTES

INDEX

Afterword

WHEN *Second Chances* was first published in hardcover last year, I expected it to spark a powerful emotional response. After all, it challenged some strongly held beliefs in modern American society. But in reading the numerous letters from readers, it was evident that I had tapped into a pool of hot concern, a wellspring of anxiety across the land. And, to my surprise, the letters revealed a new dimension of the divorce experience. The children of divorce have found a new communal voice. Now grown into their twenties and thirties, and some into their fifties and sixties, they said, in effect, "At last I understand why I am feeling this way. Thank God I am not alone."

Until now, they said, no one had acknowledged their pain. As children they had been expected to suppress their feelings, to stop bemoaning what hurts and get on with life. "Stop the pity party" was a phrase used. They were told, by their parents and by society at large, that children are naturally resilient and will of course recover from the trauma of divorce. As long as society believed there were no long-term consequences of divorce, adult children of divorce simply did not exist as a group of people with a shared identity, with like experiences, with common problems.

Second Chances not only gave this large group of people a voice but it also encouraged many to write asking where they could get help. Some wanted to know if there were groups of children of divorce who met regularly, like adult children of alcoholics. Others wrote to say that they were working with their therapists to establish such groups.

Meanwhile, therapists began saying that many men and women were coming into therapy with the book in hand. Children of divorce were using it to open areas of discussion. Adults contemplating divorce were using it to guide their decisions. "People were propelled into treatment by the book," said Deborah Resnikoff, a psychotherapist in San Francisco, "because it gave them great pause. They might go ahead with the decision to divorce but they did so better prepared. They were concerned about the long-term effects on their children."

Other colleagues noted that *Second Chances* came along when, for a variety of social and cultural reasons, many people were just starting to take divorce more seriously. According to Neil Kalter, a professor of psychology at the University of Michigan, schools nationwide are more keenly aware of the effects of divorce on children. Demand for special programs on divorce is becoming stronger, he said, as people accept that there are long-reaching effects of divorce on child development. Recently, the sixty-two principals in the Oakland archdiocese school system sought help in establishing such programs, suggesting how widespread divorce has become in recent years.

There is also renewed interest, Professor Kalter continued, in groups designed to help divorced parents understand and help their children. Parents are less apt to say that divorce won't hurt their children, according to Emily Brown, director of the Divorce and Marital Stress Clinic in Arlington, Virginia. Parents have always been concerned about their kids, she told me, but now more information is available.

Second Chances is but a small part of this new body of information, helping to place divorce squarely on the public agenda. Our thinking about divorce — as individuals and as a society — is changing. Our insights are deeper. Many of these changes and insights are reflected in the letters *Second Chances* prompted and in the early reports from groups of adult children of divorce.

People whose parents divorced tell me they are beginning to make connections between past experiences and present feelings and to understand that maybe they can break free of the past. They are beginning to realize that they never really separated emotionally from their parents but that once they do, the future holds new possibilities.

To many, it feels like an awakening:

"After twenty long years I have finally come to understand that I am not the only one who has the feelings that I have about life in general."

"I always feel an instant kinship and compassion for other children of divorce. Your results confirm for me that I am not alone. They also tell me that I'm not a failure."

Their comments reflect many things I did not know about the long-term experience of divorce when I wrote *Second Chances*. For example, several people said they have absolutely no memories of their childhood before the divorce. One young woman said life before her twelfth birthday is a total blank. Such amnesia was not evident in my study, except for one gifted young man who blocked out his sixteenth year, the year in which his parents divorced.

I was also struck by the level of concern shown for siblings. "My brother has always been a very special person in my life," says one woman, "but he has many emotional scars that may never heal. He lives ten miles away but he has not talked to my mother in five years." She continues, "My sister has been living in Norway for twenty-three years. She and my mother have never gotten along and my sister has more than her share of emotional problems. I care for all my family members so much and it causes me grief that none of them will acknowledge that the other ones exist!"

Another surprise was the extent of worry people carry into apparently happy marriages. "I have been married for eight years now to a wonderful husband. Yes, we have had our ups and downs, and I'm going to try with all my strength to make this marriage work. Still, I find myself thinking sometimes, Why try so hard, it's going to end someday, all marriages fail eventually." This woman's fear stems from an internal voice that says fear and betrayal are to be expected. Love and intimacy cannot last.

Another says: "The divorce that took place twenty-one years ago still causes repercussions today. When does the pain stop? After fourteen years of marriage and a wonderful relationship with my husband and two children I still am very scared that it might be taken away from me, as it was from my mother."

Several of the new support groups were composed of women in their late twenties and early thirties who had already had some psychotherapy. They said that issues and experiences stemming from the long-ago divorce were never explored in their individual therapy sessions. The idea that their current relationships were suffering from the legacy of divorce was largely new to them.

Now, as this idea was openly discussed in the groups, many of the young women took a fresh look at their mothers and fathers. The result was that many suddenly realized that they continued to feel responsible for their mothers' well-being, as if their fates were inextricably tied to their mothers'.

Such feelings of responsibility for a needy person were then transferred to their own adult relationships. One woman said, "I finally realized that whenever I get involved with a man, I relinquish my commitment to take care of myself. I find myself feeling increasingly victimized by life. I think what I'm doing is trading off my adult power in the world for a chance of reducing the abyss of loneliness that still traps the child." For her, and many other overburdened children of divorce, intimacy translates into giving up self. She becomes attentive to the needs of others, not to herself.

Such women are sometimes attracted to cold, denying men so they can avoid the caretaking role. To love someone nice would mean falling into the trap of self-sacrifice. Others are attracted to weak men who need caretaking and rescuing. Such marriages become frustrating as the child of divorce establishes a kind of mother-daughter dependency in her relationship with her husband.

This pattern of giving up one's childhood to care emotionally for a troubled parent can happen in any family. But it remains largely unacknowledged as a widespread phenomenon among children of divorce. The costs to the child are enormous and sometimes seem unending. "I am forty-three years old and I still get angry at myself for giving in to my mother's every whim and letting her control my life," says one woman. "I guess I'm still trying to please her, hoping that someday she will say that she appreciates me just because I am me."

Being closely tied to their mothers, many young women tended to accept the mother's version of what went wrong with the marriage. They did not question her critical descriptions of the father, allowing these hostile notions to spill over to men in general. Some were coached: Never trust men.

The young women in therapy therefore spent a great deal of time trying to formulate clearer images of their fathers. Some literally went in search of their fathers after years of little or no contact. One woman said, "Soon I'll be meeting my natural grandparents. For some reason, I feel this will fill a void in my past. And you never know, I might even be able to ask them what my father was like."

One young woman in our study, Linda, whose life is chronicled in the chapter on overburdened children, is still searching for her father. Like many adopted children, her inner search was translated into a real search. Fifteen years after the divorce, Linda drove two thousand miles to Minnesota to see her father. She got to within two blocks of his apartment when her courage failed her. "I couldn't go any further," she admitted. "I knew I couldn't do it by myself. I could only go with someone I felt safe with. I was afraid to find that what everybody said was true, that he doesn't care about us, that he doesn't love me. In my mind, I always thought he didn't come to see me because of the conflict with Mom, but that he really loved me. I always said I'd go if I could, but then I couldn't do it."

To move on in adulthood, children of divorce needed to flesh these men out rather than accept the two-dimensional stereotypes projected by their mothers. As they put together a realistic, more human picture of their fathers, their attitudes toward men in general changed. Their expectations improved, as did their relationships.

One thing that continues to astonish, however, is that children of divorce never seem to realize the extraordinary amount of support that they have given so freely to their parents. To them, it was a tacit understanding. Children are supposed to make sacrifices for their parents, not the other way around. And as young adults, they still fail to realize how heroic they were. They fail to take credit for everything they did. Tragically, they do not use their achievements to bolster their self-esteem.

Nevertheless I am encouraged by the early reports from self-help groups and from psychotherapists who are individually treating adult children of divorce. Children of divorce seem eminently treatable, motivated to change, and aware of their problems, and have access to deeply rooted feelings. Most also have access to their mothers and fathers; they are in the rare position of conducting field tests of their insights.

Many readers wrote to ask how the men, women, and children in our original study are faring. The twentieth anniversary of their divorces is coming up in 1991.

As for the children now in the third decade of life, we are not seeing any sudden closures or solutions to the problems raised in *Second Chances*. Many are doing better, others less well. There is no clear trend of the group's changing course, although individuals continue to change in ways that are striking.

The Burrelle family, the subjects in Part III, are a good example. I recently met with each of them more than fifteen years after the divorce. Betty, the mother, had sacrificed herself completely to the goal of keeping her three children sheltered and fed in the years after divorce. This was the first time I had ever seen her happy. Last summer she spent six weeks in Nepal with two of her children, and she got promoted at work. Moreover, her father had died after a long illness and left her a small but, to Betty's way of thinking and living, substantial inheritance.

"I don't want to change the way I am," she said, running her fingers through thick dark hair now laced with gray. "I'm a little worried about that. I really have been very strong, maybe too strong. I'm scared of having this money because I'm not spoiled and I don't like the way money affects people. It's not always for the best." She paused and said, "But it's good for the kids. They won't have to scratch and do without, the way we've all had to do."

I left Betty with the feeling that for the first time in fifteen years she was on an even keel. The terrible stress was behind her. Fifteen years after the divorce, she had stopped running.

Dale, the father, was now divorced from his third wife. We met in an oyster bar in Manhattan, and the whole time we talked his eyes kept roving around the room.

I asked him if he learned anything from his last divorce.

"Well," he said, bringing his eyes back to meet mine, "one of the things you learn is that if you're in the wrong relationship, you should get out. I see it in business a lot. If you're not the right person for the job, get out."

Dale seemed to subscribe to what a colleague of mine calls the head cold theory of divorce. Take two aspirin, get a little rest, and the entire problem will go away.

As we talked, I was once again impressed by how little Dale's descriptions of his children and their feelings matched up with what I knew to be true.

Steve Burrelle, the oldest child, had recently moved to New York to be closer to Dale, despite the fact that he had seen very little of his father over the years and despite his continuing sense that his father did not love him. Steve was not surprised when his father's third marriage failed. "I've seen so many marriages and divorces," he said. "I've become immune."

When I asked Steve if he ever thinks about divorce, he said, "If I thought about it, I'd probably think a lot about it. I probably wouldn't be able to do anything else. So I don't think about it. I've got other stuff to do."

I asked him if he thought the divorce had affected his life.

He stroked his forehead for a moment and gave his answer slowly. "It makes you grow up a lot faster, to make your own decisions early on. Your mom is the only one there and your dad is halfway across the country. You know," he said, "getting a letter from my dad was like getting a reward." He let the remark sink in. "I think divorce runs in families, and that worries me. It has more tendency to happen, and I only hope I can bypass that and avoid the mistakes my mom and dad made." He looked at me silently, as if to say, "Do you think I can?"

Tanya, the middle child, is a great success. The owner of a window design business, she has five people working for her. But her love life is a mess.

"I still get involved with a lot of younger men," she said, "and most of them are dependent on me. They're insecure and then become extremely jealous and possessive. That's the pattern. I take care of them. Sometimes I give them money, sometimes I give them advice, and sometimes I encourage them to go out with other women." She sounds incredibly sad. "All the time I'm not sure what I'm looking for. I'm not sure I'll ever find someone who can take care of me."

"Maybe you're not letting that happen."

"True," she said. "One of the reasons I always get involved with men dependent on me is that it gives me the upper hand. I don't have to worry about them leaving me."

"Why would you worry about that?"

Her answer was direct. "My dad left, remember?"

Of all the Burrelle children, Kyle, the youngest, still seems to be faring the best. He has few memories of the divorce. The day we met, Kyle had just returned from a football game and his cheeks were flushed.

"I think when people get married, they should know it's forever," he said emphatically. "And know it's for the rest of their lives, especially if they have kids. I just don't understand how people can get married and then end up hating each other."

I asked him what he remembered.

"Very little. I was very little. All I remember is the big house and the big back yard. It's like it never existed. It's like I once asked a guy who couldn't walk, and had never walked, what it was like. Didn't he wish that he could? And he said that he didn't miss it because he never knew what it was like. That's the way it is with me and the divorce. I don't remember them being married. You don't miss what you don't know anything about."

Kyle was clearly doing well in all aspects of his life. I look forward to seeing him again in a few years and finding out what kind of husband and father he will make.

Indeed, I had hoped to find out how all the young people in the study would fare as parents. But so far, not many have had children of their own. Eighteen years after the study began, there have been only about a dozen born to the 131 children — who are now between the ages of twenty and thirty-six — in our original study. Two of this new generation are homeless, living on the streets with their mother in Dallas. One is little Angela (described in Part II), who lives with her loving and happily married parents in Seattle. The relatively small number of children could be related to the lasting effects of divorce or it could simply be part of the social trend toward delayed childbearing. It's too soon to confirm the observation either way.

I can say, however, that as time goes on, my respect for these children of divorce only increases. They do not take relationships lightly. Despite hard knocks, they are not cynical. Having access to their feelings and memories, they are people with high levels of compassion, integrity, and morality. They know right from wrong, although they do not always act in their own best interests. Quite unexpectedly, they show reverence for the family even though they continue to feel that their own families let them down.

I also respect the men and women who poured out their life stories to me this past year. They have shown me that children of divorce can and do recover — many on their own without professional help or group therapy. They revealed some of the things that helped them.

One woman wrote of her life's work, as a way to heal herself. "My husband and I work together as teachers in a rural school in Texas. We work well together and share most aspects of our lives. We see a depressing number of teen mothers bearing children at seventeen or eighteen years old, often without partners or marriage. When they do marry, the relationships break up because of all the stresses of making ends meet. I am on the local school board, trying to improve our health education curriculum. I also work for the local Planned Parenthood and am on an advisory committee that provides services to abused children. In my career I am trying to address issues that affected my early life. I hope I can help improve options and conditions but it will take major social changes to make childhood the protected and happy time that it ought to be."

Tragically, the new generation of children of divorced families does not appear to be faring better than the last. At the Center for the Family in Transition, a personal letter goes out to every couple in the county who file for divorce, offering help in planning for their children at this time of stress. Since 1980, we have served almost three thousand divorcing families. But it is sad to report that children today are more troubled than the carefully screened children described in *Second Chances*. The children in this new generation have seen more abuse. They have experienced more neglect. Their homes are more disorganized. Many of the parents are severely troubled. Many are preparing to move out of their children's lives. Few recognize that the nature of their postdivorce relationship with each other will influence their children's emotional and moral development. Rarely are the children, of either gender or any age, protected from the destructive parental interaction. The common adult expectation continues to be that children, being children, will recover.

My intent in *Second Chances* is not to argue against divorce but rather to raise the consciousness of the community about the long-term effects of divorce on children. I do not argue that children have no chance of health or happiness after divorce, and I give instances where children have done well. But the challenges children must meet after their parents divorce are severe. Parents and society are too often unaware and unhelpful. I am deeply concerned that children are so regularly put at risk and that it is so common for them to suffer.

I am very pleased that *Second Chances* hit a raw nerve in this country, reinforcing what a lot of people already knew in their bones, because the first step in solving a problem is to acknowledge it. Only then can we get at the complex tasks that lie ahead.

Appendix

METHOD AND SAMPLE

RESEARCH SAMPLE

In 1971, each of 131 children and adolescents from 60 families, together with their parents, were studied intensively during a six-week period near the time of the marital separation, which was defined as the time when the parents physically separated and remained permanently apart.[1] Each family member was reexamined at 18 months postseparation, at five years, and again at ten years postseparation. At the time of this writing, many had also been seen at the 15-year mark. The 131 children were divided almost equally between males and females (48% boys, 52% girls). At the time of separation slightly more than half were eight years old or younger, 47% were between 9 and 18 years old. Fifty-nine mothers and 47 fathers were interviewed initially.

At the 18-month mark, contact was reestablished with 58 of the original 60 families. Because two couples had been reconciled in the intervening year and two other families declined to participate or could not be located, the first follow-up population included 56 families, with data derived from interviews with 41 fathers, 53 mothers, and 108 children. Forty-five percent of the returning youngsters were boys, 55% girls.

At the 5-year mark, contact was again established with 58 of the original families. The sample for whom we had extended interviews supplying sufficient data to permit a full psychological and social assessment consisted of 96 children from 56 families. Fifty-four mothers and 41 fathers were interviewed at the 5-year mark.

At the 10-year mark, 54 (90%) of the original 60 families were located, and members in 52 families (87%) were interviewed. Of the children, 110 were interviewed directly, and extensive data regarding another six were obtained from family members, surpassing the numbers reached at the 5-year mark. Of all the children reached, 113 met the criteria for inclusion in the analysis. These included 50 male and 63 female subjects, seen over the 2-year period

1981–1983. Of the adults, 47 women and 36 men met the criteria for full inclusion in the analysis.[2] The mean length of time since the separation was 10.9 years with a range of 9.6–13.1 years.

In the process of contacting individuals regarding authorization for a release of information in the preparation of this book, virtually all agreed to a further interview, which represented approximately a 15-year follow-up. This most recent follow-up is currently still in progress, and at the time of publication half the children and more than one-third of the parents have been interviewed. Since the 10-year follow-up, we have been saddened to learn of the death of one of the fathers in our original sample and of four of the children — two through accident and two through illness.

It is important to note that the children were screened initially for chronic psychological problems. Prior to the family rupture, all of the children in the study had reached appropriate developmental milestones in the view of their parents and teachers. They were performing at age-appropriate levels within their schools. Children who had ever been referred for psychological or psychiatric treatment were excluded from the study. The sample probably represented young people skewed in the direction of psychological health, since they had been able, by all accounts, to maintain their developmental pace within the failing marriage.

Demographics of the Original Sample

These were first marriages for all but 10% of the men and 7% of the women. The average age of the men at separation was 36.9; the average age of the women was 34.1. Couples had been married an average of 11.1 years prior to the decisive separation, ranging between 4 and 23 years, and averaged 2.2 children per family.

They were a well-educated group. One-quarter of the men held advanced degrees in medicine, law, or business administration. One-third of the women had earned a college degree, with some few holding graduate degrees. Only 18% of men and 24% of women had terminated their education with a high school diploma.

In their initial socioeconomic distribution, the families reflected the population of the suburban northern California county in which they resided. The families were largely, but not entirely, within the middle-class range. Of the original 60 families, 88% were white, 3% were black, and 9% were interracial, with one Asian spouse. The distribution of the families along social class dimensions was determined using the Hollingshead Two Factor Index of Social Position.[3] Forty-three percent of families fell into the two highest categories, 29% ranked in the middle category, and another 28% ranked at the two lowest levels.

The Population at Ten Years

The socioeconomic differences between men and women at the 10-year mark were less pronounced than those observed at the 18-month and 5-year marks, when we reported a precipitous economic decline for 60% of the women and a drop in the standard of living for the majority of the women and children. By the 10-year mark, 40% of the women and 50% of the men belonged in the two highest categories of the five-level Hollingshead scale. Women still outnumbered men significantly in the two lowest categories, where 30% of the women were ranked, compared with 17% of the men.

At 10 years, 42 women and 46 men were employed. With respect to type of employment, equal proportions (42%) were classified as professionals, although it is significant that, whereas the professional men were physicians, attorneys, and business executives, only one woman was a physician. The majority of female professionals were in fields such as teaching, nursing, or the arts, reflecting a substantial difference in both social status and income. One-quarter of the women and somewhat less than one-fifth of the men were experiencing grave financial difficulties.

Geographic Stability

Our ability to locate the children after a lapse of so many years was unexpectedly aided by the finding that a full 41% continued to reside in the county in which the initial study was done. An additional 36% had moved out of the immediate geographic area to neighboring San Francisco Bay Area counties or elsewhere within the state, so that 77% of the young people in the study had remained in California. Of the remainder, half now live in neighboring states. None were living outside the country at the 10-year mark, although at least two were outside the country at 15 years. Overall, this represents an unanticipated stability in residence.

The geographic stability of the adults was also surprising. Over half of the women (53%) and almost half of the men (49%) continued to live, a decade later, in the county where the study was initiated. When mothers did move, they were as likely to move out of the state (22%) as elsewhere in California (25%). Fathers tended to remain within the state (43%). Even taking into account some degree of mobility, the majority of men and women (67% and 63%, respectively) showed considerable stability of residence. Only 14% of women and 17% of men had a history of multiple moves and instability in this regard.

METHODOLOGY

The choice of research design, including measurement strategies and creation of variables from coding schemas, stems from decisions about which dimensions of the phenomena under study are of interest. This investigation was originally conceptualized as a hypothesis-generating study in which the goal was to explore and track the perceptions and experiences of the individual family members, particularly the children, following divorce. The qualitative focus of the study is ideally suited to this purpose, as the emphasis is on attempting to understand the complexity and variation endemic to the long-term divorce process from the point of view of the participants. The various methods of data collection and analysis, including the use of extensive clinical interviews and development of coding categories truly reflective of the richness of the clinical data, were selected for their suitability to retain and highlight the qualitative nature of the phenomena under investigation.

Initial Contact

Families in the study understood from the outset that advice in planning for the children was being offered in exchange for their willingness to participate in the research project. The roles of counselor and researcher were combined. Sources of referral were primarily attorneys and the schools. Very few litigating families were included.

Each family member was seen individually. The research objective in seeing parents and children separately and in gathering independent information from the schools was to obtain a complex and rich set of data about each family member as well as about the relationships within that family. The potential pitfalls of interviewing just one family member about that family's overall divorce experience were convincingly demonstrated throughout the history of the project. The multiple sets of data that we collected enabled us to triangulate often apparently irreconcilable data into a meaningful psychological portrait of the family and its members in the midst of divorce.

Each parent was interviewed weekly over a 6-week period; each child was seen for three or four sessions. Parent interviews ranged from an hour to one and a half hours; most child sessions were 50 minutes. Families were not excluded if one family member refused to be involved. Generally, the same clinician saw all family members, but occasionally two staff members shared parents and children, if time considerations or particular expertise dictated such an arrangement. The average number of interviews per family was 15.

The Follow-up Studies

Families were recontacted at 18 months, 5 years, and 10 years from the decisive marital separation. Family members were seen individually for a single follow-up interview, which lasted up to several hours; young children were seen for extended play sessions. By the time of the 10-year follow-up, however, even the youngest children were old enough to be interviewed. At 18 months and at 5 years, the same clinician who assessed the family originally was available to interview each family member. At the 10-year mark, three of the five original clinicians remained available, thus ensuring considerable continuity of contact for these young people and their parents. At the 18-month and 5-year follow-ups, independent school interviews were conducted; at the 10-year follow-up, parent and child questionnaires supplemented the interview material. The 15-year follow-up, still in progress, uses interview methods exclusively.

Initial Assessment

The children and their parents were seen individually by trained clinicians in semistructured clinical interviews according to a uniform outline of content areas to be covered. Data gathered from the parents initially included a broad range of material regarding each family and family member's history through the difficulties of the marriage and the decision to separate. Additionally, a major focus was on the quality and vicissitudes of parental and parent-child relationships, observations regarding responses and behaviors in the children and on the parents' stresses, coping capacities, and ability to reconstitute. Views of the future held by each parent for himself or herself and for the children were also solicited along with views on issues related to custody and visiting. All of this information, integrated with that which was unique to each family's history and situation, allowed the development of interlocking sets of formulations about the parents' own central psychological responses to the divorce and their motivation and capacities to assume or continue the parenting role within the structure of the postdivorce family.

Evaluation of the children focused on response to stresses in the divorce situation measured by the children's achievement of age-appropriate psychological and developmental milestones. What evolved and was refined in the initial phases of the project, then, was a Divorce-Specific Assessment of Children, which incorporated a basic understanding of each child's psychological functioning, focused specifically on divorce and divorce-related change. The three major areas of inquiry within this Divorce-Specific Assessment included (1) the child's unique response to and experience with his or her parents' separation and divorce; (2) continuity and change in parent-child relationships; and (3) the network of support systems available to the child outside the home.

Extensive summaries of the interviews were prepared by the clinicians, transcribed, and the transcriptions coded, using a series of rating scales and categorical items.[4] Reliability was established between trained clinicians by the consensus method. Those codes requiring clinical judgment were discussed and discrepancies resolved. After consensus was reached, the same clinical raters completed coding the transcripts.

Eighteen-Month and Five-Year Assessments

The method of assessment at 18 months and at 5 years was essentially the same as has been described for the initial time period. The same interview outline was used in semistructured interviews, with additional portions added at each time period that addressed issues relevant to the demographic and psychological status appropriate to the time elapsed. Interview portions having to do with premarital and marital history were not repeated.

Assessment at Ten Years

As at previous time periods, the interview outline was adjusted to include new areas relevant to assessment of status at 10 years. The 10-year interview outline included all items on the initial interview (except predivorce history) and those new items added at 18 months and 5 years that were still appropriate at 10 years. Thus, the semistructured interviews at 10 years were the most extensive of the follow-ups in the study. As at the earlier time periods, the interviews were transcribed and the transcriptions were coded. The coding forms at 10 years contained categories used at the earlier time periods and new categories reflecting questions added at 10 years. A total of 710 items were coded for each child and 398 items for the parents combined. See Table 1 for a summary of the domains of functioning reflected by these categories.

TABLE 1
*Summary of Domains of Functioning
Coded at the Ten-Year Follow-Up**

Children	*Parents***
Marital status/history	Marital status/history
Living situation (and custody)	Employment
Pattern of contact with father	Schooling/training
Pattern of contact with mother	Economic circumstances
Attitudes toward parent contact	Living situation
Schooling	Social relationships
Employment	Supports/needs
Economic situation	Parenting
Adolescent achievements	Current psychological functioning
Early/middle adolescent history	Treatment history
Later adolescent history	Attitude toward the divorce
Supports	Coparental relationship
Peer relationships	Interparental relationship
Sexual/love relationships	
Current psychological functioning	
Psychotherapy and health history	
Relationship with father	
Relationship with mother	
Attitude toward mother's remarriage	
Attitude toward father's remarriage	
Attitude toward the divorce	
Expectations/attitudes toward the future	

*These domains of functioning are coded in the form of clinical ratings based primarily on interview data and secondarily on questionnaire data from parents and children.
**Mother and father were rated separately.

Coding items requiring clinical judgments were reviewed extensively by trained clinical raters. Operational criteria anchoring scale points were developed and discussed thoroughly. Transcripts from 10% of the sample were selected and individually coded. Interrater reliabilities were computed using Kendall's tau b statistic for ordinal-level variables and the kappa statistic for nominal-type variables. Those variables having acceptable levels of agreement ($p < .05$) constituted 62% of the ordinal codes and 54% of the nominal codes. The remaining codes were reviewed and operational criteria further defined. Where consensus on these criteria could not be reached, the codes were eliminated from formal analyses.

ANALYSIS OF THE DATA

All parent and child data through the 5-year follow-up were computer-coded and analyzed using several statistical tests and methods, including analyses of variance, factor analysis, and other correlational techniques.

Data Reduction

Data analysis at the 10-year mark was the most extensive undertaken to that point, including both cross-sectional and longitudinal analyses.

Preliminary to tests of clinical questions, frequencies were obtained on all of the coding categories. Those categories that did not discriminate statistically were examined and eliminated if the frequencies were not meaningful clinically. Appropriate measures of association were run between remaining categories. Categories that were associated above the .80 level were either combined or collapsed. The surviving categories provided the data base.

The primary method of analysis at 10 years was assessment of the sample using the chi-square statistic, as the data are of a categorical nature. The children were assessed by sex, age group, and sibling status. The definition of age groups over the course of the investigation changed according to the dictates of statistical criteria and clinical meaningfulness. Data at the initial contact and 18-month follow-up were analyzed using six age groups at the time of the separation: 2–4 years old, 5–6 years, 7–8 years, 9–10 years, 11–12 years, and 13–18 years. At the 5-year follow-up, this was collapsed to four groups for continuing analysis: 2–5 years old, 6–8 years, 9–12 years, and 13–18 years. At the 10-year follow-up, age group was defined according to age and developmental stage at the 10-year mark rather than by original age at the time of the separation. (See Table 2.)

TABLE 2
*Age Groupings of Children
by Sex (at 10 Years)*

Age Grouping	Males	Females	Total	% of Total
11–15 years	10	16	26	23%
16–18 years	22	16	38	33%
19–23 years	12	27	39	35%
24–29 years	6	4	10	9%
	50	63	113	100%

Dependent measures were organized into several dimensions reflecting psychological, social, academic, and economic functioning, attitudes toward the divorce, expectations for the future, and perceived long-term residual impact of being a child of divorce.

A global measure of child outcome entitled Ego Cope was developed by combining two codes representing different but overlapping dimensions of functioning. One dimension, ego intactness, is an assessment of the individual's internal degree of psychological integration, affective stability, and strength of defensive structure. The second dimension, overall competence, represents the way in which an individual functions in various areas of the external environment including school, occupation, and social and family relationships.

The adults were assessed by sex, age group, and marital status. For the purpose of analysis by age group, the parents were grouped according to age at the time of the separation. At that time the women ranged in age from 22 to 53 years and the men from 25 to 65 years. Four age groups were identified, with very slight differences between men and women determined by the distribution of the sample. The age groupings for women were 22–29 years, 30–33 years, 34–39 years, and 40–53 years. For men, the groupings were 25–29 years, 30–34 years, 35–39 years, and 40–65 years.

Individual parent-child relationships were analyzed along several dimensions, including overall quality, type of identification, and feelings of rejection, love, trust, worry, and anger.

Profiles were developed that reflect combinations of parent characteristics within each divorced couple, such as patterns of psychological change, quality of life, socioeconomic status, conflict and anger, cooperation over visiting, attitude toward the ex-spouse as parent, and degree of felt responsibility for the children. The rationale behind the development of the parent profiles stemmed from our realization that many of the critical long-term effects of divorce are best conceptualized at a family level. While each person's response is in part due to individual variation and exposure to certain life experiences, it is in the history of changes in the family that significant individual transformations may be best understood. The parent profiles represent an attempt to combine information from individual parents into family-level variables that more accurately represent the reality of the postdivorce environment in which children have lived. These parent profiles were then compared with measures of child functioning in an attempt to perceive triadic or family system–level relationships.[5] An analysis of longitudinal effects among parents and children, including patterns of stability and change in functioning over time and prediction of long-term functioning, was also carried out. A dependent variable was constructed that reflected a pathway, or adequacy of psychosocial adjustment both at the time of the initial contact and at 10 years post-separation. In this manner, improvement and decline over the full span of the postdivorce years was evaluated against a subgroup of variables that emerged as psychologically meaningful or statistically significant in the course of our cross-sectional analysis.

Acknowledgments

This work represents the culmination of the efforts of many talented and dedicated people — the clinicians who interviewed the adults and the children, the researchers who helped analyze the data, the editors and the support staff who helped shape the final work. I have, for purposes of coherence and structure, presented each interview as if I had conducted it. This, of course, was not possible. The interviewing was fully shared by a group of clinicians, including myself, and I would like to express my gratitude and profound appreciation to the clinicians who contributed so richly to this work. I am grateful to each for the sensitivity and compassion that was reflected in each contact with the families over the years. At the ten-year mark, the interviewers include Shauna B. Corbin, Ph.D.; Doris Schwarz Crittenden, L.C.S.W.; Barry Feinberg, L.C.S.W.; Holly Gordon, D.M.H.; Angela Homme, Ph.D.; and Susannah Roy, L.C.S.W. Of these, Doris Schwarz Crittenden, Angela Homme, Susannah Roy, and I have been with the study continuously since its inception.

I would like to acknowledge my indebtedness to the Zellerbach Family Fund, which has supported this work from the beginning. Such longstanding support is unusual in the foundation world. I would like especially to thank Edward Nathan, executive director of the Zellerbach Family Fund, for his continued confidence and encouragement. I would also like to express my appreciation to the Marion E. Kenworthy–Sarah H. Swift Foundation, Inc., for support in the writing of this book, and to W. Walter Menninger, M.D., chief of staff at the Menninger Clinic, who encouraged me to undertake this study and helped me to obtain the additional financial support that I needed. And I also want to thank the San Francisco Foundation and the Marin County Community Foundation for their help in establishing and continuing support of the Center for the Family in Transition.

The results of the original five years of the project, which have come to be known as the California Children of Divorce Study, were published in *Surviving the Breakup: How Children and Parents Cope with Divorce* (Judith S. Wallerstein and Joan B. Kelly, Basic Books, 1980). Dr. Kelly left the project after the publication of the five-year follow-up. I am grateful to the publisher for permission to make occasional use of material from this work. Four of the papers in which I reported the ten-year findings were published in the *American Journal of Orthopsychiatry*, and I would like to acknowledge my appreciation of their courtesy for my occasional use of that material. Findings from the ten-year study have also been published in the following journals: *Behavioral Sciences and the Law, Columbia Journal of Law and Social Problems, Family Law Quarterly* (with Shauna B. Corbin), *Journal of the American Academy of Child Psychiatry, Mediation Quarterly,* and *Social Work*. Chapters with colleagues based on the study have appeared in *Advances in Family Intervention, Assessment and Theory*, vol. 4 (JAI Press, 1987) (chapter by Julia M. Lewis and Judith S. Wallerstein), and *Impact of Divorce, Single Parenting, and Stepparenting on Children*, Hetherington and Arasteh, editors (Lawrence Erlbaum Associates, 1988) (chapter by Judith S. Wallerstein, Shauna B. Corbin, and Julia M. Lewis). *Factors Affecting Similarities and Differences Among Siblings Ten Years Following Parental Divorce* (Shauna B. Corbin and Julia M. Lewis) was a paper presented at the 65th Annual Meeting of the American Orthopsychiatric Association in March 1988. Much of the material in this book has not been published elsewhere.

Papers on joint custody (by Rosemary McKinnon and Judith S. Wallerstein) have been published in the *American Journal of Orthopsychiatry* and *Behavioral Sciences and the Law*. A paper on joint custody was also presented at the 65th Annual Meeting of the American Orthopsychiatric Association ("A Rose by Any Other Name: Children's Adjustment in Joint and Sole Physical Custody Families," by Marsha Kline, Jeanne M. Tschann, Janet R. Johnston, and Judith S. Wallerstein).

Julia M. Lewis, Ph.D., served as director of research of the ten-year follow-up. Shauna B. Corbin, Ph.D., was project director for the ten-year and the fifteen-year follow-up studies. I would like to express my profound gratitude to Dr. Lewis and Dr. Corbin for their meticulous analysis of the voluminous data that we have collected and the many valuable insights which they provided as we worked together over the years. I want to underscore my gratitude to Shauna B. Corbin for her gentleness, her patience, her diligence, and her devotion over so many years. I would like to acknowledge the competent and imaginative help of Barbara Lehman, editorial assistant, and to thank Elza Burton for her help.

Sandra and I would like also to thank our editor, Katrina Kenison, for her enthusiasm, her capacity to keep us on track, her patience, and her brilliance in solving structural problems. Thanks, too, to Jan Blakeslee for her careful reading of the manuscript in its early inchoate form and for many illuminating editorial suggestions that we put to very good use.

Finally, Sandra and I want to thank our husbands, Robert S. Wallerstein and Kenneth L. Stallcup, and Sandra's children, Abi and Matt, for their almost unfailing good humor and their unflagging encouragement.

Notes

Introduction

1. In all instances, the word *divorce* is used to mean the point in time when a husband and wife no longer live together and one of them has filed for divorce. The legal divorce typically follows at least a year later.

2. Because so little was known about divorce, it was premature to plan a control group. Ours was a hypothesis-finding study designed to examine divorce as a process with an unfolding history and after-history. We decided to carry out a detailed, in-depth study using a sample of manageable size so that we could study each individual and family in their inner complex of motivations and determinants. From the findings of such a study we hoped to generate hypotheses that could then be tested in a more focused way with properly sized and selected samples and appropriate control.

3. Judith S. Wallerstein and Joan B. Kelly, *Surviving the Breakup: How Children and Parents Cope with Divorce* (New York: Basic Books, 1980); E. Mavis Hetherington, Martha Cox, and Roger Cox, "The Aftermath of Divorce," in *Mother-Child, Father-Child Relations*, ed. H. Stevens, Jr., and M. Mathews (Washington, D.C.: National Association for the Education of Young Children, 1978), 149–76; E. Hetherington, M. Cox, and R. Cox, "The Development of Children in Mother-Headed Families," in *The American Family: Dying or Developing*, ed. H. Hoffman and D. Reiss (New York: Plenum, 1978); Neil Kalter, "Children of Divorce in an Outpatient Psychiatric Population," *American Journal of Orthopsychiatry* 47 (1977): 40–51.

4. *Surviving the Breakup* (Wallerstein and Kelly; 1980) reported the findings of the California Children of Divorce Study through the completion of the five-year follow-up. Throughout the present volume, reference has been made to numerous observations, findings, and statistical results that are derived from the original book. For economy of style they will not be referenced each time. Unless otherwise indicated, material referring to the period prior to the ten-year follow-up may be presumed to be referenced to the previous book.

5. Kai T. Erikson, *Everything in Its Path: Destruction of Community in the Buffalo Creek Flood* (New York: Simon and Schuster, 1976).

6. Lenore C. Terr, "Children of Chowchilla: A Study of Psychic Trauma," *The Psychoanalytic Study of the Child* 34 (1979): 547–623; L. Terr, "Chowchilla Revisited: The Effects of Psychic Trauma Four Years After a School Bus Kidnapping," *American Journal of Psychiatry* 140 (1983): 1543–50.

7. Joan B. Kelly, Ph.D., left the project after the five-year findings were published.

Chapter 1

1. Michael Rutter, "Parent-Child Separation: Psychological Effects on the Children," *Journal of Child Psychology and Psychiatry* 12 (1971): 233–60.

2. Judith S. Wallerstein and Shauna B. Corbin, "Father-Child Relationships After Divorce: Child Support and Educational Opportunity," *Family Law Quarterly* 20 (Summer 1986): 109–28.

3. Lenore J. Weitzman, *The Divorce Revolution: The Unexpected Social and Economic Consequences for Women and Children in America* (New York: Free Press, 1985).

Chapter 3

1. In identifying the person who wanted the divorce, we did not go by who filed the divorce papers. In our experience, the person who actually files the papers is not always the one who most wants the divorce. Some people will file for divorce as a "weapon" to bring the other person back to the marriage. Their goal is to make the other person contrite or guilty over recent actions or behavior, but the tactic is likely to backfire. The person who is supposed to be punished may welcome the freedom, trapping the person who has filed the divorce papers into an unwanted decision. People also file for divorce amid the heat of family quarrels.

2. Arthur J. Norton, assistant chief, Population Division, U.S. Bureau of the Census, telephone conversation with the author, April 26, 1987.

Chapter 5

1. Shauna B. Corbin and Julia M. Lewis, "Factors Affecting Similarities and Differences Among Siblings Ten Years Following Parental Divorce." Paper presented at the 65th Annual Meeting of the American Orthopsychiatric Association, San Francisco, March 1988.

Chapter 6

1. Neil Kalter, Barbara Riemer, Arthur Brickman, and Jade Woo Chen, "Implications of Parental Divorce for Female Development," *Journal of the American Academy of Child Psychiatry* 24 (1985): 538–44.

Chapter 8

1. Lenore J. Weitzman, *The Divorce Revolution: The Unexpected Social and Economic Consequences for Women and Children in America* (New York: Free Press, 1985), 266–301. The figures regarding noncompliance cited by Weitzman are from the results of a 1981 survey conducted by the U.S. Census Bureau.

Chapter 11

1. L. Belmont and F. Marolla, "Birth Order, Family Size and Intelligence," *Science* 182 (1973): 1096–1101; L. Belmont, Z. A. Stein, and J. T. Wittes, "Birth Order, Family Size and School Failure," *Developmental Medical Child Neurology* 18 (1976): 421–30.

Chapter 13

1. Daniel J. Levinson, *The Seasons of a Man's Life* (New York: Alfred A. Knopf, 1978).

Chapter 14

1. Frank F. Furstenberg, S. Phillip Morgan, and Paul D. Allison, "Paternal Participation and Children's Well-Being After Marital Dissolution," *American Sociological Review* 52 (1987): 695–701.

Chapter 16

1. Susan B. Steinman, "The Experience of Children in a Joint Custody Arrangement: A Report of a Study," *American Journal of Orthopsychiatry* 51, no. 3 (1981): 403–14; Susan B. Steinman, Steven E. Zemmelman, and Thomas M. Knoblauch, "A Study of Parents Who Sought Joint Custody Following Divorce: Who Reaches Agreement and Sustains Joint Custody and Who Returns to Court," *Journal of the American Academy of Child Psychiatry* 24 (1985): 545–54.
2. Marsha Kline, Jeanne M. Tschann, Janet R. Johnston, and Judith S. Wallerstein, "A Rose by Any Other Name: Children's Adjustment in Joint and Sole Physical Custody Families." Paper presented at the 65th Annual Meeting of the American Orthopsychiatric Association, San Francisco, March 1988.
3. Janet R. Johnston, Marsha Kline, and Jeanne M. Tschann, "Ongoing Post-Divorce Conflict in Families Contesting Custody: Does Joint Custody and Frequent Access Help?" Paper presented at the 65th Annual Meeting of the American Orthopsychiatric Association, San Francisco, March 1988.

Chapter 18

1. Arthur J. Norton and Jeanne E. Moorman, "Current Trends in Marriage and Divorce Among American Women," *Journal of Marriage and the Family* 49 (1987): 3–14.

2. John Guidubaldi, Helen K. Cleminshaw, Joseph D. Perry, and Caven S. Mcloughlin, "The Impact of Parental Divorce on Children: Report of the Nationwide NASP Study," *School Psychology Review* 12 (1983): 300–23; E. Mavis Hetherington and Kathleen A. Camara, "The Effects of Family Dissolution and Reconstitution on Children," in *Family Relations: A Reader,* ed. Norval D. Glenn and Marion T. Coleman (Chicago: Dorsey Press, 1988), 420–31.

3. Report of the Governor's/Massachusetts Bar Association's Commission on the Unmet Legal Needs of Children (1988), 29.

Appendix

1. Wallerstein and Kelly, 1980.

2. Analysis of the families who were lost to follow-up at the 18-month and 5-year marks indicates that these families did not differ from the population that remained in the study in their race or socioeconomic status or along psychological dimensions that we were able to ascertain. However, the families lost to the follow-up at the 10-year mark did differ somewhat from those in the sample, in the lower socioeconomic status and greater psychological instability of the adults. Two families, with a total of 5 children, reconciled and therefore were excluded from the analysis at each of the follow-up points.

3. August B. Hollingshead, "Two Factor Index of Social Position," unpublished manuscript, Yale University, New Haven, Conn., 1957.

4. For details see Wallerstein and Kelly, 1980.

5. For a complete discussion of this method of data analysis, see Julia M. Lewis and Judith S. Wallerstein, "Methodological Issues in Longitudinal Research on Divorced Families," in *Advances in Family Intervention, Assessment and Theory,* vol. 4, ed. J. P. Vincent (Greenwich, Conn.: JAI Press, 1987).

Index

Father-daughter relations, 64–67, 83,
109–10; and abusive relationships in
adulthood, 119–20; daughter as
concubine in, 201–2; and diary
communications, 244; identification
and, 103, 234–35; postdivorce, 141–
42, 180–81, 242–44, 302; sexual abuse
allegations in, 197–98; and visitation,
169–71
Father-son relations: in adolescence,
82–84, 149–50, 234, 302; and college
education, 154–60; identification and,
103, 175, 234–35; and delinquency,
151–54; and mothers, 192–204;
postdivorce 76–77, 78–79, 80, 84, 85–
93, 141–42, 145–60, 175, 229–40, 283,
302; and violent behavior, 113–19,
121–25; and visitation, 229–40
Fifteen-year follow-up interviews, xx,
324
First-born children: adjustment to
divorce, 176
Five-year follow-up interviews, xvii–
xix, 323, 327
Future orientation: in children of
divorce, 156–57

Gail, 201–2
Generativity vs. stagnation (Erikson),
143
Geographic stability: of research
sample, 313
Girls, 54–67, 94–111, 161–72, 176–83,
241–55, 299; early marriages among,
170–72; father complex and attraction
to older men among, 64–67; and
fathers, 83, 109–10, 201–2 (*see also*
Father-daughter relations); guilt
feelings in, 292; idealization of absent
father by, 242–44; mothering role
assumed by, 99–100, 198–200; and
mothers, 94–111, 179–81 (*see also*
Mother-daughter relations);
promiscuity among, 161–69; and
stepmothers, 255; and sexual abuse
allegations, 197–98; and sleeper
effect, 56–64; and stepfathers,
249
Grandparents: postdivorce help from,
7, 110, 111, 182
Grief feelings, 6; mourning of
marriage, as psychological task, 279,
290–91; *see also* Bereavement
Guilt feelings, 6; in children of divorce,
13–14, 74, 77–78, 195–96, 292, 299; in
divorced parents, 26–27

Health insurance, 132
Homosexual relations: among divorced,
49

Identification: in children of divorce,
89–91, 93, 102–6, 108, 115–16, 156–57,
175, 234–35, 292; and violent
behavior, 113–25
Identity: establishing, 55, 89; loss of, in
divorce, 52–53
Infidelity: birth of child precipitating,
134–35
Intact family: divorced family vs., xii,
18, 232–33; mourning loss of, 290–91
Involvement, fear of: and betrayal
feelings in children, 25, 55, 62–64
Isolation: of older divorced men, 43–46;
of single parents, 132–34

Jan, 191–92
Jarrett, 154–60
Job opportunities: for divorced women,
137–38, 209–14, 304–308, 321–25
Johnston, Dr. Janet, 272
Joint custody, 232, 256–73, 304;
adolescents' response to, 257, 268–69;
and age of child, 267–68; and
bedtime rules, 263; best and worst
scenarios of, 270; changeover day in,
261–63, 268; children's view of, 266–
69; commitment to, 269–70; ex-
spouses and, 260–61, 263, 265–266;
costs of, 258; court-ordered, 272–73,
304; ending, 270; definition of, 256–
57; double lives for children in, 264–
65; father's commitment in, 271;
flexibility in, 269–70; motivations for,
257, 259–64; parents' view of, 259–66;
professional attitudes toward, 261,
270–71; research studies on, 259, 270;
and television watching, 263–64;
transitions in, 270–72

Karen, xii–xiii
Kelly, Joan Berlin, xiii
Kelly, Walt, 307
Kevin, 151–54
Kirk, 192–95

Last-born children: adjustment to
divorce, 173–83
Levinson, Dan, 223
Linda, 198–200
Litrovski, Larry, 113–16
Loneliness: in children of divorce, 13,
22, 67–70, 107; in older men, 43–46,
301; in older women, 49–50, 301

KENT MARSHALL

Judith S. Wallerstein, Ph.D., is the founder and executive director of the Center for the Family in Transition in Corte Madera, California, which counsels more divorcing families than any other agency in America. An internationally recognized authority on the effects of divorce, she is the author, with Dr. Joan Berlin Kelly, of *Surviving the Breakup: How Children and Parents Cope with Divorce.* For over twenty years she has been a senior lecturer at the School of Social Welfare at the University of California at Berkeley, and has been a fellow at the Center for Advanced Study in the Behavioral Sciences in Stanford, California.

Sandra Blakeslee is an award-winning free-lance science and medical writer who contributes regularly to the *New York Times* science news department and many national magazines.

34355